THE GARDEN CONSERVANCY'S

OPEN DAYS
DIRECTORY

The Guide to Visiting Hundreds of America's Best Private Gardens

2000

EDITION

Published by The Garden Conservancy, Inc.
Distributed by Harry N. Abrams, Inc., Publishers

Published in 2000 by The Garden Conservancy, Incorporated
Distributed in 2000 by Harry N. Abrams, Incorporated, New York
Book design by Richard Deon Graphic Art

ISSN 1087-7738
ISBN 0-8109-6694-8

Library of Congress Cataloging-in-Publication Data

The Garden Conservancy's Open Days Directory: The Guide to Visiting Hundreds of America's Best Private Gardens. - 6 ed.
     p. cm.
     Includes index.

1. Gardens—United States—Directories. 2. Botanical gardens—United States—Directories. 3. Arboretums—United States—Directories. 1. Garden Conservancy

    SB466.U65G37 2000   712'.07473
                         QB198-1548

Sixth Edition
This book is printed on recycled paper.
Manufactured in the United States of America.

Contents

Cover photo: Merrin Garden, Cortlandt Manor, NY

SPONSORS

The Garden Conservancy gratefully acknoweldges

for its generous sponsorship of the 2000 Open Days Program.

Our appreciation also to our Media Sponsors:

The Cultivated Gardener
&
Veranda Magazine

and to the fine garden businesses who have supported this publication through their advertising. Please consult these pages for all of your gardening needs and tell the advertisers you saw them in the *Open Days Directory*.

INTRODUCTION

WELCOME TO THE GARDEN CONSERVANCY'S 2000 *Open Days Directory*, your personal invitation to visit hundreds of private gardens in the United States.

It couldn't be easier. We've asked our Garden Hosts to provide descriptions of their gardens, the dates and hours they welcome your visit, and detailed driving directions. You do the rest!

So plan your visit to see these wonderful gardens, whether they're in your neighborhood or make for an enticing weekend getaway.

What Is The Open Days Program?

The Open Days Program is the only national program that invites the public to visit America's very best, rarely-seen, private gardens.

History

In 1995, the Garden Conservancy published the first edition of the *Open Days Directory*, listing 100 private gardens in New York and Connecticut. Since then the *Directory* has evolved into a listing of hundreds of private gardens nationwide, with plans to continue its expansion.

The Open Days Program is modeled after similar programs abroad including England's popular "*Yellow Book*" and Australia's growing Open Garden Scheme.

The mission of the Open Days Program is to increase public appreciation and enjoyment of America's gardens in all their regional diversity, and to build an audience to support garden preservation in America.

How Is The Open Days Program Organized?

Each Open Day area has at least one Regional Representative who works on a volunteer basis to recruit private gardens in his or her area and to assist with the promotion and advancement of the program. You'll find a list of Regional Representatives beginning on page 14.

The *Open Days Directory* is published by the Garden Conservancy, and distributed by Harry N. Abrams, Inc., Publishers.

If you are interested in learning more about the organization of Open Days throughout the United States, please contact The Garden Conservancy, Open Days Program, Post Office Box 219, Cold Spring, NY 10516. Telephone: 914/265-5384. Fax: 914/265-5392.

Admissions

A $4 admission fee is charged per garden. Visitors may purchase admission coupons through the Garden Conservancy at a discounted price (see order form on the last page of this *Directory*). Admission coupons remain valid from year to year. Proceeds from the Open Days Program support the national preservation work of the Garden Conservancy, as well as local not-for-profit organizations designated by individual Garden Hosts.

General Information

The Garden Conservancy's Open Days Program is simply based on a Garden Host's willingness to share his or her garden with the public on various dates throughout the gardening season. We make every attempt to open a variety of gardens, within a reasonable driving distance of each other, on the same date. There are exceptions and you will note some gardens that we simply had to include but that are off the beaten path.

We are also pleased to provide listings of public gardens in each Open Day area to round our your day of garden visiting or to enjoy at other times of the year.

Garden Listings

Those of you who have purchased the *Open Days Directory* in the past will notice some changes to its organization. This year we've arranged garden listings in the following sequence:

- alphabetically by state
- alphabetically according to Open Day Area (i.e. San Francisco Bay Area, Seattle & Vicinity, Dutchess & Columbia Counties)
- alphabetically by garden name.

To help you locate a specific garden, we've indexed them by garden name in the back of the *Directory*. There is also a master calendar in the beginning of the *Directory* that lists all Open Days for the 2000 season.

Maps

Each state section begins with a map of that state with a listing of Open Days. Each Open Day listing is preceded by a map designed to provide the general location of the gardens open on that day.

Directions given for each garden assume that garden visitors are traveling from the nearest major highway. In some cases, references from two starting points are given. Please travel with a local map.

Each private garden listing includes the name of the garden and its location. A description of the garden, the dates and times it is open, and driving directions are also included.

Public garden listings are marked with a 🏵, and include the garden name, full address, contact information, a brief description of the garden, hours of operation, and driving directions. We encourage you to contact the site directly for more information.

Information in this *Directory* was, to the best of our knowledge, correct at the time the *Directory* went to press. Since publication, some changes may have occurred. When possible, the Garden Conservancy will notify you of changes in advance; otherwise please take note of the schedule changes posted at admission tables or check the Garden Conservancy's website prior to your visit. (www.GardenConservancy.org).

Information Gathering

The information presented in the *Open Days Directory* is collected by Garden Conservancy staff and Regional Representatives around the country. We rely on Garden Hosts to provide information for their listings. Information for Public Garden listings is likewise gathered from the site's staff. The Garden Conservancy is not responsible for the accuracy of the information published within these listings.

Nominations to include gardens in the *Open Days Directory* are accepted. Please call or write for a survey form and nomination criteria.

Inquiries regarding the *Open Days Directory* should be directed to:

Open Days Program
The Garden Conservancy
P.O. Box 219
Cold Spring, NY 10516
Telephone: (914) 265-5384
Fax: (914) 265-5392

ETIQUETTE

The Garden Conservancy's Open Days Program is made possible solely through the willingness of gardeners throughout the country to share their gardens. We ask you to please respect their generosity while visiting by following these simple guidelines:

- Do not pick any plant or remove any part of a plant from the garden. If you require help identifying a plant, please ask the Garden Host.
- Do not leave litter in the garden.
- Stay on the paths.
- Follow any signs or directions provided at the garden.
- Respect the privacy of the owners.
- Please leave all pets at home.
- Children must be supervised at all times.
- Park your car so others can enter and leave the parking area.
- Please remember to check with the owner before taking photographs.
- Respect the dates and times each garden is open as listed in the *Directory*. **Do not attempt to contact the Garden Host directly**. Please contact the Open Days Program office to pursue special visiting arrangements or to bring a group to a garden.

Our last request is that you take advantage of the opportunity to visit the wonderful private and public gardens presented in this edition of the *Open Days Directory*. Enjoy!

Laura Mumaw Palmer
Director
Open Days Program

Introduction From The Chairman

Once again in 1999, the Open Days Program generated a most rewarding response, attracting more than 54,000 appreciative and keenly-interested garden visitors.

This large and ever-increasing number of visitors has significantly helped to strengthen the crucial preservation efforts of the Conservancy and also has supported the endeavors of other nonprofit organizations designated by garden owners.

Even more impressive than numbers, however, is the almost tangible level of excitement the program has engendered since its inception.

The Open Days Program has proven to be an extremely rewarding and productive experience for all participants. Visitors are tremendously grateful for the opportunity to experience the unique diversity and creativity of exceptional private gardens that the program has opened to them. Garden hosts, who so generously share their talents and enthusiasm, are gratified by and impressed with the genuine interest and knowledge of those who visit the gardens they have created and tended with such exceptional care.

Another major accomplishment of the Open Days program has been its rapid evolution into an informal forum for the valuable exchange of ideas and information, as well as a celebration of a mutual respect and love for nature and gardening.

Dedication has been the key! Our Regional Representatives form the backbone of the Open Days Program. They skillfully and diligently direct the activities of their energetic committee members, who, with Garden Hosts throughout the United States, bring you the *Open Days Directory* and the unique opportunity to expand your garden visits.

This millennium edition offers further expansion and refinements as we work to create a truly comprehensive compendium of private and public gardens of merit throughout the United States. The *2000 Directory* is the harvest of the efforts of many dedicated individuals: our visionary founder, Frank Cabot, the enterprising Regional Representatives and their hardworking committee members; the gracious, generous private and public garden hosts; and the invaluable staff of the Garden Conservancy.

The Open Days program is your entry into a whole new dimension of horticultural delights and surprises that will captivate, fascinate, enlightened, and inspire. Worlds of immense beauty and diversity await you on the other side of these now-open garden gates.

Janet Meakin Poor, Open Days Program Chairman

The Garden Conservancy

Why—and How—do We Conserve Gardens?

The Garden Conservancy was founded to answer these questions, to provide the resources necessary to preserve many of America's finest gardens and to open the gates of these gardens to the public for education and enjoyment.

Why do we conserve gardens? Anyone who gardens knows the fragile nature of the gardener's creation: Subject to the ravages of climate, weeds, erosion, pests, and other problems, even the most carefully designed gardens can vanish within just a few years when untended. When we lose an exceptional garden, we lose its beauty, but we also lose the lessons it can teach us about the gardener's era—its values, horticultural science, and aesthetic standards. We conserve beautiful gardens because they are a vital part of our nation's cultural heritage. Experts estimate that more than two-thirds of great American gardens have already been lost to the tides of time. As the first national organization devoted to garden preservation, The Garden Conservancy is working to stem that tide by identifying gardens of unusual merit across the nation-from a desert garden in California to a Japanese garden in New York-and working with their owners and other interested parties to insure the gardens' futures. Some of these gardens are national treasures, while others are important community resources; all merit conservation as part of our national legacy.

How do we conserve gardens? While the gardener is able to maintain the garden, it remains vibrant. But when the gardener can no longer invest the time, energy, and resources required, the garden and its beauty can perish. Saving a fine garden requires expertise, funding, and community support—resources The Garden Conservancy brings to bear in preserving great American gardens and opening them to the public. The Garden Conservancy works in partnership with individual garden owners as well as public and private organizations, and uses its legal, financial, and horticultural resources to secure each garden's future and to make it permanently accessible to the public.

The Garden Conservancy is a national not-for-profit organization working to preserve America's exceptional gardens.

The Garden Conservancy

The Preservation Projects Of The Garden Conservancy
2000 Garden Visiting Information

The Garden Conservancy is currently working toward the preservation of eighteen special gardens around the country. You are welcome to visit and will find a full description, visiting information, and directions for the following projects in this edition of the *Directory*:

Aullwood Garden MetroPark, Dayton, OH

The Beatrix Farrand Garden at Bellefield, Hyde Park, NY

The Chase Garden, Orting, WA

Dumbarton Oaks Park, Washington, DC

The Fells, John Hay National Wildlife Refuge, Newbury, NH

Gibraltar, Wilmington, DE

The Harland Hand Garden, El Cerrito, CA

Historic Morven, Princeton, NJ

The James Rose Center, Ridgewood, NJ

The John P. Humes Japanese Stroll Garden, Mill Neck, NY

McKee Botanical Garden, Vero Beach, FL

Peckerwood Garden, Hempstead, TX

The McLaughlin Garden & Horticultural Center, South Paris, ME

Mukai Farm & Garden, Vashon Island, WA

The Ruth Bancroft Garden, Walnut Creek, CA (San Francisco Bay Area)

Springside, Poughkeepsie, NY

Val Verde, Montecito, CA

Van Vleck House & Gardens, Montclair, NJ

2000 Open Days Schedule

Alabama (Birmingham)	May 6 & 7
Arizona (Phoenix)	April 8
California (Los Angeles)	May 6
California (San Francisco Bay Area)	May 6 & 7, June 3 & 4, September 30 & October 1
California (San Francisco Peninsula)	April 15 & May 13
Colorado (Colorado Springs)	June 24
Connecticut & Southeastern New York	May 7, May 21, June 4, June 25, July 9, July 23, September 10 & September 24
District of Columbia (Washington)	May 13 & June 24
Florida (Jacksonville)	April 29
Georgia (Atlanta)	May 6
Illinois (Chicago)	June 18, June 24, July 16 & September 24
Illinois (Hinsdale)	July 22
Illinois (Rockford)	June 24
Illinois (St. Charles)	July 9
Louisiana (New Orleans)	April 15
Maryland (Annapolis)	June 10
Maryland (Baltimore)	September 16
Massachusetts (Boston)	September 16 & 17
Massachusetts (South Dartmouth)	July 8
Michigan (Bloomfield Hills)	July 16
Michigan (Harbor Springs)	July 26
New Hampshire	July 8
New Jersey	May 13, May 20 & June 10
New York (Albany)	June 18
New York (Cambridge)	July 9
New York (Lake Champlain)	July 15
New York (Eastern Long Island)	April 29, June 17, July 15 & September 16
New York (North Shore of Long Island)	May 21
New York (Saratoga Springs)	June 17
Ohio (Cincinnati)	June 24 & July 8
Ohio (Columbus)	June 10
Ohio (Dayton)	May 20
Pennsylvania (Bucks County)	May 14
Pennsylvania (Centre Hall)	May 13 & June 11
Pennsylvania (Philadelphia)	May 13
Pennsylvania (Pittsburgh)	September 10
Tennessee (Chattanooga)	May 13
Tennessee (Nashville)	June 4
Texas (Austin)	October 14
Texas (Houston)	March 19
Vermont (Manchester)	June 10 & July 8
Washington (Seattle)	May 6 & 7, June 3 & 4
West Virginia (Charleston)	June 10
Wisconsin (Lake Country)	July 16

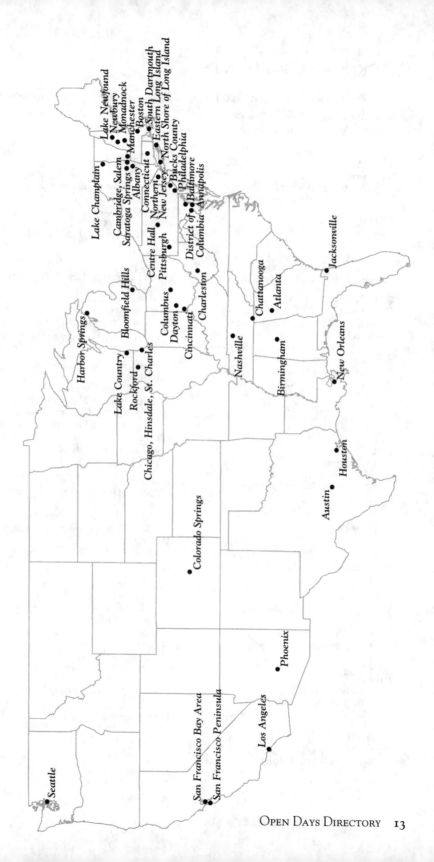

2000 OPEN DAYS REGIONS

Lake Newfound
Newbury
Monadnock
Manchester
Boston
South Dartmouth
Eastern Long Island
North Shore of Long Island
Bucks County
Philadelphia
Baltimore
Annapolis
District of Columbia
Lake Champlain
Cambridge, Salem
Saratoga Springs
Albany
Connecticut
Northern New Jersey
Centre Hall
Pittsburgh
Charleston
Jacksonville
Chattanooga
Atlanta
Bloomfield Hills
Harbor Springs
Columbus
Dayton
Cincinnati
Nashville
Birmingham
New Orleans
Lake Country
Rockford
Chicago, Hinsdale, St. Charles
Houston
Austin
Colorado Springs
Phoenix
San Francisco Bay Area
San Francisco Peninsula
Los Angeles
Seattle

Acknowledgements

Over the past six years, nearly 100 Regional Representatives have volunteered their time and energy to the development of the Garden Conservancy's Open Days Program. We are grateful for their ongoing commitment and efforts.

ALABAMA
Birmingham
   Mrs. A. Jack Allison (1998-2000)
   Mrs. John N. Wrinkle (1998-2000)

ARIZONA
Phoenix
   Mrs. Scott Crozier (2000)
   Nancy Swanson (1999)
   Gregory S. Trutza (2000)
   Mrs. Donald C. Williams (1998-1999)

CALIFORNIA
Carmel
   Mrs. Lee Meneice (1997-1998)
Los Angeles
   Mrs. Donivee Nash (1999-2000)
San Francisco Bay Area
   Sonny Garcia (1998-2000)
   Charmain Giuliani (1998-2000)
   Richard G. Turner Jr. (1998-2000)
   Tom Valva (1998-2000)
San Francisco Peninsula
   Mrs. Harvey D. Hinman (1998-2000)

COLORADO
Colorado Springs
   Mrs. Terence Lilly (2000)
   Mrs. Gene Moore (1998-2000)
Denver
   Mrs. Moses Taylor (1998-1999)

DELAWARE
Wilmington
   Mrs. George P. Bissell Jr. (1998-1999)
   Mrs. Sidney Scott Jr. (1998-1999)

FLORIDA
Jacksonville
   Carolyn Marsh Lindsay (1998 & 2000)
Vero Beach
   Mrs. Thomas S. Morse (1998-1999)
   Mrs. Henry N. Tifft (1999)

GEORGIA
Atlanta
   Virginia Almand (1998)
   George E. N. de Man (2000)
   Mrs. William Huger (1999-2000)

HAWAII
Honolulu
   Mrs. E. Chipman Higgins (1997-1998)

ILLINOIS
Chicago
   Mrs. Charles E. Schroeder (1997-2000)
St. Charles & Rockford
   Susan Beard (2000)
Hinsdale/Naperville
   Mrs. David C. Earl (2000)

INDIANA
Indianapolis
   Dr. Gilbert S. Daniels (1997-1998)

LOUISIANA
New Orleans
   Ann Hobson Haack (1998-2000)

MARYLAND
Annapolis
   Mrs. John A. Baldwin (2000)
Baltimore
   Nan Paternotte (1997)
   Mrs. Frances Huber (1998)
   Mrs. Clark MacKenzie (1999)
   Mrs. Thomas G. McCausland (2000)
Chestertown
   Mrs. Adrian P. Reed (1999)

MASSACHUSETTS
Boston
   Mrs. Henry S. Streeter (1997-2000)
South Dartmouth
   Mrs. Thomas S. Morse (1998)
   Mrs. Robert G. Walker (1999-2000)
Worcester
   John W. Trexler (1998-1999)

MICHIGAN
Ann Arbor
   George Papadalos (1998)
   Marie Cochrane (1999)
Bloomfield Hills
   Lynne Clippert (2000)
   Starr Foster (1998-1999)
   Lois Gamble (2000)
   Mrs. John Knutson (2000)
Grosse Pointe
   Mrs. John Ford (1997-1998)
   Mrs. Bragaw Vanderzee (1999)
Harbor Springs
   Mrs. John Ford (1998)
   Mrs. Frank Hightower (2000)

MINNESOTA
Minneapolis
   Mrs. John Winsor (1997)
   Mrs. Henry L. Sweatt (1997 & 1999)

MISSOURI
Kansas City
  Mrs. George Powell III (1997)
  Mrs. Dwight Sutherland (1997)
St. Louis
  Mrs. William H. T. Bush (1998)

NEW HAMPSHIRE
Monadnock
  Mrs. Story Wright (2000)
New London
  Mrs. Gusta Teach (2000)
Squam Lake
  George Carr (2000)

NEW JERSEY
  Mrs. J. Duncan Pitney (1997-2000)

NEW YORK
Albany/Schenectady
  Joanne Lenden (1998-2000)
  Mrs. Henry Ferguson (2000)
Cooperstown
  Mrs. H. Rodney Hartman (1998)
  Patricia Thorpe (1998)
Eastern Long Island
  Lalitte Scott (1996-2000)
Lake Champlain
  Mrs. James T. Flynn (1999-2000)
Salem & Cambridge
  Mrs. Henry Ferguson (2000)

NEW YORK & CONNECTICUT
  Page Dickey (co-founder)
  Penelope Maynard (co-founder)
  Jane Havemeyer (1995-2000)
  Sara M. Knight (1995-2000)
  Enid Munroe (1995-2000)
  Melissa Orme (1995-2000)

OHIO
Akron
  Mrs. W. Stuver Parry (1998-1999)
Cincinnati
  Mrs. William R. Seaman (1999-2000)
Columbus
  Mrs. Roger Blair (2000)
  Mrs. Robert F. Hoffman Jr. (2000)
  Karen K. Meyer (1999)
  Connie Page (1998)
Dayton
  Mrs. James Woodhull (1997-2000)
  Barbara Rion (1997-2000)
Granville
  Janet Oberleissen (1998)

PENNSYLVANIA
Centre Hall
  Dr. Richard Morgan (2000)
Philadelphia
  Mrs. Frank H. Goodyear (1998-1999)
  Mrs. Morris Lloyd Jr. (2000)
  Mrs. Edward Starr III (1998-1999)
Pittsburgh
  Bernita Buncher Duber (2000)
  Mrs. Joshua C. Whetzel Jr. (1998 & 2000)

SOUTH CAROLINA
Greenville
  Mrs. Nelson B. Arrington (1997-1998)
  Mrs. Samuel M. Beattie (1997-1998)

TENNESSEE
Chattanooga
  Mrs. Halbert Law (1999-2000)
  Mrs. John Stout (1999-2000)
Memphis
  Mrs. Albert M. Austin III (1999)
  Mrs. David B. Martin (1999)
Nashville
  Mr. Bob Brackman (2000)
  Mrs. Robert C. H. Mathews Jr. (2000)
  Mr. Ben Page (2000)

TEXAS
Austin
  James deGrey David (1998-1999)
  Deborah Hornickel (2000)
  Jennifer Staub Meyers (1998-1999)
  Dr. Gordon L. White (1998-1999)
Houston
  Mrs. J. Taft Symonds (1998-2000)
  Mrs. Sellers J. Thomas Jr. (1998-2000)

VERMONT
Lake Champlain
  Mrs. James T. Flynn (1999-2000)
Manchester
  Mrs. A. V. S. Olcott (1998-2000)

VIRGINIA
Charlottesville
  Mrs. Mario di Valmarana (1997)
Middleburg
  Mrs. Charles H. Seilheimer Jr. (1997)
Richmond
  Mrs. Robert A. Bristow II (1997)

WASHINGTON
Seattle
  Barbara Flynn (1999)
  Mrs. Bruce McIvor (2000)

WASHINGTON, D.C.
  Joanne S. Lawson (1997-2000)
  Mrs. John Macomber (1997-2000)

WEST VIRGINIA
Charleston
  Mrs. Herbert Jones (1997)
  Mr. & Mrs. James Rufus Thomas II
  (1998-2000)

WISCONSIN
Lake Country
  Mrs. Anthony Meyer (2000)
  Mrs. Henry Quadracci (2000)
Milwaukee
  Mrs. William Allis (1998-1999)
  Mrs. Robert W. Braeger (1998-1999)

ALABAMA

★ Birmingham

ALABAMA OPEN DAYS
May 6 & 7: Birmingham Area

Birmingham Open Days

Regional Representatives: Mrs. John N. Wrinkle & Mrs. A. Jack Allison

Saturday & Sunday, May 6 & 7

BIRMINGHAM
Brown Garden, 2760 Abingdon Road: 1 p.m. - 5 p.m.
Cooney Garden, 14 Ridge Drive: 1 p.m. - 5 p.m.
Louise & John Wrinkle, 2 Beechwood Road: 1 p.m. - 5 p.m.
The Gardens of Brookhill Manor, Five Brookhill Manor: 1 p.m. - 5 p.m.
Zoe's Garden, 1800 Mayfair Drive: 1 p.m. - 5 p.m.

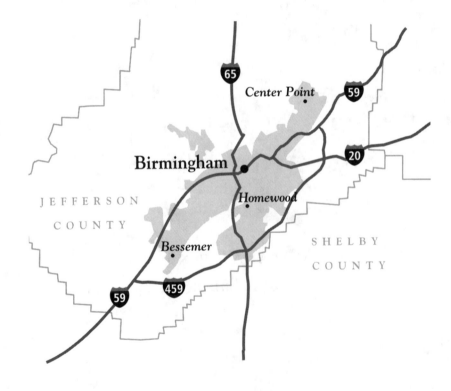

Brown Garden

2760 ABINGDON ROAD, BIRMINGHAM

This three-acre property gives the feel of a small country estate. The home and grounds, enjoyed through the years by several families with children, have been restored and amplified by the present owners. The gently curving driveway terminates in a circular parking court. A double boxwood parterre leads to the entrance, marked by a covered terrace where climbing roses abound. Opening off the rear of the house is a level area encircled by a stone wall, featuring perennial beds and zoysia grass underlining a willow oak allée. Almost hidden by boxwood and hollies, and up several steps on the left side, is a beautiful swimming pool featuring a deck of bluestone in grass.

Saturday & Sunday, May 6 & 7, 1 p.m. - 5 p.m.

From Hollywood Boulevard take Highway 280 East. Go past Cherokee Road Exit to the overpass at Pump House Road. Turn right onto Pump House Road and go .4 mile to Abingdon Road. The garden is at the first house on the right. Park on Pump House Road or Abingdon Road.

Proceeds shared with The Birmingham Botanical Society.

Cooney Garden

14 RIDGE DRIVE, BIRMINGHAM

One look up the drive and you'll suspect you've been invited into one of Birmingham's loveliest examples of English-style gardening. Once you reach the top of the drive, you'll know. Sited on five-acres of hillside, this is gardening on a grand scale, where the house and garden are a gracious complement to each other. The garden was established more than seventy years ago, and the Cooneys have presided over it for the past fifteen. During this time, Liz has restored the fountain garden to its original all-white flower grandeur and reclaimed the woods that had moved in. The rose parterre, gazebo garden, and crabapple orchard are her visions for this breathtaking example of dedicated gardening. The Cooneys have taken a grand old garden and given it new life and elegance.

Saturday & Sunday, May 6 & 7, 1 p.m. - 5 p.m.

From Mountain Brook Village, take Lane Park Road by the Botanical Gardens on the left. At the traffic light, turn right onto County Club Road and go .7 mile to Ridge Drive. Turn left onto Ridge Drive and go .4 mile to garden on the right. Park on Ridge Drive.

Proceeds shared with The Birmingham Botanical Society.

Louise & John Wrinkle

2 BEECHWOOD ROAD, BIRMINGHAM

The original house and property were developed in 1938 by Louise's parents. Twelve years ago, she and her husband moved back to her childhood home and extensively remodeled the house and grounds. A two-acre mature woodland garden features collections of hollies and vacciniums, as well as the ranunculus family. Southeastern natives and their Asian counterparts, many planted side by side for easy comparison, are subjects of equal interest. Guests may circulate freely among the upper gardens: a small boxwood parterre defined by a Belgian fence of native crabapple, a cutting garden, and an herb garden. A network of winding gravel paths leads visitors from these upper gardens to a wooded valley, where a brook flows year round.

Saturday & Sunday, May 6 & 7, 1 p.m. - 5 p.m.

From Highway 280/I-459 take Exit 19 onto Lake Shore Drive. Turn right and go through the traffic lights. The road becomes Mountain Brook Parkway. Go 1.1 miles to right onto Overbrook Road, then go .6 mile and turn left onto Beechwood. The house is on the corner of Beechwood and Woodhill. Please park on Woodhill and walk up the driveway.

Proceeds shared with The Birmingham Botanical Society.

The Gardens of Brookhill Manor

FIVE BROOKHILL MANOR, BIRMINGHAM

Five years ago a vision was created to build ten homes in a quaint English village setting in a gated community. Our individual gardens were designed to complement the personalities of the owners. The utilization of small areas was essential. Be our guests and enjoy the refreshing gardens of city living.

Saturday & Sunday, May 6 & 7, 1 p.m. - 5 p.m.

From Highway 31 in Homewood, take Hollywood Boulevard .8 mile toward Homewood Gates on right. Park on Hollywood Boulevard or in church lot across the street.

Proceeds shared with The Birmingham Botanical Society.

ZOE'S GARDEN

1800 MAYFAIR DRIVE, BIRMINGHAM

In 1944 my parents purchased this wonderful house built in 1926. Five years ago my husband and I renovated my family's house and moved back into my childhood home. The English garden I had always dreamed of could now be done. We started with a holly hedge along the 200 feet on the street. The stone pillars with gate and rose arbor invite you to a special place. The wildflower plots, including poppies, larkspur, bachelor buttons, etc. are defined by grass and stone paths laid by my husband. There are also many old fashioned climbing roses (one original to the property found in a neighbor's yard) and others from another old Birmingham garden. Many herbs grown throughout the garden are used in my restaurant, Zoe's Kitchen, located three blocks from our house. The shady stone terrace and fish pond have become the favorite place for dining and relaxing after a day of cooking or gardening, both labors of love.

Saturday & Sunday, May 6 & 7, 1 p.m. - 5 p.m.

From Lake Shore Drive take Highway 31 North .6 mile toward Homewood. Turn left onto Mayfair Drive. Go .1 mile. The garden is at the intersection of Mayfair and Roxbury. Park on Mayfair or Roxbury.

Proceeds shared with The Birmingham Botanical Society.

BIRMINGHAM BOTANICAL GARDENS &

2612 LANE PARK ROAD, BIRMINGHAM, AL 32513.
(205) 879-1227.

Birmingham Botanical Gardens features sixty-seven acres of native and exotic plants. Major collections include camellia, cactus and succulent, rhododendron, iris, fern, lily, orchid, old-fashioned and modern roses, and sculpture. There is also a conservatory, plus vegetable and herb gardens. There is a renowned Japanese garden with an authentic teahouse and cultural performance pavilion. A horticultural library and ongoing horticultural programs are available. Attractive gift shop offers unusual garden items and flower-arranging supplies. Most areas are handicapped accessible.

Year round, daily, dawn - dusk.

From I-20 / I-59 exit onto Highway 280 East. Take the Mountain Brook/Zoo/Gardens Exit. Turn left at traffic light onto Lane Park Road. The gardens are on the left. From I-65 South, take I-20 to I-59 East. Go 1 mile and turn right onto Route 280 East and follow above directions. Heading north on I-65 take Exit 250 onto I-459 East. Take Exit 19 and go 3.5 miles on Route 280 West to the Zoo Exit. Turn left at the traffic light onto Lane Park Road. The gardens are on the left.

Birmingham Museum of Art/The Charles W. Ireland Sculpture Garden &

2000 8TH AVENUE NORTH, BIRMINGHAM, AL 35203. (205)254-2565.

This multilevel sculpture garden is a unique space for the display of outdoor art. Welcoming you to this urban oasis is a lushly planted area shaded by towering water oaks. Beneath the oaks' central canopy is the striking installation, Blue Pools Courtyard, by Valerie Jaudon. Sculpture by Rodin, Botero, and others lies directly ahead as you continue your way through this extraordinary space. The final focal point is the magnificent Lithos II waterfall by Elyn Zimmerman. Within the sculpture garden is the Red Mountain Garden Area, created in 1956. Admission is free.

Year round, Tuesday through Saturday, 10 a.m. - 5 p.m.; Sunday, noon - 5 p.m.; Closed Mondays, New Year's Day, Thanksgiving & Christmas Day.

From I-20 / I-59 take the 22nd Street Exit. Turn left onto 22nd Street, go 1 block, and turn right onto Eighth Avenue North; go 1 block to 21st Street. The museum is on the corner of 21st Street and 8th Avenue North.

Cathedral Church of the Advent &

2017 6TH AVENUE NORTH, BIRMINGHAM, AL 35203. (205) 251-2324.

These gardens are an oasis in the heart of Birmingham's central business district. The larger, the Rector's Garden, is a courtyard framed by church buildings. A white garden, it also offers favorite Southern plantings, as well as fountains and statuary. The canopy of a giant oak invites visitors to garden benches for lunch, reading, and reflection. The Betsy Turner Garden is an allée of Japanese maples underplanted with shade-loving perennials. The gardens are tended by the Advent's St. Francis Guild, volunteers who show their love of gardening in this much loved place.

Year round, daily, 8 a.m. - 5 p.m; Sunday, 8 a.m. - 1 p.m.

Located at the corner of Sixth Avenue North and Twentieth Street in downtown Birmingham.

ARIZONA

★ Phoenix

ARIZONA OPEN DAYS
April 8 & 9: Phoenix

Phoenix Open Days

Regional Representatives: Mary Crozier & Gregory S. Trutza

Saturday, April 8

PARADISE VALLEY
Anne & Fred Christensen Garden, 5739 North Saguaro Road: 10 a.m. - 4 p.m.
Drake & Shelley Duane's Garden a la Monet, 3606 East Marletta
    Avenue: 10 a.m. - 4 p.m.
Ellen Gliddens Stiteler & John Stiteler's Garden, 6002 North Elizabeth
    Place: 2 p.m. - 6 p.m.
Saguaro Road Retreat, 5660 North Saguaro Road: 10 a.m. - 4 p.m.

PHOENIX
Shilo, 2332 East Quail Avenue: 10 a.m. - 4 p.m.
Tesfaye's Garden, 4432 North 30th Street: 10 a.m. - 4 p.m.
Tish Pedley Milroy's Garden, 5029 North 46th Place: 10 a.m. - 4 p.m.

Saturday & Sunday, April 8 & 9

PARADISE VALLEY
Drake & Shelley Duane's Garden a la Monet, 3606 East Marletta
    Avenue: 10 a.m. - 4 p.m.

PHOENIX
La Casa Amable, 5401 East Lafayette Boulevard: 10 a.m. - 4 p.m.
Shilo, 2332 East Quail Avenue: 10 a.m. - 4 p.m.
Tesfaye's Garden, 4432 North 30th Street: 10 a.m. - 4 p.m.
Tish Pedley Milroy's Garden, 5029 North 46th Place: 10 a.m. - 4 p.m.

Anne & Fred Christensen Garden

5739 North Saguaro Road, Paradise Valley

Our garden is a combination of family tradition and adapting to our house's setting on five acres in the desert. Our desert plantings in the front enhance our spectacular view of Camelback Mountain. Interspersed among our desert plantings, both front and back are beds full of tall bearded iris-most of the bulbs coming from my mother's garden. Also to satisfy my childhood memories are the pansies, gardenias, camellias, geraniums, roses, poppies, citrus trees, and a fig tree. We have perching places to watch the children on the swings and to rest from tennis. There are small pools with cascading fountains for the children to splash in. All the plant material from the property is turned into compost or mulch.

Saturday, April 8; 10 a.m. - 4 p.m.

Take Camelback Road to 64th Street. Travel north on 64th Street to McDonald (less than 1 mile). Travel west on McDonald 1 block to Saguaro Road. Travel south on Saguaro Road to 5739 (second driveway on the left). Please park on the property.

Proceeds shared with The Desert Botanical Garden.

Drake & Shelley Duane's Garden a la Monet

3606 East Marletta Avenue, Paradise Valley

With landscape architect Gregory Trutza, we've created a Giverny replica in the desert. A pond fed by three waterfalls is filled with water lilies, aquatic plants, and fish across which a verdi bridge arches. A faux finished curving wall embraces the garden which features weeping willows, other deciduous trees, a rose garden, verdi planters, burgeoning blossoms, and a variety of grasses. Scattered about are teak, stone, and verdi seating set against a rear, vine-covered, residential facade accented by Monet-esque shutters.

Saturday & Sunday, April 8 & 9, 10 a.m. - 4 p.m.

Traveling west from Scottsdale Road or east from Highway 51, take Lincoln to Palo Cristi/36th Street (1 traffic light east of 32nd Street. The first light west of Tatum). Travel 1 block south on Palo Cristi is Marlette Avenue. The garden is on the northeast corner of Palo Cristi and Marlette Avenue up a long driveway. Please park along Marlette Avenue and Palo Cristi.

Ellen Giddins Stiteler & John Stiteler's Garden

6002 North Elizabeth Place, Paradise Valley

Desert Gardens designed by Steve Martino. Gardens were designed for outdoor living and to complement Luis Barragan-style home.

Saturday, April 8, 2 p.m. - 6 p.m.

Take Lincoln Boulevard to Palo Cristi/36th Street turn south for .5 mile. Home is the Northeast Corner of Palo Cristi and Bethany Home Road. Park on streets bordering home.

Proceeds shared with The Desert Botanical Garden.

La Casa Amable

5401 East Lafayette Boulevard, Phoenix

Bienvenidos...Welcome. The sweet fragrance of orange blossoms, the seasons of a grand fig tree, bird filled palm trees, gnarled olive trees, and the brilliant colors of native wildflowers and bougainvillea greet La Casa Amable's visitors. We invite all to experience the magical atmosphere of the gardens of Mexico in the heart of Phoenix. The property was originally purchased by William J. Murphy in the 1800s and features towering eucalyptus trees said to be among the first grown in the valley. Greg Trutza of New Directions in Landscape Architecture has created over a period of ten years this feast for the senses, including a raised-bed organic garden featuring native heirloom vegetables.

Sunday, April 9, 10 a.m. - 4 p.m.

We are at the corner of 54th street and Lafayette Boulevard: 5401 East Lafayette Boulevard. From Camelback Road, turn south onto 56th Street. Turn right at the first traffic light onto Lafayette Boulevard. Go to 54th Street. From Indian School Road turn north onto 56th Street. Turn left at the first traffic light onto Lafayette Boulevard. Go to 54th Street. Please park on the street.

SAGUARO ROAD RETREAT

5660 NORTH SAGUARO ROAD, PARADISE VALLEY

Although surrounded by the Metropolitan City, this five-acre property gives the illusion of being in the country. Upon entering the property your first glance is of the magnificent Praying Monk on Camelback Mountain. The drive is made up of natural granite to keep with a country feel. An intimate courtyard, with fountain carved from flagstone, magnificent ironwood trees, succulents, cacti and a variety of butterfly and hummingbird attracting plants await your arrival. Flagstone pathways wind through various niche gardens—herb and vegetable garden, rose garden, citrus grove and child's playground. The property is surrounded by cacti, creosote, palo verdes, mesquites, ocotillos, palo brea and lysiloma tree. Other areas of interest: the blue lagoon cast pool and spa, hobby house, guesthouse, tennis court and putting green.

Saturday, April 8, 10 a.m. - 4 p.m.

Take East Camelback to 64th Street. Turn left onto North 64th Street which becomes North Invergorden Road. Go to McDonald. Go west 1 block and turn left onto Saguaro Road. The garden is on the west side. Please park along Saguaro.

Proceeds shared with The Desert Botanical Garden.

SHILOH

2332 EAST QUAIL AVENUE, PHOENIX

Located at the base of the McDowell Mountains at the end of Pinnacle Peak Road. The setting for this garden is on a beautiful natural desert site. It has evolved in phases over time as we seem to add a new project every year or so. I have designed natural granite paths that wind through the native desert landscape. Steps through the arroyos with surprise stop and pause points along the way like a sunset viewing ramada, a wildlife water feature, and a firepit area. Beside the various garden terraces I added around the sprawling adobe hacienda, the paths all lead to the newest addition...A lush secret garden that is entered across a bridge and through a desert moongate using natural stone from on site.

Saturday & Sunday, April 8 & 9, 10 a.m. - 4 p.m.

From Central Phoenix take Route 51 north and exit at Bell Road heading east. Travel east on Bell approximately 4.5 miles to Scottsdale Road and turn north. Travel north on Scottsdale Road approximately 4.5 miles to Pinnacle Peak Road and turn east. Travel east on Pinnacle Peak Road approximately 4.5 miles, through the traffic light at Pima Road to The Mountain. Turn left continuing along Pinnacle Peak Road about .5 mile. The property is located on the south side of the road. Drive through the wooden gates or park on street and walk in.

Tesfaye's Garden

4432 North 30th Street, Phoenix

A work of art that uses the earth for canvas, this very special garden invites the viewer to wander through paths of well-orchestrated texture and color grown mostly from seed. Arbors of wisteria, mandevilla and climbing rose enclose the intimate garden rooms. A nearby field used for growing wild bird seed in the summer transforms to a field of poppies, ranunculus, digitalis and many other traditional flowers in early spring. It is an equal opportunity garden not just for favorite traditional garden flowers. In this garden all seeds that germinate are incorporated with several desert wildflower annuals. It is not uncommon to see baby blue eyes, red flax and many other desert favorites with tulips, ranunculus and allium. A garden designed to appeal to all senses. An ever-changing garden ten years in the making and always evolving with uncommon fruit bearing trees and ornamental collectibles. Come see and expect the unexpected.

Saturday & Sunday, April 8 & 9, 10 a.m. - 4 p.m.

From North 32nd Street and Camelback take North 32nd Street go south to Campbell which is the next traffic light. At Campbell go west to 30th Street. On 30th Street go south. The garden is located just south of Campbell on 30th Street. Please park on the street or at Mountain View Christian Church. Park on the street.

Tish Pedley Milroy's Garden

5029 North 46th Place, Phoenix

Landscape architect Greg Trutza of New Directions designed the garden of my dreams. Using the principals of Feng Shui, he incorporated my love of roses with the desert, my wish for a Koi pond with an oriental teahouse and arched bridge. He understood my propensity for stuff and made it all work.

Saturday & Sunday, April 8 & 9, 10 a.m. - 4 p.m.

Major cross streets: 44th Street & Camelback. Go east on Camelback. Turn North onto 45th Place. Turn quickly onto service road/runs parallel to Camelback. Go east to 46th Place, turn north. Please park on the street.

Boyce Thompson Arboretum State Park ❧

37615 Highway 60, Superior, AZ 85273. (520) 689-2811.

Boyce Thompson Arboretum is Arizona's oldest and largest botanical garden, featuring plants of the world's deserts. Nestled at the base of Picketpost Mountain, the Arboretum was founded in the 1920s by mining magnate William Boyce Thompson. Encompassing 323 acres, are several miles of nature paths through the gardens—including the Cactus Garden, Taylor Family Desert Legume Garden, the Curandero Trail of medicinal plants. Ayer Lake is home to a variety of water fowl, as well as two species of endangered fish—the Desert Pupfish and Gila Topminnow. Other specialty gardens include the Wing Memorial Herb Garden, the Demonstration Garden and the Hummingbird/Butterfly Garden. There are surprises around every bend, from a streamside forest to towering trees. The Arboretum is a National Historic District and an Arizona State Park.

Year round, daily, 8 a.m. - 5 p.m. Closed Christmas Day

Take I-60 / Superstition Freeway east from Phoenix. The entrance is located on the south side of the highway, just west of Superior, Arizona.

Desert Botanical Garden ❧

1201 N. Galvin Parkway, Phoenix, AZ, 85008. (480) 941-1227.

Surrounded by rugged red buttes, the Desert Botanical Garden's 145 acres compromise one of the most complete collections of desert flora in the world. The garden is home to more than 20,000 plants and is a renowned research facility. The exhibition "Plants and People of the Sonoran Desert" captures the life of the area's first inhabitants. Spring is an especially beautiful time to visit, when hundreds of varieties of wildflowers burst into bloom.

October - April, daily, 8 a.m. - 8 p.m.; May - September, 7 a.m. - 8 p.m. Closed Christmas Day.

Take the McDowell Road east to Galvin Parkway and turn south. The garden is on the Galvin Parkway/64th Street just south of McDowell Road. The entrance is clearly marked on the east side of Galvin Parkway, and is just north of the Phoenix Zoo, in Papago Park.

❧ *public garden*

THE CACTUS GARDEN AT THE PHOENICIAN ❧

6000 EAST CAMELBACK ROAD, SCOTTSDALE, AZ 85251. (602) 941-8200.

Up the steps, across from the main entrance to The Phoenician resort, the cactus garden is a small gem nestled against the tail end of Camelback Mountain. Flagstone pathways wind through a wide variety of well-marked cacti and succulents, punctuated by several pieces of bronze statuary.

Year round, daily, dawn - dusk.

The entrance to The Phoenician is north off of Camelback Road, between 56th and 64th Streets. Drive into the main entrance to the resort. The garden is directly across and up the steps.

CALIFORNIA

★ San Francisco Bay Area
★ San Francisco Peninsula

★ Los Angeles

CALIFORNIA OPEN DAYS

May 6: Los Angeles
May 6 & 7, June 3 & 4, September 30 & October 1:
San Francisco Bay Area
April 15, May 13: San Francisco Peninsula

Los Angeles Open Day

Regional Representative: Mrs. Donivee Nash

Saturday, May 6

ARCADIA
Merrill & Donivee Nash, 1014 Hampton Road: 10 a.m. - 4 p.m.

LA CANADA
Dr. & Mrs. Val Clark, 900 Descanso Drive: 10 a.m. - 4 p.m.

LOS ANGELES
Cooper/Taggart Garden, 2643 Crestmoore Place: 10 a.m. - 4 p.m.
Daigre/Hamann Garden, 564 North Beachwood Drive: 10 a.m. - 4 p.m.
"El Chaparro" California Native Garden, 111 South Van Ness Avenue: 10 a.m. - 2 p.m.
Horton Garden, 256 South Van Ness Avenue: 2 p.m. - 6 p.m.
Rheinstein Garden, 435 South Windsor Boulevard: 2 p.m. - 6 p.m.

PASADENA
Archibald Young/Martin-Watterson, 808 South San Rafael Avenue: 10 a.m. - 2 p.m.
La Folie, 400 South San Rafael Avenue: 10 a.m. - 2 p.m.

SAN MARINO
Mr. & Mrs. Robert D. Volk, 1440 Orlando Road: 10 a.m. - 4 p.m.

ARCHIBALD YOUNG/MARTIN-WATTERSON

808 SOUTH SAN RAFAEL AVENUE, PASADENA

This garden was designed by A.E. Hanson for Archibald and Edith Young in 1927 in the Andalusian style to match the George Washington Smith-designed hacienda. Originally on three acres, the garden has been rescued by the current owners, George Martin and Jim Watterson. It includes mature palm trees; a 300-plus rose garden; a classic Mediterranean garden; a cactus garden; a seventy-year-old white wisteria arbor and colonnade; a hand-set, Moorish-style, rock-paved motor court; a 7,000-square-foot home and artist studio; and a pool pavilion.

Saturday, May 6, 10 a.m. - 2 p.m.

Exactly 1 mile south of the 210 Freeway going south on San Rafael Avenue from Colorado Boulevard. Take Linda Vista/San Rafael Exit from 210 Freeway East and San Rafael Exit from 210 Freeway West; or exit Avenue 64 from #110 Pasadena Freeway and take Avenue 64 north to LaLoma Road. Turn right onto LaLoma Road and go to San Rafael. Turn right onto San Rafael. The main gate is between LaLoma Avenue and Hillside Terrace.

Proceeds shared with The California Arboretum Foundation

COOPER/TAGGART GARDEN

2643 CRESTMOORE PLACE, LOS ANGELES

Our secret garden is located behind an ancient Opuntia hedge into which is set a green door on a hillside in Glassel Park. Plantings have been arranged to obscure the urban setting yet allow hillside views, creating a sense of rural peacefulness. Painterly use of color and texture abound in "garden rooms" connected by winding paths. The combination of view and terrain, old fruit trees, wild Mediterranean plantings, and rustic gravel paths conjure up the feeling of an Italian hillside in the country.

Saturday, May 6, 10 a.m. - 4 p.m.

*From the North: Take the 2 South to the Verdugo Exit in the Eagle Rock area. Turn left onto Verdugo, then right onto Eagle Rock Boulevard. At the traffic next light (which is Verdugo again) turn left. *Travel on Verdugo past the park to Avenue 35 and turn left. Avenue 35 will then turn around to the left and become Kinney. Stay on Kinney and turn left at the next street, Crestmoore Place, a dead-end street. The garden is at the second house from the bottom on the right. The number 2643 is on a beat-up mailbox. There is a cliff and a cactus hedge with a green door. Open the door and come up the* stairs. *The garden is at the top by the pond. From the South: Take the 2 North, exit at Verdugo. Stay in the right lane and cross Eagle Rock Road, onto Verdugo. Follow directions above*. Please park on Crestmoore Place.*

DAIGRE/HAMANN GARDEN
564 NORTH BEACHWOOD DRIVE, LOS ANGELES

A wide variety of unique and exuberant plant material envelopes a 1923 Spanish cottage in this typical city garden. Water features, roses, container borders and a driveway kitchen garden add to the cozy private space.

Saturday, May 6, 10 a.m. - 4 p.m.

Take the Gower Exit off of the 101 Freeway/Hollywood Freeway. Go south past Sunset and Santa Monica Boulevard to the traffic light at end at Melrose Avenue. Paramount Studios is on the left. Turn left onto Melrose then take an immediate right on Beachwood Drive. Pass the first stop sign, look for 564 in the second block, on the left. Please park on the street.

DR. & MRS. VAL CLARK
900 DESCANSO DRIVE, LA CANADA

Charming vines cover much of the English cottage house built in 1932. Surrounded by a rolling lawn, a formal rose garden, a formal garden maze of boxwood hedges. Stone patios and even a rooftop planted with vines and flowers form a secret garden for the grandchildren. Stone pieces and little surprises will delight the visitor. Perennials in deep beds, pots and roses abound in this classic, but always comfortable, storybook setting.

Saturday, May 6, 10 a.m. - 4 p.m.

Exit the 210 Freeway at Berkshire Avenue. Go west on Berkshire Place. Cross a small bridge and turn right on Berkshire Avenue. Continue west on Berkshire Avenue past three stop signs and turn right (north) on Beulah Drive. Turn left at the next intersection ("T") onto Descanso Drive. The garden is at the corner of Descanso Drive and Beulah. Please park anywhere on the street.

"El Chaparro" California Native Garden

111 South Van Ness Avenue, Los Angeles

"El Chaparro" was created to bring the botanical wilds of Southern California into an urban setting, and by so doing recreate the palette and scents of the nearby foothills and mountains. The garden is loosely organized by plant community including chaparral, desert, island and meadow. Within these groups primary plants are grown along-side their native companions, essentially surviving on rainfall alone, just as they would in nature. Structure is provided by the distinctive personalities of three native oaks, two of which were moved from the wild in an effort to save them from destruction by the proverbial "bulldozer." Added interest is provided by an arrangement of rustic pergola seats made from hickory branches, which add to the sense of "old California" that is ever present in this garden.

Saturday, May 6, 10 a.m. - 2 p.m.

From Santa Monica: Take the 10 Freeway East to La Brea. Turn north on La Brea to third Street. Turn right on third Street to South Van Ness Avenue and turn left. Go to the southwest corner of South Van Ness to the first Street. Please park on the street.

Horton Garden

256 South Van Ness Avenue, Los Angeles

A series of garden rooms surround this circa 1910 Craftsman house located four miles west of downtown Los Angeles. The back garden was designed in 1989 by landscape architect, Frances Knight. Garden designer and plantswoman Judy Horton has treated the garden as a work in progress ever since. The garden rooms or spaces consist of: an intimate terrace planted with white flowering, fragrant vines; a large Craftsman pergola; mixed borders around a rectangular lawn; a dry garden; a potting shed and naturalistic garden; various container gardens; and a front garden that relies primarily on foliage for color. Fruit trees create a theme and a feeling of abundance throughout the garden. The planting reflects the owner's interest in seasonal change in the garden.

Sunday, May 6, 2 p.m - 6 p.m.

From the Pasadena/Harbor Freeway/Route 110 take the Third Street Exit. Go west for 4 miles and take the first right after Wilton Place. From Hollywood Route 101 take the Sunset Boulevard Exit. Turn south onto Van Ness Avenue and go about 3 miles. From Santa Monica/Route 10 take the Western Avenue Exit. Go north about 3 miles to Third Street and turn left. The first traffic light is Wilton Place, turn right after Wilton Place. Please park on the street.

LA FOLIE

400 SOUTH SAN RAFAEL AVENUE, PASADENA

This is a twentieth-century interpretation of an eighteenth-century Italian/French garden, with a top note of English naturalism. Several vignettes of roses, as well as perennials and woodlands, are set on the banks of the historic "San Rafael," with bowers and niches to contemplate life's wonder. Fountains splash to accent the scent of jasmine.

Saturday, May 6, 10 a.m. - 2 p.m.

Take 134 East to San Rafael Exit. Turn right at the exit onto Colorado Boulevard. Turn right onto San Rafael and then left onto 400 South San Rafael. Please park on the street.

MERRILL & DONIVEE NASH

1014 HAMPTON ROAD, ARCADIA

The home and garden are located in the Upper Rancho area of the historic Rancho Santa Anita, a neighborhood famous for its 200- to 300-year-old oak trees. The garden is a constantly evolving entity whose backbone is several hundred roses-Austins, hybrid teas, and old English. A formal pool, tennis court, and Dumbarton Oaks-inspired summerhouse provide a framework for perennials, climbing roses, clematis, and many varieties of trees. This garden is designed with the opportunity of almost year-round outdoor living in mind, but is at its most beautiful during the roses' first bloom.

Saturday, May 6, 10 a.m. - 4 p.m.

From the west, proceed east on 210 Freeway. Exit at Rosemead North/Michillinda. Proceed north on Michillinda, cross Foothill Boulevard, turn right onto Hampton Road. Continue to intersection of Hampton and Dexter Roads. The house is #1014 Hampton on the southwest corner of the intersection. From the east, proceed west on 210 Freeway. Exit at Baldwin Avenue. Proceed north on Baldwin, cross Foothill Boulevard, turn left at the second street/Hampton Road. Follow Hampton to the intersection of Dexter and Hampton. Follow as above.

Proceeds shared with The California Arboretum Foundation.

Mr. & Mrs. Robert D. Volk

1440 ORLANDO ROAD, SAN MARINO

This one-acre property has a series of garden rooms, connected by a 150-foot corridor. The traditional perennial border includes many Austin roses and herbaceous plants. A knot garden complements the Georgian Colonial architecture of the house, but surprises the viewer with its Mediterranean plant material. The pool garden has a purple border and a diverse collection of hydrangeas. The orchard garden includes apples, pears, and citrus along with iris and lavender.

Saturday, May 6, 10 a.m. - 4 p.m.

From the Pasadena Freeway (110), go to the end and proceed north on Arroyo Parkway .5 mile to California Boulevard. Turn right and proceed 1.9 miles to Allen Avenue. Turn right and proceed 2 blocks to Orlando Road and the entrance gates to the Huntington. Turn right and proceed .4 mile to the intersection of Avondale Road and Orlando Road. From the Foothill Parkway (210), take the Hill Avenue Exit, proceed south 1.1 miles to California Boulevard. Turn left and proceed .4 mile to Allen Avenue. Turn right and proceed as above.

Proceeds shared with The Huntington Botanical Gardens.

Rheinstein Garden

435 SOUTH WINDSOR BOULEVARD, LOS ANGELES

Our back garden was designed by Judy Horton to include several distinct areas. From our old-fashioned porch, the view is serene, architectural, with clipped spheres and a quiet pool bringing a sense of order. A tree room with gravel floor and green hedge walls is another serene space. In contrast, the pool garden is "hot"-succulents, cannas, bananas, loquats, kumquats, etc. Behind a gravel garden and a screen of quinces is the hidden place to grow things willy-nilly. There are black hollyhocks, heirloom tomatoes in chartreuse tubs and an old iron Turkish tent covered in annual vines. Our garden is organic and filled with butterflies and little birds.

Saturday, May 6, 2 p.m. - 6 p.m.

Four blocks east of Rossmore. Two and one half blocks north of Wilshire, and 1.5 blocks south of Third. Please park on the street.

THE ARBORETUM OF LOS ANGELES COUNTY ♣

301 NORTH BALDWIN AVENUE, ARCADIA, CA, 91007. (626) 821-3222.

The Arboretum is a 127-acre horticultural and botanical museum jointly operated by the County of Los Angeles and the California Arboretum Foundation. The Arboretum has plants from around the world blooming in every season. It is a wildlife refuge,complete with fish, turtles, ducks, geese, and other native and migrating birds enjoy the sanctuary of Baldwin Lake and the Tropical Forest. It is Old California with historic buildings dating from 1840 that show early California lifestyles. The Hugo Reid Adobe is a California state landmark, the century-old Queen Anne Cottage is a national landmark. The Arboretum staff has introduced more than 100 flowering plants to the California landscape and boast tree collections from many countries. A daily tram runs through the grounds every thirty minutes from 11 a.m. - 3 p.m. The arboretum is constantly adding horticulture classes, culture and beauty to its acreage.

Year round, daily, dawn - dusk.

Exit the 210 Freeway exit on Baldwin Avenue. The Arboretum is in the San Gabriel Valley, freeway close to downtown Los Angeles, and right next door to Pasadena.

THE HUNTINGTON LIBRARY, ART COLLECTIONS, AND BOTANICAL GARDENS ♣

1151 OXFORD ROAD SAN MARINO, CA, 91108. (626) 405-2141.

The former estate of railroad magnate Henry Huntington showcases over 14,000 species of plants in 150 acres of gardens. Highlights include a twelve-acre desert garden, a rose garden, Japanese garden, jungle garden, and ten acres of camellias. Art and literary treasures are displayed in historic buildings on the grounds. English tea is served in the Rose Garden Tea Room.

Tuesday - Friday, noon - 4:30 p.m.; Saturday & Sunday, 10:30 a.m. - 4:30 p.m.; Summer hours (June through August), Tuesday - Sunday, 10:30 a.m. - 4:30 p.m.

Located near the city of Pasadena, approximately 12 miles northeast of downtown Los Angeles. From the downtown area, take the Pasadena Freeway (110) north until it ends and becomes Arroyo Parkway. Continue north on Arroyo for 2 blocks to California Boulevard, turn right and continue on California for 2 miles. Turn right at Allen Avenue and go straight for 2 short blocks to the Huntington gates. For recorded directions from other area freeways, call (626) 405-2274.

VAL VERDE &

MONTECITO, CA. (805) 965-3639.

Designed and built at the turn of the century by Bertram Goodhue, Val Verde has been beautifully maintained ever since. Steps are being taken to guarantee the preservation of this fine Southern California estate, including the Italianate gardens and landscaped grounds. The acknowledged masterwork of Lockwood de Forest.

Val Verde is not yet opened to the public. Call for private tour information.

A preservation project of The Garden Conservancy.

San Francisco Bay Area Open Days

Regional Representatives: Dick Turner, Sonny Garcia, Charmain Giuliani, & Tom Valva

Saturday, May 6

EL CERRITO
Harland Hand Garden, 825 Shevlin Drive: 10 a.m. - 4 p.m.

BERKELEY
Maybeck Cottage—Garden of Roger Raiche & David McCrory,
    1 Maybeck Twin Drive: 10 a.m. - 4 p.m.

OAKLAND
Sharon & Dennis Osmond, 5548 Lawton Avenue: 2 p.m. - 6 p.m.
Shaunee & Pat Power, 5935 Manchester Drive: 10 a.m. - 4 p.m.

Sunday, May 7

KENTFIELD
Geraniaceae Gardens, 122 Hillcrest Avenue: 10 a.m. - 4 p.m.

SAN FRANCISCO
Blarry House, 104 Laidley Street: 10 a.m. - 2 p.m.
Harry Stairs Garden, 47 Harry Street: 10 a.m. - 4 p.m.
Singer/Kapp Garden, 21st Street: 10 a.m. - 2 p.m.
The Pelavin Garden, 90 Woodland: 10 a.m. - 4 p.m.

Saturday, June 3

BERKELEY
Our Own Stuff Gallery Garden—Marcia Donahue, 3017 Wheeler Street:
    2 p.m. - 6 p.m.
Suzanne Porter, 2810 Webster Street: 2 p.m. - 6 p.m.

OAKLAND
Sharon & Dennis Osmond, 5548 Lawton Avenue: 2 p.m. - 6 p.m.

Sunday, June 4

KENTFIELD
Geraniaceae Gardens, 122 Hillcrest Avenue: 10 a.m. - 4 p.m.

SAN FRANCISCO
Stevens Garden, 183 Edgewood Avenue: 10 a.m. - 2 p.m.

Saturday, September 30

ALAMEDA
"Mellow Yellow"—The Madden/Thompson Garden,
   400 Haight Avenue: 2 p.m. - 6 p.m.
Watts/Coup Garden, 1000 Park Street: 4 p.m. - 8 p.m.

BERKELEY
Our Own Stuff Gallery Garden—Marcia Donahue, 3017 Wheeler Street:
   2 p.m. - 6 p.m.

EL CERRITO
Harland Hand Garden, 825 Shevlin Drive: 10 a.m. - 4 p.m.

KENSINGTON
Garden of Anderson Family, 17 Beverly Court: 10 a.m. - 2 p.m.

OAKLAND
Sharon & Dennis Osmond, 5548 Lawton Avenue: 2 p.m. - 6 p.m.

Sunday, October 1

GREENBREA
Missionor—Herb Weber's Garden, 40 Altura Way: 10 a.m. - 4 p.m.

KENTFIELD
Geraniaceae Gardens, 122 Hillcrest Avenue: 10 a.m. - 4 p.m.

SAN FRANCISCO
Blarry House, 104 Laidley Street: 10 a..m. - 2 p.m.
Sonny Garcia & Tom Valva, 423 Flood Avenue: 10 a.m. - 2 p.m.

Garden of Anderson Family

17 Beverly Court, Kensington

The Anderson Family Garden is an exciting mixture of the old and the new. First settled in the early 1920s by the Anderson family, the original garden surrounded a small cottage. That garden included a fruit orchard, rose gardens, and vegetable gardens. There was even a chicken coop. The current owner, Janet Anderson, grew up in this garden and later in life came back and retired here. Working with professional garden artists, the current garden design weaves together historic garden elements with an exotic collection of new plants, statuary and urns. Don't miss the variety of bulbs, salvias, geraniums, palms. cycads, roses, bamboos, orchids, rhododendrons, and other unique plants.

Saturday, September 30, 10 a.m. - 2 p.m.

Kensington is in the hills between Berkeley and El Cerrito in the East Bay. Take the Albany Exit (Buchanan Street Exit) off I-80N. This is the first exit north after Gilman Street Exit in Berkeley. Follow the road to the east past San Pablo Road up Marin Avenue. Take Marin Avenue to the Marin Circle (about 2 miles). Go around the circle and then up The Arlington. Follow The Arlington up to the town of Kensington. Just past the town grocery, make a "U"-turn and go back down about one-half block. Make the first right on Ardmore Road. Take Ardmore down about .25 mile and then park. Beverly Court is a small cul-de-sac on the right (it looks like a driveway and is easy to miss). Walk down to the garden from Ardmore Road.

Blarry House

104 Laidley Street, San Francisco

Blarry House is a continuing experiment with low-maintenance natives and exotics. Our small garden is multileveled with views of the city and the San Francisco Bay. A pond (also known as the raccoon bath and smorgasbord) sits aside the requisite Gunnera. A country feel lends contrast to the reality of being in the middle of the city.

Sundays; May 7, October 1; 10 a.m. - 2 p.m.

From Route 101, take Army/Cesar Chavez exit and go west on Cesar Chavez to Noe Street, traveling about ten blocks. Turn left onto Noe Street, which dead ends on Laidley. We are three houses to the left of the intersection of Laidley and Noe. The house is dark green. From Northbound I-280, follow signs to the Bay Bridge but exit at San Jose Avenue. After the first traffic light on San Jose, turn left onto Dolores and immediately left onto 30th Street. Turn left onto Noe Street and follow directions from above. We are at 104 Laidley Street. Please park along the street.

Proceeds shared with The Friends of the Urban Forest.

Geraniaceae Gardens

122 Hillcrest Avenue, Kentfield

These tranquil gardens were developed as living praise to hardy geraniums, and other rare and unusual shrubs and hardy perennials. The one-acre site began as a small flat area and long, steep slopes of bright yellow clay. It was a challenge to carve out areas of cultivation. There are two sunny perennial and shrub borders in the upper garden for hot and cool colored plants, and linking staircases to a lower woodland garden. A small nursery displays plants in the geranium family. The garden has a number of sculptures by Bay Area artists and there are many seats and a small casita for resting and talking

Sundays; May 7, June 4, October 1; 10 a.m. - 4 p.m.

From San Francisco, cross the Golden Gate Bridge on Highway 101. Continue approximately 8 miles north through Mill Valley into Corte Madera. Take the San Anselmo Exit onto Sir Francis Drake Boulevard going west. Continue as described below. Coming from the East Bay, follow I-58 west across the Richmond San Rafael Bridge. Take the second exit, Sir Francis Drake Boulevard. The road passes San Quentin Prison, and after several miles, goes underneath Highway 101. Continue as described below. From the Junction of 101 take Sir Francis Drake Boulevard west for 2 miles. At a large set of traffic lights turn left onto College Avenue. The Kentfield Fire Station is at the traffic light. Go along College Avenue past a pedestrian light and 2 stop signs. At the second stop sign, turn right onto Estelle Avenue. (West America Bank is on the right). Go up Estelle to the stop sign, and turn right onto Hillcrest Avenue. Number 122 is the second house on the right on Hillcrest. Do not block driveway. There are two gardens next door to each other, at 122 and 124 Hillcrest. Directional arrows will indicate a path through the two gardens with the exit at the beginning of the driveway. Please park on the right side of Hillcrest.

HARLAND HAND GARDEN

825 SHEVLIN DRIVE, EL CERRITO

Harland Hand's Garden was designed using the principles of fine art in a composition of interesting combinations of foliage and floral color, texture, and form. Inspired by Nature and rock formations in the High Sierras, Mr. Hand sculpted concrete steps, paths, pools, and benches. The garden has been featured in various books, magazines, newspapers, and television programs. The nearly half-acre garden is an environment to experience. Mr. Hand died in September 1998; however his garden will continue to be open to the public by appointment. Information concerning his own book, *The Composed Garden*, will also be available.

Saturdays; May 6, September 30; 10 a.m. - 4 p.m.

Take I-80 to El Cerrito, Central Avenue Exit. Turn right onto Central Avenue. Turn left onto San Pablo Avenue. Turn right onto Moeser Lane. Go up the hill, turn right onto Shevlin Drive and proceed 1.5 blocks to the garden.

🌀 *A preservation project of The Garden Conservancy.*

HARRY STAIRS GARDEN

47 HARRY STREET, SAN FRANCISCO

My house and garden sit on a little-known stairway in a part of town once known as Fairmount Heights; now it is commonly known as Noe Valley. The size of the lot is roughly one-acre. Having the good fortune to live on such a large, open property, I am able to create not one, but several different garden environments. My garden consists of four sections, all connected with bending pathways of various stepping stones. The upper section is the most formal, with a slate walkway and sitting areas around a lawn and trellises of climbing star jasmine and honeysuckle. The lower section has a slate sitting area surrounded by a variety of grasses. To the left of the grass area is a kidney-shaped rose garden and deck with chairs and reclining benches. The most spectacular part of the yard is the backdrop of Noe Valley, the San Francisco skyline, the Bay Bridge, and the East Bay hills framed by towering eucalyptus and cyprus trees. Gardening is my passion; the joy and happiness it brings me is shared with those who walk the stairs and take time out to stop and look.

Sunday, May 7, 10 a.m. - 4 p.m.

Take Noe Street south to its end at Laidley Street. Harry Street steps are directly across the intersection approximately three doors to the right of Blarry House. Park and walk up.

"Mellow Yellow" — The Madden-Thompson Garden

400 Haight Avenue, Alameda

Our yellow cottage and garden are enclosed by an antique wrought iron fence. Because I am a garden designer, my garden is a laboratory where I gleefully practice the "art of cramming." Not only do I test new and unusual plants, I also experiment using familiar plants in new ways. Two years ago, I discovered that two quadrants of the garden are infected with Oak Root Fungus. These areas have become a secondary "lab" to test plants for resistance to this fungus. Ever-expanding collections include hemerocallis and lilium hybrids and berberis. I love warm colors, using a wide assortment of yellows, oranges, and reds as well as greens of all hues and variegated foliage.

Saturday, September 30, 2 p.m. - 6 p.m.

*From the Bay Bridge/I-80 East take new San Jose/Southbound 880 lanes. Take the Broadway/Alameda Exit and stay right. Turn right at the first traffic light onto Fifth Street. Stay in the middle lane. At the Broadway traffic light, use one of the two left lanes to go under the freeway into the Webster Street Tube to Alameda. *Once through the Tube, go 6 blocks to Haight Avenue and turn right. Go 4 blocks to the corner of Fourth Street and find parking anywhere. From Freeway 880, take the Broadway Exit and bear right onto Broadway at the traffic light. Turn right at the next light onto Seventh Street. Go 2 blocks to the next signal, which is Webster Street and turn right again. Look for a sign that reads "Alameda" and take through the Webster Street Tube into Alameda. Follow directions above. From I-24/Contra Costa County follow until I-24 becomes the 980 connector. Exit at Eleventh/Twelfth Street in Oakland. Go straight to Fifth Street and turn left at the traffic light onto Broadway. At the Broadway traffic light, use one of the two left lanes to go under the freeway into the Webster Street Tube to Alameda. Follow directions above.**

Maybeck Cottage — Garden of Roger Raiche & David McCrory

1 Maybeck Twin Drive, Berkeley

The garden's collection encompasses nearly 3,000 kinds of plants from around the world. Emphasis here is on plants that thrive in Berkeley, with some pushing the cold tolerance a bit, and plants with great foliage and year-round interest. The plants are displayed in a heightened naturalistic style among constructions, or theaters, of found objects. Roger has developed and perfected the style he and David now market as "Planet Horticulture" through their firm of the same name.

Saturday, May 6, 10 a.m. - 4 p.m.

Get to Cedar street (4 blocks north of University Avenue or 4 blocks south of Gilman Street; both are exits from Highway 80). Proceed east, uphill, until Cedar Street ends at

La Loma. Turn left onto La Loma. The second street on the right is Buena Vista at a 4-way stop sign. Turn right onto Buena Vista; park along the road on Buena Vista. Maybeck Twin Drive is the first left on Buena Vista. The first house up from the corner (not center house) is #1.

MISSIONOR — HERB WEBER'S GARDEN

40 ALTURA WAY, GREENBREA

My lifelong passion for growing things and for physical labor, tools and construction has resulted in an uniquely personal home and garden. Unable to suppress my penchant for the heroic and romantic in my life, I have created a palm-lined drive-way, a pool surrounded by tree ferns, cycads, palms, bromeliads and other exotics, interspersed everywhere with rhododendrons, azaleas, magnolias, maples, conifers, flowering trees, citrus, perennials, vines and leaves; big leaves, small leaves, variegated leaves, shiny leaves and fuzzy leaves. And in winter when the pool is not so inviting I have my new 6,000 cubic foot conservatory filled with anthuriums, orchids, gesneriads, and ripening, edible bananas.

Sunday, October 1, 10 a.m. - 4 p.m.

North on Highway 101 approximately 10 miles beyond Golden Gate Bridge to Sir Francis Drake Blvd. west (toward San Anselmo) to second traffic light. Turn right on LaCuesta and proceed one block to a 5-way intersection. Turn slightly left almost straight ahead onto Los Cerros. Follow 1 block to Via Cheparo and then proceed uphill 1 long block to Altura on right. Proceed about 150 yards to palm-lined driveway labeled #40 and #50 on the curb. Please park on the street. Proceed down driveway to #40 on the left.

OUR OWN STUFF GALLERY GARDEN — MARCIA DONAHUE

3017 WHEELER STREET, BERKELEY

My twenty-year-old garden is a gallery where Mark Bulwinkle's sculpture in steel and mine in stone complement a large collection of unusual and sculptural plants. Their arrangement and interaction create an atmosphere many of my visitors and I find thrilling. Anne Raver wrote, "Art and nature are as intimately entangled here as lovers and nothing is sacred." To me, though, everything is sacred here, even sacred enough to poke fun at, and I love sharing it.

Saturdays; June 3, September 30; 2 p.m. - 6 p.m.

From I-80/580 by the San Francisco Bay, take the Ashby Avenue/Berkeley exit. After 1.5 miles look for Shattuck Avenue. There are two gas stations at the intersection of Shattuck and Ashby. Cross Shattuck and turn right onto Wheeler Street. Look for the fourth house on the left, #3017 Wheeler Street. Please park on Wheeler or Emerson Streets.

Proceeds shared with Strybing Arboretum & Botanical Gardens.

Sharon & Dennis Osmond

5548 Lawton Avenue, Oakland

Mine is a small, shady garden—intensively planted, intensely personal, and enclosed by high walls of foliage. For me, gardening here is a journey in search of memory, and so as if to illuminate that search, mirrors, like beacons, shine among the leaves, and *Pittosporum* 'Silver Sheen', which hedges the garden's path, shimmers with moving light. Foliage texture and color here make the garden a place of mysterious beauty in every season; the round pool at the patio's edge reflects the movement overhead of the branches and the flicker of hanging mirrored balls. Occasionally, a mannequin pokes her foot through shrubbery and lowers it into the water.

Saturdays; May 6, June 3, September 30; 2 p.m. - 6 p.m.

Located in the Rockridge area of Oakland just 2 blocks south from the Rockridge BART station, our house is at #5548 Lawton Avenue. From I-80, take the Ashby Avenue/ Berkeley Exit and go east on Ashby to College Avenue. Take College Avenue to Lawton and then turn east onto Lawton.

Shaunee & Pat Power

5935 Manchester Drive, Oakland

Shaunee and Pat Power lost their home and garden in the 1991 Oakland firestorm. They immediately decided to rebuild their home, and hired Harland Hand to design their garden. The garden incorporates Harland's signature design features of rocks and cement that form paths, mounds, and rooms over approximately one third of an acre. As the garden matures the rooms become more distinct and appealing. The garden contains a spectacular water feature designed by Harland as well as a sport court for family recreation purposes. Harland and Shaunee worked closely to select the plantings for the garden. Among the many varieties of plants are rhododendrons, roses, irises, azaleas, and numerous grasses, placed among many fruit trees and other trees in Harland's characteristic emphasis on color and natural effect.

Saturday, May 6, 10 a.m. - 4 p.m.

From Highway 24 East take the Broadway Exit, turn right onto Broadway, and then take an immediate left onto Ocean View. Manchester Drive is the second right turn off of Ocean View. The garden is on the right. From Highway 24 West take the Broadway Exit. Turn left onto Ocean View, the first left after the traffic light, and go 2 blocks to Manchester Drive.

Singer/Kapp Garden

21st Street, San Francisco

An entire city lot is devoted to create a park-like setting in this Noe Valley garden. Cobblestones, marble, and brick were used extensively by the previous owners to create a durable hardscape. Special care was taken to preserve many existing features when the current owners had a new house constructed on the property in 1997. A restful atmosphere complements the award-winning house designed by Turnbull, Griffin, and Haesloop which gracefully blends inside and outside spaces. Multilevel brick terraces provide ample room for entertaining large numbers of people in this private, hilltop setting, and several well-established trees provide ample shade from some of San Francisco's sunniest days.

Sunday, May 7, 10 a.m. - 2 p.m.

From the Golden Gate Bridge, take Lombard Street to Divisidero and turn right. Go south about 2 miles. Divisidero curves into Castro just 2 blocks after Haight. Follow Castro past Davies Medical Center approximately 6 more blocks. Cross Market Street and go south to 21st Street. Turn left. The garden is up hill 1 and one half blocks on the right, between Noe and Sanchez. From 101 South, take the Ceasar Chavez/Army Street Exit and drive west on Chavez for about 8 blocks. Turn right onto Dolores, just after St. Luke's Hospital (on the left). Go north about 10 blocks to 21st Street. Turn left. The garden is up hill 2 and one half blocks, between Sanchez and Noe in the middle of the block. From 280 North, take San Jose Avenue Exit. Drive approximately 1 mile to Ceasar Chavez/Army Street and turn left just after St. Luke's Hospital. Go 1 block to Dolores. Turn right. Follow directions above from Chavez and Dolores. Please park on the street.

SONNY GARCIA & TOM VALVA
423 FLOOD AVENUE, SAN FRANCISCO

Our garden is small but filled with many rare and unusual plants. It was a challenge to incorporate many good design ideas into such a small space. The emphasis in our garden is on foliage. Bold, textured, colored, and variegated plants are collected from all over the country. Intricate juxtapositions and dramatic combinations of colorful foliage keep the garden interesting year-round. We are very honored to have our garden featured in books, magazines, and television, including "The Victory Garden" on PBS, Rosemary Verey's *Secret Gardens*, and Sir Roy Strong's *Successful Small Gardens*.

Sunday, October 1, 10 a.m. - 2 p.m.

From the north, take Highway 101 South to I-280 South. Take the Monterey Boulevard exit. Go .5 miles to Foerster Avenue. Turn left onto Foerster and right onto Flood Avenue. From the South, take Highway 280 North to the Ocean Avenue exit. Turn left on Geneva Avenue and stay in the right lane. Turn left onto Ocean Avenue and immediately right onto Phelan Avenue. Follow Phelan Avenue around San Francisco City College. Turn left onto Gennessee and right onto Flood. Look for house #423.

STEVENS GARDEN

183 EDGEWOOD AVENUE, SAN FRANCISCO

This is a collector's garden—a small city one at that—built on a rocky hillside site. There is really no theme to it, or plan. I collect alpines that will survive a damp location and many tree species, some dwarf, some bonsai and many in pots. Paths are river stones; thus there is no wheelchair accessibility.

Sunday, June 4, 10 a.m. - 2 p.m.

Just a few blocks from the Strybing Arboretum. From the arboretum, go south on Ninth Avenue to Judah. Make a left (east), go past the University of California Medical Center. The first right after the Medical Center is Willard. Make a right onto Willard and proceed up a steep hill. At the top of the hill, go right onto Belmont. At the top, make a left onto Edgewood. We are #183, just past four identical garages. You may park in front of the two marked ones. I am the next house up hill.

SUZANNE PORTER

2810 WEBSTER STREET, BERKELEY

My small urban garden is both a personal refuge and a place to develop my plant palette and design style. It is a naturalistic space punctuated by a sculptural column which integrates water. There are pathways to secluded corners for contemplation. I try to maintain a delicate balance between a passion for plants, art, and design. A multi-layered color palette which concentrates on maroon, greens, and chartreuse foliage is a backdrop for the more intense oranges and golds. My garden is constantly changing, always giving me pleasures and surprises.

Saturday, June 3, 2 p.m. - 6 p.m.

From I-80/580 by the San Francisco Bay, take the Ashby Avenue/Berkeley Exit. Go approximately 2.5 miles to College Avenue. Cross College Avenue and turn right at the second street, Piedmont Avenue. Go 1 block to Webster Street and turn right. My garden is at the third house on the right.

THE PELAVIN GARDEN

90 WOODLAND, SAN FRANCISCO

Toby & Al's home sits up in the tree tops like an elegant cabin that was designed by Richard Neutra. Chip Lima has redesigned the garden into elaborate, colorful terraces filled with rare tropical plants, succulents, and roses. The view of downtown and the park-like setting are rare urban commodities.

Sunday, May 6, 10 a.m. - 4 p.m.

From Highway 101N, take the Fell Street Exit west. At the end of the Pan Handle be in the right lane to exit and turn left onto Stanyan Street. Go 8 blocks south on

Stanyan Street then turn right onto Parnassis Street. Go 1 block and turn left onto Woodland Street. Go to 90 Woodland on the left.

WATTS/COUP GARDEN

1000 PARK STREET, ALAMEDA

Ours is a small urban garden with a wisteria-covered pergola (1911?), magnolia, camellias and roses. Planting beds have been enlarged to contain an unusual mix of antique and avant garde, hot plants and old stand bys, where we enjoy pushing the limits of the expected, the intentional and the happy accident. It now includes two small water features, entomological silkscreens, a post modern Shakespeare garden, blueprints for a prison and televisions as garden lights. Recent projects have involved lighting experiments, therefore we have extended open hours for those who would like to view the garden at dusk.

Saturday, September 30, 4 p.m. - 8 p.m.

From San Francisco and Berkeley: 880 South, exit 23rd Ave. in Oakland, past the 7-11 across the Park St. Bridge, lands you on Park Street on right. Number 1000 Park is on left. From San Jose and south, 880 North exit 29th Ave in Oakland, right on Fruitvale, under freeway, over Fruitvale Bridge and straight on Tilden Way to Park St. Left on Park 6 blocks to Clinton St. Please park on Street.

DUNSMUIR HISTORIC ESTATE ❧

2960 PERALTA OAKS COURT, OAKLAND, CA 94605. (510) 615-5555.

John McLaren, designer of Golden Gate Park in San Francisco, is said to have assisted in designing the gardens at the Dunsmuir Estate for the Hellman family, who owned the estate from 1906 until the late 1950s. Today, the fifty acres of meadows and gardens are still graced with a wide variety of trees, including Camperdown elms, bunya-bunya, and hornbeam, which surround the turn-of-the-century Neo-Classical Revival-style mansion.

February - October, Tuesday - Friday. Also open the first and third Sunday, May - September. 10 a.m. - 4 p.m.

Located off I-580 East at the 106th Avenue Exit. Make 3 quick left turns to cross the freeway, then turn right onto Peralta Oaks Drive. Follow signs to Dunsmuir. From I-580 West, exit at Foothill/MacArthur Boulevard and veer to the right onto Foothill Boulevard. Turn right onto 106th Avenue and right again onto Peralta Oaks Drive. Follow signs to Dunsmuir.

Kaiser Center Roof Garden ❧

00 LAKESIDE DRIVE, OAKLAND, CA, 94612. (510) 271-6197.

The Kaiser Center Roof Garden is a three and one-half -acre park located four floors above street level on top of the Kaiser Center Garage. The garden, designed by the San Francisco firm of Osmundson and Staley, was installed in 1960. Despite a busy urban setting, boundary hedges, winding paths, bermed plantings, and a reflecting pond give the garden a quiet, oasis-like quality. A large variety of specimen trees, shrubs, perennials, and annuals provide year-round horticultural interest.

Year round, Monday - Friday, 7 a.m. - 7 p.m.

From San Francisco, take the Bay Bridge to I-580 East (toward Hayward). One mile past the bridge, take the Harrison Street exit and turn right onto Harrison Street. Go straight through three traffic lights. Lake Merritt is on your left and the Kaiser Building is ahead to the right. Continue straight on Harrison and get into the right lane. Turn right onto 20th Street and make an immediate right into the parking garage. There is also street parking in the neighborhood. Take the garage elevator to Roof Garden level.

Strybing Arboretum & Botanical Gardens ❧

9TH AVENUE, SAN FRANCISCO, CA, 94122. (415) 661-1316.

Strybing Arboretum and Botanical Gardens sprawl over fifty-five acres and feature 7,000 kinds of plants from all over the world: Chile, Australia, Cape Province, and New Zealand to name a few. Specialty gardens include the Primitive Plant Garden, the Moon-Viewing Garden, and the Garden of Fragrance. You can stroll on your own or take a free guided tour offered by the Strybing Arboretum Society. If you are still not sated, stop by the Helen Crocker Russell Library of Horticulture, a free reference library.

Library open year round, daily, 10 a.m. - 4 p.m. (Except major holidays). Gardens open Monday - Friday, 8 a.m. - 4:30 p.m.; Weekends and holidays. 10 a.m. - 5 p.m.

Located in Golden Gate Park, at the corner of Ninth Avenue and Lincoln Way.

THE BLAKE GARDEN OF THE UNIVERSITY OF CALIFORNIA &

70 RINCON ROAD, KENSINGTON, CA 94707. (510) 524-2449.

This ten and one-half-acre garden was given to the University in the early 1960s by the Blake family. The garden was established when the house was designed and built in the 1920s. It has a large display of plants ranging from drought-tolerant to more moisture-loving plants from places such as Asia. The garden is divided into the formal area, the drought-tolerant section, the Australian Hollow, the cut-flower section, and the redwood canyon.

Year round, Monday - Friday. 8 a.m. - 4:30 p.m. Closed on University holidays.

From I-80, take the Buchanan Street off-ramp east to Buchanan Street. Follow Buchanan which turns into Marin Avenue until you arrive at a traffic circle with a fountain. Take the fourth exit off the circle onto The Arlington. Travel 1.8 miles to Rincon Road on the left. Blake Garden is 70 Rincon Road.

THE JAPANESE TEA GARDEN &

GOLDEN GATE PARK, SAN FRANCISCO, CA 94117. (415) 831-2700.

The Japanese Tea Garden in Golden Gate Park, the oldest public Japanese garden in the United States, dates from 1894. Created for the California Mid-Winter Exposition to represent a Japanese village, the five-acre stroll garden includes a drum bridge, a teahouse, a pagoda, a gift shop, two gates built for the 1915 Panama Pacific Exposition, and a Temple Belfry Gate (or Shoronomon). The garden also has a notable collection of beautiful stone lanterns and a large bronze Buddha cast in 1790.

April - October, daily, 9 a.m. - 5:30 p.m. November through March, daily, 8:30 a.m. - 5 p.m.

Located in the center of Golden Gate Park near the DeYoung Museum and Academy of Sciences on Hagiwara Drive. It is 100 yards north of the North Gate of Strybing Arboretum.

THE RUTH BANCROFT GARDEN ❧

P.O. Box 3484, Walnut Creek, CA 94598. (925) 210-9663.

The Ruth Bancroft Garden rises above the status of a collection to an exceptional demonstration of the art of garden design. Working primarily with the dramatic forms of her beloved succulents, Mrs. Bancroft has created bold and varied compositions in which the colors, textures, and patterns of foliage provide a setting for the sparkle of floral color.

Open for Open Days visitors on May 6, June 3 & September 30, 10 a.m. - 2 p.m., Otherwise, open by appointment only.

Just north of Highway 24, exit I-680 on Ygnacio Valley Road. Follow Ygnacio Valley Road 2.5 miles to Bancroft Road. Turn left, pass Stratton. At the end of wooden fence turn right into #1500 Bancroft Road.

A preservation project of The Garden Conservancy.

San Francisco Peninsula Open Days

Regional Representative: Mrs. Harvey D. Hinman & Mrs. Mo Sanders

Saturday, April 15

ATHERTON
Crocker Garden, 151 Glenwood Avenue: 10 a.m. - 2 p.m.
Suzanne's Garden, 88 Selby Lane: 10 a.m. - 4 p.m.

MENLO PARK
The Woodruff Garden, 1911 Oakdell Drive: 10 a.m. - 4 p.m.

Saturday, May 13

ATHERTON
Gene & Chuck Pratt, 166 Encinal Avenue: 10 a.m. - 2 p.m.
Joan & Mo Sanders, 156 Hawthorn Drive: 10 a.m. - 2 p.m.
Lynnie & Rich Dewey's Garden, 97 Hawthorn Drive: 10 a.m. - 2 p.m.
The Garden at 130 Selby Lane: 10 a.m.- 2 p.m.

PALO ALTO
Debby & Rob Ruskin, 174 Walter Hays Drive: 10 a.m. - 2 p.m.

WOODSIDE
Creekside Garden, 121 Fox Hollow Road: 10 a.m. - 4 p.m.

CREEKSIDE GARDEN

121 FOX HOLLOW ROAD, WOODSIDE

Twenty-five years ago when we built our home we sought out a natural wooded setting because Jim, an architect, wanted to design a house for such a site. While we love the redwoods and changing light of the forest, planting a garden that withstands a few hours a day of intense sunlight is a challenge. Several years ago Peggy Hinman designed a beautiful woodland garden for us. She created terraces going down to the creek and used a lovely palette of grey-green foliage, crimson maples, and purple lavender to give us color in the forest year-round.

Saturday, May 13, 10 a.m. - 4 p.m.

Take Highway 280 to Woodside Road exit. Take Woodside Road west towards the mountains. Go through the town. Fox Hollow Road is first left past Roberts Grocery Store. We are #121 Fox Hollow Road, the third house on the left. Please park on the left side of Fox Hollow Road.

CROCKER GARDEN

151 GLENWOOD AVENUE, ATHERTON

Entering this one-and-one half-acre garden through a small gate framed by a woodland garden, the visitor is treated to an expansive, park-like vista anchored by mature evergreen trees that serve as a foil for a large variety of deciduous trees and shrubs. Brick paths lead through many interesting gardens surrounding the house, (the original part of which was the carriage house for a large Victorian estate). One experiences an incredible collection of rhododendrons, camellias, azaleas, deciduous flowering trees and shrubs, Japanese maples, and a rose collection.

Saturday, April 15, 10 a.m. - 2 p.m.

Take Highway 101, to the Marsh Road/Atherton Exit. Travel west on Marsh Road to its end at Middlefield Road. Turn left onto Middlefield Road, go .6 miles to Glenwood Avenue, turn right and look for #151 on the right. Please park along the street.

Debby & Rob Ruskin

174 Walter Hays Drive, Palo Alto

This active family garden was designed by the owner, a lover of plants, wildlife, cozy spaces, water, stone, and peaceful relaxation. The living areas include a redwood deck and gazebo, a brick patio surrounding a lap pool, gravel paths, and raised rock beds nestled into lush greenery punctuated with roses, daylilies, and other perennials.

Saturday, May 13, 10 a.m. - 2 p.m.

From Highway 101, take the Embarcadero West/Stanford Exit and proceed to Walnut Drive (after a traffic light at Louis Road). Turn right onto Walnut Drive and right again onto Walter Hays. Continue around the "U" to #174 Walter Hays.

Gene & Chuck Pratt

166 Encinal Avenue, Atherton

We have been personalizing our one-acre property since moving in more than ten years ago. Our passion for aesthetics is evident in the abundance of artistic detail that enhances the stucco walls, stone terrace, massive California live oaks, coast redwoods, arbors, and water features found throughout our garden. We are constantly evaluating, upgrading, and refining our inviting and comfortable garden rooms.

Saturday, May 13, 10 a.m. - 2 p.m.

From Highway 101, take the Marsh Road/Atherton Exit heading west. Marsh Road ends at Middlefield Road. Turn left onto Middlefield Road and continue to an elementary school on the corner of Encinal. Turn right onto Encinal and proceed to #166. Please note that parking is prohibited on the south side of the street.

Joan & Mo Sanders

156 Hawthorn Drive, Atherton

A one-acre garden that is enhanced with more than 200 rose bushes, citrus plants, and herbs. Redwood trees, honey locust, and birch predominate, but others include fruit trees and Japanese maples. A small formal garden with arches displays various clematis and climbing roses. Look for an Archie Held waterfall sculpture near the pergola in the rear garden. The garden is part of a subdivision of the old Flood summer estate.

Saturday, May 13, 10 a.m. - 2 p.m.

Take Highway 101 to the Marsh Road Exit. Go west on Marsh Road to its end and turn left onto Middlefield Road and left again onto James. Take the second right off James and look for 156 Hawthorne.

Lynnie & Rich Dewey's Garden

97 Hawthorn Drive, Atherton

For me, our garden is the greatest gift. As I wander through the many rock-lined pathways bordered by raised perennial beds, I am constantly astonished at the dazzling and subtle array of colors and textures orchestrated to create such an amazing place of peacefulness. I am immediately filled with an incredible sense of calmness, well-being, and contentment. There are beautiful views from every vantage point as you walk from one end to the other. My favorite spot is the fish pond, with its stepping-stone bridge, gentle waterfalls and fire-colored dragonflies.

Saturday, May 13, 10 a.m. - 2 p.m.

From Highway 101, take the Marsh Road/Atherton Exit. Go west on Marsh Road to its end at Middlefield Road. Turn left onto Middlefield Road and go to James Avenue. Turn left through iron gate onto James Avenue and go 2 blocks to Hawthorn Drive and turn left. The garden is at the first house on the right. Please park along road.

Suzanne's Garden

88 Selby Lane, Atherton

Take a stroll through this gardener's garden, with paths continually inviting you to explore the entertainment areas, quiet rooms, places to sit, hidden nooks and little surprises. The garden, filled with a good variety of plant material for seasonal color, display, cutting, collecting, as well as favorites from Filoli, exhibits Suzanne's enthusiasm for plants and gardening. Designed by Bruce Chan and Suzanne in 1983, emphasis was placed on areas for entertaining, flexibility for gardening and plant material, and variations in proportions and space. The mounds in the garden add depth, interest and visual focal points; the dry stone walls add texture and color. A striking feature this spring will be thousands and thousands of tulip and daffodils in bloom. Please visit and take time to enjoy it all.

Saturday, April 15, 10 a.m. - 4 p.m.

Take Highway 101 to Woodside Road/Route 84 West/Redwood City; from Route 280 take Route 84 East. Take El Camino south for .7 mile, turn right and go west on Selby Lane, which is the first right turn in Atherton. The cul-de-sac, also called Selby Lane, is at the cross street Austin (stop sign), .4 miles from El Camino Real. Turn at the sign number 98. Please park along the street or in the cul-de-sac (on the west side only).

The Garden at 130 Selby Lane

130 Selby Lane, Atherton

Rare in California, my garden is a parterre of box hedges clipped into geometric pattern with walkways and seating vistas, graced by native oaks and redwoods. Featured also is a gazebo, a wisteria arbor, topiaries and a cutting garden with trellises of climbing roses. Rhododendrons, azaleas, and hydrangeas bloom throughout the season.

Saturday, May 13, 10 a.m. - 2 p.m.

From Highway 101, take the Highway 84 West Exit/Woodside Road. From I-84 Exit El Camino Real South. Proceed to Selby Lane. Turn right onto Selby. Continue .7 mile to 130 (corner lot). From Highway 280, take the Highway 84 East Exit/Woodside Road. Proceed as above. Park along cul-de-sac (use side entrance gate).

The Woodruff Garden

1911 Oakdell Drive, Menlo Park

Azaleas, species geraniums, Japanese maples, sasanqua camellias and other shade-loving plants surround the house in raised brick planters. Step through a gate and delight in a feast for the senses! A brightly colored butterfly garden, raised rock beds, fountains, a small rose garden, arbors and trellises, a small pond and a gazebo nestled in flowering shrubs await you in this magical garden. See if you can find the slowly dripping fountain for butterflies.

Saturday, April 15, 10 a.m. - 4 p.m.

From Route 280, take the Sand Hill East/Menlo Park Exit. At the major intersection of Sand Hill and Santa Cruz Avenue, turn left. At the first light, bear right at fork, continuing on Santa Cruz Avenue. Take the first right onto Oakdell. The Woodruff garden is on the far right-hand corner at 1911. Please park on Oakdell Drive or Stanford Avenue.

ALLIED ARTS GUILD ♣

75 ARBOR ROAD, MENLO PARK, CA 94025. (650) 322-2405.

One of the San Francisco Peninsula's most enduring institutions is Allied Arts Guild with its shop and arts and crafts studios nestled in a California landmark setting of mission-style buildings and Spanish gardens. The gardens, reminiscent of those of Granada, provide an oasis of graciousness and serenity to those who come to shop, lunch, or simply bathe in their charm. The Guild benefits Packard Children's Hospital at Stanford.

Year round, Monday - Saturday, 10 a.m. - 5 p.m.

Take Highway 101 to University Avenue, turnoff in Palo Alto and drive west on University Avenue to El Camino Real. Travel north for 1 mile to Menlo Park's Cambridge Avenue. Turn west onto Cambridge and follow to the end which is the Allied Arts Guild parking lot.

EMMA PRUSCH FARM PARK ♣

647 SOUTH KING ROAD, SAN JOSE, CA 95116. (408) 926-5555,

Emma Prusch Farm Park offers visitors opportunities for recreation and to learn about San Jose's agricultural past. The park's forty-seven acres features San Jose's largest barn; more than 100 community and school garden plots; acres of open grass perfect for picnicking, kite flying, games, and relaxing; a rare fruit orchard featuring a strawberry tree, wild pear tree, and a raisin tree; a grove of international trees; close encounters with farm animals—everything from sheep, pigs, steer, ducks, chickens, geese, and rabbits; and old farm equipment displays. In addition, there are school tours, environmental education classes, and summer camps, as well as year-round special events.

Year round, daily, 8:30 a.m. - dusk.

From Highway 101, take the Story Road East Exit. Turn left at King Road and left at the next traffic light into the driveway. From Route 680, take the King Road Exit and turn onto King Road. Proceed one-half block and turn right into the driveway. From Route 280, take the King Road Exit and turn right. Proceed to the next traffic light and turn right into the driveway.

FILOLI ❧

CANADA ROAD, WOODSIDE, CA 94062. (650) 364-8300

Filoli is a 654-acre estate. It is a registered State Historical Landmark and is listed on the National Register of Historic Places. Sixteen acres of formal gardens are divided into a number of separate garden rooms.

Mid-February - October, Tuesday - Saturday, 10 a.m. - 2 p.m. Docent-led tours every Tuesday and Wednesday. Please call for information.

Located approximately 25 miles south of San Francisco off Highway 280. Edgewood Road Exit.

THE ELIZABETH F. GAMBLE GARDEN CENTER ❧

1431 WAVERLEY STREET, PALO ALTO CA, 94301. (650) 329-1356.

This two-acre urban garden, located forty miles south of San Francisco, surrounds a turn-of-the-century house and carriage house. The formal gardens have been restored from the original plans. The working gardens include experimental demonstrations and displays. Formal gardens may be rented to private parties on weekends.

Year round, daily, dawn - dusk. Access to certain areas may be restricted on weekend afternoons.

From Route 101, exit on Embarcadero West. Turn left onto Waverley Street. The parking lot is on the left. From U.S. 280, exit on Page Mill Road East, cross El Camino and continue on Oregon Expressway. Turn left onto Waverley Street. The house is on the corner of Waverley and Churchill. The parking lot is north of the house.

COLORADO

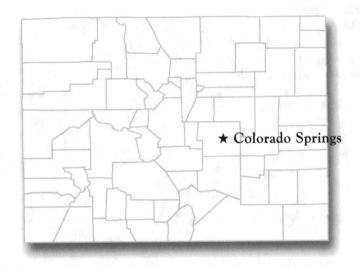

★ Colorado Springs

COLORADO OPEN DAYS
June 24: Colorado Springs

Colorado Springs Open Days

Regional Representatives: Mrs. Terence Lilly & Mrs. Gene H. Moore

Saturday, June 24

Fawn Hayes Bell's Garden, 1619 Wood Avenue: 10 a.m. - 6 p.m.
Kircher Gardens, 1514 Wood Avenue: 10 a.m. - 2 p.m.
Schulz Garden, 1325 North Cascade Avenue: 10 a.m. - 4 p.m.
The Lanes' Garden, 1535 Culebra Avenue: 10 a.m. - 3 p.m.
The Robert & Penny Smith Garden, 1723 Wood Avenue: 10 a.m. - 2 p.m.
The Yellow House Wheelchair Garden, 11 East Columbia Street: 10 a.m. - 4 p.m.

Fawn Hayes Bell's Garden

1619 Wood Avenue, Colorado Springs

My three-year-old garden fills a flat, rectangular lot in the Colorado Springs historic district, the old north end, where just over 100 years ago a treeless prairie grew. Today, mature trees and lawns and the remnants of an original irrigation ditch are testimony to gardening in a semi-arid environment. Rose and catmint hedges, wrought iron fencing, and informal paths of flagstone transition to dry creek beds and border plantings of regional natives, xeriscape and traditional plants. The garden is one of open views and character. From within my landscape architectural studio in the ninety-five-year-old carriage house to the east, I enjoy looking across the seasonal beauty and gaining insight from many planting experiments.

Saturday, June 24, 10 a.m. - 6 p.m.

From I-25 go east on the Uintah Street Exit. From Uintah Street go north on Cascade Avenue (north of Downtown and Colorado College and just to the east of I-25) Turn left (west toward the mountains) at any perpendicular street within a few blocks north of Uintah. Go 1 block to Wood Avenue: 1619 Wood Avenue is located on the east side of the street between Caramillo and Del Norte Streets. Follow the numbered addresses to the 1600 block. The house is light green and has a front deck with chairs. Please park on the street.

Kircher Gardens

1514 Wood Avenue, Colorado Springs

Our home was built in 1908 on a small rectangular lot. A brick patio and pergola connect the home visually to a two-story carriage house. A custom fountain separates a cutting garden from a grass garden that conceals the hot tub. Another garden with circular path lies to the rear of the property. Beyond that, a gate leads you to an herb, a berry, and a vegetable garden in the far west end of the property.

Saturday, June 24, 10 a.m. - 2 p.m.

Four blocks north of Uintah east of I-25. Uintah is adjacent to Colorado College. Exit I-25 at Uintah Street, go east for 2 traffic lights. Turn left onto Cascade. Travel north for 3 blocks and turn left on to Buena Ventura, for one block, turn right onto Wood Avenue. We are the third house on the west side. Please park on Wood Avenue.

SCHULZ GARDEN

1325 NORTH CASCADE AVENUE, COLORADO SPRINGS

Fifteen years ago when we purchased a beautiful 1902 vintage home with greatly neglected gardens, I began working with my hands and heart to fulfill my childhood dream of having my own "Secret Garden." My side yard, partially enclosed by a vine-covered original stone wall with metal gate, is where I have created my "Secret Garden." It includes a cistern-fed rock pool, false pond with seeping spring, a formal fountain and gazing globes, all nestled into perennial gardens. The remainder of our yard consists of three areas: the front yard with elevated flowerbeds which retains two historic irrigation grates, a work area with compost pile and garden shed, and a cutting garden along the alley. The backbone of my garden is a variety of perennials chosen by watching what grows in other local gardens, especially those that do well in shade. I keep trying to wean myself from annuals, but I continue to be addicted to their constant color. Our personal "Garden Conservancy" project is to return our yard to its original state when it contained the lot to our south. It was sold off separately when a previous owner willed the house to a local college.

Saturday, June 24, 10 a.m. - 4 p.m.

From I-25 take Exit 143, Uintah Street east. Continue approximately .2 mile to the traffic light at the top of the hill, North Cascade Avenue. Turn left onto North Cascade. Proceed 1.5 blocks to 1325 North Cascade, on the east side of Cascade Avenue. Please park in the street.

THE LANES' GARDEN

1535 CULEBRA AVENUE, COLORADO SPRINGS

When we seriously began to develop our garden ten years ago, we realized we were going to face some formidable challenges. Fortunately the property has "good bones," with nice size beds and magnificent trees. In order to use the shade to our advantage, we decided to try to develop a country/woodland garden. The garden contains a wide variety of ferns, hostas, columbines and primroses. The patio garden is planted with many fragrant flowers so on a summer day one experiences a delightful aroma as well as a visually appealing quiet spot.

Saturday, June 24, 10 a.m. - 3 p.m.

Go to 1400 block of North Cascade. Turn west on Columbia. Proceed through the 4-way stop down the hill until Columbia dead ends at Culebra. Turn right on Culebra and when the road divides (one-half block) stay left of the center planting. The house is on the right, surrounded by a white picket fence. Please park on the street.

The Robert & Penny Smith Garden

1723 Wood Avenue, Colorado Springs

This garden was "inherited" from the previous "succession" of owners, but has been modified to suit our tastes. We call it our "English cottage" garden in a Victorian house. We have added a sizable vegetable garden and raspberry patch, and enjoy a Belgian espaliered fence screening a parking lot. An espaliered apple tree is occasionally fruitful, but our peach, apricot, and plum trees are only decorative. Tomatoes and potatoes are our chief pride and joy.

Saturday, June 24, 10 a.m. - 2 p.m.

*Exit I-25 and go east on Uintah Avenue (away from the mountains) and drive to Cascade Avenue, about 3 blocks. Turn left at the traffic light and drive north about 6 blocks. Turn left onto Del Norte, go 1 block to Wood Avenue and turn right. Go to #1723. From US-24, exit onto I-25 toward Denver. Go approximately 5 miles north and exit onto Uintah Avenue. *Follow as above. Please park along the road.*

Proceeds shared with the Pikes Peak Hospice.

The Yellow House Wheelchair Garden

11 East Columbia Street, Colorado Springs

This garden is about thirty by thirty feet, including a grape arbor on one side. The beds are high enough to reach easily while sitting down. It is an octagonal shape with a brick "floor," and the center has an oval fountain. It has exuberant colors and shapes and is surrounded by a wooden fence with lattice at the top. If you are on crutches or have arthritis it is a comfortable height when you are working.

Saturday, June 24, 10 a.m. - 4 p.m.

The yellow house is 3 blocks east of I-25. The cross street is Uintah Street. Turn left onto Cascade Avenue and go north 2 blocks. Turn to the right and the house is the second house on the right. It has a blue door and a white balcony. It is a tiny house and the garden is behind it. Please park on Cascade Avenue to the west.

CHEYENNE MOUNTAIN ZOO &

4250 CHEYENNE MOUNTAIN ZOO ROAD, COLORADO SPRINGS, CO 80906.
(719) 633-9925

The Cheyenne Mountain Zoo is located at 7,000 feet on the side of Cheyenne Mountain. The horticultural efforts are focused on native plants, theme gardens, and naturalized exhibits. Two favorite gardens are the Hummingbird Garden and the Butterfly Garden. The Hummingbird Garden was featured in a book, Hummingbird Gardens, and supplies many opportunities to see these wonders up close. In Asian Highlands, Siberian tigers are featured in a large naturalistic exhibit. The area is also home to some unusual trees and shrubs. Primate World, with a large outdoor gorilla exhibit, has been used in an experimental prescribed fire. Lion's Lair was landscaped using a combination of grasses and perennials to give the feeling of the open savanna. Your trip to the zoo will feel like a trip to the Great Rocky Mountains.

Year round, daily, 9 a.m. - 5 p.m.

From I-25, take Exit 138 and drive west for 2.8 miles to the Broadmoor Hotel. Turn right at the hotel and follow signs from there.

GARDEN OF THE GODS VISITOR CENTER &

1805 NORTH 30TH STREET , COLORADO SPRINGS, CO 80904.
(719) 634-6666.

"Where the Garden Comes Alive." The red rocks of Garden of the Gods have served as a landmark to travelers for over 3,000 years. Imagine towering sandstone rock formations against a backdrop of snow-capped Pikes Peak and brilliant blue skies. That's the view form the beautiful Garden of the Gods Visitors Center. The Garden of the Gods is a unique biological melting pot where several life zones converge. The grasslands of the Great Plains meet the pinyon-juniper woodlands characteristic of the American Southwest, and merge with the mountain forests skirting 14,100-foot Pikes Peak. Around the Visitor Center can be found the various native gardens that naturally blend with this park that has been designated as a National Natural Landmark.

June 1 - August 31, daily, 8 a.m. - 8 p.m. September 1 - May 31, daily, 9 a.m. - 5 p.m.

From Denver go south on I-25. Take Exit 146 onto Garden of the Gods Road. Turn left onto 30th Street and go .25 mile. The Visitor Center will be on your left.

STARSMORE HUMMINGBIRD GARDEN ❦

2120 SOUTH CHEYENNE CANON ROAD, COLORADO SPRINGS, CO 80906. (719) 578-6146.

The garden at the Starsmore Discovery Center, which is the visitor's center for North Cheyenne Canon Park, has been turned into a hummingbird garden by the Friends of Cheyenne Canon volunteers. The original plantings of shrubs in several garden beds at the front of the center are gradually being filed in with flowering perennials, which attract hummingbirds and are native to the area. The Canon is a natural magnet for Broadtail and Rufous Hummingbirds every summer.

June - August, daily, 9 a.m. - 5 p.m.

Exit I-25 at Exit 140B (South Tejon Exit) and turn right on Tejon. Tejon becomes Cheyenne Boulevard. Travel 3 miles west on Cheyenne Boulevard. Follow "Seven Falls" signs and "Starsmore Discovery" signs to South Cheyenne Canon Road. Park in lot.

THE COLORADO SPRINGS FINE ARTS CENTER GARDENS ❦

30 WEST DALE, COLORADO SPRINGS, CO 80903. (719) 634-5581

Two gardens grace the grounds around the Southwest Deco building, both filled with sculptures. Plantings have been designed by the Broadmoor Garden Club and include many indigenous grasses, shrubs, and trees, all labeled. One garden is pocket park on a main thoroughfare. The garden is an enclosed sculpture courtyard offering a different, more protected climate.

Open free of charge on Saturday, June 24, 10 a.m. - 4 p.m. Otherwise open for an admission fee, Tuesday - Sunday.

Take I-25 through Colorado Springs and exit at Uintah, just three miles north of downtown. Go east on Uintah about three blocks and turn right (south) on Cascade. Drive through the campus of Colorado College and turn right (west) at Dale. The corner garden at Cascade and Dale is the entrance to Fine Arts Center property. Park in the lot across from the buildings entrance.

❦ *public garden*

The Colorado Springs Xeriscape Demonstration Garden ❧

2855 MESA ROAD, COLORADO SPRINGS, CO 80904. (719) 448-4651

This Xeriscape Demonstration Garden was designed in response to the need to conserve water. Since one-half of all water used annually is applied to lawns and gardens, planting with water conservation in mind was a goal. We are a demonstration garden where everyone is welcome to come see that xeriscape is a beautiful, low-water use addition to their yards. The view from the garden is also quite an attraction as we overlook the Garden of the Gods and Pikes Peak.

Year round, daily, 10 a.m. - 4 p.m.

Take Interstate 25 to Fillmore Exit. Turn west, pass Coronado High School, and proceed to the next traffic light. Turn right onto Mesa Road and go about .5 mile to the entrance.

The Demonstration Garden at the Horticultural Art Society of Colorado Springs ❧

COLORADO SPRINGS, CO 80904. (719) 596-4901

The garden was a project of the local Nurserymen's Association who banded together with a group of citizen gardeners in 1962 to form the Horticultural Art Society of Colorado Springs, Inc. It was designed to demonstrate, sometimes by trial and error, plants and shrubs that will thrive in a sheltered, semi-shaded city garden. Featured areas are perennial beds, rose beds, a fragrance garden for the handicapped, a childrens garden, a regional native plant berm, a rock garden with stream and wilding area, a ground cover display, and the All-American Selections display garden. The Demo Garden has evolved through the years as a living entity, it will continue to change, but the basic design remains much as the founders envisioned it.

Saturday, June 24, 10 a.m. - 4 p.m. with guide. Otherwise open daily.

Exit I-25 at Uintah to the east, take next right turn onto Glen Avenue. Proceed past Willow Pond and city greenhouses to the garden, corner of Glen and Mesa in Monument Valley Park. From the East, turn west off Cascade Avenue on to Cache la Poudre (at Colorado College). Cross the bridge west over Monument Creek and the garden is on the immediate right with a parking lot to the left.

CONNECTICUT & NEW YORK

Connecticut

Southeastern New York

CONNECTICUT & NEW YORK OPEN DAYS

May 7, 21 & 28, June 4 & 25, July 9 & 23
September 10 & 24, October 15

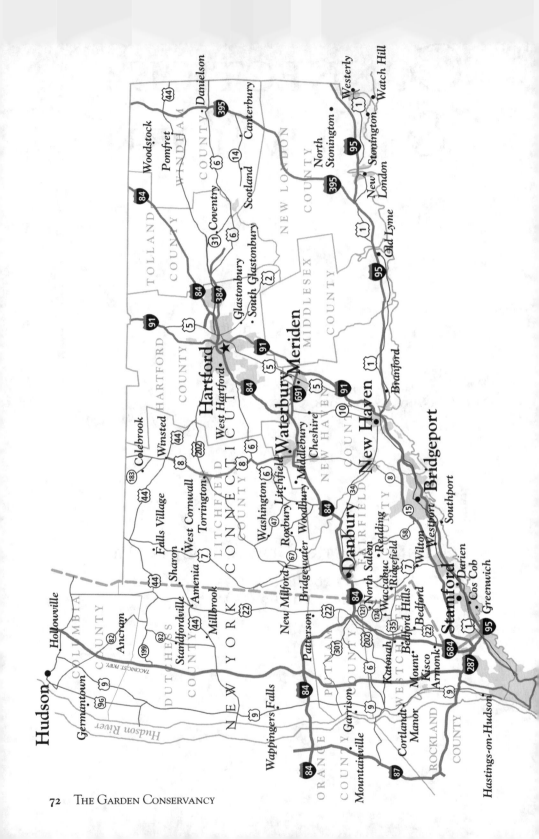

New York & Connecticut Open Days

Sunday, May 7

FARMINGTON, CT
Kate Emery & Steve Silk, 74 Prattling Pond Road: 2 p.m. - 6 p.m.

REDDING, CT
Highstead Arboretum, 127 Lonetown Road:
   guided walks 10 a.m., noon, 2 p.m. and 4 p.m.

SCOTLAND, CT
Richard Redfield, 379 Brook Road: 10 a.m. - 4 p.m.

STAMFORD, CT
Ruth & Jim Levitan, 26 Wake Robin Lane: 10 a.m. - 4 p.m.

WESTPORT, CT
Malcolm's Way, 17 Hockanum Road: 2 p.m. - 6 p.m.
Paul Held & Jane Sherman, 195 North Avenue: 10 a.m. - 6 p.m.

WETHERSFIELD, CT
Gary Berquist, 125 Jordan Lane: 2 p.m. - 6 p.m.

HASTINGS-ON-HUDSON, NY
Midge & Dave Riggs, 112 Lefurgy Avenue, Hastings-on-Hudson: 10 a.m. - 4 p.m.

MOUNTAINVILLE, NY
Cedar House—Garden of Margaret Johns & Peter Stern,
   Otterkill Road at Anders Lane: 10 a.m. - 6 p.m.

MOUNT KISCO, NY
Jane Keiter, 43 Taylor Road: 10 a.m. - 4 p.m.
Judy & Michael Steinhardt, 433 Croton Lake Road: 10 a.m. - 4 p.m.

WAPPINGERS FALLS, NY
Anne Spiegel, 299 Maloney Road: 10 a.m. - 4 p.m.

For descriptions of the New York gardens see page 286

Sunday, May 21

MIDDLEBURY, CT
John N. Spain, 69 Bayberry Road: 10 a.m. - 6 p.m.

RIDGEFIELD, CT
Garden of Ideas, 647 North Salem Road: 10 a.m. - 4 p.m.

SOUTH GLASTONBURY, CT
Brad & Toni Easterson, 124 High Street: May 21, 10 a.m. - 4 p.m.

AMENIA, NY
Broccoli Hall—Maxine Paetro, 464 Flinthill Road: 10 a.m. - 4 p.m.

ARMONK, NY
Cobamong Pond, 15 Middle Patent Road: 10 a.m. - 2 p.m.

BEDFORD, NY
Penelope & John Maynard, 210 Hook Road: 10 a.m. - 6 p.m.
Phillis Warden, 531 Bedford Center Road: 10 a.m. - 4 p.m.

COPAKE FALLS, NY
Margaret Roach: 10 a.m. - 4 p.m.

GERMANTOWN, NY
Tailings—David Whitcomb & Robert Montgomery,
    404 White Birch Road: 10 a.m. - 2 p.m.

WAPPINGERS FALLS, NY
Anne Spiegel, 299 Maloney Road: 10 a.m. - 4 p.m.

Saturday, May 27

MOUNT KISCO, NY
Henriette Suhr, 95 Old Roaring Brook Road: 2 p.m. - 6 p.m.

Sunday, May 28

REDDING RIDGE, CT
The Peonies at Poverty Hollow, Poverty Hollow Road: 9 a.m. - 6 p.m.

Sunday, June 4

BRANFORD, CT
Nickolas Nickou, 107 Sunset Hill Drive: 1 guided tour at 10 a.m. No wandering alone.

COLEBROOK, CT
Marveen & Michael Pakalik, 46 Stillman Hill Road: 2 p.m. - 6 p.m.

DANIELSON, CT
Robert Bonneville, 10 Morin Avenue: 10 a.m. - 4 p.m.

FALLS VILLAGE, CT
Martha A. & Robert S. Rubin, 55 Hautboy Hill Road: 2 p.m. - 6 p.m.

FAIRFIELD, CT
Nancy & Tom Grant, 4014 Redding Road: 10 a.m. - 4 p.m.
Sarah & Jonathan Seymour, 1534 Redding Road: 10 a.m - 4 p.m.

FARMINGTON, CT
Arline & Buzz Whitaker, 4 High Street: 10 a.m. - 4 p.m.

GREENWICH, CT
Stonybrooke, 29 Taconic Road: 10 a.m. - 4 p.m.

LITCHFIELD, CT
Dan & Joyce Lake, 258 Beach Street: 3 p.m. - 7 p.m.
Mr. & Mrs. David Stoner, 183 Maple Street: 2 p.m. - 6 p.m.

MIDDLEBURY, CT
John N. Spain, 69 Bayberry Road: 10 a.m. - 6 p.m.

REDDING, CT
Highstead Arboretum, 127 Lonetown Road:
   Guided walks 10 a.m., noon, 2 p.m., & 4 p.m.

RIDGEFIELD, CT
David Barnhizer, 153 South Salem Road: 10 a.m. - 4 p.m.

WEST CORNWALL, CT
Julia & John Scott, 52 Cream Hill Road: noon - 4 p.m.

WEST HARTFORD, CT
Sara M. Knight, 18 High Farms Road: 10 a.m. - 2 p.m.

WESTPORT, CT
Anita & Jim Alic, 6 Snowflake Lane: 10 a.m. - 4 p.m.
Barbara Carr's Garden, 31 Westway Road: 10 a.m. - 4 p.m.

WATCH HILL, RI
The Gardens at Graigie Brae, 6 Aquidneck Avenue: 10 a.m. - 4 p.m.

For descriptions of the New York gardens see page 286

WILTON, CT
Beverly Frank—Foxglove Meadow, 203 Sharp Hill Road: 10 a.m. - 3 p.m.

ANCRAM, NY
Adams-Westlake, 681 Route 7: 10 a.m. - 4 p.m.

ARMONK, NY
Mrs. John C. Sluder, 9 Half Mile Road: 10 a.m. - 2 p.m.

BEDFORD, NY
Ann Catchpole-Howell, 448 Long Ridge Road: 10 a.m. - 4 p.m.

AMENIA, NY
Broccoli Hall—Maxine Paetro, 464 Flinthill Road: 10 a.m. - 4 p.m.

COPAKE FALLS, NY
Margaret Roach: 10 a.m. - 4 p.m.

GERMANTOWN, NY
Mark A. McDonald—Runningwater, 67 Wire Road: noon - 6 p.m.

GHENT, NY
David Lebe & Jack Potter, 104 May Hill Road: 2 p.m. - 6 p.m.

HOLLOWVILLE, NY
Adele & John Slocum, 119 Catskill View Road: 10 a.m. - 2 p.m.

KATONAH, NY
Barbara & Tom Israel, 296 Mount Holly Road: 10 a.m. - 4 p.m.
Cross River House, 129 Maple Avenue: 10 a.m. - 2 p.m.
Roxana Robinson—Willow Green Farm, 159 North Salem Road: 10 a.m. - 4 p.m.

NORTH SALEM, NY
Carol Goldberg—Artemis Farm, 22 Wallace Road: 10 a.m. - 4 p.m.
Duck Hill, 23 Baxter Road: 10 a.m. - 6 p.m.
Keeler Hill Farm, North Salem: 10 a.m. - 4 p.m.

Sunday, June 25

BETHLEHEM, CT
Baker/Linder Garden, 217 Arch Bridge Road: 2 p.m. - 6 p.m.

BRIDGEWATER, CT
Maywood Gardens, 52 Cooper Road: 10 a.m. - 2 p.m.

CANTERBURY, CT
Westminster Gardens—Eleanor B. Cote & Adrian P. Hart,
    26 Westminster Road: 1 p.m. - 5 p.m.

CORNWALL BRIDGE, CT
Michael Pollan, Pritchard Road: 2 p.m. - 6 p.m.

FAIRFIELD
Nancy & Tom Grant, 4014 Redding Road: 10 a.m. - 4 p.m.

NEW CANAAN, CT
Sandra & Richard Bergmann, 63 Park Street: 10 a.m - 6 p.m.

POMFRET, CT
Lt. Col. Paul G. & Mrs. Ann B. Hennen, 52 Putnam Road: 10 a.m. - 6 p.m.
Robert & Joan Macneil, 73 Cooney Road: 10 a.m. - 4 p.m.

RIVERSIDE, CT
Susan Cohen, 7 Perkely Lane: 3 p.m. - 6 p.m.

STONINGTON, CT
Mr. & Mrs. Juan O'Callahan, 40 Salt Acres Road: 10 a.m. - 2 p.m.

SOUTHPORT, CT
Enid & Harry Munroe, Fleming Lane: 2 p.m. - 6 p.m.

WARREN, CT
May Brawley Hill, 184 Brick School Road: 10 a.m. - 2 p.m.

WASHINGTON, CT
Charles Raskob Robinson & Barbara Paul Robinson, 88 Clark Road: 2 p.m - 6 p.m.
George Schoellkopf, Nettleton Road: 2 p.m. - 6 p.m.
Gael Hammer, 63 River Road: 10 a.m. - 4 p.m.
Linda Allard, 156 Wykeham Road: 10 a.m. - 4 p.m.

WEST REDDING, CT
Hughes-Sonnenfroh Gardens, 54 Chestnut Woods Road: 2 p.m. - 6 p.m.

WOODSTOCK, CT
Judith & Robert Gries, 486 Route 169: 10 a.m. - 4 p.m.

BEDFORD, NY
Phillis Warden, 531 Bedford Center Road: 10 a.m. - 4 p.m.

GARRISON, NY
Ross Gardens, Snake Hill Road, Travis Corners: 10 a.m. - 4 p.m.

KATONAH, NY
Cross River House, 129 Maple Avenue: 10 a.m. - 2 p.m.

MILLBROOK, NY
John H. Whitworth Jr., 506 Altamont Road: 2 p.m. - 6 p.m.

Sunday, July 9

COLEBROOK, CT
Steepleview Gardens—Kathy Loomis, Route 182: 10 a.m. - 4 p.m.

COVENTRY, CT
David & Julia Hayes, 905 South Street: 10 a.m. - 4 p.m.

EASTFORD, CT
Emberborne—Garden of Susan Burns & Bob Williams, 126 Halls Pond Road: 10 a.m. - 4 p.m.

GREENWICH, CT
Mrs. Philip McCaull, 221 Round Hill Road: 2 p.m. - 6 p.m.

SHARON, CT
Kathleen & James Metz, Cobble Pond Farm: 2 p.m. - 6 p.m.
Lee Link, 99 White Hollow Road: 2 p.m. - 6 p.m.

WEST CORNWALL, CT
Michael Trapp, 7 River Road: 10 a.m. - 4 p.m.

WOODSTOCK, CT
Judith & Robert Gries, 486 Route 169: 10 a.m. - 4 p.m.
Upperbrook Farm, 170 Lyon Hill Road: 10 a.m. - 5 p.m.

AMENIA, NY
Jade Hill, 13 Lake Amenia Road: 10 a.m. - 4 p.m.

BEDFORD, NY
Mrs. John E. Lockwood, 32 St. Mary's Church Road: 10 a.m. - 2 p.m.

MOUNT KISCO, NY
Jane Keiter, 43 Taylor Road: 10 a.m. - 4 p.m.
Judy & Michael Steinhardt, 433 Croton Lake Road: 10 a.m. - 4 p.m.

GERMANTOWN, NY
Mark A. McDonald—Runningwater, 67 Wire Road: noon - 6 p.m.

HOLLOWVILLE, NY
Laurence Sombke & Catherine Herman Garden, 258 Connecticut: 10 a.m. - 4 p.m.

Sunday, July 23

AVON, CT
Green Dreams—Garden of Jan Nickel, 71 Country Club Road: 10 a.m. - 4 p.m.

FALLS VILLAGE, CT
Bunny Williams, Point of Rocks Road: 2 p.m. - 6 p.m.

MERIDEN, CT
George Trecina, 341 Spring Street: 10 a.m. - 2 p.m.

RIDGEFIELD, CT
Donna Clark, 264 North Salem Road: 10 a.m. - 4 p.m.
Garden of Ideas, 647 North Salem Road: 10 a.m. - 4 p.m.

SHARON, CT
Lynden B. Miller, 1 Williams Road: 10 a.m. - 2 p.m.

SOUTHPORT, CT
Enid & Harry Munroe, Fleming Lane: 2 p.m. - 6 p.m.

STONINGTON, CT
Mrs. Frederic C. Paffard, Jr., 389 North Main Street: 10 a.m. - 2 p.m.

WASHINGTON, CT
Gael Hammer, 63 River Road: 10 a.m. - 4 p.m.
George Schoellkopf, Nettleton Road: 2 p.m. - 6 p.m.

BEDFORD, NY
Phillis Warden, 531 Bedford Center Road: 10 a.m. - 4 p.m.

MILLBROOK, NY
Belinda & Stephen Kaye, Deep Hollow Road: 10 a.m - 4 p.m.

CORTLANDT MANOR, NY
Carol & Raymond Rocklin's Garden, 20 Rocky Ridge: 10 a.m. - 2 p.m.
Vivian & Ed Merrin, 2547 Maple Avenue: 10 a.m. - 5 p.m.

STANFORDVILLE, NY
Ellen & Eric Petersen, 378 Conklin Hill Road: 10 a.m. - 2 p.m.
Zibby & Jim Tozer, Uplands Farm, Hunns Lake Road: 10 a.m. - 2 p.m.

SALT POINT, NY
Ely Garden, Allen Road: 10 a.m. - 2 p.m.

Sunday, September 10

AVON, CT
Green Dreams—Garden of Jan Nickel, 71 Country Club Road: 10 a.m. - 4 p.m.

COS COB, CT
Florence & John Boogaerts—Mianus Dawn, 316 Valley Road: 1 p.m. - 5 p.m.

FARMINGTON, CT
Kate Emery & Steve Silk, 74 Prattling Pond Road: 2 p.m. - 6 p.m.

LITCHFIELD, CT
Mr. & Mrs. David Stoner, 183 Maple Street: 2 p.m. - 6 p.m.

MERIDEN, CT
George Trecina, 341 Spring Street: 10 a.m. - 2 p.m.

RIDGEFIELD, CT
Garden of Ideas, 647 North Salem Road: 10 a.m. - 4 p.m.

SOUTHPORT, CT
Enid & Harry Munroe, Fleming Lane: 2 p.m. - 6 p.m.

WESTPORT, CT
Barlow Cutler-Wotton, 79 King's Highway North: 10 a.m. - 4 p.m.
Malcolm's Way, 17 Hockanum Road: 2 p.m. - 6 p.m.

WETHERSFIELD, CT
Gary Berquist, 125 Jordan Lane: 2 p.m. - 6 p.m.

WINSTED, CT
Rita & Steve Buchanan, 317 Colbrook Road: 2 p.m. - 6 p.m.

ANCRAM, NY
Adams-Westlake, 681 Route 7: 10 a.m. - 4 p.m.

BEDFORD, NY
Ann Catchpole-Howell, 448 Long Ridge Road: 10 a.m. - 4 p.m.
Laura Fisher, Wildflower Farm, 44 Broad Brook Road: 10 a.m. - 4 p.m.

COPAKE FALLS, NY
Margaret Roach: 10 a.m. - 4 p.m.

GHENT, NY
David Lebe & Jack Potter, 104 May Hill Road: 2 p.m. - 6 p.m.

HUDSON, NY
Hudson Bush Farm, 154 Yates Road: 10 a.m. - 4 p.m.

LEWISBORO, NY
The White Garden, 199 Elmwood Road: 10 a.m. - 4 p.m.

NORTH SALEM, NY
Dick Button, Ice Pond Farm, 115 June Road: 10 a.m. - 6 p.m.

PATTERSON, NY
The Farmstead Garden, 590 Birch Hill Road: 10 a.m. - 2 p.m.

WACCABUC, NY
James & Susan Henry, 36 Mead Street: 10 a.m. - 4 p.m.

Sunday, September 24

WESTPORT, CT
Barlow Cutler-Wotton, 79 King's Highway North: 10 a.m. - 4 p.m.

WINSTED, CT
Rita & Steve Buchanan, 317 Colbrook Road: 2 p.m. - 6 p.m.

Sunday, October 15

ARMONK, NY
Cobamong Pond, 15 Middle Patent Road: 10 a.m. - 2 p.m.

Anita & Jim Alic

6 Snowflake Lane, Westport

This secluded woodland property was developed by eclectic collector gardeners. Evolving from a Connecticut "jungle" and turned into a series of loosely defined rooms, it includes an entry garden, an extensive rose garden, a shade garden, a shrub garden, a perennial and grass garden, and pool plantings.

Sunday, June 4, 10 a.m. - 4 p.m.

From the Merritt Parkway, take Exit 42. Go north on Route 57, 1 mile to first traffic light/Lyons Plain Road; turn right. Go 200 yards, then bear right onto Coleytown Road. Go .5 mile to North Avenue and turn left. Snowflake Lane is 200 yards ahead on the right. The house, #6, is at the end of Snowflake on the right. Please parallel park on grass along road.

Arline & Buzz Whitaker

4 High Street, Farmington

The gardens surround and complement this house, the former Whitman Tavern built in 1786. Shrubs and a perennial garden surround a small fish pond and terrace. The beds in the center of the yard are six years old and contain some new and tried and true older favorites. A pet memorial is under the grape arbor. The drought of 1999 and hungry varmints that are enjoying perennial plant roots are driving the garden to a more specialized shrub one. Hopefully the next few years will see blooming shrubs and trees from spring through fall.

Sunday, June 4, 10 a.m. - 4 p.m.

From I-84 take Exit 39. Go west on Route 4 for about 1 mile. High Street is the first left. The garden is at #4, the first on the right. Please park in the adjacent shopping center.

Baker/Linder Garden

217 Arch Bridge Road, Bethlehem

This four-acre garden, forty-years-old, has been our property for ten years. A spectacular thirty-five-mile view has been kept in mind when planning this garden which includes a formal boxwood hedge garden, three connecting perennial gardens, swimming pool beds, and container plantings. Shade gardens have been developed beneath the inherited large conifers by cutting away undergrowth and forming hidden rooms for shade-loving plants.

Sunday, June 25, 2 p.m. - 6 p.m.

From I-84 take Exit 15/Southbury. At exit ramp take Route 6 East for 5 miles and turn left onto Route 47. Go 1 mile, and bear right at fork onto Route 132 to Bethlehem. Go 4.4 miles to Carmel Hill Road and turn left. Go .8 mile to Arch Bridge Road and turn right. Please park along street.

Barbara Carr's Garden

31 WESTWAY ROAD, WESTPORT

We purchased the property in June of 1972. The weekend we moved in, a freak storm caused the nearby tidal pond to overflow its banks. Our house appeared to be a floating island. When the waters receded, plant damage was obvious, In my determination to bring things back to life, I learned to garden and love it. My garden is fun, whimsical, and full of wonderful specimen plants. It brings me great pleasure, and I hope you will enjoy your visit. It was recently featured in Time-Life's *Designing Beds and Borders.*

Sunday, June 4, 10 a.m. - 4 p.m.

From I-95 traveling north, take Exit 19/Southport. At end of ramp, turn right onto Center Street. Go to intersection and turn right onto Pequot Avenue. Turn right onto Westway Road. At the intersection, turn left onto Westway Road/Oxford Road. Look for #31 on the mailbox. From I-95 traveling south, take Exit 19/Southport to traffic light. Turn right onto Post Road. Just before Pequot Motel turn left onto Center Street. Go under I-95 overpass and follow directions above. Please park on side street only.

Barlow Cutler-Wotton

79 KING'S HIGHWAY NORTH, WESTPORT

A country garden with open vistas across a lawn under a canopy of seventy-five-year-old apple trees to perennial borders and meadow gardens with mowed paths and screening by shrubs and trees. Early September highlights the billowing, white "sweet" clematis climbing through shrubs, with ripening grasses, and tall purple salvia 'Indigo Spires.' Pink 'Autumn Joy' Sedum in hedges darkens to rosy hues, with accents of white boltonia in late September. Bordering the lawn under the apple trees are dark green yews with gnarled trunks, planted as seedlings by the gardener's mother in 1931.

Sundays, September 10 & 24, 10 a.m. - 4 p.m.

From the Merritt Parkway, take Exit 41. Turn south onto Route 33. Follow to traffic light at junction of Route 57. Turn right onto King's Highway North. Pass a cemetery. The garden is at the top of the hill, across from a long white picket fence. Look for a stone wall and #79 on the mailbox. The house is a grey-shingled colonial on the right. Park across the street in front of the white picket fence.

Proceeds shared with The Aspetuck Land Trust.

Beverly Frank — Foxglove Meadow

203 Sharp Hill Road, Wilton

Stroll through the wildflower meadow that grows as high as an elephant's eye or, if you prefer, soar above it on a swing for an aerial view. Meander along the herbaceous borders: one straight, one serpentine along a winding stone wall. Tired after an active day of garden viewing? Then lie back in a hammock under a canopy of birch leaves or sip iced tea beneath the cool bough of a giant spruce in the company of birds and butterflies. All this plus a 200-foot allée of crab apples.

Sunday, June 4, 10 a.m. - 3 p.m.

From the Merritt Parkway, take Exit 41 to Wilton/Route 33 North. Turn right at the traffic light onto Route 53, bearing left at fork onto Route 106. Go up hill past Lakeland Farm. Turn left at fork onto Sharp Hill Road/Route 106. The garden is at the fourth house on the left. Please park on Buckingham Ridge Road.

Brad & Toni Easterson

124 High Street, South Glastonbury

Once the site of an old mill, this garden runs along a brook for 300 feet. It encompasses a series of perennial, shrub, and mixed borders with emphasis on native material, naturalistic plantings, and organic gardening practices. The south garden has an extensive collection of ornamental grasses.

Sunday, May 21, 10 a.m. - 4 p.m.

From Hartford take Route 2 east to Route 17 to South Glastonbury. At the Congregational Church, turn right onto High Street. Travel .25 mile to the brook. The house is #124. Park on High Street.

Bunny Williams

Point of Rocks Road, Falls Village

Various gardens surround nineteenth-century buildings. A sunken formal garden has mixed borders and a small reflecting pool. Walkways lead to a conservatory filled with tender plants and flanked by a potager. A newly established woodland garden with pond and a vegetable garden are located near a "working" greenhouse used for winter storage of plants and propagation.

Sunday, July 23, 2 p.m. - 6 p.m.

From Route 7 North, go to Falls Village. Turn left at the blinking traffic light onto Main Street/Route 126. Bear right (still on Route 126). Go to stop sign at Point of Rocks Road. The driveway is directly ahead. Please park in field adjacent to house.

Charles Raskob Robinson & Barbara Paul Robinson

88 Clark Road, Washington

Brush Hill, included in Rosemary Verey's book *The Secret Garden* and *House & Garden* (October 1997), is set between an eighteenth-century Connecticut farmhouse and barn amidst old stone walls. The garden includes a rose walk featuring old roses and climbers, a fountain garden planted in yellows and purples, herbaceous borders, and a terraced garden planted in hot colors leading up to a garden folly, through a woodland arch to a developing woodland walk with a newly created series of cascading pools. There is an old Lord & Burnham greenhouse, along with a white wisteria-draped bridge over the pond with water lilies and grass borders.

Sunday, June 25, 2 p.m - 6 p.m.

From I-84, take Exit 15 at Southbury. Take Route 6 North to Route 47 and turn left. Go 4 miles, passing Woodbury Ski Area on left, and turn right onto Nettleton Hollow Road. Go 4.1 miles, pass intersection of Wykeman and Carmel Hill Roads, and take next sharp left onto Clark Road (deadend). The house, #88, is the first and only one on left. Please park along Clark Road before driveway.

Dan & Joyce Lake

258 Beach Street, Litchfield

Blessed as we are with thirty-two acres of diverse terrain and the ownership of a horticultural business, we have used our surroundings to develop four large naturalistic ponds, wetlands, and forest. Viewers can enjoy more than twenty perennial beds, both sunny and shady, a large Locust arbor, grass garden, pond-side expressions, and woodland shade gardens. Although in its nascent stages, a 700-foot woodland stroll garden is available for the visionary. We have extensive amounts of native mountain laurel and have many large boulders in our landscape. We have a landscaped container nursery with an allée and a formal design with tasteful accents.

Sunday, June 4, 3 p.m. - 7 p.m.

In Litchfield, at traffic light on Route 202 by Stop & Shop turn onto Milton Road. After .25 mile, fork right onto Beach Street. Go 2 miles, and Horticultural Center is on the right. There are stone columns, stone walls and large maple trees. We are 2 miles from Milton Road, 2.25 miles from Route 202.

David Barnhizer

153 South Salem Road, Ridgefield

The house is a 1750 saltbox set on an unfinished railroad spurline. From an eighteen-foot granite cliff splashes a recirculating waterfall providing dramatic focus to the naturalistic gardens created by Stamats Landscaping Design. There are many native shrubs as well as woodland perennials such as rodgersia, ligularia, hosta, ferns, foamflower, and arisaema.

Sunday, June 4, 10 a.m. - 4 p.m.

From the intersection of Routes 35 and 123, travel north on Route 35/South Salem Road. Go .6 mile to mailbox that reads #153 on right. From the intersection of Route 33 at the landmark fountain go south on Route 35/South Salem Road. Go 1.4 miles to mailbox that reads #153 on the left. Please park on grass shoulder of Route 35 or on Old South Salem Road.

Proceeds shared with The Weir Preserve.

David & Julia Hayes

905 South Street, Coventry

Sculptor David Hayes, whose work is found in many public and private collections in this country and in Europe, lives and works on this old farm. Hayes displays his completed works in an old orchard, by the pond, in a large hayfield, and behind the house. They are in or near informal gardens of herbs, wildflowers and ferns, roses (mostly old roses), annuals, perennials, and vegetables. Wear comfortable shoes as the paths are not all smooth.

Sunday, July 9, 10 a.m. - 4 p.m.

From I-84 traveling east, take Exit 59/Route 384. Follow Route 384 to the end (approximately 8 miles). Take Route 44 about 3.5 miles, then turn right onto Silver Street (signs there for Caprilands and Hale Homestead). Follow about 2 miles to end, turning left onto South Street (go to right at stop sign after Hale Homestead). Go 4.5 miles to #905. Park along street. The driveway is available for those with walking difficulties. From Route 32 traveling west, go through Willimantic to junction with Route 31 in Coventry. Turn left onto Lake Street and go to South Street. Turn left onto South Street and go approximately .6 mile to #905.

Proceeds shared with the East Catholic High School Scholarship Fund.

DONNA CLARK

264 NORTH SALEM ROAD, RIDGEFIELD

These romantic English-style gardens are in an informal country setting. Follow the flowing lines of the gardens to find many varieties of old favorites and the very newest perennials and annuals intertwined with whimsical sculptures. These ever-changing gardens are a continuous creation from the heart. Stepping through a garden gate into the vegetable and cutting gardens, you are welcomed by three miniature donkeys, who will come to the fence with the encouragement of carrots pulled from the garden.

Sunday, July 23, 10 a.m. - 4 p.m.

From Route 35, turn onto Route 116/North Salem Road. The garden is 1 mile from that intersection on the right. Please park in the paved area.

EMBERBORNE—
GARDEN OF SUSAN BURNS & BOB WILLIAMS

126 HALLS POND ROAD, EASTFORD

The house is in the Gothic Revival style and the gardens are Victorian having been inspired by the writings of Andrew Jackson Downing. There are several gardens with winding walks connecting one to the other. Also included are arbors, seats, fences, sculpture, a bottle tree, a bridge, and a Gothic-style wood house. The July garden features daylilies. The surrounding eight acres feature an understory of native blueberries. The garden is filled with birds, butterflies, and other wildlife.

Sunday, July 9, 10 a.m. - 4 p.m.

From I-84 take Exit 69/Willinton. Turn right onto Route 74. Go 8 miles to Route 44 in Ashford. Turn left onto Route 44 and continue to Route 89 and turn right. Take an immediate left around the island onto Slade Road. Go up the hill and turn left at the top onto Bebbington Road. Turn right at the first road onto Kennerson Reservoir Road. Go straight to the stop sign. Note your mileage here. Go 2 miles to three newspaper boxes at the bottom of the driveway on the left. On a tree there is the #126. Go up the driveway 600 feet. When the driveway splits take the middle drive. Please park so circular drive is free.

Proceeds shared with The Eastford Public Library.

Enid & Harry Munroe

Fleming Lane, Southport

Informal, our beautiful shade and mixed border gardens change throughout the season as we experiment with perennials, herbs, shrubs, ground covers, ornamental grasses, and tropical plants. We have more than 100 container plants, many with "black" foliage or blooms. The gardens were an inspiration for Enid's book, *An Artist in the Garden: A Guide to Creative and Natural Gardening.*

Sundays; June 25, July 23, September 10; 2 p.m. - 6 p.m.

From the Merritt Parkway, take Exit 42/Westport/Weston. From the west, turn left; from the east turn right. Bear left as road forks to right, keeping Daybreak Nursery greenhouse on the right. Turn left at the "T" onto Cross Highway. At third stop sign, make a sharp right onto Sturges Highway. Take the second left onto Fleming Lane. The garden is the second on the right. Please park along street.

Florence & John Boogaerts — Mianus Dawn

316 Valley Road, North Mianus, Cos Cob

This tiny, steep site overlooking the Mianus River is an exuberant combination of her lavish Gertrude Jekyll perennials and his Edwin Lutyens architectural stone-work. The garden is a sequence of terraces carved into the wooded hillside: a fern grotto, niches and ramps, a flower garden, a boxwood parterre, a potager, a grape arbor, and an espalliered apple orchard.

Sunday, September 10, 1 p.m. - 5 p.m.

From I-95, take Exit 4, turn onto Indian Field Road (north, towards Greenwich). Travel .7 mile, turn right (Mobil station) onto East Putnam Avenue. Travel .5 mile, turn left (Gulf station) onto Orchard Street, bear right at triangle, turn right at next intersection, Valley Road. Travel 1.6 miles, after second stop sign, to 4th house, #316 on left. From Merritt Parkway, Exit 33, Eastbound (New Haven) bear right onto Den Road, at Roxbury Road turn left at stop sign, (1.7 miles) to Westover Road. Westbound (to NYC), right on Den Road (.5 mile) to Bangall Road; turn left, continue, with red barn horse farm on the right (.5 mile), to Riverbank Road, turn left, cross over the Merritt Parkway. Riverbank Road becomes Westover Road. Go 1.7 miles to Mianus Road, turn right. Mianus Road becomes Valley Road. Go 1.7 miles to #316 on right. Please park along road.

GAEL HAMMER

63 RIVER ROAD, WASHINGTON DEPOT

This is a cottage garden designed to engulf the house with flowers and shrubs, which provide different spaces for outdoor living. Special areas include oversized borders, a grass garden, a white moon garden, an enormous "step" garden and container gardens on an old-fashioned porch and sunny deck. The garden has been featured in Martha Stewart Living and House Beautiful.

Sundays; June 25, July 23; 10 a.m. - 4 p.m.

From Route 109, travel to Washington Depot. Take River Road .5 mile from town. Please park in front of the house.

GARDEN OF IDEAS

647 NORTH SALEM ROAD, RIDGEFIELD

Twelve years ago this spot was covered with Kentucky bluegrass and poison ivy-infested woods. Today a fine collection of both woody and herbaceous ornamental plants grow here, along a stunning natural marsh. A large raised-bed vegetable garden produces a bounty of delicious edibles from April through November. Stroll through shade and sun, ponder poetic verse displayed along the way, and relax in one of many secluded nooks. Other points of interest include hand-built cedar structures, whimsical statuary, water features, unusual annuals, and lots of birds and bugs. Recent completion of a plankway across the marsh allows exploration of heretofore uncharted garden territory.

Sundays; May 21, July 23; September 10, 10 a.m. - 4 p.m.

From Route 35 in Ridgefield, take Route 116 for 2.9 miles. The garden is on the left. From Route 121 in North Salem, take Route 116 into Connecticut. The house is on the right, 1.3 miles from the New York border. Please park in the paved parking area.

GARDENS AT GRAIGIE BRAE

6 AQUIDNECK AVENUE, WATCH HILL, RI

My gardens fill a rather small piece of property overlooking Foster's Cove on Little Narraganset Bay facing west. The terrain is varied, so we have created garden rooms. By the front door I have a "walk-through" English garden, followed by a green garden with a small fish pond for quiet repose. Through a pergola and a gate there is a wide perennial border—across from which is a large herb garden featuring a knot garden backed with old-fashioned English roses. Below the swimming pool is a small, shady retreat.

Sunday, June 4, 10 a.m. - 4 p.m.

From Thomas Moore's home in Stonington, CT: Turn left from Moore's driveway. Go to the traffic light. Turn left onto A-1-A. Go about 3 miles to the stop sign in Westerly. Turn right and follow signs to Beaches. Proceed about 2 miles up a hill to Beach Street, go past Smith's Florist, and keep going to stop sign. Go straight through, approaching Watch Hill. Proceed to a yellow house on the right. The second street after the house will be Neowan Avenue on the right. Take this 1 block to Aquidneck Avenue. Turn left. The house is the second on the right. There is a #6 on the door.

GARY BERQUIST

125 JORDAN LANE, WETHERSFIELD

This half-acre garden has three ponds, two streams and nine waterfalls, with Koi in one pond and goldfish in others. Rare trees and plants are found among the stepping-stone paths and rock-lined berms. A white Victorian bridge leads into the garden, which is anchored by a screened gazebo. Part shade garden, part butterfly garden, part water garden and rock work offer something for everyone.

Sundays; May 7, September 10; 2 p.m. - 6 p.m.

Exit 28 off I-91. Take immediate right onto Route 99 south exit. Come to stop light. Go right on Jordan Lane; #125 is on left before overpass.

GEORGE SCHOELLKOPF

NETTLETON ROAD, WASHINGTON

A true plantsman's garden, filled with striking combinations of unusual plants in an eclectic and distinctive design.

Sundays; June 25, July 23; 2 p.m. - 6 p.m.

From I-84, take Exit 15 at Southbury. Take Route 6 north through Southbury and Woodbury. Turn left on Route 47 north. Go 4 miles, pass Woodbury Ski Area on left and turn right onto Nettleton Hollow Road. Go 1.7 miles. The house is on the right. Please park along road.

George Trecina

341 SPRING STREET, MERIDEN

A professional landscape designer's display and trial gardens, with one-third acre of continuous mixed borders containing more than 300 varieties of woody plants and perennials, some unusual. The planting schemes are enhanced with an assortment of annuals, tender perennials, and container plantings with a decidedly tropical theme. The sloping front yard-structured with paths, walls and stairways-features a white garden and a "wild" garden.

Sundays; July 23, September 10; 10 a.m. - 2 p.m.

From I-91 take Route 691 West to Exit 6/Lewis Avenue. Turn right to end. Turn right onto Hanover Street to the first traffic light. Turn left onto Columbus Avenue and go to second stop sign. Turn left onto Prospect Avenue and then turn at the first right onto Spring Street to the fourth house on the right, #341. From I-84, take Route 691 East to Exit 5/Chamberlain Highway. Go right to the end. Turn left onto West Main Street to the first traffic light. Turn right onto Bradley Avenue and go to the first stop sign. Turn left onto Winthrop Terrace and past the traffic light onto Columbus Avenue. Continue as above. Please park along Spring Street.

Green Dreams—Garden of Jan Nickel

71 COUNTRY CLUB ROAD, AVON

My garden, developed during the last twenty years, is a blend of color, thoughts, and dreams. A mixture of formal and informal, plantings and sculpture; the garden lends itself to many rooms. The side gate leads to a secluded seating area and water garden. Enter through the trellised, bi-level deck to witness a spectacular obelisk garden. The front walkway leads to a ribbon of grass bordered by an array of unusual perennials enclosing a woodland garden. The crab tree garden is done in shades of green and white, along with the sundial garden in shades of burgundy, yellow, and green. Stone, concrete, iron, and unusual containers are used throughout; along with a vast mix of perennials, grasses, and shrubs.

Sundays; July 23, September 10; 10 a.m. - 4 p.m.

From I-84, take Exit 39/Farmington/Route 4. From the intersection of Routes 10 & 4, go .5 mile to the third traffic light and turn right onto Farm Road/Tilletson Road. Go past farm to Old Farms Road, approximately 3 miles. Turn left onto Old Farms Road and stay right at the fork. Go past the school to Country Club Road and turn left. Go .3 mile to #71 Country Club Road. Please park across Country Club Road on Tamara Circle.

Proceeds shared with The Animal Friends of Connecticut.

HIGHSTEAD ARBORETUM

127 LONETOWN ROAD, REDDING

A high place, indeed, the arboretum is thirty-six acres of relatively undisturbed Connecticut woodland, meadow, wetland and rock ledge. In May, a collection of fourteen species of deciduous azaleas (fenced for protection from deer) is to be enjoyed for its color and fragrance. In June, an expansive understory of mountain laurel follows, with a special Kalmia exhibit featuring more than sixty cultivars and three of the seven laurel species. Woodland trails and a boardwalk through the wetland allow appreciation of multiple habitats and the plants, birds and wildlife dwelling there.

Sundays; May 7, June 4; guided walks 10 a.m., noon, 2 p.m., and 4 p.m.

From I-95 or the Merritt Parkway/Route 15, take Route 7 North. Turn right onto Route 107 for six miles (be sure to follow signs for Route 107 as it crosses Route 53). Pass police station, an elementary school, and the Redding Country Club. Take the second driveway on the left after the Country Club, # 127 Lonetown Road. Follow signs into arboretum. Follow signs for parking.

HUGHES-SONNENFROH GARDENS

54 CHESTNUT WOODS ROAD, WEST REDDING

Despite deer and drought frustrations, the anticipation and planning for next year's Garden Conservancy inspires me with hope and renewed energy. A recent trip to Rocky Mountain National Park taught me how gardeners everywhere must learn how to embrace Mother Nature and coexist somehow with the animal population. Everywhere Tim and I drove around the awesome town of Estes Park, we saw tidy cedar and wire fences protecting the plants from the herds of elk. Beautiful as they are, they eat almost everything you don't want them to eat (sound familiar)? So if you come to visit our beloved five acres in the year 2000, you might see new fencing to protect our precious flowers, more ornamental grasses, and deer- and drought-resistant plants. Gardening has always been a challenge and next year will be the best so far. Hope to see you then!

Sunday, June 25, 2 p.m. - 6 p.m.

From Route 84, take Exit 3/Route 7 South. Go 3 miles to the traffic light at junction of Route 35. Bear left through the light, continuing on Route 7 South. Go 1.5 miles. At third traffic light, turn left onto Topstone Road. Go .25 mile, down hill, cross railroad tracks and bear left up hill, continuing on Top Stone Road for .5 mile. Take second left onto Chestnut Woods Road. The house, #54, is the second on the right. Please park along the second driveway and walk back to the main entrance.

Proceeds shared with The Redding Garden Club.

John N. Spain

69 Bayberry Road, Middlebury

Garden areas include a rock garden, a woodland garden with paths, an outdoor (winter hardy) cactus garden, planted walls and troughs. The rock garden combines dwarf conifers with hardy cacti and many unique rock garden plants. There is also a thirty-two-foot landscaped greenhouse of cacti and succulents.

Sundays; May 21, June 4; 10 a.m. - 6 p.m.

From I-84, take Exit 17. Go straight on Route 64 to the second traffic light. Turn right onto Memorial Drive. At end, turn left onto Kelly Road. Go .25 mile to the 2nd street on the right, Three Mile Hill Road. Continue on Three Mile Hill Road to the third street on the right, Bayberry Road. The house, #69, is the second on the right. Park along the road.

Judith & Robert Gries

486 Route 169, Woodstock

These country gardens work in concert with an historic house and barn. The formal lines of the beech, yew, and privet hedges create outdoor garden rooms where lush and informal borders of sprawling signature roses, clematis, perennials and herbs are punctuated with sentinel evergreens. These "garden rooms" are connected by intersecting pathways or allée of trees, which are accented with trellises, arbors, and statuary. These pathways allow vistas to adjacent rooms, drawing a visitor forward with a sense of discovery, while attention to detail holds the visitor within the room. There are shady borders under the shelter and guard of stately old trees, while other borders include water features, hostas, and woody shrubs.

Sundays; June 25, July 9; 10 a.m. - 4 p.m.

From I-84 North, take Exit 73. Turn right onto Route 190 to Route 171 in Union. Turn right onto 171 East, continue for about 3 miles to Route 197. Bear left onto Route 197. Continue to Route 169 (about 6.7 miles). Turn right onto Route 169 to Route 486 (about 3 miles). Please park in the circular driveway in front of the house.

Proceeds shared with The Woodstock Garden Club.

JULIA & JOHN SCOTT

52 CREAM HILL ROAD, WEST CORNWALL

Over many years the owners have transformed this precipitous, rocky hillside terrain with a sixty-foot waterfall into a series of very different gardens. The upper garden adjoining the millpond has traditional shrubs, perennial beds, and a stone-edged cutting garden. This is linked by terraced gardens and an orchard to the lower pond and water garden. An early spring and wildflower garden borders the waterfall. It has magnificent views and is a garden full of surprises!

Wednesday, June 4, noon - 4 p.m.

Take Route 7 to Route 128 in West Cornwall. Turn east for 1-2 miles after covered bridge. Take first left, by Cornwall School (Cream Hill Road). Number 52 is on the right side (red board fence.)

KATE EMERY & STEVE SILK

74 PRATTLING POND ROAD, FARMINGTON

Our ambitious but embryonic one-acre garden on a sloping site in woods reflects a fascination with using colorful foliage to create season-long interest. Numerous sun and shade mixed borders are connected by meandering paths and a dry, gravel streambed. Features include a tulip walk, lilac garden, shrub border, a fall garden and stone patio with unusual container plantings.

Sundays; May 7, September 10; 2 p.m. - 6 p.m.

From I-84 East or Westbound, take Exit 39. Move to the right lane of exit ramp. At end, take right turning lane toward UConn Health Center. Go approximately 100 yards, turn left onto Prattling Pond Road (across from entrance to commuter parking lot) continue straight to #74, last driveway on right. Please park in driveway or on the road past driveway.

KATHLEEN & JAMES METZ

COBBLE POND FARM, SHARON

Cobble Pond Farm features both formal and informal herbaceous borders. Several garden rooms, in pastoral settings, are defined and accented by stone wall hedges, clipped yews, sweeping lawns, mature trees, flagstone paths, and open fields. The fifteen acres were designed by the Olmsted Brothers Firm. The secret garden in the Italian style; a sunken garden, and pergola continue to reflect the plan.

Sunday, July 9, 2 p.m. - 6 p.m.

Take I-84 to Route 22 North to Route 343 in Amenia, New York. Turn right onto Route 343 and go 5 miles to the Sharon Clock Tower. At the 4-way stop turn right onto South Main Street. Go .9 mile and turn left onto West Woods Road. The entrance is the third driveway on the left. Please park on West Woods Road.

LEE LINK

99 WHITE HOLLOW ROAD, NEW YORK

Three stone walls cascade down a sunny hillside. The space between each is planted with perennial borders which bloom with the flowering seasons of spring and summer. One level is set off by a water garden, which reflects a winter conservatory on the hill behind it.

Sunday, July 9, 2 p.m. - 6 p.m.

From the junction of Routes 7 & 112, turn onto Route 112. Go about 2 miles on Route 112 until you see a sign "Entrance to Lime Rock Race Track." Turn left onto White Hollow Road and travel 2.5 miles. The house #99, is on the right, opposite a white fence.

LINDA ALLARD

156 WYKEHAM ROAD, NEW YORK

High on a hillside, with a panoramic view of the Litchfield Hills, this garden has old-world charm. Surrounded by stone walls covered with espaliered fruit trees and climbing roses and hydrangeas, the garden is partly formal and partly potager. A lush rose arbor filled with pale pink and white roses interwoven with clematis separates the two. Boxwood hedges define the white formal garden enhanced by a variety of green textures. Geometric beds overflowing with fruits, vegetables, herbs and flowers are a true depiction of potager. This part of the garden changes yearly; plantings are worked by color and color combination.

Sunday, June 25, 10 a.m. - 4 p.m.

From Washington Green-at Gunn Memorial Library turn onto Wykeham Road. Follow for about 1.5 miles until Old Litchfield Road forks left. Stay right on Wykeham for about .25 mile. Go up a small hill, to a red barn on the right side of the road. The entrance to the garden is opposite the red barn. Number 156 is on the stone wall; proceed through the gate to the garden.

Lynden B. Miller

1 Williams Road, Sharon

This country garden features mixed herbaceous borders backed by a yew hedge, a daylily walk, a meadow, a woodland, a raised garden, and a cottage garden for unusual plants. The garden is designed for year-round interest and is at its fullest in summer and fall.

Sunday, July 23, 10 a.m. - 2 p.m.

From Route 41 North, go through Sharon, past shopping center on the left and a Texaco station on the right. Take the first right onto Calkinstown Road. Go .7 mile and turn left onto Williams Road. The house (#1) is on the left corner. Please park off road or along road the shoulder.

Lt. Col. Paul G. & Mrs. Ann B. Hennen

52 Putnam Road, Route 44, Pomfret

These gardens, with various degrees of formality, cover three acres. Oriental and Occidental influences, coupled with appropriate garden ornaments and statuary, are present. Featured are perennial borders, stone pathways, a woodland path and brook garden, ponds with fountains, shrubs and natural borders, a bonsai display, a rock garden, and more. Work on new gardens and other projects may be in progress during visit.

Sunday, June 25, 10 a.m. - 6 p.m.

From I-84, take Exit 69/Route 74 South to Route 44. Take Route 44 East to the 4-way stop at the intersection of Route 44, Route 169, and Route 97. Turn right onto Route 44 East toward Putnam. The Pomfret Post Office is a short distance from the intersection on the right. The house #52, is the second past the post office. Park on premises or at the post office lot.

Proceeds shared with The Pomfret Historical Society.

Malcolm's Way

17 Hockanum Road, Westport

If you practice medicine and raise rhododendrons for a lot of years, you learn that some truths apply to both enthusiasms. Nature is remarkable and caring makes a difference. For more than forty-five years I have had an increasing interest and pleasure in watching things grow. My particular delight has been in cloning and collecting rhododendrons and azaleas. My Schlippenbachi are more than seven feet tall, as are my Scintillation, grown from Dexter's 1959 clones. The garden, set between two ponds, has merged in an unstructured melding of color, texture and variety.

Sundays; May 7, September 10; 2 p.m. - 6 p.m.

*From the Merritt Parkway take Exit 42/Westport. At the traffic light, turn left onto Weston Road if traveling north, turn right if traveling south. *Continue straight to blinker, Easton Road. Daybreak Nursery will be on the right. Continue to the "T" at Cross Highway and turn left. Turn at the next left onto Hockanum Road. The first driveway on right, #17, is Malcolm's Way. From I-95 take Exit 18/Sherwood Island. Turn left. At third traffic light, turn left onto Route 1. At the first traffic light (McDonalds), turn right onto Roseville Road. Go 1.9 miles to "T" at Cross Highway; turn left. Almost immediately, turn right onto Hockanum Road. The first driveway on the right, #17, is Malcolm's Way. Please park in available space on adjacent roads.*

Martha A. & Robert S. Rubin
55 Hautboy Hill Road, Falls Village

This land must have been a settler's nightmare back in the eighteenth century, a steep north-facing hillside of glacial ledge, scattered stones, watery chasms, and bog. The woods of maple, oak, and ash were too dense to get a wagon through, but there was water in a fast-flowing stream, plenty of rock to build walls and foundations, wood for a house, a barn, an icehouse, a shed. So it became a farm. Today, the land offsets its geological irregularities in more aesthetic ways. It bestows a glorious view and features winding, hidden footpaths through woodlands over streams to distant ponds and waterfalls. It has bowed to its human caretakers by allowing gardens of vegetables, shrubs and flowers, an orchard, berry patches, and a contemplative garden surrounding a Japanese teahouse. But all that human hands have rendered accede to the natural aspect that made it possible. Martha Adams Rubin is the author of *Countryside Garden and Table*.

Sunday, June 4, 2 p.m. - 6 p.m.

Take Route 7 to Cornwall Bridge. At Cornwall Bridge, bear right onto Route 4 (or left if you are coming from the north). Continue about 4 miles to a flashing traffic light and then continue straight ahead onto Route 43. Continue another 4 miles to a cemetery on the right and a Civil War monument on the left. Just beyond the monument, turn right onto Hautboy Hill Road. The Rubin house is .6 mile on the left, #55. Alternate: On Route 63 drive 6 miles north of Goshen, CT and turn left onto Hautboy Hill Road (or right if you are coming from the north). The Rubin house is .3 mile on the right.

Marveen & Michael Pakalik

46 Stillman Hill Road, Colebrook

One lovely, open, sunny acre with distant views of the Berkshires, this garden features three long herbaceous perennial/shrub borders, each devoted to the seasons, and a new evergreen shrub border that keeps mysteriously expanding. A lovely all-white woodland garden blends with native flora. A stone patio features unusual container plantings.

Sunday, June 4, 2 p.m. - 6 p.m.

From Route 8 North or Route 44 West, travel to Winsted, then take Route 183 North to Colebrook. At the intersection of Routes 182 & 183, turn left and go to the top of hill. The house #46, is the first white house on the right. From Route 44 East to Norfolk, bear left at George's Norfolk Garage and take Route 182 approximately 4 miles (just past Route 182A) to top of hill. The house, #46, is a white house on left. Please park on the street.

May Brawley Hill

184 Brick School Road, Warren

My garden includes a fenced, old-fashioned perennial garden in front of a barn, a dooryard garden, and borders around the house, a potager, a woodland garden featuring species primula, and a pond.

Sunday, June 25, 10 a.m. - 2 p.m.

From Kent/Route 7, take Route 341 east toward Warren. Take the third left after Warren town line onto Brick School Road. Bear right at fork. The house (#184) is 1 mile on left past fork. From Warren/Route 45 north, take the fourth left onto Brick School Road. Bear left at stop sign. The house (#184) is 1 mile further on the right. Please park along the road.

Maywood Gardens

52 Cooper Road, Bridgewater

This property displays gardens of various design. Included are a formal rose garden, a perennial garden, a woodland garden, an annual garden, and a large greenhouse complex.

Sunday, June 25, 10 a.m. - 2 p.m.

From I-84 take Exit 9 and travel north on Route 25 toward Brookfield Village. Turn right onto Route 133 East toward Bridgewater. Cross Lake Lillinonah Bridge and take the first right after the bridge onto Wewaka Brook Road. Go .75 mile and turn right onto Beach Hill Road to the end. Turn right onto Skyline Ridge. Go .5 mile and turn right onto Cooper Road. Please park on the right across from the greenhouse complex.

MICHAEL POLLAN

PRITCHARD ROAD, CORNWALL BRIDGE

This garden is a work in progress, an effort to colonize an unruly landscape. It unfolds along a path linking the house to a small hut in the woods. Mr. Pollan is the author of books *Second Nature* and *A Place of My Own*.

Sunday, June 25, 2 p.m. - 6 p.m.

From Route 7, travel 1 mile south of Cornwall Bridge. Turn left onto Route 45 South. Continue on Route 45 South for 2 miles to the top and turn left onto Flat Rocks Road. Go .3 miles to the second left, Pritchard Road. The house is the first driveway on the right, an unpainted clapboard house with a barn in the back.

MICHAEL TRAPP

7 RIVER ROAD, WEST CORNWALL

This old-world-style garden is intimate, with cobbled paths, terraced gardens, raised perennial beds, and reflecting pools. Overlooking the Housatonic River, the property has a distinct French/Italian flavor.

Sunday, July 9, 10 a.m. - 4 p.m.

From Route 7, take Route 128 East through the covered bridge into West Cornwall. Continue on Route 128, taking the 2nd left onto River Road. The house is yellow with gray trim. It is the first on the left and sits behind the Brookside Bistro. Park in front or along the road.

MR. & MRS. DAVID STONER

183 MAPLE STREET, LITCHFIELD

This garden is twelve years old and could best be described as informal cottage style. It overlooks a pond and Prospect Mountain. In addition to perennial beds, there are more than sixty roses and fifty peonies, and a variety of small trees and shrubs. The vegetable garden is large and beautiful.

Sundays; June 4, September 10; 2 p.m. - 6 p.m.

From the west, take Route 202 east through Bantam to the first left across from Ristorante. Follow to Maple Street and go north for .75 mile. The house, #183, is on the west side of the street. Please park in driveway or along street.

Proceeds shared with The Bellamy-Ferriday House.

Mr. & Mrs. Juan O'Callahan

40 Salt Acres Road, Stonington

The four-acre seaside garden consists of grass with trees and border gardens along stone walls. There are six large cutting beds with a variety of flowers and bulbs, and four large rose beds enclosed in a yew hedge. A "secret garden" is built into the rock ledge next to the seawall. The greenhouse holds succulent plants in the summer. The view of Watch Hill, Sandy Point, and Fishers Island is spectacular.

Sunday, June 25, 10 a.m. - 2 p.m.

From I-95, take Exit 91/Stonington Borough Village. At end of ramp, if coming from north, turn left; from south, turn right. Go .25 mile, turn left onto North Main Street. Continue for about 2 miles across Route 1 to stop sign and turn left onto Trumbell Street. At the next stop sign, turn right over the bridge (railroad tracks) into the village. Follow Water Street to Church (Noah's Restaurant), and turn left. Go 2 blocks, then turn left onto Orchard Street. Turn right at next block onto East Grand Street. Continue to the end. Please park under the trees.

Proceeds shared with The Pregnancy Support Center, Inc. of Groton.

Mrs. Frederic C. Paffard, Jr.

389 North Main Street, Stonington

A ninety-year-old boxwood hedge one-quarter-mile long, a rose arbor, and an old fashioned garden are highlights. There is also a formal perennial garden edged with boxwoods and a water garden. Interesting old outbuildings, a greenhouse, a vegetable garden, a natural pond with resident otters and blue herons, and a meadow are adjacent. English boxwood and perennials will be available for sale, with ten percent of the proceeds to be donated to the Garden Conservancy.

Sunday, July 23, 10 a.m. - 2 p.m.

From I-95, take Exit 91. Go south to North Main Street, then turn left toward Stonington Borough. Go approximately 1.5 miles to #389 North Main Street. From Route 1, turn north onto North Main Street at the traffic light. Number 389 is the second driveway on right. Park anywhere.

Mrs. Philip McCaull
221 Round Hill Road, Greenwich

Walking this beautiful property, you will be reminded of an English manor house, yet there are distinctively southern touches. Interesting specimen trees, a boxwood garden, a vegetable garden, an herb garden, and a cutting garden of roses, lilies, and annuals grace the grounds and flagstone patio. A pond and pool complete this paradise.

Sunday, July 9, 2 p.m. - 6 p.m.

From the Merritt Parkway, take Exit 28/Round Hill Road. Go south 1 mile. The house, #221, is on the east side of the road. Please park along Round Hill Road.

Proceeds shared with The Garden Education Center of Greenwich.

Nancy & Tom Grant
4014 Redding Road, Fairfield

Our garden is an extension of an eighteenth-century reproduction Fairfield, Connecticut, Georgian house we built in 1972. Despite the fact that the house is new, it is listed in the historic and architectural survey of Fairfield, Connecticut, by the Connecticut Historical Commission. We have tried to create an eighteenth-century feel to our garden to complement the house. What was once a vegetable garden has been taken over by more than 100 roses and peonies, perennials, shrubs, herbs and annuals. We start many plants from seed and continually divide and change. Our newest project is a deer-proof garden outside the fenced area. We maintain the gardens ourselves.

Sundays; June 4 & 25, 10 a.m. - 4 p.m.

From the Merritt Parkway, take Exit 44/Fairfield from New York turn left off ramp and then left at the traffic light onto Route 58/Black Rock Turnpike. From New Haven turn left off ramp and right at traffic light onto Route 58/Black Rock Turnpike. Go north towards town of Redding for 1.9 miles to North Street/Division Street. Turn left onto North Street and proceed west past two stop signs for 1.5 miles. At third stop sign, turn right onto Redding Road. Go north for .3 mile to 4014 Redding Road. The garden is on the southeast corner of Redding Road and Mile Common Road. Please park on Mile Common Road.

NICKOLAS NICKOU

107 SUNSET HILL DRIVE, BRANFORD

This garden features many species and varieties of mature rhododendrons and azaleas. In addition, there are many rare trees and shrubs from China and Japan, coupled with woodland flowering plants and ferns.

Sunday, June 4, 1 guided tour at 10 a.m. No wandering alone.

From I-95, take Exit 55 to Route 1. Go east .4 mile and turn right onto Featherbed Lane; continue to end. Turn left, go 200 feet, then turn right onto Griffing Road, which runs into Sunset Hill Drive. (Ignore the first right onto Sunset Hill Drive.) The yellow hydrant on the left marks the driveway. Park along the road.

PAUL HELD & JANE SHERMAN

195 NORTH AVENUE, WESTPORT

Sloping terrain and dappled sunlight make a perfect environment for growing some precious, rare plants. This garden includes a delightful mix of shrubs and ground covers, both alpine and woodland. It is home for the largest collection of *Primula sieboldii* in North America and Europe. It is also home for the American Hepatica Association. Hepatica is a woodland flower treasured by adults and children alike.

Sunday, May 7, 10 a.m. - 6 p.m.

Take the Merritt Parkway to Exit 42. Go under the parkway if coming from the north; turn left off exit if coming from the south. Go to Route 136 and go north to the first stop sign, which is North Avenue. Turn right onto North Avenue and go .3 mile to #195 on the tree or mailbox. Please park on the street on the dirt curb.

RICHARD REDFIELD

379 BROOK ROAD, SCOTLAND

This large woodland garden includes a small stream bordered with candelabra primroses. The higher ground includes native and exotic woodland plants. There is also a sunny area with creeping phlox and other sun-lovers. Mature, slow-growing conifers and a raised bed area constructed in an old barn foundation are additional features.

Sunday, May 7, 10 a.m. - 4 p.m.

From the center of Scotland (opposite the Green), Brook Road leaves Routes 14 & 97 between the Congregational and Roman Catholic churches. Follow Brook Road approximately 1.8 miles. Park in the yard on lawn.

Rita & Steve Buchanan

317 COLEBROOK ROAD, WINSTED

This one-acre garden, started in 1993, has been featured in *Country Living Gardener* and other publications. Surrounding a pond and bordered by a creek and woodland, it includes stone-walled terraces filled with large drifts of perennials, native wetland wildflowers and shrubs, and hardy broadleaf evergreens and conifers. There is a greenhouse and kitchen garden. The Buchanans write and illustrate garden books and have done all the work on the garden themselves.

Sunday, September 24, 2 p.m. - 6 p.m.

From Route 44 (west of Winsted), travel north on Colebrook Road/Route 183. Go 2.1 miles. The house, #317, is on the west side of the road. Please park in the driveway or along the road.

Robert Bonneville

10 MORIN AVENUE, DANIELSON

My garden is situated in a residential-commercial area but is well isolated by a strategic planting of trees and by ornamental fences. It is comprised of several different themes including the following: several small brooks and ponds, some oriental influence, perennial garden, organic vegetable garden and various other themes as well as a small greenhouse full of tropical plants. There are several small outbuildings, including a small grist mill, scattered about-all made of old bard boards. (Note that the word small is often used as all this is confined to one acre). Also included in the tour is a woodworking shop where I spend the winter months when gardening is out of the question. There are more than 100 azaleas scattered throughout the gardens and approximately two dozen bonzai specimens.

Sunday, June 4, 10 a.m. - 4 p.m.

Take Interstate 395 from south to Exit 92. Turn left onto Route 6 and go approximately .5 mile to right on Route 12. Go approximately .5 mile to second left, Morin Avenue. First house on right. From North take right on Route 6 then same as above. Parking on street or lot across street at Larry's Automotive.

Robert & Joan Macneil

73 Cooney Road, Pomfret Center

Started in 1991, these Oriental-style gardens contain fish ponds, dry as well as wet brooks, and paths that wind along stone walls connecting beds of shrubs and perennials. The gardens incorporate the natural landscape, blending in native plants, ferns, mosses, and lichen-covered rocks. The setting is designed to provide restful spots with natural seating and peaceful views of the garden. A combination of perennials and annuals infuse color throughout the season. For contrast, a Zen garden offers the simplicity of shades of gray, welcoming meditation and offering consistency throughout the year. Most recently a new section of garden has been constructed, with raised beds that will provide kitchen herbs and edible flowers as well as vegetables. Always a work in progress, the gardens change each year to include other varieties of plants, additional sections of the property, and new ideas.

Sunday, June 25, 10 a.m. - 4 p.m.

From I-84 take Exit 69. Turn right onto Route 74 East and go to Route 44. Turn left onto Route 44 East and go to Route 101. Turn right onto Route 169 South. Go approximately 1 mile to Kearny Road and turn left. Go to stop sign and turn right onto Cooney Road (dirt road). Go .3 mile to left onto paved drive. There is a mailbox with sunflowers on it. Please park in front of the house.

Ruth & Jim Levitan

26 Wake Robin Lane, Stamford

This unique, one-acre woodland garden is covered by dogwoods and azaleas blooming over a carpet of old-fashioned spring perennials and biennials. It was created over a forty-year period by the owners, both dedicated amateur gardeners.

Sunday, May 7, 10 a.m. - 4 p.m.

From the Merritt Parkway, take Exit 35/High Ridge Road. Go 50 yards north and turn left onto Wire Mill Road. Continue about .5 mile, crossing a small bridge, and turn right onto Red Fox Road. Go up the hill 1 block and turn left onto Wake Robin Lane. Park in the street.

SANDRA & RICHARD BERGMANN

63 PARK STREET, NEW CANAAN

The architect's modernist garden, recently published in *House Beautiful* magazine, has a highly ordered geometry serving as an extension to the 1836 Greek Revival-style house. An abstract but formal composition using a series of stepped terraces which merge, join, and enfold space on the one-third acre in-town site. Keeping to the minimalist theme, abundant summer annuals are limited to two colors. The serene, landscaped rooms are formalized by yew parterres, serial hedges, stone and painted brick walls, a bosque of pruned crab apple trees, a topiary folly of cones and pyramids, raked gravel. The introduction of the conversational patter of water is the newest element this year. The garden's geometry contrasts with the thick, random woodland of mature pines and hemlocks. A screen of European beech separates the entry from the landmark building.

Sunday, June 25, 10 a.m - 6 p.m.

From I-95, take Exit 11 at Darien. Turn left if coming from New York (right if coming from New Haven) onto Post Road. Go to Mansfield Avenue, turn left. Mansfield becomes South Avenue* in New Canaan and deadends at Elm Street. Turn left onto Elm Street and go 1 block. The railroad station is at the intersection. Turn right onto Park Street intersection. We are the first house on the left at the corner of Park and Seminary. From the Merritt Parkway, take Exit 37 at Darien and turn left onto South Avenue. Follow directions above.* Please park across the street at the free municipal parking lot.

SARA M. KNIGHT

18 HIGH FARMS ROAD, WEST HARTFORD

This garden was developed over a twenty-year period. It boasts hostas under a giant yew along the driveway, a front cottage garden, a heather bed, and a formal area with roses under the pool. There is also a small hexagonal herb garden, a forty-foot perennial border with a long blooming span, and a short woodland walk with rhododendrons and azaleas underplanted with myrtle and wildflowers.

Sunday, June 4, 10 a.m. - 2 p.m.

From I-84, take the Park Road/West Hartford Center Exit. Turn left at the traffic light at end of ramp. Go straight, past 5 traffic lights. The road changes names from Park to Sedgwick to Mountain and bends around to the right. High Farms Road is the second left after the fifth traffic light. The house, #18, is the third on the right. Park along the street.

SARAH & JONATHAN SEYMOUR

1534 REDDING ROAD, FAIRFIELD

Our gardens were begun seventeen years ago. They have evolved from deep wood-land to partial- and full-sun gardens. The goal for us is to marry the surrounding woods with our garden and house. As of this writing one of the original sections is going through a complete overhaul. I have not been happy with it for a long time and have tried using plants to make it right, but that wasn't the answer. Jonathan's talents as a terrace and stonewall builder, I hope, are the answer. The shrub border is now two years old, and the only area that was watered during the drought of 1999, so it should be filling in. Once again to all the people who have come to visit us over the years a heartfelt thank-you for appreciating what we have tried to accom-plish and, of course, we would love to see you again. To those who are new to the Garden Conservancy tours, come wander in the gardens, chat with Roger Raymond the beekeeper, pet our beloved cats and dogs, see Jonathan's amazing birdhouses and have some iced tea or lemonade. As always, we are proud to say we do all our own design, planting, and stone work.

Sunday, June 4, 10 a.m - 4 p.m.

From the Merritt Parkway, take Exit 44/Fairfield; from New York take a right off ramp onto Congress Street; from New Haven take a left off ramp, left at traffic light, go under Merritt and right onto Congress Street. Follow Congress approximately 2.25 miles to Cross Highway. Turn left. At first stop sign, go left onto Redding Road. Driveway is .3 mile on left, just past Melin Drive. There are five mailboxes across the street from driveway. Please park along the Seymour's section of the driveway.

STEEPLEVIEW GARDENS — KATHY LOOMIS

25 STILLMAN HILL ROAD, COLEBROOK

Our gardens at Steepleview were created in a former cow pasture at the top of a sunny hill to showcase an ever-changing rainbow of floral colors that complement one another. Interesting plant habits and foliage textures are featured in the more than twenty cottage-style gardens displaying hundreds of different hybrid daylilies, stunning six-foot spikes of delphinium, and a very large collection of familiar and unusual perennials. Butterflies and hummingbirds are frequent garden visitors, lured to the flowers planted specifically to attract them. Bright beautiful colors are the main theme of the gardens at Steepleview.

Sunday, July 9, 10 a.m. - 4 p.m.

From Winsted on Route 44, turn right onto Route 183/Colebrook Road. Continue for approximately 3 miles to the 4-way intersection with Route 182. There is a large barn on the left. Turn left onto Route 182. Steepleview Gardens will be at the third house on the left (gray farmhouse at the top of hill.) From Norfolk on Route 44, turn left onto Route 182 just before George's Norfolk Garage. Travel approximately 4 miles. Look for the

Pinney Street sign on the right. Do not take this road, but begin counting houses after it. Steepleview Gardens will be the third house on the right. Please park on the road.

Proceeds shared with The Colebrook Historical Society.

STONYBROOKE

29 TACONIC ROAD, GREENWICH

Twenty-six years ago, we fell in love with this rambling old property of waterfalls, rock outcroppings, and open space. It was the site of Caleb Meade's saw mill, which, in the eighteenth and nineteenth centuries provided lumber and fine paneling for this and many a house in Greenwich. During the Depression, the house was restored and enlarged by architect Richard Henry Dana for the Carleton Granberrys. The modest gardens enhance the natural landscape. You may see dwarf conifer collections, old fashioned perennials, roses, and a long row of seventy-year-old peonies. You may walk along the stoney brooke, passing the old dam and self-sown foxgloves growing willy-nilly. Or you may just sit and reflect in the old white pine grove, on the hill overlooking the orchard, or on the lawn with a view.

Sunday, June 4, 10 a.m. - 4 p.m.

From the Merritt Parkway, take Exit 31/North Street south toward town. Take the second road on the left, Taconic Road. Go down the hill to Byfield Lane on the right, and park. Stonybrooke begins just past Byfield. There are a few spaces to park near the entrance. Those who have difficulty walking may go up the drive to park on the level.

Proceeds shared with The Green Fingers Garden Club.

SUSAN COHEN

7 PERKELY LANE, RIVERSIDE

Overlooking a tidal inlet, this small, sloping property has been shaped over the past twenty years by its current owners, who first removed overgrown shrubs and vines to create a garden in harmony with its waterfront setting. Susan Cohen, a landscape architect, created a fountain grotto from the old foundation walls of a derelict boat house, regraded parts of the land and designed flowering borders to surround the house. Four raised beds provide growing space for vegetables, herbs, and roses.

Sunday, June 25, 3 p.m. - 6 p.m.

From I-95, take Exit 5. Turn right onto Post Road/Route 1. Turn right again at the first intersection onto Sound Beach Avenue. Continue into Old Greenwich. Turn right at the traffic light onto West End Avenue. A Mobil station will be on the right. At the traffic circle, go left onto Riverside Avenue; there is a boatyard on the left. Turn left onto Marks Road and then take the first left onto Perkely Lane. The house, #7, is the second on the right. Please park on Marks Road, beyond Perkely Lane.

The Peonies at Poverty Hollow

POVERTY HOLLOW ROAD, REDDING RIDGE, CT

More than 425 varieties of peonies (tree, herbaceous, and intersectional) flourish among ledges, mature trees, stone walls, and winding paths on several acres of hillside and plateau. Shade gardens and small seating groups are scattered along the way for quiet overviews and reflection. As a *Country Living* cover story in 1996 and featured again in 1998, this property continues to evolve. A bed of native peonies from France and another from England have been added recently. In the March 1999 issue of *Connecticut Magazine*, garden columnist Rea Lubar Duncan suggests that perhaps nowhere else in a private garden is there such a variety of peonies. A member of the Board of Directors of the Peony Society, author/owner R. Kennard Baker devotes much of his time to this love of earth and beauty.

Sunday, May 28, 9 a.m. - 6 p.m.

From the Merritt Parkway/Exit 44, travel 10 miles north on Route 58/Blackrock Turnpike to the stop sign at the Episcopal Church and Church Hill Road. Turn right onto Church Hill Road and travel down a steep and winding hill. Bear right onto Poverty Hollow Road and go over the bridge where an officer will direct parking. From Georgetown, follow Route 107 to Redding Nursery. Exit right onto Cross Highway. Go past blinking traffic light to Route 58/Blackrock Turnpike. Cross over Route 58 onto Church Hill Road and follow as above.

Upperbrook Farm

170 LYON HILL ROAD, WOODSTOCK

A former dairy farm situated on a rolling hillside, Upperbrook has a variety of gardens: woodland paths with hostas, rhododendron, azaleas, and other shade-loving shrubs; a rose garden; daylilies; hosta; and shrub borders. You will also find a formal perennial and herb garden in an old barn foundation. Throughout the garden one will discover garden buildings, statuary, fountains and potted urns.

Sunday, July 9, 10 a.m. - 5 p.m.

From Route 395 take Exit 97 and go west on Route 44 for 1 mile. Go west on Route 171 for 3 miles, then north on Route 169 for 5 miles to Route 197. Go 200 feet, turn left onto English Neighborhood Road. Go 1 mile and turn left onto Cherry Tree Corner Road. Turn left onto Lyons Hill Road-first house on right. From I-84 take Exit 73/ Union. Turn right onto Route 190, and go 2 miles to Route 171. Turn right onto Route 171. Go to Route 197, then 5 miles to Bean Loft to Route 197, go to Route 169. Go 6 miles left on Route 169, and proceed as above. Please park on the street.

Proceeds shared with the Woodstock Garden Club.

WESTMINSTER GARDENS—
ELEANOR B. COTE & ADRIAN P. HART

26 WESTMINSTER ROAD, CANTERBURY

The area surrounding the house has border plantings of dwarf evergreens, rhododendrons, azaleas, other shrubs, and perennials. There is also a stone terrace with a waterfall. The back area is approximately three acres. It has nearly an acre of woodland gardens with crushed stone walkways, 350 different varieties of hosta, and many astilbes, pulmonarias, ferns and other shade-loving plants. The remaining area has twenty gardens planted with tall bearded iris, Japanese iris, Siberian iris, daylilies, peonies, ornamental grasses, various shrubs, perennials and annuals. An Oriental garden with a goldfish pond is located next to the woods. Benches have been placed throughout the gardens so visitors may stop to rest.

Sunday, June 25, 1 p.m. - 5 p.m.

From I-395 South, take Exit 89. Turn right at the bottom of ramp. Follow Route 14 about 6 miles to the stop sign at the bottom of the hill. Turn right. Go over bridge to 4-way stop at intersection of Routes 169 & 14. Go straight on Route 14. From I-395 North, take Exit 83. Turn left at bottom of ramp. Follow Route 169 for approximately 10 miles to intersection of Routes 169 & 14. Turn left onto Route 14/Westminster Road. Number 26 is the second house on the left after the Mobil station. Please park along the road. Handicapped may park in the driveway.

BALLARD PARK & GARDEN &

TOWN OF RIDGEFIELD, ROUTE 35, 400 MAIN STREET, RIDGEFIELD, CT 06877. (203) 431-8156.

This semiformal garden was donated in 1964 to the town of Ridgefield by Mrs. Edward L. Ballard. It is maintained by the Ridgefield Garden Club. It is a garden of long bloom period perennials, compact shrubs, and easy-care annuals. The park has a Fletcher Steel-designed pergola.

Year round, daily, dawn - dusk.

Entrance in middle of town on Route 35. Park at Grand Union. Entrance to the park on North end.

Bartlett Arboretum ❦

151 Brookdale Road, Stamford, CT 06903-4199. (203) 322-6971.

This sixty-three-acre garden is a living museum embracing natural woodlands, perennial borders, flower gardens, and an educational greenhouse. The arboretum offers a wide variety of programs and courses, a plant information service, and guided tours.

Year round, daily, 8:30 a.m. - dusk

From the Merritt Parkway take Exit 35. Take High Ridge Road/Route 137 North for 1.5 miles to Brookdale Road on left.

Bates-Scofield House ❦

45 Old King's Highway North, Darien, CT, 06820. (203) 655-9233.

The herb garden, adjacent to the Bates-Scofield house museum, was planted and is maintained by the Garden Club of Darien. It contains many varieties of culinary, medical and strewing herbs known to have been used in Connecticut in the eighteenth century.

Year round, daily, dawn - dusk.

Take I-95 to Exit 13. Turn left onto Post Road. At the second traffic light, turn left onto Brookside Road. Bear right at curve; the house and parking lot are on the left.

Bellamy-Ferriday House & Garden ❦

9 Main Street North, Bethlehem, CT 06751. (203) 266-7596.

The Ferriday Garden is a romantic, nine-acre landscape comprised of interesting woody and herbaceous plants. The garden was initially designed circa 1920 and developed through the early 1980s. Since 1992, the Antiquarian and Landmarks Society staff have been busy restoring the large collections of lilacs, old roses, peonies, and perennials. A formal yew and chamaecyparis parterre connect an orchard and meadow, creating a pleasing stroll through the garden.

May - October; Wednesday, Friday, Saturday, & Sunday. 11 a.m. - 4 p.m.

From I-84 take Exit 15/Southbury. At exit ramp take Route 6 east for 13 miles to Route 61. Go left onto Route 61 North. At intersection of Route 61 and 132, stay on Route 61 and take the first left onto the driveway.

Boothe Memorial Park— Wedding Rose Garden &

P.O. Box 902, Stratford, CT 06614. (203) 381-2046.

A brick pathway, lined with seasonal perennials, annuals, and shrubs, leads to the exuberant Wedding Rose Garden. Separated into two garden rooms, the Wedding Garden has a restored fountain and displays Love, Honor, and Cherish roses. The Rainbow Room features a colorful explosion of thirty-four varieties. Climbing roses on trellises and an arbor enclose the garden.

Year round, daily, dawn - dusk.

From I-95 West take Exit 38/ Merritt Parkway. Continue to Exit 53. Go south on Route 110 to Main Street, Putney which forks to the right. Head south on main Street for .25 miles to the park on the left. From I-95 East take Exit 33. Follow Ferry Boulevard, bear left at fork, and go under thruway. Bear right onto East Main Street/Route 110 to its end (Main Street Putney). Go .7 mile to the park on the right.

Bowen House—Roseland Cottage &

556 Route 169, Woodstock, CT 06281. (860) 928-4074.

The gardens were laid out in 1850 as part of the landscape of Henry Bowen's summer "cottage" built in 1846. Boxwoods border the twenty-one beds of annuals and perennials, forming a "parterre" garden. Landscape designer Andrew Jackson Downing's theories inspired the design of the ribbon and carpet-bedding plantings. Noteworthy trees and shrubs include a tulip tree, a Japanese maple, a Chinese wisteria, and old-fashioned roses.

Year round, daily, dawn - dusk.

From I-395 take Exit 97 for Route 44 West for 1 mile. Go west on Route 171 for 3 miles and north on Route 169 for 1 mile. House is on the left.

Brookfield Historical Society Museum Garden &

165 Whisconier Road, Brookfield, CT 06804. (203) 740-8140.

Designed by Dr. Rudy J. Favretti, this nineteenth-century herb garden complements the 1876 museum it adjoins. The focal is a sundial surrounded by coral bells and thyme. There is a brick walk throughout the property. The garden was created and is maintained by the Brookfield Garden Club.

Year round, daily, dawn - dusk.

Located on the corner of Routes 25 & 133 in Brookfield.

Caprilands Herb Farm ♣

534 SILVER STREET, COVENTRY, CT 06238. (203) 742-7244.

More than thirty world-famous theme gardens illustrate the use of shrubs, annual flowers, herbaceous plants, vegetables, and herbs in numerous creative and decorative arrangements and settings. Highlights include a butterfly garden, a large botanic garden, a naturalists' garden, a silver garden, saints garden, a small arboretum, and a 400 foot post and beam greenhouse displaying many herbal varieties suitable for northern gardens. The gardens are framed by a sheep meadow with a flock of Scottish Blackface sheep, complementing the dyers' and weavers' gardens.

Year round, daily except holidays, 9 a.m. - 5 p.m. (10 a.m. in the winter months).

The farm is on Silver Street in North Coventry, south of Routes 44 and 31. Route 31 is accessed from I-84. Route 44 is accessed from I-384E.

Connecticut Audubon Birdcraft Museum ♣

40 UNQUOWA, FAIRFIELD, CT 06430. (203) 259-0416.

America's oldest private songbird sanctuary was founded in 1914. The five-acre sanctuary (originally fourteen acres), planted to attract birds with trees and shrubs, was designed by Mabel Osgood Wright (1859-1934), a pioneering American conservationist, photographer, and author. Demonstration plantings to attract birds and a butterfly meadow restoration in progress.

Year round, Tuesday - Friday, 10 a.m. - 5 p.m.; Saturday & Sunday, noon - 5 p.m.

Take I-95 to Exit 21/Mill Plain Road. Go north on Mill Plain Road for .5 miles to stop sign. Turn right onto Unquowa Road and proceed for .5 miles to parking entrance immediately on left after I-95 overpass.

CONNECTICUT COLLEGE ARBORETUM &

WILLIAM STREET, NEW LONDON, CT 06320. (806) 439-5020.

The Connecticut College Arboretum was established in 1931. In addition to being a recreation area, the arboretum serves the college and the public with a unique blend of horticulture, conservation, and ecological research. Self-guided tour pamphlets are located in a box on the notice board inside the main entrance. The primary collection is of eastern North American native woody plants.

Year round, daily, dawn - dusk.

From I-95 northbound take Exit 83: left at the traffic light at end of ramp onto Williams Street. Turn right onto Route 32 North at the first traffic light (top of hill, at Coast Guard Academy). Turn left into the college main entrance at the second traffic light. From I-95 southbound: Exit 84N at end of Goldstar Bridge (over Thames River between Groton and new London) which becomes Route 32. Turn left at second light into the main college entrance. From I-395 southbound: take Exit 2.5 miles south. Turn right at second traffic light into college main entrance.

CRICKET HILL GARDEN &

670 WALNUT HILL ROAD, THOMASTON, CT 06787. (860) 283-1042.

A visit to this garden/nursery has been likened to stepping into a scroll painting of Chinese tree peonies. See more than 200 named varieties of tree peonies in an array of color, flower forms, and fragrances. Free catalog available.

May - June, Wednesday - Sunday, 10 a.m. - 4 p.m.

Take I-95 or I-84 to Route 8 North. Go to Exit 38/Thomaston, turning left at the bottom of the ramp onto Main Street. Turn left at the third traffic light onto Route 254. Go .5 miles on Route 254 to a blinking yellow light. Turn left onto Walnut Hill Road. Go up hill 1 mile and see our sign on the right.

ELIZABETH PARK ROSE & PERENNIAL GARDEN&

ASYLUM AVENUE, HARTFORD, CT 06103. (860) 242-0017.

This 15,000-specimen rose garden is the oldest municipal rose garden in the country. Other gardens include perennials, rock gardens, heritage roses, herb garden, wildflower garden, and annual displays. The Lord & Burnham greenhouses offer seasonal displays. The new cafe is also open year round.

Year round, daily, dawn - dusk. Greenhouse only: Monday - Friday, 8 a.m. - 3 p.m.

From I-84 take Exit 44 for Prospect Avenue. Head north on Prospect. The Park is on the corner of Prospect and Asylum Avenues.

GERTRUDE JEKYLL GARDEN AT THE GLEBE HOUSE MUSEUM 🍂

P.O. Box 245, Woodbury, CT 06798. (203) 263-2855.

In 1926 the famed English horticultural designer and writer Gertrude Jekyll was commissioned to plan an "old-fashioned" garden to enhance the newly created museum dedicated to the election of America's first Episcopal bishop. Although small in comparison with other elaborate designs she completed in England and Europe, the Glebe House garden includes 600 feet of classic English-style mixed border and foundation plantings, a small formal quadrant, and an intimate rose allée.

April - November, Wednesday - Sunday, 1 p.m. - 4 p.m.

From I-84 take Exit 15. Take Route 6 East for ten minutes to the town of Woodbury. Look for the junction of Route 317. Take Route 317 to the fork, bear left and the Glebe House Museum is 100 yards ahead.

HILL-STEAD MUSEUM'S SUNKEN GARDEN 🍂

35 Mountain Road, Farmington, CT 06032. (860) 677-4787. WWW.HILLSTEAD.ORG.

This 1901 Colonial Revival country house, now a museum, was the former home of Alfred Atmore Pope and his wife Ada Brooks Pope and contains their collection of Impressionist painting by Cassatt, Degas, Manet, Monet, and Whistler. The Sunken Garden is based on a design by Beatrix Jones Farrand, circa 1916, and features more than seventy-five varieties of perennials and other flora in the texture, foliage, and color combinations (blues, pinks, whites, purples, and grays) preferred by Farrand.

Year round, daily, 7 a.m. - dusk. Museum: May - October, Tuesday - Sunday, 10 a.m. - 5 p.m.; November - April, Tuesday - Sunday, 11 a.m. - 4 p.m.

From I-84 east or west, exit 39 (Route 4 West). Go to second traffic light and turn left onto Rt. 10 South. At next traffic light turn left onto Mountain Road. Museum entrance is .25 miles on the left.

HILLSIDE GARDENS 🍂

P.O. Box 614, Norfolk, CT 06058. (860) 542-5345

Hillside gardens is home to horticulturists Fred and Mary Ann McGourty. Their extensive garden, set around an old farm with stone walls, has more than twenty borders arranged with imaginative plant combinations. There are also areas for trial and evaluation of new perennials. The associated nursery specializes in a wide range of choice and uncommon plants.

May 1 - June 30, daily except holidays, 9 a.m. - 5 p.m.

Located on Route 272, 2.5 miles south of the center of Norfolk.

KEELER TAVERN MUSEUM— CASS GILBERT HOUSE & GARDEN ❧

P.O. BOX 204, RIDGEFIELD, CT 06877. (203) 438-5485.

A "Charleston Garden" is what architect Cass Gilbert called this garden setting that he designed circa 1910. A garden house looks down on a sunken garden with brick walls, arches, and a reflecting pool. The award-winning flower beds have been restored and are maintained by the Caudatowa Garden Club, using more than 100 varieties of annuals and perennials.

Year round, daily, dawn - dusk.

At the intersection of Route 33 and Route 35.

LAUREL RIDGE FOUNDATION ❧

WIGWAM ROAD, LITCHFIELD, CT

This display of the genus Narcissus was planted over approximately ten acres in 1941. The original 10,000 daffodils have naturalized for the past fifty years. The current owners have maintained the display and welcome visitors to drive by and share its splendor.

April - May, daily, dawn - dusk.

Take Route 118 east from Litchfield to Route 254. Turn right onto Route 154, go 3.5 mile and turn right onto Wigwam Road. The planting is about 1 mile on the left.

LEE MEMORIAL GARDEN/ GARDEN CENTER OF NEW CANAAN ❧

89 CHICHESTER ROAD, NEW CANAAN, CT 06840.

The Garden Center of New Canaan owns and maintains the Olive and George Lee Memorial Garden. This garden is a beautifully planted woodland offering visitors a splendid view of the many azaleas, rhododendrons, daffodils and wild flowers at their colorful best during the spring and summer.

Year round, daily, dawn - dusk.

Take the Merritt Parkway to Exit 36. Go north on Route 106. Bear left at the fork onto Weed Street. After approximately 2.5 miles, turn left onto Wahackme Road. Turn right onto Third Street, Chichester Road. Park off road at entrance.

New Canaan Nature Center &

144 Oenoke Ridge Road, New Canaan, CT 06840. (203) 966-9577.

Two miles of trails crisscross natural areas of this forty-acre site, providing access to unusual habitat diversity—including wet and dry meadows, two ponds, wet and dry woodlands, dense thickets, and an old orchard and cattail marsh. Highlights include a bird and butterfly garden, a large herb garden, a wildflower garden, a naturalists' garden, a small arboretum, and a 400-foot solar greenhouse.

Year round, daily, dawn - dusk.

Take Exit 37 off the Merritt Parkway and follow Route 124 through town. Located on Route 124, 1 mile north of the New Canaan town center.

Noah Webster House &

227 South Main Street, West Hartford, CT 06107. (203) 521-5362.
HTTP://WWW.CTSTATEU.EDU/-NOAHWEBSTER.HTML.

The Noah Webster House as a raised-bed teaching garden planted with herbs and other plants available to the Websters during the middle of the eighteenth century. A small demonstration plot of vegetables is also grown. Plants are labeled, so visitors may guide themselves through the garden.

Year round, daily, dawn - dusk.

Located 1 mile south of I-84 off of Exit 41. Follow signs at the end of the exit and travel for 1 mile. The museum is on the left.

Painter Ridge Perennials &

35 Painter Ridge Road, Roxbury, CT 06783. (860) 355-3844.

These country perennial gardens bloom continually from May to November. Included are fruit trees, old-fashioned lilacs and roses, herbaceous perennials, and an organic vegetable garden. Owners are in the process of creating a maze throughout a two-and-one-half to three-acre plot. Plants and cut flowers are available for sale.

May - October, daily, 10 a.m. - 4 p.m.

From Roxbury/Southbury, take Route 67 to Route 317 to Painter Hill Road to Painter Ridge Road, approximately 3 miles. From Washington/Woodbury, take Route 47 to Painter Ridge Road.

Pardee Rose Gardens ♣

180 Park Road, Hamden, CT 06518. (203) 946-8142.

The Pardee Rose Garden covers about three acres in East Rock Park. The rose beds are laid out geometrically, leading to a three-tiered central brick rose garden, and are planted with 1,500 rose bushes. More than 400 named varieties are currently grown. There are two greenhouses, as well as annual and perennial flower plantings.

Year round, daily, dawn - dusk

From I-95 take I-91 to New Haven. Take Exit 5 and continue north on State Street for 2 miles. Turn left onto Farm Road. The garden is 1 block up the hill.

Shoyoan Teien —
The Freeman Family Garden ♣

343 Washington Terrace, Middletown, CT 06459-0435. (860) 685-2330. www.wesleyan.edu.east

Shoyoan Teien is a Japanese-style viewing garden designed and built by Stephen Morrell in 1995. Inspired by the "dry landscape" aesthetic, the garden's raked gravel riverbed evokes the prominent bend in the Connecticut river as it flows through wooded hills near Middletown. Japanese tea ceremonies are periodically performed in the adjacent tatami room.

Open Days Event with Stephen Morrell: May 21, 10 a.m. - noon. Weekends during the academic year: Saturday, Sunday 2 p.m. - 5 p.m. Call for specific open dates.

From the north, take I-91 South to Exit 22 (left exit) to Route 9/Exit 15 and follow the signs to Wesleyan. From the south, take I-95 to I-91 North/Exit 18 or take the Merritt/ Wilbur Cross Parkway (Route 15) to Route 66 East and follow the signs to Wesleyan. From the northeast, take the Massachusetts Turnpike/I-90 West to I-84 West to Hartford; I-91 South to Exit 22 South (left exit); south on Route 9 and follow signs to Wesleyan/Exit 15. Or, take I-95 South through Providence, R.I. to Route 9 North/Exit 15, and follow signs to Wesleyan.

St. Paul's Church Garden of Bible Plants ♣

174 Whisconier Road, Brookfield, CT 06804. (203) 775-9587.

In the Spring of 1997, members of St. Paul's Church designed and created a Bible Garden in front of the church to grow herbs and flowers mentioned in the Bible, thereby forging a link between today and those distant and hollowed times. The garden also contains plants of historical legend associated with biblical characters and times. The garden is designed in the shape of a cross, forty feet by forty feet, with flagstone paths and a circle in the center. The plants are all identified as to their place in the Bible and labeled accordingly. Behind the church is a columbarium (burial ground) for church members. A traditional New England stone wall surrounds the maintained gardens. A ten-foot granite cross highlights the center of the garden.

Year round, daily, dawn - dusk

Located .25 miles north of the intersection of Routes 25 & 133 in Brookfield.

Stamford Museum & Nature Center ♣

39 Scofieldtown Road, Stamford, CT 06903. (203) 322-1646.

The Stamford Museum and Nature Center's 118 acres include woodland trails and a 300-foot boardwalk winding along a stream to provide a trail walk experience for parents with strollers, the elderly, and people in wheelchairs. A garden with plants indigenous to Connecticut is at the boardwalk entrance. On the early-New England farm, herbs and vegetables grow. The setting for the entire property includes flowering trees, shrubs, and ground covers, as well as a small lake, a waterfall, a marble fountain, and sculpture.

Year round, Monday - Saturday & holidays; 9 a.m. - 5 p.m. Sundays 1 p.m. - 5 p.m.

From I-95 take Exit 7 to Washington Boulevard/Route 137 North to Merritt Parkway. Located .75 mile north of Exit 35 on the Merritt Parkway at the junction of High Ridge Road (Route 137) and Scofield Road.

The Bird & Butterfly Demonstration Garden at The Nature Center for Environmental Activities ♣

10 Woodside Lane, Westport, CT. (203) 227-7253.

The garden serves as an example of well behaved plants that do not threaten the Connecticut environment. Both native and well behaved non native plants were selected for their function: To feed and protect birds and butterflies. The promise to promote the balance of nature has been kept. It is a pesticide free garden. The garden was installed in 1995.

Monday - Saturday, 9 a.m. - 5 p.m.; Sunday, 1 p.m. - 4 p.m.

From I-95 (Connecticut Turnpike) Exit 17, turn left at the end of the ramp onto Route 33 North. Go 1.5 miles to the intersection with Route 1. Turn left onto Route 1, go .5 miles to the second traffic light. Turn right onto Kings Highway North. Take the 1st left onto Woodside Avenue (becomes Woodside Lane). Go .9 mile to The Nature Center.

THE GARDEN EDUCATION CENTER OF GREENWICH/MONTGOMERY PINETUM &

BIBLE STREET, P.O. BOX 1600, COS COB, CT 06807. (203) 869-9242.

The 102-acre pinetum, formerly the estate of renowned plant collector Colonel Robert H. Montgomery, now a town of Greenwich park open to the general public, contains fine conifers, rock gardens, and woodland trails. The Garden Education Center has an auditorium/gallery, library, two garden shops, and a teaching greenhouse.

Montgomery Pinetum: year round, daily. Garden Education Center: September - December, Monday - Friday, 9 a.m. - 4 p.m.; Saturday, 10 a.m. - 2 p.m., closed Sundays; January - June, Monday - Friday, 9 a.m. - 4 p.m., closed Saturdays and Sundays. Closed July and August.

From I-95 take Exit 4/Indian Field Road. Follow Indian Field Road to end at traffic light. Turn right onto Route 1/Post Road/Putnam Avenue. At fourth traffic light turn left onto Orchard Street. Proceed .2 mile and turn right onto Bible Street. Follow Bible Street .7 mile; the entrance is on your left.

THE OGDEN HOUSE MUSEUM AND GARDEN &

1520 BRONSON ROAD, FAIRFIELD, CT 06430. (203) 259-1598.

This authentic colonial garden features over 100 medicinal and culinary plants that would have been necessary for the survival of the Ogden family in the late 1700s. A raised bed kitchen garden, a native wildflower walk and other beds surround the Ogden House, a 1750 saltbox farmhouse which is listed on the National Register of Historic Places. The gardens are designed and maintained by the Fairfield Garden Club.

May - October and year round by appointment, weekends, 1 p.m. - 4:30 p.m.

From I-95 South/Exit 21, at the end of ramp, turn left onto Mill Plain Road. Bear left on Sturges Road. Turn right onto Bronson Road. Ogden House is 1.3 miles on the right. From the North: At the end of ramp, proceed straight ahead on Sturges Rd. (Then, same as south).

WEIR FARM NATIONAL HISTORIC SITE 🐌

735 NOD HILL ROAD, WILTON, CT 06897. (203) 834-1896.

From 1882 to 1919, Weir Farm was the summer home of the American Impressionist painter J. Alden Weir. Sixty acres have been preserved of the landscape that inspired Weir and his contemporaries - Childe Hassam, John Twachtman, and Albert Pinkham Ryder. A self-guided tour allows visitors to explore the sites where some of their paintings were done. Guided tours are available of the art studios and the circa 1915 restored rustic enclosed garden. A Colonial Revival sunken garden, built by Weir's daughter in the 1930s, was rehabilitated in the spring of 1998 and is adjacent to the visitor center.

Call for tour schedule.

From I-84 take Exit 3/Route 7 South. Follow for 10 miles into the Branchville section of Ridgefield and turn right at light onto Route 102 West. Take the second left onto Old Branchville Road. Turn left at the first stop sign onto Nod Hill Road. Follow for .7 mile; the site is on the right and the parking is on the left.

WHITE FLOWER FARM 🐌

P.O. BOX 50, LITCHFIELD, CT 06759. (860) 567-8789.
WWW.WHITEFLOWERFARM.COM.

White Flower Farm is best known as a mail-order nursery, but it's also a great place to visit. In addition to the working nursery, the grounds are home to an impressive collection of mature trees and shrubs. There are also numerous display gardens featuring perennials, tender perennials and annuals, bulbs and roses. Tour maps are available at the Visitor Center or the Store.

Year round, daily, 9 a.m. - 6 p.m.; April - October, 10 a.m. - 5 p.m. November - March.

The garden is located on State Route 63; it's .7 mile north of Route 109, and 3.3 miles south of Route 118. Watch for the signs, and please park in the lot just north of the store.

DISTRICT OF COLUMBIA

Washington ★

DISTRICT OF COLUMBIA OPEN DAYS
May 13 & June 24: Washington, D.C. Area

Washington Area Open Days

Regional Representatives: Joanne Seale Lawson & Mrs. John Macomber

Saturday, May 13

ARLINGTON, VA
Burnet-Deutsch Garden, 716 North Edgewood Street: 10 a.m. - 4 p.m.
Cozy Shack, 3219 North 4th Street: 10 a.m. - 4 p.m.

WASHINGTON, D.C.
Caroline & John Macomber, 2806 N Street, NW: 10 a.m. - 4 p.m.
Jane MacLeish's Garden, 3743 Upton Street, NW: 10 a.m. - 2 p.m.
Mr. & Mrs. Eric Weinmann, 3244 Nebraska Avenue, NW: 10 a.m. - 4 p.m.
Mr. & Mrs. Robert W. Duemling, 2950 University Terrace: 10 a.m. - 2 p.m.
Sarah S. Boasberg, 3136 Newark Street, NW: 10 a.m. - 2 p.m.

Saturday, June 24

ARLINGTON, VA
Burnet-Deutsch Garden, 716 North Edgewood Street: 10 a.m. - 4 p.m.
Cozy Shack, 3219 North 4th Street: 10 a.m. - 4 p.m.
Hilltop Cottage, 2046 Rockingham Street: 10 a.m. - 4 p.m.

BETHESDA, MD
Kefauver Garden, 4831 Park Avenue: 10 a.m. - 4 p.m.

Burnet-Deutsch Garden

716 North Edgewood Street, Arlington

This intimately structured outdoor living space appears deceptively larger than its modest 7800 square feet. Extensive renovations to the 1920s bungalow and garden occurred simultaneously as one design effort. The result of this multi-disciplined effort is a seamless flow of hardscapes and landscape beds strategically integrated with the main house structure. Three separate and distinct "garden rooms" extend indoor entertaining to the outdoors. The sunken garden, the oval garden and the family garden and patio all offer individualized environments in which diverse rich plantings are artfully displayed. Throughout the garden there are elements of surprise, delights, vistas and focal points. The major component of the sunken garden is a round water feature offering neutralizing effect on the surrounding quasi-urban setting. Surely, this creation is proof that grand solutions can be achieved in restricted spaces.

Saturdays; May 13, June 24; 10 a.m. - 4 p.m.

From Beltway (495) in Virginia, east on Route 267 to Route 66 East to Exit 71 (Glebe Road/Fairfax Drive). Stay straight on Fairfax Drive crossing Wilson Boulevard (Merit Gas Station on right corner). Street name changes to North 10th Street. Go to second traffic light and turn right onto Northern Washington Boulevard. Go to next traffic light (approximately .25 mile) and turn right onto North Pershing Drive to the first right, North Edgewood Street. Go to #716 (sixth house on left). From Washington D.C., cross into Virginia, from Georgetown, Via The Key Bridge. Proceed and at slight fork veer right under overpass and at top of hill merge to right lane to access Route 50 West. At first traffic light (approximately 1 mile) turn right on North Pershing Drive. Go through first intersection and turn right at first street, North Edgewood. Go to #716 (sixth house on left). Please park on the street.

Proceeds shared with The Lyon Park Citizens Association.

Caroline & John Macomber

The design of this narrow garden reflects the serene Federal style of the house; a water runnel and a line of river birch accentuate its simple lines, which unite three seating areas. The plantings are designed to be more cultivated near the house and to have a more woodland character at the far end. Trees, shrubs, and a selection of bulbs and perennials are planned especially for fall, winter, and spring interest.

Saturday, May 13, 10 a.m. - 4 p.m.

The garden is in central Georgetown and can be reached from main roads such as Canal Road from the west, Wisconsin Avenue from the north, and Pennsylvania Avenue or M Street from the east. Number 2806 is on the south side of N Street, between 28th and 29th Streets.

Proceeds shared with The Georgetown Garden Club.

Cozy Shack

3219 North 4th Street, Arlington

Cozy Shack is a small natural garden featuring a large fish pond, Tennessee crab paving, sweeps of perennials, grasses, and sedges, and lots of informal plantings. The garden won a 1999 Grand Award in the Landscape Contractors Awards Competition. Garden owners are Doug Mearns and Thom Mannion of Tom Mannion Landscape Design, Inc.

Saturdays, May 13 & June 24, 10 a.m. - 4 p.m.

Ashton Heights, Arlington is a Northern Virginia suburb of Washington, DC. The garden is near the intersection of North Jackson Street and Pershing Drive. Please park on the street.

HILLTOP COTTAGE

2046 ROCKINGHAM, MCLEAN

We bought an old house with an even older, very neglected, once-great garden. Its strength was classic Virginia: one dramatic spring display of hundreds of azaleas, rhododendrons, and mountain laurel. To enjoy the garden throughout the year, we have redesigned it, adding two water gardens (one for koi; one for goldfish), two perennial gardens, shade gardens, and an evergreen hillside—all connected by paths, focal points, and rest spots. The garden today is a complex series of rooms on different levels that have to be sought out to be enjoyed. Intentionally, one cannot read the garden with a single glance or from a single perspective. In 1999, the garden was described as a standout by *The Washington Post*. This year the garden was published in a new book *Big Ideas for Small Spaces: Pocket Gardens* edited by James Trulove.

Saturday, June 24, 10 a.m. - 4 p.m.

From Washington DC, take Route 66 west. Exit at Sycamore Street and turn right onto Sycamore. Go 1 mile to the traffic light at Williamsburg and the Williamsburg Shopping Center. Go straight on Williamsburg for 5 blocks. Turn left onto Kensington. Go 5 blocks and turn left onto Rockingham. Hilltop Cottage is the second house on the right after Rhode Island. From the Beltway, take Route 66 east and exit at Westmorland Street. Turn left onto Westmorland. At the first traffic light turn right onto Williamsburg. Go .75 mile. At the traffic light at the Williamsburg Shopping Center, turn left to continue on Williamsburg for 5 blocks. Follow directions above.

JANE MACLEISH'S GARDEN

3743 UPTON STREET, NW, WASHINGTON

This small garden was developed to provide a variety of inviting, seductive, and surprising spaces for an active family. There is a choice of places to eat, a lawn for croquet, and beds filled with a collection of plants. Shapes gently woven with plant material are so subtle that many miss them. An old limestone temple is tucked in the rear of the garden. The sound of water greets visitors in this ever-changing garden.

Saturday, May 13, 10 a.m. - 2 p.m.

From I-495, take the Connecticut Avenue Exit south towards Chevy Chase. Go 4.5 miles to Van Ness Street. Turn right and go through one traffic light; at the next corner (37th Street) turn left. Go one block to Upton Street and turn right. Number 3743 is sixth house on the right. Please park along the road.

KEFAUVER GARDEN
4831 PARK AVENUE

The Kefauver Garden is situated in Bethesda, nesteld under an old oak tree on a quiet street. Entering the front garden you are greeted by an enormous boulder sculptured by nature to impress. A variety of blooming plants, shrubs and trees complement an excellent hardscape design of steps, retaining walls, patios, and walks. Let the walks lure you into the back garden with a deck and trellis overhead of an unusual shape. Sit down for a while and take in the shimmering light of the unusual plant material around you. Refreshments will be served during visiting hours. The Garden was designed with lots of attention to detail by Corinna Posner and Nicholien van Schouwen of European Garden Design.

Saturday, June 24, 10 a.m. - 4 p.m.

Take the Beltway to exit at River Road south towards Bethesda. Follow River Road south to Western Avenue, turn right on to Western Avenue and take your first right on to 4831 Park Avenue. The house is on the right hand side.

MR. & MRS. ERIC WEINMANN
3244 NEBRASKA AVENUE, NW, WASHINGTON

Our three-acre garden within the city has developed over the last twenty years. We have created a sweep of lawn, herbaceous borders enclosed by a trellis, a *trompe l'oeil* allée of willows, vegetable and cutting gardens, and a shade garden. A wide pebble terrace runs the length of the house.

Saturday, May 13, 10 a.m. - 4 p.m.

From Route 495 West, take the Connecticut Avenue Exit. Go south on Connecticut Avenue to Nebraska Avenue. Turn right and go around Ward circle and continue on Nebraska Avenue. Number 3244 is just beyond the fourth traffic light on Nebraska Avenue at the corner of Foxhall Road. Please park on Nebraska Avenue opposite the house.

Proceeds shared with GROW (Garden Resources of Washington).

Mr. & Mrs. Robert W. Duemling
2950 University Terrace, Washington

This new house and garden has been constructed in a two-acre landscape of mature spruces, hollies, and tulip poplars. Secluded and private, the garden feels more like the country in a city location. Terrace beds and containers are planted to complement and "extend" the house, while peripheral areas display a wide variety of perennials and shrubs, with an emphasis on cutting material for use in the house.

Saturday, May 13, 10 a.m. - 2 p.m.

Take Massachusetts Avenue to Ward Circle. At the circle, pick up Nebraska Avenue going west. Pass American University. Go past three traffic lights. Nebraska Avenue becomes Loughboro Road. University Terrace is the second left after the third traffic light. If you reach Arizona Avenue (where there is a stop sign), you've gone one block too far.

Proceeds shared with The Georgetown Garden Club.

Sarah S. Boasberg
3136 Newark Street, NW, Washington

This city shade and woodland garden, on a hillside of oaks and beeches, has been developed gradually over twenty years. The owner, a garden designer and former chairman of the American Horticultural Society, tries to have something in bloom at every time of year. The planting is necessarily informal, using many different shade-tolerant plants. Most of the garden is not handicapped-accessible; the paths are narrow and the steps are steep.

Saturday, May 13, 10 a.m. - 2 p.m.

Located at 3136 Newark Street, between Connecticut Avenue and 34th Street, N. W. The nearest Metro is at Cleveland Park.

Proceeds shared with The Friends of the National Arboretum.

American Horticultural Society at George Washington's River Farm ♣

7931 EAST BOULEVARD DRIVE, ALEXANDRIA, VA 22308. (703)768-5700.

Once part of George Washington's property, this twenty-five-acre garden overlooking the Potomac River now serves as headquarters for the American Horticultural Society. The gardens include: The Interactive Children's Gardens; the George Harding Memorial Garden; the Wildlife Garden; rose, herb, perennial and annual display beds; a picnic area; art exhibits; a visitor's center and gift shop.

Year round, Monday - Friday, 8:30 a.m. - 5 p.m. Closed on Holidays.

River Farm is located approximately 4 miles south of Old Town Alexandria, just off the George Washington Memorial Parkway. Exactly .5 miles after going under the Stone Bridge, make a left off the Parkway at the Arcturus/East Boulevard/Herbert Springs Exit. Turn left at stop sign. Entrance is on the right.

Dumbarton Oaks & Dumbarton Oaks Park ♣

1703 32ND STREET, NW, WASHINGTON, DC 20007. (202) 339-6401.

The Dumbarton Oaks Gardens and Dumbarton Oaks Park were designed as one project by noted architect Beatrix Farrand in cooperation with her clients, Mr. & Mrs. Robert Woods Bliss, who purchased the property in 1920. The design, mostly completed in the 1920s and 1930s, progressed from formal terraced gardens near the house, to an informal, naturalistic landscape in the stream valley below, with designed views between them. In 1940, the Blisses gave the house and related formal gardens to Harvard University as a research center and conveyed the twenty-seven-acre, naturalistic landscape to the National Park Service. Dumbarton Oaks Park is managed by the Rock Creek Park Division of the National Capital Region of the National Park Service.

April - October, daily, 2 p.m. - 6 p.m.; November - March, daily, 2 p.m. - 5 p.m.

Garden entrance: Located at R and 31st Streets, NW, 1.5 blocks east of Wisconsin Avenue. Please park along the street. Park Entrance: North on Lovers Lane from R Street, east of 31st Street; Lovers Lane runs between the Dumbarton Oaks Gardens east wall and the west edge of Montrose Park. Entrance is on the left at the bottom of the hill.

🌼 A preservation project of The Garden Conservancy.

HAMILTON COURT ❧

1220-1236 31st STREET, NW, WASHINGTON D.C.

One of the first projects of landscape architects Oehme Van Sweden, this courtyard is a tranquil oasis in the heart of Georgetown. The buildings surrounding the courtyard are a handsome knit of historic preservation and new construction. The sweet bay magnolias and other magnificent trees and plantings are now very well established.

Saturdays, May 13 & June 24, 9 a.m. - 6 p.m.

Travel south on Wisconsin Avenue toward Georgetown. Turn left onto N Street, NW and then right onto 31st Street. The entrance to Hamilton Court is on 31st Street between N Street, NW and M Street, NW.

TUDOR PLACE HISTORIC HOUSE & MUSEUM GARDEN ❧

1644 31st STREET, NW, WASHINGTON, DC 20007. (202) 965-0400.

Tudor's Place's five-and-one-half-acre garden retains its original Federal period flavor while it reflects the evolution of 180 years of family ownership by descendants of Martha Washington. The extensive, sloping South Lawn has centuries-old specimen trees surrounded by nineteenth-century shrubs. The formal north garden is divided into rooms with box circle and "flower knot" that date from the earliest design.

Monday - Saturday, 10 a.m. - 4 p.m.; Sundays in April, May, September, and October, 12:30 p.m. - 4 p.m. Closed major holidays.

Located between Q and R Streets in Georgetown, a 20-minute walk from Dupont Circle or Foggy Bottom Metrorail Stops. Metrobus stops are nearby at Q and 31st Street and Wisconsin Avenue. Street parking only.

UNITED STATES NATIONAL ARBORETUM ❧

3501 NEW YORK AVENUE, NE, WASHINGTON, DC 20002.
(202) 245-2726. WWW.ARS-GRIN.GOV/NA. JARVISM@ARS.USDA.GOV

This is America's Arboretum, 446 acres of gardens and collections in the heart of the city. There are extensive collections of native and Asian plants in natural settings. The National Herb Garden and the National Bonsai and Penjing Museum are world renowned as is the Gotelli collection of Dwarf and Slow Growing Confers. Azalea, dogwood, magnolia and native plant displays are spectacular in the spring. Perennials, flowering shrubs and trees and an extensive aquatic plant display provide color throughout the summer months.

Year round, daily, 8 a.m. - 5 p.m. The Bonsai & Penjing Museum open daily, 10 a.m. - 3:30 p.m. Closed December 25.

Located in northeast Washington, D.C., off New York Avenue/Route 50 and Bladenburg Road. Gates are located on the New York Avenue service road and on R street, off Bladenburg Road. Parking is free.

WASHINGTON NATIONAL CATHEDRAL— BISHOP'S GARDEN ❧

WISCONSIN & MASSACHUSETTS AVE, NW, WASHINGTON, DC 20016.
(202) 244-0568.

The Bishop's Garden, often described as an "oasis in the city," includes a rose garden, two perennial borders, a yew walk, three herb gardens, the bishop's lawn and the shadow house. Tours are offered by All Hallows Guild, founded in 1916 to maintain and beautify the gardens and grounds of the cathedral. Plants are based on Christian myths and legends, on historical interest, or are native to America. Frederick Law Olmsted, Jr. designed the gardens.

Year round, daily, dawn - dusk. Tours offered without reservations, April - October, Wednesdays, 10:30 a.m. Group tours offered by reservation only.

Take Massachusetts Avenue NW to Cathedral Close (at intersection of Wisconsin Avenue NW). Turn onto Cathedral Grounds (close) at South Road. Gardens are entered through arch (on foot) approximately 300 feet from Wisconsin on South Road. Self-guided garden tour brochure available in herb cottage gift shop nearby.

FLORIDA

★ Jacksonville

FLORIDA OPEN DAYS

April 29: Jacksonville

Jacksonville Open Day

Regional Representative: Carolyn Marsh Lindsay

Sunday, April 29
Baker Garden, 4915 Ortega Boulevard: 10 a.m. - 4 p.m.
Gardens of Los Cedros, 4157 Ortega Boulevard: 10 a.m. - 4 p.m.
The Hicks Garden, 4705 Ortega Boulevard: 10 a.m. - 4 p.m.

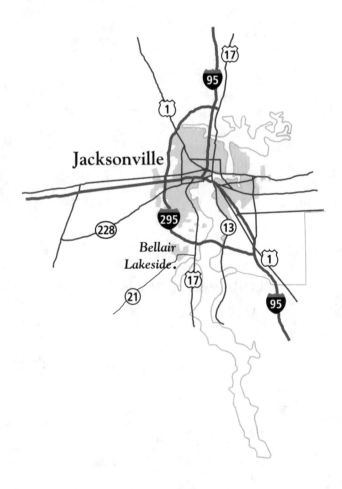

BAKER GARDEN

4915 ORTEGA BOULEVARD, JACKSONVILLE

A formal garden on the St. Johns River, the Baker Garden has brick pathways complementing the brick house and walls, rose-filled arbor, and white wisteria-wrapped pergola. A formal arrangement of hedges, flowering trees, shrubs, and perennials enclose the north and south rooms, which contain only white flowering plants. The Kingswood boxwood patterned garden sets off the statue by artist Malvena Hoffman. The river laps at the edge of the hybrid tea rose garden with its masses of blooms.

Sunday, April 29, 10 a.m. - 4 p.m.

Take Roosevelt Boulevard/Route 17 to Robert Gordon Road. Turn left to deadend street at Ortega Boulevard; across the street is #4915. Please park on Ortega Boulevard and Robert Gordon Road.

Proceeds shared with The Late Bloomers.

GARDENS OF LOS CEDROS

4157 ORTEGA BOULEVARD, JACKSONVILLE

A beautiful Italian fountain at the end of the cedar-lined driveway awaits your arrival at Los Cedros, which was built in 1924. The Mediterranean entrance leads to a pair of English urns circa 1870 by Jay Pulham with religious decorations that frame the garden pavilion. Another pair of circa 1860 urns with topiaries is near the English garden that spreads under the grotto, which is wrapped in wisteria. Three statues by Faith Winters, an English artist, adorn the brick paths. The English armillary circa 1880 stands guard over the new part of the formal knot garden containing miniature azaleas, mondo grass, and low junipers. Upon leaving the magnificent grounds, a reflective moment can be spent at the Italian Garden Temple.

Sunday, April 29, 10 a.m. - 4 p.m.

Take Roosevelt Avenue/Route 17 to Verona. Take Verona east to Ortega Boulevard. Please park on Pawnee, Arapahoe or Choctaw.

Proceeds shared with The Late Bloomers.

THE HICKS GARDEN

4705 ORTEGA BOULEVARD, JACKSONVILLE

The 1928 Cape Cod-style home is linked to a 1960s Georgian with a loggia designed by Atlanta architect Norman Askins. The loggia is host to beautiful pots of orchids and seasonal flowers. Strolling up the driveway under the live oaks, one passes the white fence surrounded by azaleas, holly trees, and boxwood. The lawn leads off to the right, with formal gardens edged in brick. The gardens are gracefully curved and one arrives at the oval terrace featuring a wishing well from the Warner estate in Bel Air. The azaleas, holly, ferns, and foxglove contrast with the old Carolina brick and Pennsylvania bluestone used throughout the gardens. On the waterside is an impressive view of the downtown skyline, which can be enjoyed from the pool or from under the limestone-columned arbor. Hydrangeas and azaleas define the oval lawn below, and a set of circular English steps with thyme growing between the bricks leads to a parterre rose garden at the edge of the St. Johns River.

Sunday, April 29, 10 a.m. - 4 p.m.

Take Roosevelt Boulevard/Route 17 east to Verona. Go to Ortega Boulevard and turn right to #4705 Ortega Boulevard. Please park on Pawnee or Arapahoe.

Proceeds shared with The Late Bloomers.

McKEE BOTANICAL GARDEN 🐾

350 U.S. 1, VERO BEACH, FL 32962-2905. (561) 794-0601.

The garden is now eighteen acres of what was originally an eighty-acre tropical hammock along the Indian River. McKee Botanical Garden was originally designed by landscape architect William Lyman Phillips in the early 1930s. Phillips created the basic infrastructure of streams, ponds, and trails. Native vegetation was augmented with ornamental plants, and for years McKee Jungle Gardens was one of Florida's most popular attractions. The garden went into decline during the 1970s due to competition from new larger-scale attractions. The land, all but the last eighteen acres, was sold to condominium developers, but fortunately, the historic core of the garden remains. Plans are underway to reopen in the summer of 2000 as a public botanical garden.

Please call for the 2000 schedule.

The garden is located at 350 South US 1 at the southern gateway to Vero Beach, on the mainland.

A preservation project of The Garden Conservancy.

GEORGIA

Lookout Mountain & Chattanooga, TN Area

★ Atlanta

GEORGIA OPEN DAYS
May 6: Atlanta

Atlanta Open Days

Regional Representatives: Mrs. William Huger & George de Man

Saturday, May 6

ATLANTA
Franklin's Outhouse Garden, 2060 Cottage Lane: 10 a.m. - 2 p.m.
Garcia Garden, 1315 Metropolitan Avenue SE: 10 a.m. - 2 p.m.
Hugh & Mary Palmer Dargan, 2595 Forrest Way: 10 a.m. - 2 p.m.
Plomgren Garden, 3018 Vinings Forest Way: 10 a.m. - 2 p.m.

CRABAPPLE
Rooster's Ridge Farm, 400 Dorris Road: 10 a.m. - 2 p.m.

DECATUR
The Garden of Ryan Gainey, 129 Emerson Avenue: 10 a.m. - 2 p.m.

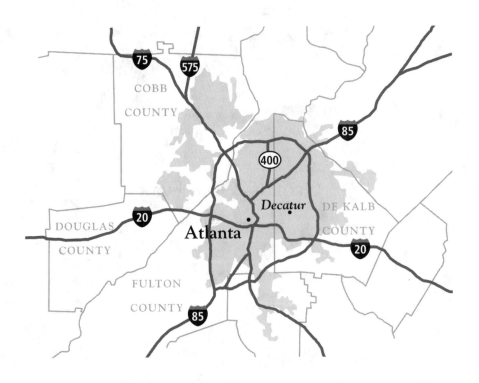

Franklin's Outhouse Garden

2060 Cottage Lane, Atlanta

This is a small in-town garden that has been developed over the last thirteen years. Key elements include a white lattice fence that provides enclosure for the garden, a large stone terrace for entertaining, a small grass area surrounded by six-foot perennial and annual flower beds, a fountain and fish pond, a wildflower area, planted pots which add interest and color, and a screened garden house which is fondly referred to as the "Outhouse." The garden provides an extensive collection of flowering trees and shrubs selected for seasonal interest and fragrance.

Saturday, May 6, 10 a.m. - 2 p.m.

From I-75/take Exit 10A (Northside Drive/Route 41 North). Go .6 mile to Collier Road. Turn right on Collier Road and travel .1 mile to Cottage Lane. Turn left and the house #2060, is on the left. Please park along the road.

Garcia Garden

1315 Metropolitan Avenue SE, Atlanta

The Gardener's Cottage is a cottage style garden surrounding a 1930s brick bungalow. There is an "X" boxwood pattern that greets visitors at the front door. On the corners, stand an enormous specimen deodara cedar and two American hollies that were planted when the house was built. Under these trees is a shade garden. The rest of the garden is filled with unusual perennials, vines and shrubs with roses abounding as well. Interesting structures and fences create a framework for the garden started in 1994. Of note is the pleached American beech hedge along one side of the drive underplanted with unusual bulbs. Not to be missed is the "pit" greenhouse under the deck. The garden is a constant work in progress, so there is always something new to see.

Saturday, May 6, 10 a.m. - 2 p.m.

Travel on I-75/85 south through Atlanta. Take I-20 East towards Augusta. At Exit 28-A which is Moreland Avenue South turn right off ramp, after leaving the interstate. Take the second street on your left (Long John Silver is on one corner and the Martha Brown United Methodist Church is on the other). Go through the traffic light and look for the East Atlanta post office on the right. Number 1315 is 6 houses past the post office on the right on the corner of Metropolitan Avenue and Haas Avenue.

Hugh & Mary Palmer Dargan

2595 Forrest Way, Atlanta

Visitors won't be surprised to learn that this couple spent many years gardening in Charleston, for the influence of that city's courtyard garden is obvious. In the front garden, dubbed The Perennial Sweep, boxwood balls anchor the arabesque curves of the planted borders. The backyard garden has a charming blue and white theme, carried out not only in the plantings, but in well-chosen garden accessories. Hand-painted tiles created by the Dargans show that this is very much an artist's garden.

Saturday, May 6, 10 a.m. - 2 p.m.

From I-85 South turn right onto Lenox Road. Turn left onto Buford Highway and then right onto Sidney Marcus Boulevard. Go .3 mile and turn right onto Lindbergh Drive. Go .7 mile and turn right onto Forrest Way.

Plomgren Garden

3018 Vinings Forest Way, Atlanta

This award-winning garden was created in stages with the help of local designers, the latest of whom is Jeremy Smearman of Planters. The newest section of this garden is an addition to an antique greenhouse designed to accommodate Mr. Plomgren's collection of specimen camellias. The added conservatory will house more than 150 camellias. The upper and lower gardens are divided by a stacked stone retaining wall. The upper garden has flowering perennial borders with roses, herbs and shrubs. The lower garden is filled with a boxwood knot garden and an arbor covered with New Dawn roses. The upper garden houses a New England-style garden house. In the past years this garden has been featured in Southern Living and was a Golden Trowel Merit Winner in Garden Design Magazine.

Saturday, May 6, 10 a.m. - 2 p.m.

Take Paces Ferry Road past the Lovett School and turn left at new Paces Ferry. Cross over to Randall Road, which dead ends into Randall Farm. Take a left turn onto Randall Farm. Turn right onto Vikings Forest Way which is the first street on the right.

Rooster's Ridge Farm

400 DORRIS ROAD, CRABAPPLE

This Crabapple, Georgia garden encircles the owners' fieldstone and cedar shake and shingle home, situated on a ridge overlooking their cattle farm. Privacy is afforded not by the evergreen hedges or stone walls of the city, but by pastures and wooded hills. The landscaped acreage reflects forty years of experimentation with the enormous number of flowering perennials, shrubs, and trees adaptable to Zone 7b.

Saturday, May 6, 10 a.m. - 2 p.m.

On GA 400 North from Atlanta, exit at Haynes Bridge Road #9. At top of ramp turn left. Continue to shopping center on left, at intersection of Haynes Bridge and Old Milton Parkway, Turn left onto Old Milton. Cross Main Street at next traffic light, and continue straight for 2.9 miles to Broadwell Road. Turn right onto Broadwell and follow to traffic light at Crabapple Corners. Continue straight, passing a Shell station on the left and an antique store on the right, and go 1.3 miles on GA 372 to Dorris Road and turn left. (Do not turn onto Old Dorris Road, which is gravel.) Continue .5 mile to #400 on the right. The driveway is gravel, and a grey barn with red roof is clearly visible at the entrance.

The Garden of Ryan Gainey

129 EMERSON AVENUE, DECATUR

The garden has an extensive plant collection, beautifully integrated into rooms and thoughtfully designed to show classic garden style yet exuberant color. The garden has received national and international publicity and has been featured on HGTV (an eight-part series for PBS), The Victory Garden, and Audrey Hepburn's Gardens of the World.

Saturday, May 6, 10 a.m. - 2 p.m.

From I-75/I-85 (south of the center of Atlanta), take the Freedom Parkway Exit. Do not exit at Carter Center, but stay on Freedom Parkway until it ends on Ponce De Leon. Turn right onto Ponce De Leon. When Scott Boulevard splits off to the left, bear right and stay on Ponce De Leon. At the third street on the right, turn right onto Drexel and then left at the next street. This is Emerson and the house, #129, will be on the left. Please park along the road.

Proceeds shared with The Atlanta History Center.

ATLANTA BOTANICAL GARDEN ♠

1345 PIEDMONT AVENUE N. E., ATLANTA, GA 30309. (404) 876-5859

At the Atlanta Botanical Garden you will find collections of roses, herbs, summer bulbs, ornamental grasses, conifers, and much more. A highlight of any trip to the garden is a tour through the Dorothy Chapman Fuqua Conservatory. Inside are collections of exotic tropical plants such as palms, cycas, ferns, orchids, and epiphytes. The adjacent Desert House showcases Old World succulents, including botanical rarities. The two-acre children's garden is new this year.

Year round, Tuesday - Sunday, 9 a.m. - 6 p.m.

From I-75 / I-85 take the 14th Street Exit and proceed east until it dead ends on Piedmont Avenue. Turn left and the garden entrance will be .5 miles on the right.

ATLANTA HISTORY CENTER ♠

130 WEST PACES FERRY ROAD, NW, ATLANTA, GA 30305.
(404) 814-4000.

Thirty-three acres of beautiful gardens, woodlands, and nature trails show the horticultural history of the Atlanta region. Gardens include the Mary Howard Gilbert Memorial Quarry Garden with native plants, wildflowers, bridges, and a stream; the Tullie Smith Farm garden featuring period vegetables, flowers, herbs, and antique species rarely seen elsewhere; the Swan House gardens featuring formal boxwoods and classical statuary; the Swan Woods Trails, labeled for nature study; the Garden for Peace featuring the Soviet Georgian sculpture "The Peace Tree;" the Frank A. Smith Memorial Rhododendron Garden featuring dozens of species of rhododendrons and azaleas; and the Cherry-Sims Asian-American Garden featuring species from the southeastern United States and their Asian counterparts, including many cultivars of Japanese maples.

Year round, Monday - Saturday, 10 a.m. - 5:30 p.m.; Sunday, noon - 5:30 p.m.

From I-75 take the West Paces Ferry Road Exit. The Center is located 2.6 miles east of the Interstate in Buckhead.

♠ *public garden*

Illinois

★ Rockford
St. Charles ★ ★ ★ Chicago
Hinsdale

Illinois Open Days

June 18 & 24, July 16: Northern Chicago
June 24: Rockford
July 9: St. Charles
July 22: Hinsdale

Hinsdale Open Day

Regional Representative: Mrs. David C. Earl

Saturday, July 22

HINSDALE
Burke Garden, 316 East Sixth Street: 10 a.m. - 4 p.m.
Musso Garden, 242 East Third Street: 10 a.m. - 4 p.m.
The Gardens of Kellie & Barry O'Brien, 527 West Maple Street: 10 a.m. - 4 p.m.

LA GRANGE
Catherine & Francis Donovan, 320 South Waiola: 10 a.m. - 4 p.m.

OAK BROOK
Susan & Ken Beard, 3711 Madison Street: 10 a.m - 4 p.m.
Tom Keck, 3421 Spring Road: 10 a.m. - 4 p.m.

BURKE GARDEN

316 EAST SIXTH STREET, HINSDALE

Our garden is a peaceful oasis in our busy suburban lives. The compact space is filled with inviting places to sit alone or with others. Bluestone and brick walkways connect small and larger entertaining areas to a beautiful screened gazebo with a copper roof. Whether we sit soothed by the sounds of the fountain in the walled courtyard, stroll through the woodland path connecting a hidden herb garden to a white shade garden, view the various perennial borders, or entertain our friends or ourselves in the gazebo, we are surrounded by nature and a sense of peace.

Saturday, July 22, 10 a.m. - 4 p.m.

From I-94, take Ogden Avenue west to the second traffic light (Garfield Avenue/York Road). Turn left. Drive approximately 1.5 miles (through the Village of Hinsdale) to 6th Street. Turn left, go 2.5 blocks. The house is a large English Tudor with a circle drive. It is located on the right side between Elm and Oak Streets. From Route 83, take 55th Street east to County Line Road (approximately .3 mile). Turn left. Go to Sixth Street, turn left. The house is 1.5 blocks on the left between Oak and Elm Streets. Please park on the street.

Proceeds shared with The Wellness House.

CATHERINE & FRANCIS DONOVAN

320 SOUTH WAIOLA, LA GRANGE

An English-style garden surrounds our Victorian-style house built in 1890. Through a tall hedge, you enter the Parlor Garden with its thyme lawn and herbaceous border. A long corridor leads you to the pond with surrounding shade garden. Across the terrace is a floral allée. The gardener's service area and small vegetable gardens are to the left. An open lawn leads to the Circle Garden of mostly roses.

Saturday, July 22, 10 a.m. - 4 p.m.

From Route 294 take the Ogden Avenue Exit east. At the third traffic light, turn right onto Brainard. At the third stop sign, turn left onto Maple. Travel 2 blocks to Waiola and turn right. It is the third house on the right. Please park on the street

Musso Garden

242 East Third Street, Hinsdale

The Musso's 1800 Victorian-style house sits on the corner of a three-quarter-acre lot in the village of Hinsdale. On the west side of the house is a brick path that winds through a bermed garden bordered on one side with a Victorian-style child's playhouse and on the other side with large trees and bushes which give the garden privacy and provide a sense of serenity. Meandering through one of the rose-covered arches, the path opens onto a large brick patio with iron furniture and planters surrounding a trickling three-tiered fountain. As you walk past the coach house, you enter the oldest section of the garden. Four flagstone squares house antique roses, clematis, perennials, and a variety of vegetables and annuals. Along the back yard and east side there is a row of apple trees and mature bushes which house many birdhouses and form a backdrop for the perennial garden that runs the length of the property. Stone and iron benches offer a retreat on a hot summer day.

Saturday, July 22, 10 a.m. - 4 p.m.

From Route 294, take Ogden Avenue west. After 2 traffic lights, turn left onto York Road (Shell station and Dunkin Donuts). Follow York Road past "S" curve, over train tracks to a 4-way stop sign. Turn left onto Third Street and go 2 blocks. The garden is at the southwest corner of Third Street and Elm Street, at a 2-story gray house with burgundy, white, and green trim. Please park on the street.

Susan & Ken Beard

3711 Madison Street, Oak Brook

We have lived and gardened on these three acres in Oak Brook for twenty-nine years. Each year we tackle a new project in the garden, tying to make a private oasis for our family and grandchildren. This year we added a nineteen-foot bridge which made the flow of the garden more interesting. An arbor with an eight-foot opening was also completed in an effort to keep the deer out. Most of the property is in various degrees of shade, which lends itself to hosta and many other woodland plants (ferns, epimedium, corydalis, etc.) that border paths lined with flag stone and wood chips. I am a hosta collector with 280 plus varieties and climbing. The garden has been designed to play down the old swimming pool, that was here when we moved in, and to give views with focal points from every room in the house and during every season.

Saturday, July 22, 10 a.m - 4 p.m.

Take Route 294 to Ogden Avenue. Go west towards Hinsdale, pass York Road to next traffic light, which is Madison Street. Go right approximately .6 mile across from far end of Brownswood Cemetery. The garden is at the rough cedar and stone two-story house on right side of the street. Park on east side of the road.

The Gardens of Kellie & Barry O'Brien

527 West Maple Street, Hinsdale

This three-quarter-acre garden reflects the lifestyle and personality of Kellie O'Brien and her husband Barry. Fifteen years ago they transformed their 1950s ranch home into a stately tudor, which created the background for the continuous perennial gardens weaving throughout their property. The front sunny borders are a combination of unusual evergreens and perennials. In the spring thousands of daffodils and tulips announce the beginning of a new season. Hydrangeas, roses and buddleias all add to the ongoing changes from early spring to late fall. Special attention to combining different textures is evident in the grouping of these plants. Walking through the hosta walk to the back 2,000-foot bluestone patio, you will pass an English fish pond, rose-covered balustrades, and many groupings of container gardens. This area is where the O'Briens host many family celebrations and spend hours with their five grandchildren, introducing them to the world of plants. The back gardens are mainly shade gardens with huge mature hostas, astilbes, hydrangeas, and a variety of unusual shade plants. The shed and vegetable gardens are a reflection of Kellie's farm background. The swing under the mulberry tree is where quiet moments are spent at the end of the day looking through the "magic window" created by an opening in the trees facing west. The garden has speakers throughout to further enhance this peacefulness that a gardens brings.

Saturday, July 22, 10 a.m. - 4 p.m.

The garden is between Madison and Monroe, 1 block north of Chicago Avenue or 4 blocks south of Ogden Avenue. The house is a red brick tudor on the north side of Maple. Please park on the street.

Proceeds shared with The Illinois Citizens for Life.

Tom Keck

3421 Spring Road, Oak Brook

This two-acre garden is oriented toward fall colors and the selection of trees and shrubs is slanted toward fall coloration. Grasses (approximately eighty different types) provide a year-round attraction but complement the tree selection. The hostas show well through August, but my latest interest is in conifers, of which a small selection has been introduced.

Saturday, July 22, 10 a.m. - 4 p.m.

Take Route 83 to Ogden Avenue. Travel east to Madison at the second traffic light. Travel north to the end of Madison and cross Spring Road. Continue into the driveway at the intersection of Spring Road and Madison.

THE MORTON ARBORETUM ♣

4100 ILLINOIS ROUTE 53, LISLE, IL 60532-1293. (630) 719-2400.

The Morton Arboretum is a 1,700-acre non-profit outdoor museum of woodlands, wetlands, gardens, and a restored native prairie. Established in 1922, the Arboretum's mission is to collect and study trees, shrubs and other plants from around the world, to display them in naturally beautiful landscapes for people to study and enjoy, and to teach people to grow them in ways that enhance our environment. The Arboretum also offers year-round education opportunities for customers of all ages. Families can enjoy the Arboretum by driving its eleven miles of roads or hiking its extensive pathways. The Arboretum also conducts annual special events throughout its four seasons of beauty.

Year round, daily, dawn - dusk

The Morton Arboretum is located at I-88 and Route 53 in the Village of Lisle, 25 miles west of Chicago.

Northern Chicago Open Days

Regional Representative: Mrs. Charles E. Schroeder

Sunday, June 18

LAKE FOREST
Gwill & Bruce Newman, 1213 South Estate Lane: 10 a.m. - 4 p.m.

WILMETTE
Craig Bergmann & James Grigsby, 1924 Lake Avenue: 10 a.m. - 4 p.m.

WINNETKA
Dorothy & John Gardner, 94 Indian Hill Road: 10 a.m. - 4 p.m.
Helen & Dick Thomas, 82 Indian Hill Road: 10 a.m. - 4 p.m.
Penny & Jim De Young, 22 Indian Hill Road: 10 a.m. - 4 p.m.

Saturday, June 24

LAKE BLUFF
Crabtree Farm, Sheridan Road: 10 a.m. - 4 p.m.

WINNETKA
Helen & Dick Thomas, 82 Indian Hill Road: 10 a.m - 4 p.m.
Liz & Bob Crowe, 1228 Westmoor Road: 10 a.m. - 4 p.m.

Sunday, July 16

EVANSTON
Bent Oaks, 1233 Crain Street: 10 a.m. - 4 p.m.

LAKE FOREST
A Garden on Old Meadow Lane, 285 West Laurel Avenue: 10 a.m. - 4 p.m.

METTAWA
Mettawa Manor, 25779 North St. Mary's Road: 8 a.m. - 2 p.m.

Sunday, September 24

LAKE FOREST
Camp Rosemary, 930 Rosemary Road: 10 a.m. - 4 p.m.
Little Orchard, 225 North Mayflower Road: 10 a.m. - 4 p.m.

METTAWA
Mettawa Manor, 25779 North St. Mary's Road: 8 a.m. - 2 p.m.

A Garden on Old "Meadow Lane"

285 West Laurel Avenue, Lake Forest

We moved into the big brick house with seven acres of land east of our present residence in 1954. The house was built in 1930 and planted in the English manner with American elm, white pine, and spruce, some of which still stand. Today on our remaining two and one-half acres, an extensive garden is maturing around the much smaller passive solar house we built in 1984 and live in now. Landscape architect Anthony Tyznik's beautiful design formed the bones of this garden, incorporating the existing tennis court and swimming pool and adding a pond in the northwest corner below wetland cottonwoods. Tony returned many times to design additions including the new kitchen garden and the campfire. In the early 1990s the espalliered apple orchard was started on dwarfing rootstock. The beehives were added for pollination, although to my chagrin, the bees prefer the pollen and nectar from Open Lands which borders our land to the south and which you can stroll into from the gate cut into the stockade fence.

Sunday, July 16, 10 a.m. - 4 p.m.

Take Route 41 to Westleigh Road in Lake Forest; go east on Westleigh to Green Bay Road. Turn left onto Green Bay and continue about .5 mile beyond the traffic light at Deerpath to Laurel Avenue. Turn left onto Laurel Avenue, where you must park on one side of the street. Visitors with disabilities may be driven to our house which is at the end of a narrow, unmarked cross street where you turn south and follow the cul-de-sac to the last of 5 houses, 285 West Laurel Avenue. Cars cannot be left at the house.

Proceeds shared with Madoo Conservancy, Sagaponack, NY.

Bent Oaks

Our garden, which encompasses an acre and one-half behind a 1909 house designed by architect Ernest Mayo has a number of features. Entering the garden through a gate in the east wall, you will step into a formal area with a rose garden, a small fountain, and an herb bed. Descending from the terrace steps, a sloping border on either side leads onto a checkerboard path of bluestone and grass squares encircling a small rose bed, and continues to a pergola (c. 1930), which frames our swimming pool. In one corner, a small two-level pond planted with shade-loving perennials, descends from a wooded copse. Azaleas, rhododendron, cornelian cherry, hydrangeas, and perennials, frame a green lawn with twenty-one ancient oak trees, which were slightly bent by a long-ago tornado. Amid this lawn sits our "folly," a domed gazebo that for fifty years sat atop the Evanston City Hall. The building was demolished in 1979 and we acquired its cupola and had it moved to our garden. This folly is especially dear to us since the old city hall was also an Ernest Mayo design. We feel that his cupola "has come home to roost!"

Sunday, July 16, 10 a.m. - 4 p.m.

*From the Tri-State Tollway/I-294 or the Edens Expressway/I-94 exit at Dempster Street East and continue several miles into Evanston to Ridge Avenue (Beth Emet synagogue is on the southwest corner). Turn right and go 1 block to Crain Street. *Turn right and go to the end of the short block to 1233 Crain Street. From Lake Shore Drive, travel north to Hollywood exit to Sheridan Road. Travel north on Sheridan Road into Evanston. Continue on Sheridan Road about 10 blocks to Greenleaf Street. Turn left onto Greenleaf and go 1 mile to Ridge Avenue. Turn right and go 1 block to Crain Street. *Follow from above. Please park on the street.*

Camp Rosemary

This garden was designed by Rose Standish Nichols in the 1920s and is made up of wonderful garden rooms partitioned by pines, yews, and boxwood hedges. A sweeping lawn and luscious container plantings at the front steps are the first hints of delightful discoveries inside: a charming box-edged parterre, a thyme garden, an urn brimming with roses, perennials, and annuals set against an ancient yew hedge affectionately called "the couch." Other areas include a chapel-like white garden with two reflecting pools, a vine-and-rose entwined pergola garden, three exuberant borders surrounding a small pool, an enchanting cottage garden, and a small herb garden. During the spring of 1998, work began in earnest on the walled garden which now graces the area surrounding the pool house. Elegant wide grass steps, paired rose borders, a linden alley, intricately patterned knot gardens, and four well-planted perennial borders, are all key elements of this new landscape. In contrast to the softer colors of the perennial beds near the pergola, these borders reflect a stronger palette of red, orange, violet, and blue. Some wonderful burgundy and silver foliage plants complement the whole scheme. Beyond the walled garden is a lush wooded ravine. A meandering path traces the ravine's edge beginning at the grass labyrinth and ending in a small glade, which overlooks the ravine. From this vantage point, a magnificent statue of Diana, the huntress, watches over the whole garden.

Sunday, September 24, 10 a.m. - 4 p.m.

From Route 41, take the Deerpath Road Exit going east. Proceed through town, over the tracks to the stop sign at Sheridan Road. Turn right. Go .5 mile, past Lake Forest College, past blinking yellow light, past Rosemary Road on the right. Go one-half block to Rosemary Road on the left. Turn left. Number 930 is in the middle of the block on the left. Please park in the front driveway area.

CRABTREE FARM

SHERIDAN ROAD, LAKE BLUFF

These gardens surround estate buildings designed in 1926 by David Adler. They are located on Crabtree Farm, the only remaining farm in Illinois that overlooks Lake Michigan. The gardens include a cottage garden by Ellen Shipman, a neoclassical folly house, and an original greenhouse and potting shed next to the cutting and vegetable garden. There is an indoor tennis court with espaliered ivy walls and an enclosed walled garden. The garden also has vistas, pathways, and a golfing area in its woodland and wildflower settings. A ravine walk and raised walkways lead to a private Lake Michigan beach.

Saturday, June 24, 10 a.m. - 4 p.m.

From Route 41 take the Lake Bluff Exit to Route 176. (Driving northbound take the first exit past the underpass. Driving southbound on Route 41, take exit to Route 176). Go east on Route 176 to Sheridan Road. Go north on Sheridan Road .5 mile to Crabtree Farm. Drive between ponds and follow signs to park in the field.

CRAIG BERGMANN & JAMES GRIGSBY

1924 LAKE AVENUE, WILMETTE

A very small "secret garden" at the office and home of two garden designers is all but concealed from the busy street. This intimate garden provides the setting for many unusual evergreen and woody plants—including a sixty-year-old *Magnolia x soulangiana*—herbaceous perennials and tender plantings. The old Lord & Burnham greenhouse (c. 1900) was the first greenhouse ever used by New Trier High School in nearby Winnetka. The garden has been featured in Rosemary Verey's book *The American Man's Garden, Horticulture*, and *House & Garden* magazines.

Sunday, June 18, 10 a.m. - 4 p.m.

From Edens Expressway/I-94 take the Lake Avenue Exit if traveling northbound or the Skokie Road Exit to Lake Avenue if traveling southbound. Continue east on Lake Avenue approximately 1.5 miles. The house is at Lake Avenue and Columbus Street (1924 Lake Avenue). Entry to the garden is at the rear of the house. There is limited parking on Columbus Street and in driveway. Additional parking is at the church parking lot east at Lake and Ridge Road. Entry to the garden is at the rear of the house.

DOROTHY & JOHN GARDNER

94 INDIAN HILL ROAD, WINNETKA

This second-generation garden was designed by John's mother in 1926. The original landscape garden and design are based on the principles of focus and axis. A sweeping park-like view in the front extends west to the expanse of the golf course. Five small but distinct gardens behind the house provide a good example of how to maximize the use of one acre. The second generation added a swimming pool designed as a reflecting pool and integrated into the garden by an allée of columnar maples. Gardens include a small white garden off the canopied north terrace, four parterres of roses, three parterres of vegetables and herbs, and a perennial cutting garden.

Sunday, June 18, 10 a.m. - 4 p.m.

From the Edens Expressway/I-94 take the Lake Avenue Exit if traveling northbound. Take the Skokie Road Exit to Lake Avenue if traveling southbound. Go east to Ridge Avenue. From Lake Avenue at Ridge Road, turn left (north) and drive .9 mile to the entrance of Indian Hill Road (#100-55). Please park in the lot by the gate next to paddle courts and walk a short distance to #94. No cars will be allowed to park on the road.

GWILL & BRUCE NEWMAN

1213 SOUTH ESTATE LANE, LAKE FOREST

The potting shed and foundation walls of the old greenhouses of the Albert Lasker estate (built 1920s) provide the basic structure for our complex of twelve small gardens. We began our designing, planting, and maintaining of these gardens without professional help in 1988, after the completion of the first of numerous additions to the former potting shed. On our two-thirds of an acre we have eliminated all lawn area and have continued to develop new gardens, using only plants that can survive the traumas of the weather of northeastern Illinois.

Sunday, June 18, 10 a.m. - 4 p.m.

From Route 41, take the Route 60 Exit. Go west on Route 60 to Waukegan Road. Go south on Waukegan to Everett Road. Travel west on Everett Road to Estate Lane. Go south on Estate Lane to Kennett Lane. On the south side of Kennett Lane, there is a black mailbox with #1213, and a small swan on or near the mailbox. A gravel driveway leads through a small woods to the house. Please park on street.

HELEN & DICK THOMAS

82 INDIAN HILL ROAD, WINNETKA

We inherited the fine bones of this garden several years ago when we became the second owners of this lovely French-style house. The bluestone terrace as well as the Hawthorne allée were all part of the original landscape plan in 1956. With the help of landscape designer Janet Meakin Poor we added a low entrance wall and inserted the two charming knot gardens in the front courtyard. The small standard lilacs (*Syringa patula* "Miss Kim") anchor these petite gardens. Two more knot gardens were added in the south terrace, echoing those in the front of courtyard, and feature small crab apples (Malus "Tina"). With the addition of a sunroom, a brick terrace area was created to form an intimate kitchen garden where lush herbs, climbing roses, clematis, and colorful perennials spill over the pink brick borders. Six boxwood-edged gardens surround a vibrant display of our favorite roses and form the entrance of the new pool area. The east-west perennial gardens enhance the south end overlooking the brussel block pool deck. A lattice fence frames the vegetable garden at the rear and, a unique pair of Chinese lions handsomely guard the Oriental-inspired pergola. On the shaded east perimeter of our property, a flagstone path winds through our woodland garden.

Sundays, June 18 & 24, 10 a.m - 4 p.m.

From the Edens Expressway/I-94, exit east onto Lake Avenue. The exit is Skokie Road if traveling north. Travel east on Lake Avenue to Ridge Road*. Turn left onto Ridge Road and continue to Indian Hill Road on the left. Follow Indian Hill Road to Number 82 about .5 mile. From Sheridan or Green Bay Road turn west onto Lake Avenue. Follow directions from above.*

LITTLE ORCHARD

225 NORTH MAYFLOWER ROAD, LAKE FOREST

Ours is an historic property on a bluff overlooking Lake Michigan. The house was designed in 1897 by Howard Van Doren Shaw; the garden by Ellen Biddle Shipman. It was on the Garden Club of America tour in 1933. Unfortunately, exhaustive research revealed that there were no remaining drawings or plans for the house or the garden. We moved to the property in 1992 and immediately focused on the restoration of the house and, three years later, the garden. The central feature of the property is the dramatic walled garden with reflecting pool. They are the only two remaining elements of the original landscape. The owner, trained in botany, has been working with Craig Bergmann to create new parterre gardens for this unique space and to develop an extensive collection of woody plant materials uncommon to the area.

Sunday, September 24, 10 a.m. - 4 p.m.

Take Route 41 to the Deerpath Road Exit going east. Go through town, over the tracks. The second stop sign will be Sheridan Road. Stay on Deerpath as it starts to wind around. Mayflower Road is about .25 mile east of Sheridan Road. Go south on Mayflower past Illinois and Maplewood Roads on the right. Number 255 is the second driveway on the left past Maplewood Road. Follow the long driveway back to the lake. Please park at the old garage on the right fork of the driveway.

Proceeds shared with The Chicago Botanic Garden.

LIZ & BOB CROWE

1228 WESTMOOR ROAD, WINNETKA

"A vista from every window" was the goal in the creation of our new small garden. The "bones" consist of a latticework fence, an arbor, a pergola, terraces and a small shed. These design elements are used in various parts of the garden for interest, variety and focal points, with resting places for enjoyment throughout. Foliage color and texture are high on our list as we continue to select and refine choices of plant material. Two young yellowwood trees grace the front yard, whitebuds shield us from neighbors, a golden raintree shadows the terrace, and a red chestnut tree is gaining in scale. The garden was designed and is completely maintained by its owners.

Saturday, June 24, 10 a.m. - 4 p.m.

From the north, take the Eden Expressway/I-94 South to Tower Road Exit. Go 1.4 miles east on Tower Road to Hibbard Road (3-way stop) and turn right. Take the second left onto Westmoor Road. The house is the third on the right. From the south, take Eden Expressway/I-94 to Willow Road East Exit. Go .75 mile east on Willow Road to Hibbard Road and turn left. Go .8 mile to Westmoor Road and turn right. The house is the third one on the right. Please park on Westmoor Road.

Mettawa Manor

The house and grounds were built in 1927 as a family compound. The current owners, only the second in the Manor's rich history, have been working for the past nine years to refurbish some garden areas and create new ones. The centerpiece of the garden is a newly built, walled, English-style garden with forty-foot perennial borders on either side of a sunken lawn that leads to a spring walk and rose room centered on an old fountain. Outside the east gate is a golden garden and an orchard/meadow underplanted with 20,000 narcissi and bordered by a fenced potager/cutting garden and a circular herb garden. The seventy-five-acre property has two ponds, a woodland garden, an eight-acre prairie, a parkland of specimen trees, and is surrounded by a newly reclaimed oak-hickory forest. Catch the beauty of morning light in the garden with this year's earlier opening hours.

Sundays; July 16, September 24; 8 a.m. - 2 p.m.

Take the Edens Expressway/I-94 to the Milwaukee Tollway/Route 94. Exit at Route 60 West/Town Line Road and follow 1 mile to St. Mary's Road, turn left just past the horse stables to Open Days signs on the left side of St. Mary's Road marking the private driveway entrance (on the left side of St. Mary's Road).

PENNY & JIM DE YOUNG

22 INDIAN HILL ROAD, WINNETKA

Designed by the architect Edwin Clark, the brick English Tudor-style house, built in 1927, is complemented by a sweeping bent lawn, shagbark hickory trees, and a har-tru tennis court. Flowering crab apple trees, Sargent crabs, pagoda dogwoods, Japanese tree lilacs, Washington hawthorns, witch hazel, several varieties of viburnum, a unique azalea, a fringe tree, and a Magnolia tripetala highlight this property. Ground covers of Euonymus vegetus, Euonymus coloratus, and pachysandra complement many of the above plantings. Pink and white peonies are prominent in four sizable mixed borders, and each bed features a variety of annuals and perennials that provide a colorful tapestry throughout the seasons. Spaced in the beds are hibiscus, buddleia, cotinus, and caryopteris. The rose garden, set around a circular pool, displays tea and floribunda roses, while shrub roses line the bed to the south of the tennis court. A variety of unique daylilies dominates the west side of the tennis court, and climbing the tennis court fence are an espaliered pear and an unusual selection of clematis.

Sunday, June 18, 10 a.m. - 4 p.m.

From the Eden's Expressway/I-94 North exit at Willow Road East and follow to Hibbard Road. Turn right and go south on Hibbard Road to Hill Road. Turn left and travel east on Hill Road to stop sign at Locust Street. Cross Locust and continue east to the bend on the road; just past the bend, turn right onto Indian Hill Road. Number 22 Indian Hill Road is the third house on the right. The driveway is just before the 3-way stop sign. From the Edens Expressway/I-94 south, exit at Lake Avenue East. Take Lake Avenue to Hibbard Road. Turn left and go north on Hibbard to Hill Road. Turn right and travel east on Hill Road to stop sign at Locust Street. Follow directions above. Please park along the road.

GRANDMOTHER'S GARDEN ❧

FULLERTON AVENUE (2400 NORTH) AND STOCKTON DRIVE (50 WEST), CHICAGO, IL 60624. (312) 747-0740

Wide, undulating, island beds of annuals, perennials, and grasses are set off by broad expanses of lawn weaving the gardens together. These lovely, free-form beds are a fine counterpoint for the formal plantings at the Lincoln Garden across the street.

Year round, daily, dawn - dusk.

Take Fullerton Avenue to Stockton Drive. The garden is located on the west side of Stockton Drive, south of Fullerton, near the entrance to the Lincoln Park Zoo.

CHICAGO BOTANIC GARDEN ❧

1000 LAKE COOK ROAD, GLENCOE, IL 60022. (847) 835-5440.

The garden, a living museum, covers 385 acres and features twenty-three specialty gardens including a rose garden, a waterfall garden, an English walled garden, a horticultural therapy garden, a bulb garden, a three-island Japanese garden, a fruit and vegetable garden, prairies, lagoons, and the 100-acre Mary Mix McDonald Woods. Nine islands on seventy-five acres of waterways and six miles of shoreline are distinguishing features of this "garden on the water". The living collections include more than 1.2 million plants, representing 7,000 plant types. Demonstration gardens showcase plants best suited for the Midwest. Research trail gardens hold plants being evaluated for performance in Chicago's environment. Conservation areas feature native and endangered flora of Illinois. Facilities include classrooms, an exhibit hall, an auditorium, a museum, a library, production and education greenhouses, the Daniel F. & Ada L. Rice Plant Resource Center, an outdoor pavilion, a carillon, bell tower, food service, and a gift shop. Services include adult education, programs for schoolchildren, tram tours of the garden, horticultural therapy and plant information. Owned by the Forest Preserve District of Cook County and managed by the Chicago Horticultural Society.

Year round, daily, 8 a.m. - dusk. Closed Christmas Day.

Lake Cook Road in Glencoe is located one-half mile east of the Edens Expressway. From Chicago, Metro trains (312-322-6777) and PACE buses (847-364-PACE) bring visitors to the Garden's entrance.

CRAIG BERGMANN'S COUNTRY GARDEN

700 KENOSHA ROAD, BOX 424, WINTHROP HARBOR, IL 60096. (847) 746-0311.

A garden center and perennial farm dedicated to the art of fine gardening. One thousand-one hundred herbaceous perennials hardy to the Midwest and 700 annuals and tender plants are offered in a park-like setting. There are five demonstration gardens: a sun garden devoted to full-sun perennials grouped around a clematis bower; a shade garden in the shadow of two giant Bur oaks; a rock garden comprised of plants which prefer a hot and dry situation; a rose and herb garden with rustic fencing and footbridge dedicated to plants which come into peak during the fall. Refreshments and antique garden ornaments are available in the Tea House.

April 21 - October 23, 8 a.m. - 4 p.m. Closed Monday and Tuesday.

Located about one hour from Chicago or Milwaukee. Take I-294 and exit east on Route 173. Continue east to Kenosha Road. Turn left and travel about 1.5 miles north. Garden center located on west side of street, set back in a meadow.

GARFIELD PARK CONSERVATORY &

300 NORTH CENTRAL PARK AVENUE, CHICAGO, IL 60624.
(312) 746-5100.

The historic Garfield Park Conservatory built in 1907 by Jens Jensen, is one of the largest conservatories of its kind in the world. Its eight exhibit houses display plants-some several centuries old-found in climates that range from rainforest to desert. Along with hosting five flower shows a year, the Conservatory offers guided tours for schools and other groups, and a variety of community and educational activities.

Year round, daily, 9 a.m. - 5 p.m.

From I-290 Eisenhower Expressway exit at Independence/Exit 26A and go north. Take Independence to Washington Boulevard and turn right. Take Washington east to Central Park Avenue and turn left.

MICHIGAN AVENUE PLANTINGS &

CHICAGO, IL

Stretching thirty city blocks, these island beds fill Michigan Avenue with big, bold, and beautiful seasonal plantings designed by Douglas Hoerr Landscape Architecture. Tulips underplanted with violas herald spring. Masses of annuals, perennials, and grasses celebrate summer. Kale and chrysanthemums added to the fall-blooming perennials and grasses announce fall, creating a stunning effect for miles along this stately avenue. These plantings are funded and maintained by The Michigan Avenue Streetscape Association, a not-for-profit organization of Michigan Avenue property owners and merchants.

Year round, daily, dawn - dusk.

From the north take Lake Shore Drive south to Michigan Avenue Exit. Central median planters from 11th Street north to Oak Street.

THE LINCOLN GARDEN &

CHICAGO PARK DISTRICT, 425 EAST MCFETRIDGE DRIVE, CHICAGO, IL
60605. (312) 747-0698.

Set amid a broad expanse of lawn in Lincoln Park, these gardens are at the foot of a sculpture of Abraham Lincoln (1897). The six raised beds were established in 1989 and measure thirty feet by 360 feet. There are eighty varieties of perennials. Annuals are added to provide seasonal color and interest. The six segments have alternating warm and cool color schemes. The gardens remain standing in the winter, with hardy perennials and ornamental grasses giving form and color to the landscape.

Year round, daily, dawn - dusk.

North State Parkway at North Avenue (1600 North).

The Rosenbaum Garden ❧

Chicago Park District, 425 East McFetridge Drive, Chicago, IL 60605. (312) 747-6290.

The gardens were designed to complement the existing old trees in this small city park overlooking Lake Michigan. Handsome flowering trees and shrubs give form and structure to the perennial plantings. Vibrant masses of daffodils in the spring give way to sweeps of colorful perennials and grasses in summer and fall. Lovely benches invite contemplation and repose.

Year round, daily, dawn - dusk.

Take Lake Shore Drive south to the Michigan Avenue Exit. Turn left at the first traffic light, which is Oak Street.

The Shakespeare Garden ❧

2703 Euclid Park Place, Evanston, IL60201. (847) 864-0655.

Designed by Jens Jensen in 1915 and surrounded by the original hawthorn hedges planted in 1920, the garden is romantic, secluded, and especially beautiful in June and July when its eight flower beds are filled with roses, lilies, pansies, artemesia, herbs, campanula, forget-me-nots, and daisies, all evocative of Shakespeare's poetry. Listed on the National Register of Historic Places in 1988, this garden said to have been "loved into existence" by the members of the Garden Club of Evanston, who continue to care for it eighty years later.

Year round, daily, dawn - dusk.

From either the north or the south enter Evanston along Sheridan Road and proceed to Garrett Place (2200 North). Park on Garrett Place (about mid-campus), east of Sheridan Road. The garden is reached by a bluestone walk on the east side of the Howe Chapel (on the north side of the street). Enter along this walk; the garden is not visible from either Sheridan Road or Garrett Place.

Rockford Open Day

Regional Representative: Susan Beard

Saturday, June 24

MT. MORRISON
Sharon Pierce's Garden, 112 Emily Street: 10 a.m. - 4 p.m.

OREGON
Heuer's Hosta Garden, 589 South Harmony Road: 10 a.m. - 4 p.m.
Jim & Rita Hermes, 1206 South Harmony Road: 10 a.m. - 2 p.m.

ROCKFORD
Garden of Oak Hill Cottage, 1622 Oakes Avenue: 10 a.m. - 4 p.m.
The Garden of Pauline & Paul Clausen, 2715 Karen Drive: 10 a.m. - 4 p.m.
The Hoel Garden, 1508 Sandy Point Drive: 10 a.m. - 4 p.m.
The Jean & Mary Ewaldz Garden, 2922 Carriage Lane: 10 a.m. - 4 p.m.

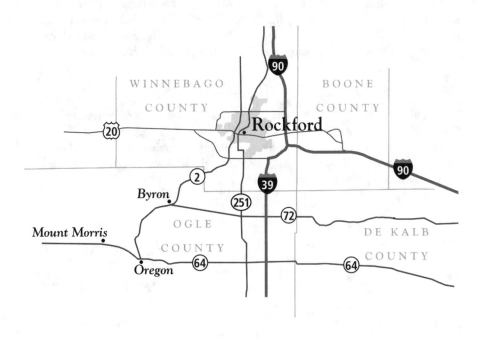

Garden of Oak Hill Cottage

1622 OAKES AVENUE, ROCKFORD

My cottage garden was created for a sense of peace, tranquility, and a life-long passion for gardening. A sanctuary for many birds, butterflies, and animal life who visit the ponds, fountains, towering oaks, and flowers along the garden paths. From the serene beauty of the moss garden to the riot of color and activity of the butterfly gardens, each of the garden rooms are unique. An old stone retaining wall, cobblestone paths, garden arbors spilling over with flowering vines, and a romantic little cottage nestled in the pines complete this unique garden setting.

Saturday, June 24, 10 a.m. - 4 p.m.

From I-251/North Second Street go to the Sinnissippi Greenhouse traffic light and turn east onto Ethel Avenue. Go to Oakes Avenue and turn right. Continue up the hill for 1 block and the garden is on the left. Please park on the street.

Heuer's Hosta Garden

589 SOUTH HARMONY, OREGON

Two full-sun perennial beds include flowers, grasses, foliage, vines and herbs. One rugosa bed blends into a hosta bed, and five hosta and shade perennial beds wind through heavy woods. Decorative ironwork and sculpture provide accent throughout.

Saturday, June 24, 10 a.m. - 4 p.m.

From Oregon, Illinois, travel west on Route 64 from city center and the junction of Routes 2 and 64. Continue 1 mile west to Oregon Trail Road. Turn left and go 3 miles to "T" at Oregon Trail Road and Harmony Road. Turn left and go 1 mile south to mailbox with #589 and hosta planted around it. Turn left and go down the long lane. Please park on the north side of lane leading to house.

Proceeds shared with The Mt. Morris Public Library.

Jim & Rita Hermes

1206 South Harmony Road, Oregon

Our garden has been designed around a ten-acre section of old white and live oak. We have added white pine and spruce over the past twenty-five years, lending structure and green all year long. The garden began with a sunny border ten years ago, and its full array of iris, daylilies, sedum, coneflowers, and hundreds of others mixed with annuals create a lively, colorful display all season. Our many paths guide you around a 10,000-gallon pond full of fish and plants, then continue around shade-loving buds of hosta, ferns, ginger, bloodroot, and pulmoneria collections. The combination of trees, flowering shrubs, and moving water creates a soothing sanctuary for many birds and butterflies and all humans that visit.

Saturday, June 24, 10 a.m. - 2 p.m.

Take Highway Route 2 South to White Pines black top. Turn right and follow signs to White Pines State Park for 5 miles to Harmony Road. Turn right at the Lake LaDonna sign and continue 1 mile north on left. Please park at the bottom of the hill.

Sharon Pierce's Garden

112 Emily Street, Mt. Morris

I started out with a single row of petunias around a birdbath. Next year I made a five-foot bed around the birdbath. To save money and work I used perennials. That was the beginning of my addition. The next year the sandbox turned into a garden. Then behind the garage, then by the fence, and next to the deck. All of the sudden, they all connected! Lilies, ferns, hosta, tansy, sedums, delphiniums, and many more I had not even heard of a few years before. I now have an addition and exercise program all wrapped in one. This year is the first year I have chosen not to make the garden bigger; instead there are plans to raise some beds and make a fountain.

Saturday, June 24, 10 a.m. - 4 p.m.

From Route 64, turn north onto Seminary Street. Travel 1 block and turn west onto Emily Street. The garden is at the second house from the end of that block. Please park on the south side of Emily Street.

Proceeds shared with Mt. Morris Library Expansion Fund.

The Garden of Pauline & Paul Clausen

2715 Karen Drive, Rockford

Our thirty-nine-year-old garden is a passionate plant collector's dream. An extensive collection of rare and unusual herbaceous perennials display a mixture of brilliant color combinations, an abundance of bloom, diverse foliage textures, and heady fragrances. It is augmented by trickling water into the pond under the majestic old spruce tree. A leisurely stroll through the garden presents the visitor with spectacular scenery. Special attention is given to the micro-climates and niches. A number of perennials rated for warmer zones than ours are grown in the garden's southerly exposure, including terrestrial *Bletilla striata* orchid, *Begonia grandis*, *Cyclamen hederifolium*, and *Arisaema candidissimum*. Statuary is strategically interspersed through the garden to enhance the plantings. Birds have an important place in the garden and are provided with many feeders, houses, and baths. Accenting annuals are planted in containers placed around the brick patio. May you find enjoyment and inspiration from this collector's paradise!

Saturday, June 24, 10 a.m. - 4 p.m.

From I-90 take the Rockford Exit/#64/East Riverside Boulevard. Turn left onto Riverside Boulevard and go 6.5 miles, passing through Loves Park, crossing the Rock River, and Route 2 to Rockton Avenue. Turn left onto Rockton Avenue and go 1 block. Turn right onto Karen Drive and go 1.5 blocks. The garden is on the right side of the street, #2715. Please park on the street.

The Hoel Garden

1508 Sandy Point Drive, Rockford

You are invited to wander our garden, born in a cornfield and bathed in sunshine. This eight-year-old garden offers you a taste of prairie plants, conifers, and a variety of viburnums and crab apple trees, as well as flowering perennials and grasses. The gardens were designed by my wife and me to provide year-round food for birds, as well as offer the beauty and enjoyment of the flowers. A pond with a small waterfall provides a habitat for waterlilies, iris, and Koi, as well as bullfrogs, toads, and ducks during the nesting season; even an occasional green heron pays a visit to test his fishing skills. Trellises hold bittersweet, clematis, trumpet vine, wild roses, and wisteria. A small limestone wall and two berms (heavily planted with a combination of conifers, red twig dogwood, viburnums, and tall hedge) divide the back yard into two garden rooms. The front yard contains some of the newest garden areas as grassy areas give way to a courtyard surrounded by spireas, lilies, roses, and low-growing evergreens interspersed with bellflowers, ajuga, blue lyme, and Japanese blood grasses.

Saturday, June 24, 10 a.m. - 4 p.m.

From I-90 take the Riverside Exit and turn west. Follow Riverside across the Rock River to North Main Street/Route 2. Turn right and go to Old River Road. Turn right and then right again onto Fenceline Drive. Turn right onto Turkey Run and then left onto Sandy Point Drive. Please park on the street.

Proceeds shared with Klehm Arboretum & Botanic Garden.

The Jean & Mary Ewaldz Garden

2922 Carriage Lane, Rockford

The scent of 140 rose bushes reaches you as you enter our garden through a vine-covered pergola. We have chosen sixty varieties of hybrid tea and floribunda roses to fill our terraced beds. Bordering the entire garden are eight shrub roses of diverse types: hardy Canadian, Austin English, heirloom, and modern varieties. We also have eighteen rose cultivars hybridized by the late Dr. Griffith Buck at Ames, Iowa. The shrub roses were carefully selected for their delightful fragrance, repeat blooming pattern, and for their winter hardiness. As companion plants for our roses, we have delphinium, clematis, iris, lilies, and many other perennials and annuals. Our garden is at its peak for abundant blooms and fragrance in the third and fourth week of June.

Saturday, June 24, 10 a.m. - 4 p.m.

From I-90 take the Rockford Exit/#64/East Riverside Boulevard. Turn left onto Riverside Boulevard and go 6.5 miles, passing through Loves Park, crossing the Rock River, and Route 2 to Rockton Avenue. Turn left onto Rockton Avenue and go 1 block. Turn right onto Karen Drive and go 2 blocks. Turn left onto Packard Parkway and go 1 block to Carriage Lane. Please park on the street.

St. Charles Open Day
Regional Representative: Susan Beard

Sunday, July 9
Charles & Patricia Bell, 39W 582 Deer Run Drive: 10 a.m. - 4 p.m.
Mark & Linda Pawelski, 5N 985 Oak Run Court: 10 a.m. - 4 p.m.

Charles & Patricia Bell

39W582 Deer Run Drive, St. Charles

In a semi-rural area west of Chicago, amid the tall oak trees and open vistas, we have established a series of gardens on two acres featuring numerous sun- and shade-tolerant perennials. Colors and textures are combined to accent and highlight how our collection of more than 400 varieties of daylilies can interact with other sun-loving plants. Several hundred varieties of perennials, decorative grasses, and flowering shrubs provide a constantly changing view in the gardens during the growing season. In the shade gardens, spring brings Virginia bluebells, bleeding hearts, primrose, brunnera, epimedium, and other shade lovers, giving way to hostas, astilbe, and ferns to provide various shades of green and variegated leaf patterns throughout the summer and fall. Various annuals are used throughout the gardens and in containers for constant color. A garden is a personal expression that is meant to be shared with others-our gardening principle.

Sunday, July 9, 10 a.m. - 4 p.m.

*From I-90 take Randall Road to Bolcum Road (about 9 miles) turn right. *Continue to Denker Road and turn right. Turn left onto the first street, which is Deer Run Drive, and continue to the first house on the right. From I-88 take the Farnsworth Road Exit. Travel north on Farnsworth Road approximately 5 miles to Fabyan Parkway and turn left. Travel approximately 3.5 miles and turn right onto Randall Road. Take Randall Road to Bolcum Road (approximately 3 miles north of Route 64) and turn left. *Follow directions from above. Please park on the street.*

Mark & Linda Pawelski

5N 985 Oak Run Court, St. Charles

The garden is a mixed-border perennial garden of one and one-half acres, consisting of informal cottage-style flower beds, specimen trees, a rectilinear herb garden, a bog garden, and many unusual woody plants. The garden has both sun and shade perennial borders, and has been in existence for six years.

Sunday, July 9, 10 a.m. - 4 p.m.

From I-90, Exit Randall Road South, go 9 miles south to Bolcum/Ridgewood. Turn left onto Ridgewood Drive and turn right at the "T" intersection. Turn right onto Oak Run Court to 5N985 Oak Run Court. From I-88, exit Farnsworth North to Fabyan Parkway, turn left (west) onto Fabyan Parkway to Randall Road. Go right (north) onto Randall Road approximately 9 miles to Bolcum/Ridgewood. Turn right onto Ridgewood Drive, at the "T" intersection go right; go right on Oak Run Court to 5N 985 Oak Run Court. Please park in front of the house and on cul-de-sac.

LOUISIANA

★ New Orleans

LOUISIANA OPEN DAYS

April 15: New Orleans

New Orleans Open Day

Regional Representative: Ann Hobson Haack

Saturday, April 15

Ann & Frederick Haack, 1224 Jackson: 10 a.m. - 4 p.m.
Mr. & Mrs. James O. Gundlach, 1238 Philip Street: 10 a.m. - 4 p.m.
Mrs. Frank Strachan, 1134 First Street: 10 a.m. - 4 p.m.
Wendy & Boatner Reily's Garden, 2221 Prytania Street: noon - 5 p.m.

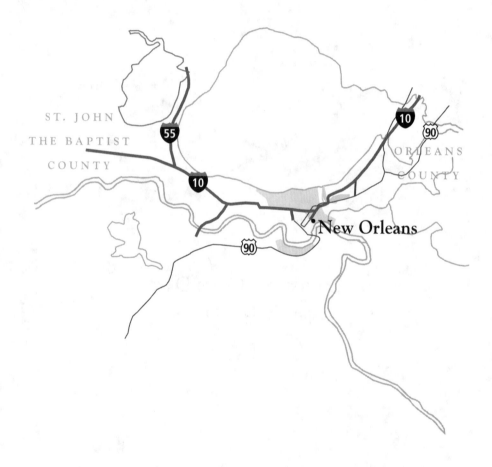

Ann & Frederick Haack Garden

1224 JACKSON AVENUE, NEW ORLEANS

The fragrance of sweet olive and confederate jasmine lure you to the front of and around the Greek Revival-style villa built in 1867. *Magnolia virginiana*, agapanthus, and dietes with a ground cover of trailing violets complete the front plantings. Pineapple guava shade the flagstone walk on the way back to the garden. The garden has a central tapis vert edged by a deep border of fragrant southern plants. The border includes sweet olive, cape jasmine, camellias, English and antique roses, *Magnolia fuscata*, and vines of stephanotis. The old flagstone terrace with pots of strawberry guava, lemon and lime trees joins the house to the garden.

Saturday, April 15, 10 a.m. - 4 p.m.

Driving from downtown New Orleans or the Greater New Orleans/Mississippi River Bridge Expressway, take St. Charles Avenue to Jackson Avenue. Go one-half block past Jackson and make a U-turn on St. Charles back to Jackson Avenue. (No left turn is permitted at Jackson.) Turn right at Jackson and go three and one-half blocks. The house is between Chestnut and Camp Streets on the right.

Mr. & Mrs. James O. Gundlach

1238 PHILIP STREET, NEW ORLEANS

Our home, in New Orleans' Garden District, is in the classic Greek Revival style and dates from 1853-1854. There is an addition in the Italianate style dating from 1869. The formal entrance has a two-tiered flower bed that leads to a free-flowing side garden. One-hundred-year-old boxwood and large magnolia trees provide a curtain of privacy. The cast iron archway is covered with bougainvillea. Plants include rare varieties of camellias, sweet olive trees, crepe-myrtles, a Chinese fringe tree, a parsley hawthorne tree, cleyera, Burford holly, shell ginger, coppertone plants, oak leaf and lace cap hydrangeas, Chinese palms, agapanthus, and a variety of tropical plants. A focal point on the patio is an intriguing bit of southern Americana, a plant bed made from the brick foundation of the old cistern.

Saturday, April 15, 10 a.m. - 4 p.m.

Driving from downtown New Orleans or the Greater New Orleans/Mississippi River Bridge Expressway, take St. Charles Avenue to First Street. Turn left toward the river and go 3 blocks to Chestnut Street. Turn left and travel 1 block. The house is on the corner of Philip and Chestnut. Please park along the road.

Mrs. Frank Strachan

1134 First Street, New Orleans

Flanked by sweet olive bushes (*Osmanthus fragrans*), an iron gate is the entry to these grounds, which surround the double-galleried Greek Revival-style house where Confederate President Jefferson Davis died. The garden has evolved over the past seventy years. The forty-five-year-old plan of garden rooms by Umberto Innocenti is apparent. The rose garden and plantings of indigenous and exotic materials can be observed and reflected in the pilastered mirrors of a teahouse facing the croquet lawn. Beyond the high garden wall are the orchid house, potting shed, and bath-house for the swimming pool area, which features palms and plumbago.

Saturday, April 15, 10 a.m. - 4 p.m.

From downtown New Orleans or the Greater New Orleans/Mississippi River Bridge Expressway, take St. Charles Avenue to First Street. Turn left towards the river and go 4 blocks to #1134 First Street, on the corner of Camp Street, in the Garden District.

Wendy & Boatner Reily's Garden

2221 Prytania Street, New Orleans

The house was built as a villa in 1850, but our garden wasn't developed until after 1910. The tall brick wall, live oak trees and hollies give privacy in the middle of the city. Old native roses, Old Blush and Mme. Carriere, climb on the Chinese trellis. On the house side is a small parterre planted in patterns of seasonal color. In the middle is a sundial from Versailles surrounded by pots of color. On the end is a tub (that was originally in the house) made from a single piece of carrara marble and filled with calla lilies. There is a boxwood knot garden along the lawn. Many different azaleas form the other borders with Indian hawthorn, camellias, dogwood, crape myrtle, and magnolia. Splashing water is a large part of our garden as it masks the traffic sounds. The terrace has pots of gem magnolia and ivy. A walled garden that surrounds the guesthouse is filled with cleyera, sweet olive, azaleas, impatiens, begonias, and petunias.

Saturday, April 15, noon - 5 p.m.

Driving from downtown New Orleans or the Greater New Orleans Mississippi River Bridge Expressway, take St. Charles Avenue to First Street. Turn left toward the river and go 1 block to Prytania Street. Turn left and go 1 block to Philip Street. The house is on the next block, #2221 Prytania Street, on the left. Please park on the street.

BEAUREGARD-KEYES HOUSE &

1113 CHARTRES STREET, NEW ORLEANS, LA 70124. (504) 523-7257.

Built by Joseph Le Carpentier in 1826, the Beauregard-Keys House is at the corner of Chartres and Ursuline Streets. The original garden was described as a "jungle." The present garden is a formal parterre and consists of ferns, lilies, camellias, azaleas, and irises. Two cast iron sofas under the iron arbor have a statue of St. Francis between them, and in the center of the garden is a cast iron fountain. The garden is designed to have seasonal blooms against a background of various evergreens.

Year round, Monday - Saturday, 10 a.m. - 3 p.m.

Located opposite the Old Ursuline Convent on Chartres Street in New Orleans.

LONGUE VUE HOUSE & GARDENS &

7 BAMBOO ROAD, NEW ORLEANS, LA 70124-1065. (504) 488-5488.

Longue Vue House and Gardens is an historic city estate created by Mr. & Mrs. Edgar B. Stern during the period 1939-1942. Mr. Stern was a very successful cotton broker in New Orleans who married Edith Rosenwald, daughter of Sears & Roebuck entrepreneur Julius Rosenwald, in 1921. The House and gardens reflect the collaborative artistic and design vision of the Sterns, as well as that of Ellen Biddle Shipman, one of the leading landscape designers of the period, and the architects William and Geoffrey Platt.

Year round, Monday - Saturday, 10 a.m. - 4:30 p.m.; Sunday, 1 p.m. - 5 p.m. Closed major holidays.

From the I-10 Expressway, take Exit 231A to Metairie Road or take Canal Street and Metairie Road buses.

THE NEW ORLEANS BOTANICAL GARDEN ❦

CITY PARK, #1 PALM DRIVE, NEW ORLEANS, LA 70124. (504) 483-9386.
WWW.NEWORLEANSCITYPARK.COM/BOTANICAL.HTML

The New Orleans Botanical Garden in historic City Park is a rare and valuable surviving example of public garden design dating from the WPA and Art Deco periods of the 1930s. Having undergone major restoration during the last decade, it preserves the original work of three noted men: architect Richard Koch; landscape architect William Wiedon; and artist-sculptor Enrique Alferez. An extensive plant collection is featured in its numerous garden rooms.

Year round, Tuesday - Sunday, 10 a.m.- 4:30 p.m.

From I-10 West, take Metairie Road / City Park Exit, turn left onto City Park Avenue. From I-10 East, take I-610 to Canal Boulevard Exit, turn left onto City Park Avenue. From I-10 Crescent City Connection, take Metairie Road / City Park Exit, turn right onto City Park Avenue. From the French Quarter, drive-up Esplanade Avenue, over Bayou St. John, turn right onto Wisner Avenue, enter at Wisner and Friedrichs.

MARYLAND

★ Baltimore
★ District of Columbia Area
★ Annapolis

MARYLAND OPEN DAYS
June 10: Annapolis
September 16: Baltimore

Annapolis Open Day

Regional Representive: Mrs. John A. Baldwin

Saturday, June 10

Annetta Kushner's Garden, 2030 Homewood Road, Ferry Farms: 10 a.m. - 2 p.m
Bretton Gardens, 855 B & A Boulevard: 10 a.m. - 2 p.m.
Gately Garden, 1917 Holly Beach Farm: 10 a.m. - 2 p.m.
Holly Beach, 1800 Holly Beach Farm Road: 10 a.m. - 2 p.m.
Richardson Garden, 43 Franklin Street: 10 a.m. - 2 p.m.

Annetta Kushner's Garden

2030 Homewood Road, Ferry Farms, Annapolis

There is always something in bloom in this residential garden. It is a collector's garden filled with a variety of flowering trees, shrubs and perennials: stachyrus, corylopsis, hamamelis, viburnums, hydrangeas, roses, euphorbias, asarums and epimediums. Enclosed by antique iron fencing and accented by metal and wood furnishings and ornaments, the landscape also includes areas devoted to shade-loving plants, roses, troughs and miniature gardens. Also featured is a double pond, a new pergola garden and a greenhouse. The garden maker wants the visitor to linger, sniff and smile.

Saturday, June 10, 10 a.m. - 2 p.m.

From Baltimore, take I-97 toward Annapolis. At the intersection of I-97 and US Route 50, go East on Route 50 toward the Bay Bridge. Take Exit 27, (a right exit after crossing the Severn River Bridge) to Route 450 South, Naval Academy. At the first traffic light, turn left onto MD 648. Go up a short hill to the first sharp right at the sign for Ferry Farms Road. This will be Homewood Road which will turn left. The Kushner garden, #2030, is three-quarters of the way down the street on the left. From the Bay Bridge, take Route 50, West toward Annapolis to Exit 27A, MD Route 450 South, Naval Academy. Turn left onto Route 450 follow directions as above. From Washington, take Route 50 East toward Annapolis, go past all Annapolis exits until Exit 27/MD 450 South/Naval Academy and follow directions as above. Park on the street but please be mindful of neighbors' lawns.

Bretton Gardens

855 B & A Boulevard, Annapolis

Bretton Gardens is a large kitchen garden of narrow raised beds-full of interesting herbs, vegetables, and flowers-which over the years has evolved into a teaching garden. While similar to a French potager in appearance, the garden relies on Native American wisdom, as passed on to me through my Cherokee heritage. This way of gardening strives for spiritual harmony which, along with companion planting, keeps plants disease-free. Many people come to the garden to meditate and to feel the peace and beauty of a garden spiritually balanced.

Saturday, June 10, 10 a.m. - 2 p.m.

From Baltimore take I-97 to Annapolis, go east on Route 50 toward the Bay Bridge. Take Exit 27/Route 2 North to Jones Station Road (approximately 4 miles) and turn left. Go 1 block then turn right onto Baltimore-Annapolis Boulevard. The garden is .5 mile on the right behind Cafe Bretton Restaurant. Park in Cafe Bretton parking lot.

Gately Garden
1917 Holly Beach Farm, Annapolis

Situated on the Chesapeake Bay with a splendid view of the Bay Bridge, this garden provides a lesson on how to make a garden that sings but doesn't upstage the main attraction. A spacious lawn, graced with old shade and fruit trees, sweeps down to the water's edge where wildflowers are encouraged. Nestled near the large, rambling farmhouse, garden beds of all sorts have been made, with special emphasis given to a small, prettily fenced, mostly perennial garden, which is always colorful, comfortable and inviting.

Saturday, June 10, 10 a.m. - 2 p.m.

Take Route 50 east to Exit 32. Turn right to top of ramp. Turn right and go to end and turn right again. Holly Beach Farm Road is on the left. The house is 2 miles down the private road on the left.

Holly Beach
1800 Holly Beach Farm Road, Annapolis

In the 1920s and 1930s, the Holly Beach gardens overlooking the Chesapeake Bay were well known throughout Maryland. At the time we purchased the property in 1995 there was little of value remaining in the gardens except for the "bones." We have reestablished the gardens under the guidance of landscape architect Gay Crowther, assisted by old photos and local knowledge. The present English style garden consists of six "rooms" to include perennial, pond, rose, hydrangea and hillside gardens. Mature trees and ivy covered walls give the garden an old-world feeling.

Saturday, June 10, 10 a.m. - 2 p.m.

Take Route 50 East; right before the Bay Bridge, take Exit 32. At stop sign at end of exit ramp, turn right. At next stop sign, turn right onto Skidmore Road. Make first left onto Holly Beach Farm Road. Go through the private gatewall and go 1 mile and turn right onto gravel road by barn/garage. Park by barn and follow signs to garden.

Richardson Garden
43 Franklin Street, Annapolis

This city garden has two parts. A formal garden is defined by large boxwoods and enclosed by a brick wall with crape-myrtles and hornbeams. The adjoining, less formal garden, contains a pool. Throughout, plantings are adjusted for sun or shade and space is given to a variety of culinary plants, including herbs and fruit trees.

Saturday, June 10, 10 a.m. - 2 p.m.

From Route 50, exit onto Rowe Boulevard and come to center of downtown to church circle. Take Franklin Street. The garden is 3 blocks from circle at 43 Franklin Street. Unrestricted street parking is available.

LONDON TOWN GARDEN ❧

839 LONDONTOWN ROAD, EDGEWATER, MD 21037. (410) 222-1919.
LONDNTWN@CLARK.NET.

Vistas of the South River and shady glades characterize London Town's woodland gardens. An unusual and artful combination of native and exotic plants, the gardens are spectacular in spring and fascinating year-round. Noteworthy plant collections include one of the most extensive selections of magnolias on the East Coast, an array of peonies including rare tree peonies, and the 10,000 narcissus that great spring at London Town.

Year round, Monday - Saturday, 10 a.m. - 4 p.m.; Sunday, noon - 4 p.m. Closed major holidays.

Take US 50/Route 301 to Route 665/Exit 22/Aris T. Allen Boulevard. Stay in the right lane and exit onto Route 2 South/Solomon's Island Road. Go over South River Bridge. Continue about .6 mile and turn left at the third traffic light onto Mayo Road. Go approximately .8 mile and turn left at the second traffic light onto London Town Road. Go about 1 mile to the end of the road.

WILLIAM PACA HOUSE & GARDEN ❧

186 PRINCE GEORGE STREET, ANNAPOLIS, MD 21401. (410) 263-5553

Twenty years ago this two-acre site was a hotel and parking lot. The walled and terraced garden is the re-creation of the eighteenth-century town residence of William Paca, a Maryland signer of the Declaration of Independence, based on historical and archaeological research. The two-story octagonal summer house at the foot of the garden is the focal point of the four formal parterres, planted with historically accurate flowers, shrubs, and trees. An elegant Chinese-style bridge crosses the spring-fed ornamental pond surrounded by informal plantings. Herb, vegetable, and fruit gardens reflect the practical aspects of town life, as do the other outbuildings on the site.

March - December, daily, 10 a.m. - 4 p.m.; Sunday, noon - 4 p.m. Call for winter hours. Closed Thanksgiving, Christmas Eve, & Christmas Day.

Take Route 50 to Exit 24. Turn onto Rowe Boulevard, toward Annapolis. At the end of Rowe Boulevard, turn left onto College Avenue. At the first traffic light, turn right onto King George Street and at the bottom of the hill turn right onto Randall Street. At the traffic light, turn right onto Prince George Street. The garden entrance is through the William Paca House. Two hour parking is available on Prince George Street.

Baltimore Area Open Day

Regional Representative: Mrs. Thomas G. McCausland

Saturday, September 16

Breezewood, 3722 Hess Road: 11 a.m. - 4 p.m.
Foxgloves, 16135 Old York Road: 11 a.m. - 4 p.m.
Garden of Jean & Tom McCausland, Remare Road: 11 a.m. - 4 p.m.
Pindale Collector's Gardens, 2117 Blue Mount Road: 11 a.m. - 4 p.m.
South Meadows, 16730 J.M. Pearce Road: 11 a.m. - 4 p.m.

BREEZEWOOD

3722 HESS ROAD, MONKTON

The garden at Breezewood began in the 1930s with an English-style layout. Radiating allées of yew hedges and a ha-ha wall capture the remarkable countryside of My Lady's Manor. Later, in the 1950s, A.B. Griswold began an extensive Oriental garden featuring pagodas, ponds, rocks and a wide variety of specimen plants.

Saturday, September 16, 11 a.m. - 4 p.m.

Take Jarrettsville Pike to Hess Road. Travel west on Hess Road to #3722 on the right; there is a stone wall with ivy and 2 mailboxes. Please park in the field on left side of drive.

FOXGLOVES

16135 OLD YORK ROAD, MONKTON

These gardens were developed gradually to complement a rambling country house, which is partly a rebuilt historic stone mill. There are two smaller garden "rooms" which open off of the house. One is a small garden with a stone wall off of a double-hanging porch, and the other a kitchen-area flower garden enclosed in a picket fence with a topiary yew hedge. The most recent area is a work in progress-a dry lagoon, reminiscent of southern coastal areas, created by reshaping an old roadbed. This is a spring garden and has as its focal point a piece of "found sculpture" that washed up on Nantucket after the sinking of the Andrea Doria. The most ambitious area is a formal quatrefoil-shaped secret garden with a fountain and pavilion. The whimsical benches were designed by the owner. It has an aerial hedge of dogwood and geometric topiaries of variegated boxwood given to the owner by the gardener at Green Animals in Rhode Island. This is also a spring garden and is being restored after losing 600 boxwood plants to the blight.

Saturday, September 16, 11 a.m. - 4 p.m.

Leaving Ladew Gardens turn left onto Jarrettsville Pike. Go 2 miles to the traffic light. Turn right onto Hess Road. Go 2.2 miles to dead end. Turn right onto Old York Road, pass Manor Tavern and turn right (still Old York Road). Go .5 miles to Foxgloves.

Garden of Jean & Tom McCausland

REMARE ROAD, MONKTON

Our garden has developed over a period of forty years as a complement to our French-style house. Principal items are yew hedges to delineate areas, topiaries as focal points, espaliered fruit trees edging the potager, and architectural features such as garden houses, obelisks, columns, and stone steps. The buildings create a village effect.

Saturday, September 16, 11 a.m. - 4 p.m.

From Ladew Gardens Exit turn left (south) onto Jarrettsville Pike and go 2 miles to the traffic light at Hess Road. Turn right (west) on Hess Road and go 2.2 miles to the dead end at Old York Road. Turn right. Pass the Manor Tavern on the right and go straight up the hill past the St. James Church onto Monkton Road. Proceed about 3 miles to Monkton. Just before Monkton there is a stop sign. Go left up the hill through the village. Cross the hike-bike trail and look for private road on the right (Remare Road). Turn right. McCauslands is on the right. Go past the entrance to the house to the opening to parking field on the right.

Pindale Collector's Gardens

2117 BLUE MOUNT ROAD, MONKTON

Our six-year-old garden is a plant collector's paradise! As owners of a wholesale perennial nursery, we use the garden to learn about and evaluate the new plants that we collect from around the world. Surrounded by woods, the gardens have many water features, all enhanced by an abundance of our native soapstone. A seven-foot waterfall, a meandering stream, a cactus garden, and a "formal" room garden are some of the highlights. Many plants are labeled so visitors can learn the names of our unusual plants.

Saturday, September 16, 11 a.m. - 4 p.m.

From Ladew Gardens turn left onto Jarrettsville Pike. Go 2 miles to Hess Road and turn right. At the deadend turn right onto Old York Road and continue straight up the hill (past St. James Church) onto Monkton Road. Take the first right onto Markoe Road. Go 1 long block to J.M. Pearce Road. Turn left (past South Meadows), cross Shepperd Road, and continue straight on Gerting Road to deadend at Wesley Chapel Road. Turn right and go up hill a short distance to Blue Mount Road. Turn left and go to 2117 on the left.

South Meadows

16730 J.M. PEARCE ROAD, MONKTON

This mostly sunny informal garden, planted over many years, is separated from cornfields and pastures by a split-rail fence. Sunny beds are mixed with trees, shrubs, perennials, and annuals. Shade-loving plants are found under trees and a woodland walk. Bloom begins in February with witch hazel and hellebores, followed by daffodils, peonies, daylilies, dahlias, anemones, and asters.

Saturday, September 16, 11 a.m. - 4 p.m.

From the Baltimore Beltway take Route 83 north to Hereford/Mount Carmel Road. Turn right onto Mount Carmel and turn right onto York Road. Turn left onto Route 138. Continue on Route 138 through the village of Monkton and continue straight on Route 138, which turns into Shepperd Road. Continue to the four-way stop. Turn right on J. M. Pearce Road. The garden is at the second driveway on the right and practically at the intersection. From Ladew Topiary Gardens, turn left onto the Jarrettsville Pike. Turn right onto Pocock Road and then turn right onto Hutchins Mill Road. Turn left onto Houcks Mill Road, and right onto Old York Road. Bear left onto Troyer Road and then left onto Shepperd Road. Turn left onto J. M. Pearce Road. The garden is at the second driveway on the right. Please park in driveway, along the road, and by the barn.

Cylburn Arboretum & Park &

4915 GREENSPRING AVENUE, BALTIMORE, MD 21209. (410) 396-0180.

Cylburn Arboretum & Park covers 176 acres with large wildflower trails, a butterfly garden, collections of magnolias and maples, and an All-American Selections Display Garden. There are nature trails through the wooded areas and wildflower preserves. On the second floor of the Central Building is a bird museum. An annual rare plant sale on the Saturday before Mother's Day is an event not to be missed.

Year round, daily, 6 a.m. - 9 p.m.

From I-695, take the exit for Route 83 South to Northern Parkway. Go west on Northern Parkway to a left on Greenspring Avenue.

LADEW TOPIARY GARDENS ❦

3535 JARRETTSVILLE PIKE, MONKTON, MD 21111. (410) 557-9466.

Ladew Topiary Gardens is considered "the most outstanding topiary garden in America" by the Garden Club of America, with fifteen thematic gardens on twenty-two acres. The crowning glory is the topiary, including the famous hunt scene complete with hounds, horses and fox streaking across a field. Harvey Ladew's historic Manor house is filled with English antiques and fox hunting memorabilia and the oval library is listed as one of the "most beautiful rooms in America." The Nature Walk at Ladew opened in fall 1999 and is a one and one-half mile self-guided interpretive trail through the woods and fields of the 250-acre Ladew estate.

Mid-April - October 31, Monday - Friday, 10 a.m. - 4 p.m.; Saturday & Sunday, 10:30 a.m. - 5 p.m.

From I-695 take Exit 27B/Dulaney Valley Road North and cross over the Loch Raven Reservoir. Bear left onto Jarrettsville Pike/MD 146. Ladew Gardens is located on the right between Hess Road and MD 152. From I-83 take Exit 27/Mt. Carmel Road east .5 mile to deadend at the York Road traffic light. Turn right and go 1 block to Monkton Road. Turn left and go approximately 6 miles to Hess Road (sharp left). Continue 2.2 miles to traffic light at Jarrettsville Pike. Turn left and Ladew Gardens is 2 miles on the right.

MASSACHUSETTS

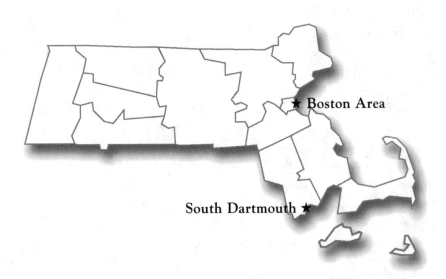

★ **Boston Area**

South Dartmouth ★

MASSACHUSETTS OPEN DAYS

July 8: South Dartmouth
September 16 & 17: Boston Area

Boston Open Days

Regional Representative: Mrs Henry S. Streeter

Saturday, September 16

BROOKLINE
Ralph & Corliss Engle, 26 Edgehill Road: 9 a.m. - 5 p.m.

CHESTNUT HILL
Greville Garden, 20 Glenoe Road: 9 a.m. - 5 p.m.
Dalton Garden, 74 Fernwood Road: 9 a.m. - 5 p.m.

DOVER
Cairn Croft, 81 Wilsondale Street: 9 a.m. - 5 p.m
Waterman Garden, 4 Brook Road: 9 a.m. - 5 p.m.

NEEDHAM
Taylor Garden, 372 Warren Street: 9 a.m. - 5 p.m.

WESTWOOD
Ferguson Garden, 541 Gay Street: 9 a.m. - 5 p.m.
Joseph Hudak & Kenn Stephens,
    64 Churchill Road: 9 a.m. - 5 p.m.
McFarland Garden, 299 Clapboardtree
    Street: 9 a.m. - 5 p.m.

Sunday, September 17

MANCHESTER
Appletrees, 6 Jersey Lane: 9 a.m. - 5 p.m.
The Garden at 9 Friend Street: 9 a.m. - 5 p.m.
The Rocks, 65 Harbor Street: 9 a.m. - 5 p.m.
Southgate Garden II, 22 School Street: 9 a.m. - 5 p.m.

MARBLEHEAD
Gardens of Donald & Beverly Seamans, 10 Harbor View: 9 a.m. - 5 p.m.
The Parable—Ellen Cool's Garden, 19 Circle Street: 9 a.m. - 5 p.m.

MARBLEHEAD NECK
Grey Gulls, 429 Ocean Avenue: 9 a.m. - 5 p.m.
Kearney Garden, 13 Flint Street: 9 a.m. - 5 p.m.
Low Woods, 405 Ocean Avenue: 9 a.m. - 5 p.m.

SWAMPSCOTT
"North Star"—The Garden of Mr. & Mrs. John Goldsmith,
    55 Galloupe's Point: 9 a.m. - 5 p.m.
Wilkinson Garden, 29 Little's Point Road: 9 a.m. - 5 p.m.

APPLETREES

6 JERSEY LANE, MANCHESTER

The Appletrees estate was built in 1896 on an old apple orchard, and was thus named by its first owner. The garden was originally laid out in the early years of the twentieth century by William Ernestus Bowditch, a landscape architect from Milton, Massachusetts. While this park-like property has had some changes over the years, many of the original features remain. These include an allée of ironwood trees, ancient yew hedges, a sunken garden, and many old and beautiful specimen trees, such as ginkgo, albizia, catalpa, dogwood and copper beech, among others. The formal, walled sunken garden was recently renovated and has a beautiful antique fountain in the center surrounded by lovely perennial beds and seating areas for rest and relaxation. The current owners have continued to enhance this three-and-one-half acre landscape, adding, among other things a cottage garden set against a clipped privet hedge, a shade garden surrounding an old shed, and various garden benches set throughout upon which to enjoy the views.

Sunday, September 17, 9 a.m. - 5 p.m.

North on Route 128 to Exit 16 (Pine Street/Manchester). Take Pine Street to the end at the center of Manchester. Take a right onto Route 127 for approximately .8 mile, just past a large open meadow. Take a right onto Jersey Lane. Appletrees is at #6, the third driveway on the left, about 100 yards up the lane. Please park in the driveway, left side near entrance.

CAIRN CROFT

81 WILSONDALE STREET, DOVER

My garden is a personal garden. The cairns mark its location, and croft means "a special place within." My design intention for the garden is to have guests enter and quickly forget from where they have come. It is a place of unspeakable joy. Cairn Croft has been featured in *Fine Gardening* Magazine, *Horticulture*, and *The Victorian Garden*.

Saturday, September 16, 9 a.m. - 5 p.m.

Take Route 128 to Exit 16 B. Travel 1 mile or less on Route 109 West and take the second right onto Summer Street. Travel 1 mile to end. Turn left onto Westfield. Travel 300 yards; turn left onto Wilsondale Street. Travel .2 mile. Watch for cairns on the left at #81. Please park beyond the house on the opposite side of the street. Please note: The Taylor garden in Needham is 1.4 miles from Cairn Croft-left onto Westfield Street from Wilsondale, first right on Chestnut Street second right onto South Street and first left onto Warren-The Taylor Garden, 372 Warren Street in Needham. Please park in the street.

FERGUSON GARDEN

541 GAY STREET, WESTWOOD

In this Tom Wirth-designed garden, the terrace leads east to the swimming pool area, beyond which lies the cutting garden. An ornamental pond with meadow are beyond to the south. In the woods, gazebo and pagan gardens are connected by woodland paths. In 1992 the garden was awarded the Massachusetts Horticultural Society's Gold Medal, and in 1994 received an Honorable Mention from *Landscape Architecture* magazine.

Saturday, September 16, 9 a.m. - 5 p.m.

From Route 128, take Exit 16 west onto Route 109. Go approximately 1.5 miles to Gay Street. Turn left on Gay Street approximately 1.1 miles to #541 on the right. Please park in the driveway. Park in the driveway or on the street.

GARDENS OF DONALD & BEVERLY SEAMANS

10 HARBOR VIEW, MARBLEHEAD

A walk through the garden is full of surprises. You come upon bronze sculptures of animals, birds, and children nestled in natural settings or as fountains recirculating water in the pool. Entering the path from the driveway that leads to the house is a small rock garden. To the right is a vegetable and cutting garden. To the left is a glade of pachysandra with rhododendrons. Beside the house are pools with a mermaid fountain flowing into a small upper pool, which flows into a lower pool with water and goldfish. Two bronze children pour buckets of recirculating water on either end. Over this pool is a bridge which leads to two gardens. Follow a rocky path to the right and find a daylily garden, clematis, a dwarf Japanese cut-leaf maple, a shade garden containing ferns and hosta, and a variety of heather on a low ledge. Go straight after the bridge to view the harbor; note the semi-circular flower garden backed by *Rosa rugosa*. Beyond is a natural field where viburnum, witch hazel, blueberry bushes and wildflowers grow. A gazebo sits on a rock terrace with thyme, lavender, and daisies, the perfect place to stop and rest.

Sunday, September 17, 9 a.m. - 5 p.m.

From Route 128 east, take 114 east to end (in Marblehead). Go right on Route 129 for one block. At light, turn left at Atlantic Avenue. Go past big church on left and turn right on Chestnut Street (at hardware store). At top of hill, turn right on Harbor View. The house is #10, on the water side of the street.

GREVILLE GARDEN

20 GLENOE ROAD, CHESTNUT HILL

This suburban garden is designed by the owner to provide private family space as well as interesting plant compositions. Under a canopy of mature oaks on one-half acre, it contains a series of garden rooms encircling the house. Starting with crocus and miniature spring bulbs in the rock garden, tulips and daffodils, etc. in the parterre garden, shrubs and perennials in the formal circle, and a clematis trellis along the east-facing woodland garden, each area creates a different feeling. In September, the *Viburnum wrightii* berries are fabulous.

Saturday, September 16, 9 a.m. - 5 p.m.

From Route 128, take Route 9 east toward Boston (3 miles). Turn right onto Hammond Street.* Glenoe Road is the 3rd Street on the left. From Boston, take Route 9 West/ Boylston Street for 5-6 miles. At the second set of traffic lights after the Chestnut Hill Road intersection, turn left onto Hammond Street. There is a CVS and Exxon on the corners. Follow from * above. Please park on the street.

GREY GULLS

429 OCEAN AVENUE, MARBLEHEAD NECK

Set above a rocky coastline, this collector's garden presents a diverse array of uncommon bulbs, perennials, heirloom vegetables, distinctive containers, hedges and (in winter) a wattle fence, which is necessary to protect the garden from the elements. Channing Blake landscaped the property (1990-1992), creating a modern design of sinuous beds in harmony with the surrounding curves of shore and sea.

Sunday, September 17, 9 a.m. - 5 p.m.

Take Route 128 to Exit 25/Route 114 East. At the traffic light in Marblehead take a right onto Ocean Avenue. Cross the causeway and stay right for 1.5 miles to traffic circle. Bear right at traffic circle and go to 429 Ocean Avenue (number painted on rock). House is on right. Please park on the street.

JOSEPH HUDAK & KENN STEPHENS

64 CHURCHILL ROAD, WESTWOOD

Nearly twenty-five years from its raw beginning, today this suburban acre presents a year-round collection of common and unique plants in an entirely secluded setting. Organized by the landscape architect Mr. Hudak, and embellished with garden artifacts of distinction by Mr. Stephens, this collection blends trees, shrubs, perennials, and bulbs into seasonally interesting combinations rarely found elsewhere. The design is a "funnel" concept, which enlarges as you proceed from the front entrance to the rear of the lot. Grand sweeps of lawn connect the front yellow garden to the red garden and climax in the "Paisley Patch" in the lower garden.

Saturday, September 16, 9 a.m. - 5 p.m.

From Route 128, take Exit 16B/Route 109 West and go approximately 1 mile. Turn left onto Churchill Road which deadends. The garden is near the top of the hill on the left. Park only on the house side of Churchill Road.

Proceeds shared with The International Design Symposium

KEARNEY GARDEN
13 FLINT STREET, MARBLEHEAD NECK

Seven years ago Randall Wieting transformed this one acre garden, half of which was a thicket of juniper and Norway maple, into rolling lawns surrounding rocky outcrops. The planting is primarily trees and shrubs, accented by perennials appropriate to a shingled summer "cottage" built early in this century-shrub roses, hydrangeas, lavender, etc. Rest on the old porch for a moment or enjoy the view of Boston from the deck.

Sunday, September 17, 9 a.m. - 5 p.m.

Whether you enter Marblehead from Pleasant Street or Atlantic Avenue, turn right onto Ocean Avenue. Cross the causeway to Marblehead Neck. Bear left at the fork, go slowly and turn right at the first street, Flint Street. The house is 200 yards on the right. Please park on the street.

LOW WOODS
405 OCEAN AVENUE, MARBLEHEAD NECK

Low Woods is a naturalist's waterfront property designed in the 1880s. One would guess it was designed by the Olmsted firm; however the actual landscape architect is unknown. The two-acre property includes a teahouse surrounded by *Juniperus virginiana*, bayberries, blueberries, and honeysuckle. There are multiple terraces and winding paths leading the visitor to breathtaking water views and restful gardens.

Sunday, September 17, 9 a.m. - 5 p.m.

Take Route 128 to exit 25 (Route 114 East). At the fourth traffic light in Marblehead take a right onto Ocean Avenue. Cross the causeway and stay right for 1.5 miles to traffic circle. Bear right at traffic circle and follow long stone wall to first opening to right, #405 Ocean Avenue. The grey house sits high up. A large copper beech is evident from the road. Park along the road.

McFarland Garden

Construction of the garden began in 1986 with a series of garden rooms, designed by Gary L. Koller. The house was originally the stable of a nearby estate. The gardens take advantage of the rolling terrrain and the setting of the house. Boulders and natural stone are an integral element of the design, as is the unusual plant material. A waterfall garden flows from the naturalistic swimming pool, and the house is surrounded by a terrace and walled garden as well as a yellow foliage parterre garden.

Saturday, September 16, 9 a.m. - 5 p.m.

Take Route 128 south from Boston Exit 16B/Route 109 West. Go through 3 traffic lights and turn left onto Nahatan Street. (1.5 miles from exit) Pass Westwood High School on left and at the 4-way stop turn right onto Clapboardtree Street to the 3rd house on the left, #299. Please park across the street on the right side of the road.

Proceeds shared with The New England Wildflower Society.

"North Star" — The Garden of Mr. & Mrs. John Goldsmith

55 GALLOUPE'S POINT, SWAMPSCOTT

A pine grove and gathering of blue spruce hide the surprises that await the visitor. A contemporary house of dramatic proportions embraces gardens and lawns planted in great splashes of old-fashioned trees, shrubs, and perennials.

Sunday, September 17, 9 a.m. - 5 p.m.

From Boston: Follow Route 1A to Route 129. In the town of Swampscott, take the right fork at the Citgo station onto Puritan Road. Follow .9 mile to Galloupe's Point on right. At the bottom of hill is #55. From Marblehead: Take Route 129/Atlantic Avenue to Swampscott and turn left onto Puritan Road. Proceed as above.

Ralph & Corliss Engle

26 EDGEHILL ROAD, BROOKLINE

This city/suburban site in an historic district is enhanced with Olmsted traditions and is close to the Boston skyline. This is a collector's garden designed to be viewed from above, with emphasis on foliage color and texture. The walk from Cumberland Road allows one to see from the street an Olmsted Brothers garden on the corner of High Street and Edgehill Road.

Saturday, September 16, 9 a.m. - 5 p.m.

From Route 128, take Route 9 East to Brookline Village, close to the Boston Line. Turn right at the traffic light at Dunkin Donuts and the fire station onto High Street. Take the

3rd left onto Cumberland. From Boston, take Route 9 West to Brookline Village. Turn left at the traffic light below the pedestrian overpass, going behind the fire station. Turn left onto High Street and follow the directions above. Park on Cumberland.

Proceeds shared with The Arnold Arboretum.

SOUTHGATE GARDEN II
22 SCHOOL STREET, MANCHESTER

A small half-acre garden. The land sloped away from the house and ended in a spongy wet area, so wet in fact that the owner was mired in it and had to yell for help! The problem was solved by digging a pond, which has provided joy for frogs and grandchildren. The entrance to the property is graveled; steps descend to the garden proper, which is guarded by a stone lion in the style of the fifteenth century, that has been bumped around and even stolen once.

Sunday, September 17, 9 a.m. - 5 p.m.

From Route 128 take the School Street Exit. Follow School Street to #22 on the right. Please try to park in the town lot behind the Town Hall. Our little driveway will be totally inadequate. This garden is just down School Street from The Garden at 9 Friend Street.

Proceeds shared with The Manchester Woman's Club Scholarship Fund.

TAYLOR GARDEN
372 WARREN STREET, NEEDHAM

Every inch of space is part of the design of this four-season garden located in a densely populated suburban neighborhood. Perennials, annuals, wildflowers, tropicals, and bulbs are artfully woven together into a bold tapestry of color, shape, and size. Visitors coming down the multi-level path are treated to many elements of surprise and curiosity, including lush and unusual container plantings and brilliant late-season color combinations. There are no fences or barriers to separate this garden from its close neighbors. Of special interest are a very shady rock garden under a deck, distinct sitting areas, a grove of eight different Japanese maples, small water features, a grist-wheel stone, and a newly created greenhouse in a former garage.

Saturday, September 16, 9 a.m. - 5 p.m.

From Route 128 take Exit 17/Needham/Natick/Route 135. At stop sign at end of ramp turn toward Needham. Go 1.4 miles through 2 traffic lights to the hospital sign on left. Turn at the sign and go 1 block to stop sign. Turn left and go .4 mile to garden on left. Park on closest side street, Laurel Drive.

The Dalton Garden

Diane and David Dalton bought this two-acre Chestnut Hill property in 1980 which was originally landscaped by Frederick Law Olmsted. Since then, they have put in more than 600 different hostas, working regularly with noted horticulturalist Allen Haskell. In their shady areas, they have a profusion of hostas and ferns. In sunnier locales, their favorites are rare rhododendrons, azaleas, dogwood, epidmediums, astilbes, and yellow daisies.

Saturday, September 16, 9 a.m. - 5 p.m.

From Route 128, take Route 9 East toward Boston. Turn right onto Hammond Street. The Longwood Cricket Club will be across the intersection and on the left. Follow Hammond to Heath Street and turn left. Turn right onto Warren and then veer to the right to take Clyde Street. Turn right onto Fernwood. Look for #74. From Boston, take Route 9 West. Turn left onto Hammond Street and follow directions above. Please park as directed.

Proceeds shared with The Tower Hill Botanic Garden.

The Garden at 9 Friend Street

MANCHESTER-BY-THE-SEA

The first garden at 9 Friend Street was laid out in 1928 for the present owner's grandfather. Mr. Frederick Rice, a floral and garden designer and lecturer, has made major changes during the past fifteen years. The English cottage-style garden, ablaze with color and awash with texture, is laid out in a series of rooms furnished with an extraordinary variety of perennials, annuals, roses, vines, and deciduous and ever-green shrubs. Brick and stone patios have been constructed for outdoor living. There are two fish ponds, a pavilion, and a teahouse. The garden was featured in the 1996 summer issue of Country Home-Country Gardens Magazine.

Sunday, September 17, 9 a.m. - 5 p.m.

Route 128 north to Exit 15, School Street, Manchester, MA. Right onto School Street at the end of exit. Pass Essex County Club on the left and proceed through the blinking red light-cemetery on left, down hill. Friend Street is the second right beyond Sacred Heart Catholic Church. The house, #9, is gray with black shutters, on the right— the only house on the street with a white picket fence. Please park on Friend Street or in lot behind Sacred Heart Church. Park on Friend Street. Just down School Street from Southgate Garden II.

Proceeds shared with The Manchester Council on Aging.

THE PARABLE — ELLEN COOL'S GARDEN

19 CIRCLE STREET, MARBLEHEAD

In the oldest part of Marblehead, beside a 1720 house of historic interest, there is a garden gate that leads into a highly developed and very personal landscape. Here are examples of the buildings, structures, tools, materials, and books that, together with the gardens, comprise the setting for a landscape designer's life and work. Many unusual early-, late- and long-blooming plants combine with artifacts of stone and wood into satisfying compositions from April until November.

Sunday, September 17, 9 a.m. - 5 p.m.

From the South: Take Route 1A North to 129 E (becomes Atlantic Avenue in Marblehead); just past the Mobil Station on the left, turn right onto Washington Street, and follow it to the Old Town House, then same as below. From the North or West: Take Route 114 E to the end at the Old Town House in the middle of Washington Street, then right onto State Street, to the Marblehead Harbor, then left onto Front Street. Circle Street will be the third and fourth left-better to take the fourth. Look for parking soon on Front Street, as the parking on Circle Street is very limited. The walk by the water is in any case very pleasant. Number 19 is half way up from the water on the right side.

THE ROCKS

65 HARBOR STREET, MANCHESTER

The Rocks is a turn-of-the-century estate that was restored over the last four years. It enjoys spectacular ocean views from the new seawall garden and original lawn terrace. Fairly mature plant material merges old garden into new, deceiving most visitors into believing the site was largely untouched by the intense reconstruction of the magnificent house. Stroll over granite and lawn, cobblestone and pebble with beautiful views in every direction. The garden offers the opportunity to see fine details in brick and limestone, granite and bluestone, wrought iron and lead-some old, some new. Garden ornaments and lovely pots filled with colorful annuals personalize this three-acre garden. Across the street is a parterre garden behind a handsome trellis fence.

Sunday, September 17, 9 a.m. - 5 p.m.

From Route 128 take Exit 16/Pine Street. Take Pine Street toward Manchester to a "T" intersection at Route 127. Turn right onto Route 127. Go approximately .75 mile out of town and turn left onto Harbor Street at the Old Corner Inn. Cross bridge over the railroad tracks to a stop sign. The Rocks is immediately ahead through stone pillars. Park along Harbor Street.

WATERMAN GARDEN

4 BROOK ROAD, DOVER

Set in a suburban location blessed with rich, moist soil, this naturalistic garden has evolved to accommodate my passion for plant collecting, color, and privacy, and our children's need for recreational space. Woody and herbaceous plants with long bloom time, handsome form, abundant berries, fall color, exceptional bark, and variegated or colored foliage assure many seasons of interest. The garden consists of long mixed borders designed with carefully contrived color schemes, shrub borders, a brook, and a brick terrace, home to a large collection of containers filled with unusual tender perennials and annuals, many grown from seed and cuttings and all arranged in daring, as well as subtle, combinations.

Saturday, September 16, 9 a.m. - 5 p.m.

From Route 128/Route 95, take Exit 21/Route 16/Washington Street west to Wellesley. Stay on Route 16 for approximately 4 miles, going through Wellesley and into South Natick. At the traffic light in South Natick turn left onto Pleasant Street. The Elliott Church is on the right and the Bacon Library on the left. Cross over the Charles River and turn onto Dover Road, second left. The third right is Brook Road. The garden is at the second house on the left. Park on the road.

WILKINSON GARDEN

29 LITTLE'S POINT ROAD, SWAMPSCOTT

Two families, Littles and Proctors, have owned Blythswood from 1909 to the present. Simplicity reflects change from many gardeners to one part-time man. He plans and cares for the lawn, rose garden, flower beds and urns. The house, terraces, garden beds and ocean view are closely related. One peony came from China in 1829 and is doing well.

Sunday, September 17, 9 a.m. - 5 p.m.

Easy to find from the town of Swampscott. With ocean on the right take Puritan Road for 1 mile. Little's Point is on the right. Look for "Marion Court Junior College," which uses same driveway as "Blythswood." Please do not park on the grass. From Marblehead, take Route 129/Atlantic Avenue and turn left onto Puritan Road. Proceed as above.

Arnold Arboretum
of Harvard University ♣

125 The Arborway, Jamaica Plain, MA 02130. (617) 524-1718.

The 265-acre Arnold Arboretum displays North America's premier collection of more than 14,000 hardy trees, shrubs and vines. The grounds were planted and designed by the Arboretum's first director, Charles Sprague Sargent, and America's first landscape architect, Frederick Law Olmsted. Highlights include crab apple, conifer, lilac, rhododendron and bonsai collections.

Year round, daily, dawn - dusk.

From the Storrow Drive take the Fenway / Park Drive Exit. Follow signs to the Riverway, which becomes the Jamaicaway and then the Arborway / Route 1. From I-95 / Route 128 exit onto Route 9 East. Follow Route 9 for 7 miles to the Riverway / Route 1 South. From the Southeast Expressway / Route 93 take Exit 11/Granite Avenue/ Ashmont onto Route 203. Follow past Franklin Park. This site is also accessible by public transportation. Please call for details.

Garden in the Woods
of the New England Wildflower Society ♣

180 Hemenway Road, Framingham, MA 01701. (508) 877-7630. or recorded info, (508) 877-6574.

Garden in the Woods, New England's premier wildflower showcase, displays the largest landscaped collection of native plants in the Northeast. Forty-five acres with woodland trails offer vistas of wildflowers, shrubs, and trees. Sixteen hundred varieties of plants, including more than 200 rare and endangered species, grow in protective cultivation. Garden in the Woods also has the largest wildflower nursery in New England.

April 15 - June 15, daily with extended hours in May to 7 p.m.; June 16 - October 31, Tuesday - Sunday, 9 a.m. - 5 p.m. Last admission to garden trails, one hour before closing.

From the North, South and East: Take Route 128 to Route 20 west; go 8 miles on Route 20 to Raymond Road (second left after traffic lights in South Sudbury); 1.3 miles to Hemenway Road. From the West: Take the Massachusetts Turnpike / Exit 12 to Route 9 East; go 2.4 miles to Edgell Road (Route 9 overpass); 2.1 miles to traffic lights; take a right onto Water Street and a left onto Hemenway Road. Follow garden signs.

Lyman Estate, The Vale &

185 Lyman Street, Waltham, MA 02154. (781) 891-4882.

The Lyman Estate, known as The Vale, is one of the finest examples in the United States of a country property laid out according to the principles of eighteenth-century English naturalistic design. The greenhouses were built from 1800 to 1930, and contain century-old camellias and grapevines, as well as tropical and subtropical plants. Unusual plants available for sale year round. Please call for the dates of specialty sales. The Vale is a property of the Society for the Preservation of New England Antiquities.

Year round, Monday - Saturday, 9:30 a.m. - 4 p.m.

Take Route 128 to Exit 26 / Route 20 East to Waltham / Boston. Follow Route 20 (it becomes Main Street) through the center of Waltham about 1.7 miles. At the Kentucky Fried Chicken, turn left onto Lyman Street. Follow Lyman .5 miles to a rotary and bear immediately right into the Estate driveway (check for a SPNEA sign). NOTE: Access to grounds is limited if a wedding is in progress.

Mount Auburn Cemetery &

580 Mt. Auburn Street, Cambridge, MA 02138. (617) 547-7105.
JHEYWOOD@MTAUBURN.COM

Mount Auburn Cemetery, founded in 1831, is America's first landscaped cemetery. One hundred and seventy-four acres contain more than 5,000 native and exotic trees identified and tagged. Many important and famous people are buried here. A fascinating place to visit and wonderful for birdwatching. Audio tour available for rent or purchase.

Year round, daily, 8 a.m. - 5 p.m. (7 p.m. during the summer)

The entrance is on Mount Auburn Street near the boundary of Cambridge and Watertown, approximately 1.5 miles west of Harvard Square, just west of Mount Auburn Hospital and Fresh Pond Parkway. The cemetery is easily reached by public transportation from Harvard Square (Number 71 or 73 bus).

THE 1768 JEREMIAH LEE MANSION GARDENS ❧
170 WASHINGTON STREET, MARBLEHEAD, MA 01945. (781) 631-1768.

The beautiful gardens now surrounding the Jeremiah Lee Mansion are designed after eighteenth-century models. They feature an herb garden, a sunken octagonal sundial garden, a large upper terrace with a colorful perennial border, and a spacious lower garden with a variety of trees, shrubs, vines, groundcovers, and wildflowers. The gardens have been designed and maintained by volunteers from the Marblehead Garden Club since 1938.

Year round, daily, dawn - dusk

From Boston, take Route 1A North to Route 129 East through Swampscott. Continue several miles on Atlantic Avenue into the business district of Marblehead. Turn left at the Texaco gas station, and take the next right onto Washington Street. Bear left at fork, drive up hill and down. The Jeremiah Lee Mansion will be on the left, a large gray building.

THE SEDGWICK GARDENS AT LONG HILL ❧
572 ESSEX STREET, BEVERLY, MA 01915. (978) 921-1944.
WWW.THETRUSTEES.ORG

From 1916-1979, Long Hill was the country estate of the Sedgwick family. It was first purchased by noted author and editor (1909-1938) of Atlantic Monthly magazine, Ellery Sedgwick, and his first wife, Mabel Cabot Sedgwick, an accomplished horticulturist and author of The Garden Month by Month. The gardens were first designed and planted by Mrs. Sedgwick. After her death in 1937, Mr. Sedgwick's second wife, the former Marjorie Russell of England, a distinguished gardener and propagator of rare plants, added many plants to the gardens including unusual species and varieties of trees and shrubs, many introduced by the Arnold Arboretum. Today, the Sedgwick Gardens reflects the collective interests and tastes of both women. Five acres of cultivated grounds are laid out in a series of separate garden areas surrounding the house, each distinct in its own way and accented by a tremendous diversity of garden ornaments, structures, and statuary. These areas are flanked on all sides by over 100 acres of woodland (containing two miles of trails and footpaths) as well as an apple orchard and meadow. More than 400 species of plants are grown, many very unusual.

Year round, daily, dawn - dusk, with occasional restricted access during weddings. Guided garden tours are offered seasonally; call for regular and group rates.

From Route 128, take Route 22 /Essex Street north 1.3 miles. Bear left at fork in road and continue for 0.2 miles to brick gate posts and entrance drive on left.

South Dartmouth Open Day

Regional Representative: Mrs. Robert G. Walker

Saturday, July 8

Ferry House Garden, 254 Potomska Road: 10 a.m. - 2 p.m.
Ginny & Stephen Spiegel, 238 Little River Road: 10 a.m. - 2 p.m.
Nonquitt Farm, Smith Neck Road: 10 a.m. - 2 p.m.

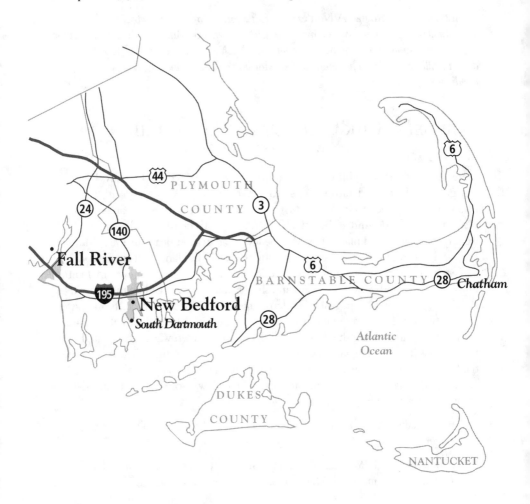

FERRY HOUSE GARDEN

LITTLE RIVER ROAD, SOUTH DARTMOUTH

Enclosed by hedge and fence, my small seaside garden is protected from strong winds. The garden, abundant in perennials, was created to complement the 1760 Ferry House. Soft hues of lavender and blue surround a large granite millstone, and granite steppingstones provide small paths throughout the garden and grape arbor. Beyond is a vast sweep of lawn leading your eye to the sea. A path leads by the waterlily pond to my romantic and happiest creation—a folly of columns, statues, and benches set in a grove of cedars overlooking sea, pond, and meadow. The garden was awarded the Mary B. Wakefield gold medal for a small garden by the Massachusetts Horticultural Society in 1996.

Saturday, July 8, 10 a.m. - 2 p.m.

From Boston: Take Route 24 south to Route 140. Turn right at the end of the exit ramp toward New Bedford. Go to the end of Route 140 and turn right onto Route 6. Go .7 miles. Turn left at traffic lights (Bishops Stang High School on left, Cumberland Farms on right). Go 2.7 miles and turn left onto Elm Street. Just past Cumberland Farms left the police station is on the right. Go 1.4 miles on Elm Street. Turn right onto Bridge Street (second stop sign). Cross the bridge and turn left onto Smith Neck Road. Go 3.4 miles to Little River Road on the right just past Round Hill, and turn right. Go 1 mile and turn left immediately after bridge. Please park in the field by the house.

GINNY & STEVEN SPIEGEL

LITTLE RIVER ROAD, SOUTH DARTMOUTH

This exposed seaside garden between an estuary and a saltwater marsh includes a sunken pool area with a flowering border, a small perennial garden, a rose garden, and a rock garden. There are several stone walls encompassing the property. The house is eighty years old, built on a rock, with a wonderful view of the Elizabeth Islands.

Saturday, July 8, 10 a.m. - 2 p.m.

Take I-95 to Route 140 South. At the end of Route 140 go right on Route 6. Continue .7 miles to Slocum Road. Turn left onto Slocum (Bishop Stang High School). Go 2.7 miles to Elm Street. Turn left onto Elm Street (Gulf station on left, police station on right). Go 1.4 miles to Padanarom Village Center. Turn right onto Bridge Street and cross the harbor bridge. Turn left after bridge onto Smith Neck Road. Go 3.4 miles to Little River Road. Turn right onto Little River, .9 miles, last driveway on left before crossing bridge. Please park in the front lawn area.

Nonquitt Farm
SMITH NECK ROAD, DARTMOUTH

The gardens surrounding Herb and Janet Sarkisian's circa 1790 colonial farmhouse overlooking Padaranam Harbor is a combination of new beds and old peripheral plantings and is a delight to explore. Stone walls, arbors and pathways direct and define the landscape. Wisteria meanders over stone walls and roses over trellises. The formal garden with its stone-lined fish pond is peaceful and has an elegant sense of space. An old apple orchard at the rear of the property has been pruned to be ornamental rather than fruit producing.

Saturday, July 8, 10 a.m. - 2 p.m.

Take I-195 to Route 140 South. From the end of Route 140 at traffic light turn right onto Route 6. Turn left at next traffic light onto Slocum Road that becomes Russell Mills Road at Friendly's Pizza. Just past the police station turn left onto Elm Street. Follow Elm Street to the second stop sign and turn right onto Bridge Street. Turn left after crossing bridge onto Smith Neck Road. Continue for .5 mile to the first driveway on the right. The garden will be to the right. Please park behind neighbor's garage on your left in the vacant lot.

Rotch-Jones-Duff House & Garden Museum ❧
396 COUNTY STREET, NEW BEDFORD, MA 02740. (508) 997-1401.

The property encompasses a full city block of urban gardens surrounded by a traditional board fence. The centerpiece of the gardens, a wooden pergola, is surrounded by a formal cutting garden, a wildflower walk, a boxwood specimen garden, and a boxwood rose parterre garden. Restoration of the rose garden was initiated in 1966 under the direction of Stephen Scaniello, noted rosarian at the Brooklyn Botanic garden, with the planting of more than 200 rose bushes. New rose beds were added in 1999. A replica of a historic wooden apiary with interior exhibit space serves as the Garden Educational Center.

January - May, Tuesday - Sunday, 10 a.m. - 4 p.m. Closed major holidays.

Take Route 128 South to Route 140 South to end. Go past lights to Hawthorne Street and turn left. Go 1.5 miles and turn left onto County Street for 1 block. Large yellow house on right. Take Route 195 East to Exit 15/Route 18. At the second set of traffic lights turn right onto Union Street to crest of hill. Turn left onto County Street for 5 short blocks. The museum is on the left.

MICHIGAN

★ Harbor Springs

Bloomfield Hills ★

MICHIGAN OPEN DAYS

July 16: Bloomfield Hills
July 26: Harbor Springs

Bloomfield Hills Open Day

Regional Representatives: Lynne Clippert, Lois Gamble, Mrs. John Knutson

Sunday, July 16

BEVERLY HILLS
Betty Sturley, 20705 Smallwood Court: 10 a.m. - 3 p.m.

BIRMINGHAM
The Dr. Alice R. McCarthy Garden, 1450 Pilgrim Road: 2 p.m. - 6 p.m.

BLOOMFIELD HILLS
Jack Krasula, 4530 Charing Cross: 10 a.m. - 6 p.m.
Judy's Garden, 3916 Cottontail Lane: 10 a.m. - 4 p.m.
Larry & Sandy Mackle, 460 Goodhue Road: 10 a.m. - 4 p.m.
LongView, 3610 Franklin Road: 10 a.m. - 4 p.m.

FRANKLIN
Hickory Hill, 26705 Irving Road: 10 a.m. - 4 p.m.

Betty Sturley

20705 SMALLWOOD COURT, BEVERLY HILLS

In 1984 we built our present house, a Williamsburg-style Colonial, on a heavily wooded one-acre lot, with the idea of reproducing the feel and sense of the old eighteenth-century Virginia capital. Adding to the impression is the handmade picket fence surrounding the propagation garden that replicates an actual Colonial Williamsburg design. The finishing touch is the clapboard garden shed that resembles an eighteenth-century outbuilding. Although I love the formal Colonial garden style, I have only maintained that tradition in the front of the house. I am a professional artist with a passion for plants, and diversity, beauty, and freedom of form have dominated the development of my gardens. I have an extensive collection of old-fashioned and David Austin roses, a hosta garden, and a four-tiered water garden, complete with two waterfalls and a bridge.

Sunday, July 16, 10 a.m. - 3 p.m.

Smallwood Court is south of 14 Mile Road about half way between Cranbrook Road/ Evergreen Road and Lahser Road. Turn south off 14 Mile Road onto Eastlady. Go 1 block and turn left onto Smallwood Court.

Hickory Hill

26705 Irving Road, Franklin

Designed around our historic 1894 Greek Revival-style farmhouse, our gardens at Hickory Hill capture the imagination in all seasons. Our three-and-one-quarter-acre property features a spring garden, an iris and peony border, a rose garden, a brilliantly colored midsummer perennial bed, and a treasured sunken white garden, complete with flowing fountain, wisteria arbor, and black stone paths. Further afield from our house is an organic raised-bed vegetable garden, a meadow for our beehives, a small wood, and large pond with a developing bog garden. Near our back porch, a classic herb garden provides fragrance and culinary herbs for the kitchen. Boxwood hedges, a 1930 Lord & Burnham greenhouse, old stone walks, and stairwells charm us to keep up the hard work. In the planning stages: a children's garden honoring our new grandchild, Maxine Rose.

Sunday, July 16, 10 a.m. - 4 p.m.

From the corner of Telegraph Road and Maple Road, go west approximately 2 miles to Franklin Road. Turn south, pass Cider Mill, cross Fourteen Mile Road (flashing red light) continuing past gas station to Wellington Road. Turn right onto Wellington to the fourth street, Irving Road. Turn right onto Irving. Hickory Hill is the second house on the left side of the street.

Jack Krasula

4530 Charing Cross, Bloomfield Hills

This beautiful home is a four-and-one-half-acre park-like setting designed and planted with more than 150 different conifers, many specimen trees, and shrubs. There are more than 500 hostas, including many of the newest varieties. Paths have been made throughout the raised beds. Flower beds are included, with many different varieties. A truly spectacular garden.

Sunday, July 16, 10 a.m. - 6 p.m.

Charing Cross is approximately .25 mile north of Big Beaver Road/Quarton Road east of Woodward Avenue. Turn east off Woodward Avenue onto Charing Cross. Go past the blinking traffic light at Kensington Road. The garden will be on the left just before Charing Cross ends at Wattles Road.

Judy's Garden

3916 COTTONTAIL LANE, BLOOMFIELD HILLS

This spectacularly diverse property contains a woodland garden, a sun garden, and a two-tiered, 10,000-gallon water garden. More than 150 varieties of hosta, unusual specimen evergreens and shrubs, wildflowers, numerous varieties of fragrant flowers, ferns, grasses, and an interesting integration of textures, shapes, and colors complement the curved lines of the beds. This visually stimulating arrangement is augmented with garden art, sculpture, birdhouses, a unique shed, and the constant sound of the waterfall.

Sunday, July 16, 10 a.m. - 4 p.m.

Located between Lahser and Telegraph Roads north of Maple Road. Travel east on Maple Road from Telegraph Road to the second traffic light. Turn left onto Gilbert Lake Road. At the third street on the left, turn left onto Cottontail Lane. The garden is the first driveway on the right. Please park on the street.

Larry & Sandy Mackle

460 GOODHUE ROAD, BLOOMFIELD HILLS

In 1972 we moved into our house built in 1929. The landscaping on the two acres was 1929 vintage, overgrown and included what nature planted. Our garden displays more than 500 hostas, 1000 plus daylilies, 140 conifers, and large number of companion plants, perennials, and annuals. There is a pond and rock garden and garden statuary, most of which is in dappled sunlight.

Sunday, July 16, 10 a.m. - 4 p.m.

Goodhue Road is south of Lone Pine Road between Cranbrook and Lahser Roads. Turn south on Goodhue Road off Lone Pine Road to the first house on the left. Goodhue Road is directly opposite St. Dunstans Theatre Pavilion.

LONGVIEW

3610 FRANKLIN ROAD, BLOOMFIELD HILLS

LongView takes its theme from the peaceful sunset viewpoint on Long Lake. The south entry, through an artist's gate, past a kitchen garden on the right, opens onto a small garden with an Oriental harmony containing a small pond, a cairn fountain and the first view of the lake. A stairway by a huge oak tree leads down to the lakeshore and a gravel garden of lavender. Perennials on the terrace behind are chosen to withstand the afternoon sun and strong winds. A flagstone walk goes along the shore to a waterfall. A pond eighteen feet above, which is surrounded by tree peonies and alpine plants, feeds a stream and the waterfall. A perennial border walk leads to the finale, a wind-protected green garden of holly, conifers, and flowering Japanese plum trees.

Sunday, July 16, 10 a.m. - 4 p.m.

From the corner of Telegraph Road/Route 24 and Long Lake Road, go west on Long Lake Road .1 mile to Franklin Road. Turn right. The house is located .25 mile on the left. Park as directed or along Franklin Road.

THE DR. ALICE R. McCARTHY GARDEN

1450 PILGRIM ROAD, BIRMINGHAM

There were no gardens on this beautiful property in 1968; however the one-acre site had magnificent trees-please note the Norway maple. Now the garden has my dwarf conifer collection plus ten Alberta spruce eight to fifteen feet tall. There are nine garden areas with many small flowering trees and shrubs and two 100-foot perennial gardens nine feet deep with a five-foot path between them. My specialty is clematis and I'm starting with antique roses and tree peonies. I like to think the individual gardens are something like English gardens I have visited, with room-like settings. I've designed the gardens myself and they reflect my interest in style, art, and horticulture. I've placed sculpture by several nationally known artists in the gardens. Enjoy!

Sunday, July 16, 2 p.m. - 6 p.m.

Pilgrim Road is between Woodward Avenue and Cranbrook Road, south of Quarton Road. Turn south onto Pilgrim Road from Quarton Road. The garden is at the third house on the left. Please park on the street.

CONGREGATIONAL CHURCH OF BIRMINGHAM ❧

1000 CRANBROOK ROAD, BLOOMFIELD HILLS, MI 48301.
(248) 644-8065.

Within a nine-acre property we have created the most interesting group of gardens, blooming from early spring with bulbs to asters in the fall. We have award-winning displays of tree and herbaceous peonies. Included are five kinds of irises, lilium beds, several hosta beds, daylily beds, and a memorial garden. Rose beds complement specimen trees and shrubs. This is a must-see, all-season garden.

Sunday, July 16, 10 a.m. - 4 p.m.

Cranbrook Road is west of Woodward between Lone Pine and Long Lake Roads. The Congregational Church is on the southwest corner of Cranbrook Road and Woodward Avenue. The entrance is on Cranbrook Road.

CRANBROOK HOUSE & GARDENS ❧

P.O. BOX 801, BLOOMFIELD HILLS, MI 48303-0801. (248) 645-3147.

Stroll through the forty acres of gardens that surround historic Cranbrook House, the 1908 Arts and Crafts-style manor house of Cranbrook's founders, George and Ellen Scripps Booth. The formal gardens and terraces are enhanced by sculptures, fountains, paths, lakes, and streams. Tended solely by volunteers, the gardens are even more exquisite today then when the Booths created them.

May - August, Monday - Sunday, 10 a.m. - 5 p.m.; September and October, call for hours. Guided tours may be arranged.

Lone Pine Road is between Lahser Road and Woodward Avenue. The Cranbrook Gardens are just west of Cranbrook Road on the north side of Lone Pine Road across the street from Christ Church Cranbrook. Please park in the Christ Church parking lot.

Harbor Springs Open Day

Regional Representative: Mrs. Frank Hightower

Wednesday, July 26

HARBOR SPRINGS
A Woodland Garden, Bester Road: 10 a.m. - 6 p.m.
Hermann, 333 Glenn Drive: 10 a.m. - 6 p.m.
Northome, 21 Beach Drive: 10 a.m. - 6 p.m.

GOOD HART
The Schoolhouse Garden, Island View Road: 10 a.m. - 6 p.m.

PETOSKY
Hameisters' Edgewater Garden, 2200 Bayside Drive: 10 a.m. - 6 p.m.

WALLOON LAKE
Marcia & William Howell's Walloon Lake Garden,
739 South Shore Drive: 10 a.m. - 6 p.m.

A Woodland Garden

BESTER ROAD, HARBOR SPRINGS

A quarter-mile driveway through Black Forest Farm makes for a dramatic entrance. A woodland garden enhances a gracious French country home, Overlooking little Traverse Bay, the house is just outside the Harbor Springs city limits. Cutting gardens, lily and hosta beds, and berms have towering hardwoods and hemlocks as a majestic backdrop.

Wednesday, July 26, 10 a.m. - 6 p.m.

From M-119 take Hoyt Street north for .75 miles. Turn right onto Bester Road. The entrance to Black Forest Farm is 1100 feet on the right. Look for a big sign.

Hameisters' Edgewater Garden

2200 BAYSIDE DRIVE, PETOSKEY

Our garden was planned to enhance the God-given beauty of the site: Lake Michigan shores and fabulous sunsets. We borrowed the "no dirt shows" philosophy of the English; rabbits' dining habits make this impossible at times. We have perennial beds, a white garden, a secret English garden, and we cater to butterflies. Unusual annuals maintain color in our short growing season. Artists love to capture the vista.

Wednesday, July 26, 10 a.m. - 6 p.m.

From U.S. 31 North or South, look for the intersection of Division Road-1.5 miles northeast of Downtown Petoskey at the edge of Bay View (a summer community). Bay View/Petoskey Country Club and a Holiday gas station are on either corner. Turn toward the Lake Chittle Traverse Bay. Continue to the end of Division Road to the last house on right. The number 2200 is on the garage, with a "welcome" flag. Please park on the roadside, on either side of the driveway.

Marcia & William Howell's
Walloon Lake Garden

739 SOUTH SHORE DRIVE, WALOON LAKE

This magical garden will be open as a special tribute to William and Marcia Howell, who died in September 1999. Marcia's dream of creating a garden became a reality in 1997, and she continued to enhance its beauty. The area was originally an overgrown, pine-encircled meadow next to the home on the shore of Walloon Lake. It is now a colorful perennial garden of flowers and shrubs that like the cool Michigan weather. The garden is surrounded by a fond du lac stone wall, behind which are flowering fruit trees and shrubs. The garden entrance is enhanced by a rustic, hand-hewn cedar archway covered with climbing white hydrangeas. Hand-hewn cedar benches add to the rustic charm of this garden. The Howells worked with John Hoffman Landscaping in Petoskey.

Wednesday, July 26, 10 a.m. - 6 p.m.

From Petoskey, take Route 131 south for 8 miles. Turn right at blinking traffic light and sign showing Walloon Lake; this is Route M75. Follow Route M75 through the village of Walloon and approximately 1.5 miles after the village will be South Shore Drive on the right, which drops down to the Lake. Follow South Shore Drive for another 1.5 miles to 739 South Shore Drive. The entrance has a split rail fence and a wrought iron sign reading "W.B. Howell." Please park along road and walk down the driveway to house and garden.

Northome

21 BEACH DRIVE, HARBOR SPRINGS

After purchasing Northome cottage in 1996, we worked with Historical Courtyards and Gardens to design a garden to fit our long and narrow lot (715' by sixty-five feet). We wanted a cottage-garden feel. The result is a shade garden bordering the house and a rock-lined drive that opens up into a large cottage garden divided by gravel paths. Many different perennials and annuals typical of cottage gardens are used, including roses, hydrangea, delphiniums, nasturtiums, foxglove, rudbeckia, and poppies. The driveway ends at an arbor with an antique gate that opens to a path through the woodland area at the back of the property.

Wednesday, July 26, 10 a.m. - 6 p.m.

Entering Harbor Springs on Route 119 turn left at the Deer Park onto Zoll Street which leads to the water's edge. Bear left onto Beach Drive.

THE HERMANN GARDEN

333 GLENN DRIVE, HARBOR SPRINGS

Our garden was originally created in 1960 with a great deal of Japanese influence. Although we have retained a bit of this feeling, we have allowed the garden to become more natural and less structured. The house is on a hill looking south over Lake Michigan, but most of the gardens are on the entrance side beginning at street level. There is only a hint of what lies beyond as you go up the winding drive. The interesting aspect of the garden to me is the unusual play of light with its many different shapes and may shades of green. It is restful but exciting and a very enjoyable place to experience.

Wednesday, July 26, 10 a.m. - 6 p.m.

From Main Street in the center of Harbor Springs go west on Main Street to the end. Turn left onto Traverse Street and go 2 blocks. As the street "dog legs" past the entrance to Harbor Point, it becomes Glenn Drive. Turn right onto Glenn Drive. After only 50 feet, go to the first driveway on the left.

THE SCHOOLHOUSE GARDEN

ISLAND VIEW ROAD, GOOD HART

My garden is a border of many different perennials against a background of large old lilac bushes. These are supplemented by annuals to provide a continuous, varied flow of color. A row of white hydrangeas accents the ninety-year-old red school-house.

Wednesday, July 26, 10 a.m. - 6 p.m.

From Harbor Springs go north on State Road/C-77 for approximately 15 miles to Island View Road. Turn left and drive about a mile to Vorce Road. The Schoolhouse is on the corner, the first drive on the right (3981 Vorce Road). Alternate route: Take Shore Drive/M119 north for 15 miles (5 miles north of Good Hart) to Island View road, then 1 mile east to Vorce Road. Park on Vorce Road.

St. John's Episcopal Church &

3RD STREET & TRAVERSE STREET, HARBOR SPRINGS, MI 49740.

St. John's Episcopal Church was consecrated on July 19, 1883. The charming garden was donated by Mr. & Mrs. John McCoy ten years ago. A raised perennial bed fills a corner area. A sculpture by Charlotte Price of Louisville is set amid the hostas and lady's mantle. The grassy area is furnished with teak settees and chairs, providing a lovely quiet place to sit. The whole area is surrounded by a white picket fence. The church will also be open so visitors may see the antique wooden interior and beautiful needlepoint kneelers that are being worked by parishioners. The designs are of Michigan wildflowers and foliage and a variety of crosses. Volunteers at the church will assist with directions to the other gardens.

Wednesday, July 26, 10 a.m. - 6 p.m.

From M119/Main Street, go west on Main Street to its end. Turn right onto Traverse Street. The church is at the corner of Third Street.

NEW HAMPSHIRE

NEW HAMPSHIRE OPEN DAYS

Saturday, July 8: Monadnock
Saturday, July 8: New London
Saturday, July 8: Squam Lake

Monadnock Open Days

Regional Representative: Mrs. Story Wright

Saturday, July 8

ACWORTH
The Gardens on Grout Hill, Grout Hill Road: 10 a.m. - 4 p.m.

DUBLIN
Crocker Garden, East Lake Road: 10 a.m. - 4 p.m.
Marilyn B. Bean, Pierce Road: 10 a.m. - 4 p.m.

PETERBOROUGH
Gardens of Stanley & Cheryl Fry, 69 Pine Street: 10 a.m. - 4 p.m.
Rosaly's Garden, Route 123: 10 a.m. - 4 p.m.

CROCKER GARDEN

EAST LAKE ROAD, DUBLIN

Our garden, which represents a collaboration between us and Kristian Fenderson, is situated between the slopes of Mount Monadnock and historic Dublin Lake. It is a collector's and flower arranger's garden, featuring raised perennial beds and gravel paths. A variety of specimen tress and shrubs are seen. Sun exposure is limited due to the mountain so that grass is not attempted, relying instead on wood chips and low growing vegetation. Everything is carefully labeled for informative viewing. You are invited to follow the gravel path around the house.

Saturday, July 8, 10 a.m. - 4 p.m.

From Keene on Route 101 pass Dublin Lake on the right, making a sharp turn, with a cemetery on the left. At the top of the rise there is a road to the right, East Lake Road. Follow, with the Lake on the right, for .8 mile. Pass a fence on the right and we are the next drive to the left, marked with the name Crocker. Proceed up the hill a short distance. The house in visible on the left. There will be people to assist in parking. From Peterborough on Route 101, go through the 'center' of town where there is a flagpole on an oval plot. The Town Hall and Library are on the left, a Community Church and Yankee Magazine (red buildings) are on the right. Proceed to the top of the hill, passing a road to Jaffrey on the left. The next left is East Lake Road. Follow as above.

GARDENS OF STANLEY & CHERYL FRY

69 PINE STREET, PETERBOROUGH

The garden consists of several individual areas on a site that is quite steep. Several styles of gardens range from formal near the house to wild gardens, a number of water features and a quite large perennial garden. Many of the garden areas have been designed by Gordon Hayward and include such striking features as a 400-foot sycamore allée and a series of semicircle terraces bordered by standard Korean lilacs.

Saturday, July 8, 10 a.m. - 4 p.m.

From Route 101 East (Nashua), proceed to Peterborough, past the intersection of Route 123 and turn right (.5 mile) onto Pine Street. The garden is at the third driveway on the left. From Route 101 West (Keene), proceed through Peterborough, pass the intersection of Route 202. Continue east on Route 101, Pine Street is on the left. The gardens are at the third driveway on the left. Please park on the street.

Marilyn B. Bean

Pierce Road, Dublin

The gardens (herb, vegetable, and flower) that surround my 1816 farmhouse and barn are now and will continue to be a work in progress. Just one of my many interests is arranging leaf combinations (size, color, shape, texture) in my garden beds.

Saturday, July 8, 10 a.m. - 4 p.m.

The garden is .7 mile south on Pierce Road from Old County Road. White farmhouse and barn on the right side. Please park on the south side of the house.

Rosaly's Garden

Peterborough, NH 03458

Set in the heart of the Monadnock Region with a dazzling view of Mount Monadnock is Rosaly's Farmstand surrounded by an acre of flowers offering more than 80 varieties of annuals and perennials. Wide grass pathways lead through the colorful rows. Each variety is labeled with its name, notes on its culture and the best way to pick it. There are several meditative and pleasing herb gardens as well, one based on a Sanskrit Design with culinary and medicinal herbs, and herbal tea garden and a water garden featuring Chinese herbs.

Saturday, July 8, 10 a.m. - 4 p.m.

Look for blue state signs for Rosaly's Farmstand on Route 101 in Peterborough. Go south on Route 123 toward Sharon. There is a blinking light at this intersection. Rosaly's Farmstand is several hundred yards up on the right on Route 123.

The Gardens on Grout Hill

The gardens on Grout Hill were developed by owners G. Kristian Fenderson and Alston Barrett over a period of thirty years from an abandoned farm and home dating from the 1790s. The gardens and other planted areas are several acres in extent. They serve as a laboratory for Kristian's landscape design business and also showcase the owners' personal favorites. The garden features many mature examples of rare and unusual woody and herbaceous plants in a variety of environments. Seasonal annuals and containers also form a large part of the summer display. Azaleas, rhododendrons, viburnums, conifers, magnolias, beech trees, and old roses are just a few of the areas of emphasis.

Saturday, July 8, 10 a.m. - 4 p.m.

From Route 10 to Route 123A, turn left and go approximately 3 miles. Bear left following Route 123A along the river for less than .5 mile. At the first crossroad, turn right onto Grout Hill Road. Cross the wooden bridge and go up hill passing Russell Road on the right and Ball Road on the left. Please park at the first left driveway after the small red Grout Hill Schoolhouse.

New London Open Days

Regional Representative: Mrs. Gusta Teach

Saturday, July 8

ELKINS
Cottage Rock, 42 Wilmot Center Road: 10 a.m. - 4 p.m.
Martha Andrea & Ralph Lapham, 23 Elkins Road: 10 a.m. - 4 p.m.

NEWBURY
Moonstone Farm, 253 Bowles Road: 10 a.m. - 4 p.m.

NEW LONDON
Richards', 5 Meadow Lane: 10 a.m. - 4 p.m.
Tomie dePaola's Garden, 300 County Road: 10 a.m. - 4 p.m.
Wellspring, Shaker Street: 10 a.m. - 4 p.m.

WILMOT
Whitney Brook Farm, Woodland Lane:
    10 a.m. - 4 p.m.

COTTAGE ROCK

42 WILMOT CENTER ROAD, ELKINS

This garden was designed around some very large granite boulders, and slopes gently down to the east and south. I love collecting new and unusual plants, and have developed beds in shade and sun to accommodate them. Working the topography of the land has helped make a natural-feeling setting. Grasses and chamaecyparis are of particular interest.

Saturday, July 8, 10 a.m. - 4 p.m.

From Route 11 in the New London area travel 1.3 miles down Elkins Road, which becomes Wilmot Center Road. Stay straight on this same road past the beach post office, up small hill to small tan and white house on right. Park on street or at parking lot just beyond my driveway. Small sign reads 42 on tree.

MARTHA ANDREA & RALPH LAPHAM

23 ELKINS ROAD, ELKINS

Our gardens have evolved over the past twenty years and surround an 1835 Cape Cod-style house in a pastoral setting on a lovely stream and historic mill pond. At the front of the house a stone-walled terrace encloses a shady area housing numerous pots and urns of agapanthus, topiaries, tuberous begonias, and impatiens. Many varieties of daylilies follow the picket fence, which encloses a small, hand-dug pond planted with water lilies and other tropical water plants. The pond abounds with tadpoles, goldfish, and snails; bull frogs, newts, and minnows mysteriously arrived on their own. The backyard deck is covered with mixed containers of herbs and annuals, and steps lead down to the stone-walled perennial beds that continue to terrace down to the stream and natural pond. Several arbors covered with morning glories and wild grapes serve as pathways to varied perennial beds. A stone step leads up to the garden, which features tall dahlias and giant sunflowers. A footbridge that crosses the stream leads to a small woodland shade garden followed by a sunny pasture and small fenced vegetable garden. There is a natural unruly aspect to our gardens, creating a habitat for wild creatures and birds. Our menagerie includes a peacock, goose, raven, and chickens that wander freely, while sheep and others stay in their fenced area.

Saturday, July 8, 10 a.m. - 4 p.m.

From Highway 89 take Exit 11 and travel east toward New London. Go approximately 2.25 miles, passing Colonial Farm Inn on the left. Turn left onto Elkins Road and follow the road approximately .75 miles, noticing Pleasant Lake on the left. Turn right at the gazebo. The garden is at the fourth house on the right past Mesa International. It is a white Cape Cod-style house with a long white picket fence. Please park on Elkins Road in front of house.

MOONSTONE FARM
253 BOWLES ROAD, NEWBURY

Carved from rocks and woods, our hilltop farm overlooking Lake Sunapee represents our varied interests. We have created places for labor, play, and relaxation. Abundant fruit and vegetables, peaceful pastures, flower beds, and a productive sugar bush surround our home, barn, and sugar house. These areas, all organic, favor animals and art and optimize our short growing season. Our flower beds are exceptional blends of fragrance, form, and color. They unify the diverse elements of our farm.

Saturday, July 8, 10 a.m. - 4 p.m.

From Route I-89: Take Exit 12 (from south turn left, from north turn right) to Route 103A. Left on Route 103A. Drive approximately 4 miles to Blodgett Landing Road. Turn right, Go .2 miles, turn left on Bowles Road. Drive .7 mile. Driveway is on left; it is blacktop and goes up a hill. At the bottom are three upright granite pieces. Look for signs for parking.

RICHARDS'
5 MEADOW LANE, NEW LONDON

This new garden was carved out of a wooded hillside four years ago. The perennial garden starts with colorful plants to suggest the tropics, then moves uphill to the green temperate zone, and ends in the cold arctic, with gray plantings and rocky outcrops. Surrounding the lawns before the woods are many rhododendrons, azaleas, laurel, and other shrubs. Functioning as a backdrop is a collection of trees including metasequoia, many varieties of pine, chamaecyparis, thuja, and weeping conifers such as spruce, hemlock, and juniper. There are also many varieties of unusual deciduous trees. Like most gardens this is a work in progress, with a vernal pool and a patio/terrace in the works.

Saturday, July 8, 10 a.m. - 4 p.m.

From Newbury, take County Road/Route 103A North. After passing under I-89, turn right at the second road, which is Meadow Lane. The garden is at 5 Meadow Lane. Please park on the street.

TOMIE dePAOLA'S GARDEN

300 COUNTY ROAD, NEW LONDON

Although my yard is private, it is an open space. My yard has views of Mounts Sunapee and Kearsarge. My gardens have been designed to provide optimal viewing from the house and from the elaborate deck off the house. The gardens are quite simple, filled with rather common northern New England perennials and annuals (grown in my greenhouse by seed). They are constantly in progress. But the setting is lovely and they very much please me. They are no "Giverney," but then again, I'm not Monet.

Saturday, July 8, 10 a.m. - 4 p.m.

From I-89, take Exit 12 (Not Exit 12A). At end of exit, follow sign to New London. At blinking yellow light (Exxon gas station on far left corner), turn left. Number 300 County Road is the first property on right. Please park in driveway, along the road, and by the barn.

WELLSPRING

SHAKER STREET, NEW LONDON

Landscape architect Roger Wells and his wife Sandy have re-created and interpreted a New England compound of three collected, handmade eighteenth-century structures, surrounded by a series of unique gardens. They converted an original seven-acre flat hayfield and sloping woodland into a flowing sequence of stone-walled terraces, fine lawns, undulating wildflower meadows, walks, paths, and accent gardens that include: a hybrid daylily border, a sunken English herbaceous garden, a heather hill, a formal herb garden, a kitchen garden and a small orchard, a New England rock garden, and a man-made brook with four ponds and a contemplative retreat.

Saturday, July 8, 10 a.m. - 4 p.m.

From I-89, take Exit 11. Go east on King Hill Road/Route 11. Go over hill, past blinking traffic light at Seaman's Road to Shaker Street (approximately 2 miles). Turn right onto Shaker Street (across from Colonial Farm Inn) and bear right at Mountain Road. Continue on Shaker Street. The garden is at the first house on the left, a white Cape Cod-style with a burgundy barn. Enter driveway with a sign that reads "Wellspring." Please park in front of barn.

Whitney Brook Farm

WOODLAND LANE, WILMOT

Our farmhouse and gardens are at the end of a country road and are surrounded by eighty acres for total privacy. The herb garden has a large collection for cooking and healing and is enclosed by a picket fence with wonderful arbors and a chicken house. There is a large organic vegetable garden with a garden house and nursery for growing rhododendrons. A pond is home for huge frogs, dragonflies, otters, and lily pads. There are natural trails in the surrounding woods with views of the mountain. We love outrageous plants like sunflowers that grow eight feet tall and vines that grow over everything. Our garden has most often been described as magical.

Saturday, July 8, 10 a.m. - 4 p.m.

From Route 89 take Exit 11 East and travel 3.8 miles. Turn left onto Village Road and the next left onto Woodland Lane. Go to the end of Woodland Lane to Whitney Brook Farm. Please park as directed.

The Fells at the John Hay National Wildlife Refuge 🦆

ROUTE 103A, NEWBURY, NH 03255. (603) 763-4789.

These extensive gardens, developed from 1914 to 1940 as a showplace country estate, had fallen into decline in recent years. After seven years of work by Garden Conservancy staff and dedicated volunteers, the profile of this historic design has reemerged.

Year round, daily, dawn - dusk. Call ahead for special events and educational programs.

Take I-89 North to Exit 9/Route 103 and go west to Newbury. Take 103A north for 2.2 miles. The Fells is on the left. Please park in the parking lot and walk down the driveway to the house and gardens.

A preservation project of The Garden Conservancy.

Squam Lake Open Days

Regional Representative: George Carr

Saturday, July 8

ASHLAND
Shirley Splaine's Garden, Winona Road: 10 a.m. - 4 p.m.

HOLDERNESS
Burleigh Farm Gardens, Burleigh Farm Road: 10 a.m. - 4 p.m.
Mr. & Mrs. Thomas H. Choate, Choate Road: 10 a.m. - 4 p.m.

CENTER HARBOR
Hillcrest Farm, Route 25B: 10 a.m. - 4 p.m.
"Serenity"—A Woodland Wildflower Garden,
    16 Slade Lane: 10 a.m. - 4 p.m.

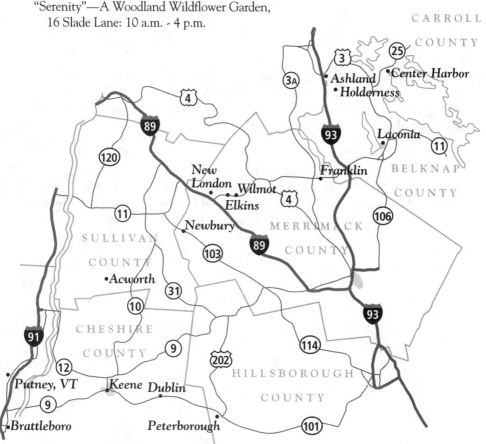

BURLEIGH FARM GARDENS

Burleigh Farm is an old summer estate and farm. There are three separate garden areas on the farm. There is a restored rock garden, a formal garden with a pool and a lovely border garden at the adjacent homes of Mr. & Mrs. Laurence J. Webster and Mr. & Mrs. Peter S. Kampf; and there are perennial borders, a wildflower area, and a cottage garden at the 1840 farmhouse of Mr. & Mrs. Robert E. Grady.

Saturday, July 8, 10 a.m. - 4 p.m.

From Route 93 North take Exit 24 toward Ashland. Go through Ashland to Route 3 and turn left. Go on Route 3 to Route 113. Take Route 113 for 3 miles to Burleigh Farm Road and turn left. Go to the first driveway, Laurence Road. The Webster & Kampf houses are the only ones on Laurence Road. The Grady gardens are at the top of Burleigh Farm Road. Please park on Burleigh Farm Road.

HILLCREST FARM

ROUTE 25 B, CENTER HARBOR

This farm landscape is evolving from an inhospitable site into a country garden with varied vistas and interesting plant combinations. Designed to attract native wildlife and to be enjoyed by family, friends and pets, this garden includes many native plants, as well as more traditional favorites.

Saturday, July 8, 10 a.m. - 4 p.m.

Take 93 North to Exit 23 towards Meredith on Route 104. Route 104 deadends into Route 3 North. Turn left onto Route 3 and continue through town of Meredith, and turn right onto Route 25-B, 2 miles north of town. Hillcrest Farm is on the left 2 miles from the town. Please park as noted in the field beyond the farm.

Mr. & Mrs. Thomas H. Choate

CHOATE ROAD, HOLDERNESS

Our original small border was in front of a stone wall, between the house and the lake. It was not suitably placed, according to the late Grace Kirkwood who moved it nearer to the house, forming a large perennial garden with added annuals. The pond gardens evolved from a well struck by lightning, making the water undrinkable. An unused well, being unacceptable to my husband, was eventually put to use, and over several years the two ponds and plantings were formed again with the valuable help of Mrs. Kirkland. The upper pool can be used for swimming and is a great source of entertainment for young children.

Saturday, July 8, 10 a.m. - 4 p.m.

Take Route 113 leaving Holderness, going towards Sandwich. About 4 miles from Holderness there is a farm on the left. Next there is a sign that says Choate Road. Our drive is just past sign. Please park on premises.

"Serenity"—
A Woodland Wildflower Garden

16 SLADE LANE, CENTER HARBOR

I started my woodland garden in the 1970s on our property on Lake Winnipesaukee. Over the years a veritable wooded "jungle" has been gradually transformed into a natural woodland setting for wildflowers, ferns, mosses, and native shrubs. Today more than 175 plant species and fifty different kinds of hardy ferns are represented. There are two man-made bog areas and a waterfall pool within the garden. This garden was designed by me and executed with the invaluable help of my husband, children, and friends. My aim is to present a natural look. I have been careful to blend textures, forms, shades of green, and colors in effective placements to create a lush, serene woodland on our quarter-acre area. Even after twenty years, I am discovering new ideas and treasures, thus subscribing to Alan Haskell's mantra on gardeners: "We are all beginners to the end!"

Saturday, July 8, 10 a.m. - 4 p.m.

From Route 25, travel 1.7 miles beyond Center Harbor going east toward Moultonboro; look for Moultonboro Neck Road on the right, opposite Aubuchon Hardware. Travel 2.6 miles and turn right at the Windward Harbor sign. Go .6 mile and turn left onto Jacobs Road. This follows a natural curve to the right and becomes Colby Road. Turn left onto Long Point Road and go .5 mile to Hauser Estates Road. Turn right and keep bearing right to Slade Lane. Turn left and the garden is on the immediate right, #16 Slade Lane with a Traylor sign on a tree next to the driveway. Please park on the street.

SHIRLEY SPLAINE'S GARDEN

WINONA ROAD, ASHLAND

Mine are hobby gardens and I am the sole gardener. I raise vegetables and fruits as well as flowers, concentrating on perennials, attempting to have continuous bloom throughout our growing season. My special loves are daylilies and hosta, although I love trying new plants. I have a small greenhouse and raise many of my plants from seed under lights and in the greenhouse.

Saturday, July 8, 10 a.m. - 4 p.m.

Take I-93 North to Exit 24/Ashland. Turn right after exit and travel down the main street of Ashland to the Civil War Monument. Turn right and pass fire station on the right, go straight, yield at intersection, then turn left onto Winona Road. Go about 4 miles. The house is a red Cape on the left. Please proceed past house and take next left onto Hawkins Pond Road. Please park on Hawkins Pond Road.

KIRKWOOD GARDENS 🌿

SQUAM LAKES SCIENCE CENTER BOX 173, HOLDERNESS, NH 03245. (603) 968-7194.

Designed by the famous landscape designer "Sonny" Kirkwood in the 1990s. The gardens offer visitors the Squam Lakes Natural Science Center lavish display of ornamental shrubs, old-fashioned roses, hybrid daylilies and colorful annuals. A flagstone terrace fountain and a pergola give another opportunity to relax and observe the birds and butterflies which visit the garden daily.

May - November, daily, dawn - dusk

100 Miles north of Boston MA in the Lakes Region of New Hampshire, Route 3, Holderness, N.H.

THE MCLAUGHLIN GARDEN & HORTICULTURAL CENTER 🌿

101 MAIN STREET, SOUTH PARIS, ME. (207) 743-8820.

Bernard McLaughlin spent a lifetime creating and maintaining lilacs, lilies, iris, hosta, and native wildflowers that comprise this three-acre perennial garden. Following McLaughlin's death, the community successfully rallied to preserve the garden and its fifty-year-old "open door" visiting tradition.

May - September, daily, 8 a.m. - 8 p.m.

Located at the junction of Western Avenue and Route 26 in South Paris, .8 mile north of the Oxford Hills Comprehensive High School. Parking is available along Western Avenue.

🌐 A preservation project of The Garden Conservancy.

New Jersey

Northern New Jersey

New Jersey Open Days

May 13, May 20 & June 10: Northern New Jersey

Northern New Jersey Open Days

Regional Representative: Mrs. J. Duncan Pitney

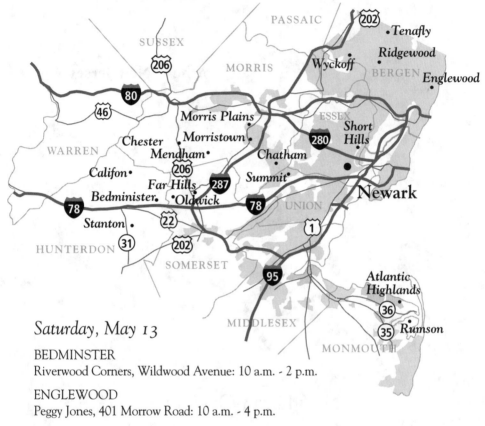

Saturday, May 13

BEDMINSTER
Riverwood Corners, Wildwood Avenue: 10 a.m. - 2 p.m.

ENGLEWOOD
Peggy Jones, 401 Morrow Road: 10 a.m. - 4 p.m.

MORRIS PLAINS
Watnong Gardens, 2379 Watnong Terrace: 10 a.m. - 4 p.m.

SUMMIT
Allen Garden, 107 Bellevue Avenue: 10 a.m. - 4 p.m.

SHORT HILLS
Garden of Dr. & Mrs. George E. Staehle, 83 Old Hollow Road: 10 a.m. - 2 p.m.
Winter's Garden, 28 Dryden Terrace: 10 a.m. - 4 p.m.

TENAFLY
Patricia Silverman, 30 Mayflower Drive: 10 a.m. - 4 p.m.

WYCKOFF
Tall Trees—Garden of Janet Schulz, 16 Colonial Road: 10 a.m. - 4 p.m.

Saturday, May 20

CALIFON
Frog Pond Farm, 26 Beavers Road: 10 a.m. - 4 p.m.

STANTON
Kallas Garden, 91 Dreahook Road: 10 a.m. - 4 p.m.

Saturday, June 10

ATLANTIC HIGHLANDS
Mrs. Sverre Sorensen, 1 Hill Road: 10 a.m. - 4 p.m.

BEDMINSTER
Riverwood Corners, Wildwood Avenue: 10 a.m. - 2 p.m.

CHATHAM
Jack Lagos, 23 Pine Street: 10 a.m. - 4 p.m.

FAR HILLS
Kennelston Cottage, 48 Post Kennel Road: 10 a.m. - 6 p.m.

MENDHAM
Mr & Mrs. Alan Willemsen, Pleasant Valley Road: 10 a.m. - 2 p.m.
Mr. & Mrs. James M. Porter, 304 Pleasant Valley Road: 10 a.m. - 2 p.m.
Pitney Farm, 1 Cold Hill Road: 10 a.m. - 4 p.m.

MORRIS PLAINS
Watnong Gardens, 2379 Watnong Terrace: 10 a.m. - 4 p.m.

OLDWICK
Creek House, 88 Rockway Road: 10 a.m. - 6 p.m.

RIDGEWOOD
Gayle & Frank Smith, 490 Hanks Avenue: 10 a.m. - 4 p.m.
The Handley Garden, 342 Franklin Turnpike: 10 a.m. - 4 p.m.

RUMSON
King & Leigh Sorensen, 7 North Ward Avenue: 10 a.m. - 2 p.m.
Linden Hill, 138 Bingham Avenue: 10 a.m. - 4 p.m.

SHORT HILLS
Winter's Garden, 28 Dryden Terrace: 10 a.m. - 4 p.m.

TENAFLY
Linda Singer, 170 Tekening Drive: 10 a.m. - 6 p.m.
Richard & Ronnie Klein, 133 Essex Drive: 10 a.m. - 4 p.m.

WYCKOFF
Tall Trees-Garden of Janet Schulz, 16 Colonial Road: 10 a.m. - 4 p.m.

ALLEN GARDEN

Until five years ago, this garden, with a mix of sun and shade, was a flat, square, suburban back yard featuring a boggy corner, piles of rocks, and a few stately trees. Realizing the potential of a low stone wall and a borrowed landscape, the owners asked Ann Granbery, of New Vernon, to design a garden for three seasons only: fall, winter, and spring. Two rock gardens, apple trees espaliered against the garage, a topiary garden "gate," and some unusual plants are features.

Saturday, May 13, 10 a.m. - 4 p.m.

From Route 24, take the Summit Avenue Exit. Go 1 block and turn right onto Bellevue Avenue. Go around the bend to a brick ranch at #107. Please park on the street. Walk down the driveway; the garden is in the back.

CREEK HOUSE

Cottage style gardens front the road and surround a cluster of stone and shingle buildings, some dating back to the 1700s. A thatched cottage marks the entrance. Functionally separate garden areas are linked by an informal planting style, aimed at conveying the sense of continuity in time and space, and providing interest year round. Roses and vines climb ornamental fences and a pergola; mixed borders feature both old-fashioned and uncommon plant varieties. The bank of Rockaway Creek, across the road from the residence, is the setting for a naturalistic planting of native shrubs and perennials.

Saturday, June 10, 10 a.m. - 6 p.m.

From I-78 take Exit 24; take fork in the direction of Oldwick. Head North on Route 523 and continue straight ahead (after 1 mile the road becomes Route 517 North) for 1.5 miles to the center of Oldwick. Turn left onto King Street (at Tewksbury Inn) and proceed for 1.6 miles to intersection with Rockway Road and continue for .5 miles to a green steel bridge). Turn right onto Rockway Road and continue for .5 miles to second bridge, bearing right at the fork. Travel another .3 miles to #88 on your right. Please park on the lawn.

Frog Pond Farm

26 Beavers Road, Califon

In a peaceful countryside hollow, a one-half-acre spring-fed pond reflects the beauty of the natural scene. The drama is heightened with introduced flowering trees, azaleas, rhododendrons, and uncommon shrubs. There are separate areas for many types of iris, primula, and wildflowers. Crossing a brook on a footbridge, you will see rock gardens and all-season perennial borders plus a blueberry house. Adding interest to the flag patio during the growing season are many tender container plants started in the small greenhouse.

Saturday, May 20, 10 a.m. - 4 p.m.

Take I-78 to Exit 24. Turn right (if coming from east) onto Route 523 toward Oldwick. Continue straight ahead as the road becomes Route 517. Continue through the village of Oldwick and on, with no turns (6 miles from interstate) to traffic light. This is Fairmont, with Fairmont Church on the right corner. Turn left onto Route 512 and go about 1 mile to Beavers Road (bend in road with fence). Turn right onto Beavers Road traveling about 1 mile to #26 at foot of hill. The number is on the mailbox and there is a pond in front of house. Please park on Beavers Road.

Garden of Dr. & Mrs. George E. Staehle

83 Old Hollow Road, Short Hills

Our garden is in an old quarry. Over the years we have cleared and planted it ourselves, after a local landscaper told us it was impossible, and to "let it stay wild." We started about forty years ago with azaleas, rhododendrons, and wildflowers, then went on to hosta, hellebores, daylilies, geraniums, primula and other perennials. We continue to collect and plant experimentally.

Saturday, May 13, 10 a.m. - 2 p.m.

Take Route 24 West to the Hobart Gap Road Exit. Turn right at traffic light onto Hobart Gap Road. At blinking traffic light the road name changes to White Oak Ridge Road. At the next traffic light (1 mile) turn right onto Parsonage Hill Road. Continue to "T" junction. Turn left onto Old Short Hills Road and go about .5 mile to second street on right which is Old Hollow Road. The garden is at #83, the fifth house on right. Please park along the street.

GAYLE & FRANK SMITH

490 HANKS AVENUE, RIDGEWOOD

Gayle and Frank Smith's garden is a shared endeavor that begins with early tulips, daffodils and iris, later shows its spectacular face with 125 hybrid daylilies, with roses during the hot months. Front garden is shrubs, bulbs, peonies, old roses. Back yard's berm has bulbs, daylilies, roses, foxgloves, and lilies. Borders have vitex, crape-myrtle, a tree peony section, hydrangeas with pulmonaria and violets, a shade garden of wildflowers, an urn with rose trellis and lilacs, fountain with ferns, raspberry patch, pieces of homemade sculpture, one with a hosta garden. Behind the garage, a Tennessee Homestead Fantasy, an heirloom architectural piece with viburnum, peonies, roses, clematis and lilacs.

Saturday, June 10, 10 a.m. - 4 p.m.

From the George Washington Bridge take Route 4 West to Route 17 North. Take 17N to Ridgewood Avenue/Ridgewood Exit. Follow East Ridgewood Avenue toward Ridgewood. Turn left onto South Van Dien Avenue (stone church on your left) and go one block. Turn right onto Hanks Avenue. House is #490 Hanks Avenue. Please park on the street.

JACK LAGOS

23 PINE STREET, CHATHAM

I have been developing this one-acre property, which backs into a lovely woods, for twenty-five years. The first garden and Island perennial border, is now one among many. A 100-year-old barn is backdrop for shade-loving plants and on its sunny sides lies an herb garden and another perennial border. Ten graceful clemitas vines climb beautifully designed lattice fencing that defines the dwarf conifer collection. A woodland garden is my latest project.

Saturday, June 10, 10 a.m. - 4 p.m.

From the Garden State Parkway or the New Jersey Turnpike, take Route 78 West to Route 24 West. Take the Chatham Exit (immediately after the Short Hills Mall). Follow signs to Route 124 West/Main Street and at the fifth traffic light turn left onto Lafayette Avenue. Go all the way to the top of the hill, and when Lafayette Avenue bends to the right, turn right onto Pine Street. Number 23 is the fourth house on the left. From Route 287 exit onto Route 24 East. Continue to the "The Mall at Short Hills" Exit. At the bottom of the exit ramp turn right onto River Road. At the first traffic light bear right and continue straight (River Road becomes Watching Avenue) to the fifth traffic light. Turn left onto Lafayette Avenue. At the top of the hill where the road bends to the right turn right onto Pine Street. Number 23 is the fourth house on the left. Please park on the street.

KALLAS GARDEN

91 DREAHOOK ROAD, STANTON

Approximately one and one-half acres are under cultivation. Herbaceous borders, annuals, woody ornamentals. The main feature is approximately 1,000 specimens of 200 different rhododendron and azalea cultivars.

Saturday, May 20, 10 a.m. - 4 p.m.

From Route 78 West take the Whitehouse/Oldwick Exit and turn left onto Route 523 South. Go to Route 22 and turn left at traffic light, approximately 1000 feet. Turn right onto the continuation of Route 523 South and go approximately 2 miles to Dreahook Road. Turn right and go 2.5 miles. The driveway is on the left between Cushetunk Road and Springtown Road. Please park on Cushetunk Road (unless handicapped).

KENNELSTON COTTAGE

48 POST KENNEL ROAD, FAR HILLS

The gardens surrounding the turn-of-the Century main residence take their inspiration from the English Tudor architecture of the house and the European tradition of creating garden rooms. Following strong axial lines, these gardens we designed as enclosures within walls, fences or plant masses, each for a different function. There is a courtyard garden, a vegetable /herb garden, a conservatory terrace garden and a pool garden. Further away, a shade garden assumes less formal lines, and a sunken garden is set within an old stone foundation. The property also features an 1800s gatehouse, an English greenhouse by Alitex and a small nursery/cutting garden framed with a twig fence, gate and arbor.

Saturday, June 10, 10 a.m. - 6 p.m.

From I-287, take Exit 26/Liberty Corner/Mt. Airy Road/Bernardsville and go 200 yards to traffic light. Turn left onto Whitenack Road and continue 2.0 miles to end at Route 202. Turn right onto Route 202 North and proceed for 200 yards to Douglass Avenue. Turn left onto Douglass Avenue and continue uphill for 1.3 miles to T-intersection at the stop sign. Turn right onto Post Kennel Road and proceed to the third driveway in the right, #48, bordered by a stone wall and a beige and green gatehouse. Follow signs for parking.

King & Leigh Sorensen

7 North Ward Avenue, Rumson

The house is a former windmill adjacent to a river. The landscape design includes a raised perennial bed with shrubs and flowering trees in the background. The garden was featured in the January 1983 issue of House Beautiful. There are espaliered apple trees near King's vegetable garden that features five varieties of lettuce. Leigh has a collection of bonsai and King raises honeybees. Many ornamental grasses are incorporated into the gardens, which flood at times of extreme high tides.

Saturday, June 10, 10 a.m. - 2 p.m.

Exit 109 on the Garden State Parkway. Turn left onto Newman Springs Road and after 1.5 miles turn left onto Broad Street. After .75 mile turn right onto Harding Place and continue east for 5 miles (the road name changes to Ridge, then Hartchorne). At the end, turn left onto North Ward Avenue. Our driveway is a continuation of North Ward Avenue. The house, #7, is marked on an oar in a grass garden.

Linda Singer

170 Tekening Drive, Tenafly

I designed this romantic garden to include bluestone walks and patios, fieldstone sitting walls, rose-and-vine-covered arbors and trellises, stone ornaments, a swimming pool, and a small vegetable garden enclosed by a white picket fence. There are perennial and mixed borders. A cottage garden is of special interest for a wide variety of flowering shrubs. The greatest challenge is thwarting the legions of moles, voles, field mice, and rabbits who love the garden as much as I do.

Saturdays; May 13, June 10, 10 a.m. - 6 p.m.

From the Palisades Parkway drive north and get off at first exit (Englewood/Palisades Avenue). Turn right at the first light onto Sylvan Avenue/Route 9W, and drive north approximately 3 miles and turn left at the light onto East Clinton Avenue. Drive .5 miles and turn right onto Ridge Road. Drive one block and turn right onto Berkeley Drive. Drive one block and turn left onto Highwood Road. Drive two blocks and turn right onto Tekening Drive. The house is the third on the right. Sign with #170 is high on a tree. Please park on the street.

Proceeds shared with Wave Hill.

LINDEN HILL
138 BINGHAM AVENUE, RUMSON

Linden Hill provides a special and unexpected landscape, with numerous garden areas that spread over eight acres. Great specimen trees rise over the level property. No one structure, garden, or style dominates the terrain. The Colonial-style house, built in the early 1890s, is gracefully surrounded by garden beds, impeccably maintained lawns, and arbors of fruit trees. More than 2,500 varieties of flowers, plants, shrubs, and trees infuse this horticulturally rich landscape. Although flowers permeate the entire property, there are ten garden sections that stand out. Reaching beyond traditional forms, Linden Hill provides a horticultural impression that is inventive and pleasurable through an overall effect of cultivated informality.

Saturday, June 10, 10 a.m. - 4 p.m.

From the New Jersey Turnpike South take Exit 11/Garden State Parkway South. At the toll after the Raritan River stay right on road marked "Local-All Exits." Take Exit 109/ Red Bank, turn left at the traffic light after paying toll and follow Newman Springs Road/ Route 520 to the end. Turn right onto Broad Street. Turn left at the first traffic light onto White Road. Take White Road to end. Turn left at the stop sign onto Branch Avenue. Turn right at blinking traffic light onto Rumson Road. Go about 3.2 miles to sign for Route 8A. Turn left onto Bingham Avenue. Linden Hill is the third driveway on the left, #138.

MR. & MRS. ALAN WILLEMSEN
PLEASANT VALLEY ROAD, MENDHAM

This charming cottage-style garden was designed by the owners to complement their 1830s farmhouse. A tall white picket fence protects the planted areas from the deer. Principal features include perennial borders, a raised-bed vegetable garden using an adaptation of the French intensive gardening method, a trough collection, and a gracious terrace garden. Pre-Revolutionary War maple and ash trees enhance the landscape of this working farm.

Saturday, June 10, 10 a.m. - 2 p.m.

From I-287 South, take Exit 35. Follow Route 510 around Morristown Square to Old Route 24/Route 510. Approximately 7 miles from the square at the traffic light, turn left onto Hilltop Road. Follow Hilltop to Pleasant Valley Road. Turn right onto Pleasant Valley Road. Go .8 mile. Follow signs for parking.

Mr. & Mrs. James M. Porter

304 Pleasant Valley Road, Mendham

Views of the rolling meadows and distant hills create the setting for this converted barn and gardens. Begun in 1981, the gardens have grown and changed over the years. Old stone walls of the original barnyard frame the entrance court, centered by an old millstone which is now a fountain. This area is planted with perennials, shrubs, roses, vines, ornamental grasses, and flowering trees. All grassed areas have recently been replaced with gravel. Double shrub borders along the drive lead to the enclosed herb, vegetable, and cutting garden. A terrace is planted with dwarf conifers, ground covers, and vines.

Saturday, June 10, 10 a.m. - 2 p.m.

From I-287 South, take Exit 35. Follow Route 510 around Morristown Square to Old Route 24/Route 510. Approximately 7 miles from the square, turn left onto Hilltop Road. Follow Hilltop to Pleasant Valley Road. Turn right onto Pleasant Valley Road. Go .8 mile. Turn left into Wendover Farm. Follow signs for parking.

Mrs. Sverre Sorensen

1 Hill Road, Atlantic Highlands

Nestled in the hills (the highest coastal point from Maine to Florida) overlooking Sandy Hook Bay to New York City is a mature, natural woodland garden created by the owner and her late husband, Sev. Years ago plants were started by cuttings and seeds (many by daughter Sandy Sorensen Henning). Today, charming paths flanked with brunnera, epimediums, and phlox wind in and about rhododendrons, azaleas, skimmias, laurel, and dogwood-all with spectacular vistas of the ocean beyond.

Saturday, June 10, 10 a.m. - 4 p.m.

Take the Garden State Parkway South to Exit 114. Turn left after the ramp and right onto Nutswamp Road. Turn left onto Neversink River Road across Route 35, onto Locust Point Road. DO NOT go over Oceanic Bridge to Rumson. Go straight through the intersection with the Red Country Store entrance on the right, bear right downhill, through the traffic light at Route 36, up Grand Avenue, under Stone Bridge, and turn right onto Ocean Boulevard/Scenic Drive. Turn at the second right onto Hill Road to # 1, the first driveway on the right. Look for high stone walls and gravel driveway. Please park along the street.

Patricia Silverman

30 Mayflower Drive, Tenafly

Over the past eight years this irregularly shaped, hilly lot has been extensively recontoured and replanted to take advantage of the diverse growing conditions (sun, shade, woodland, and bog). As a graduate of several certificate programs from The New York Botanical Gardens and a volunteer at Wave Hill, I have become a passionate plant lover. My goal after renovating our house was to maximize the garden views from each window of the house. My eclectic tastes, combined with the nature of the site, has allowed me the luxury of pursuing new ideas, expanding existing beds, creating totally new beds, as well as amending and editing the plantings. Added interest is provided by the hardscape elements of the garden-stone and brick walls, huge boulder steps, a masonry patio, dry riverbed, and strategically placed statuary.

Saturday, May 13, 10 a.m. - 4 p.m.

Take the George Washington Bridge into New Jersey via the upper level. Stay right and exit onto the Palisades Parkway North. Take Exit 1 and turn right onto Sylvan Avenue/Route 9W. Travel 1.7 miles into Tenafly. Turn left onto East Clinton Avenue. Proceed .8 miles to Woodland and turn left. Travel .5 miles to Churchill and turn right. Travel .7 miles and turn left onto Leroy. Turn left at the next street onto Mayflower. The house, #30, is the third house on the right.

Proceeds shared with Wave Hill.

Peggy Jones

401 Morrow Road, Englewood

This rolling hillside encompasses a variety of gardens, ranging from a formal rose garden to a wild woodland garden where the Japanese primrose and shooting stars dance with the hellebores. Other highlights include a rock garden, a living wall, a small enclosed courtyard with wonderful climbing hydrangeas and an elliptical herb garden in the center of the back lawn. Come and discover a wealth of unique trees, shrubs, and perennials. Find the split-leaf beech in the expansive front lawn. In the rear of the garden look for the old moss-covered stone steps that lead to the outdoor fireplace nestled under a canopy of large oaks. Look to the left and you will see the sorrel tree.

Saturday, May 13, 10 a.m. - 4 p.m.

From I-95/I-80 East (local lanes), exit at Broad Avenue/Englewood. Follow Broad Avenue north until it ends at a traffic light at Palisades Avenue. Turn left onto Palisades Avenue and then a quick right at traffic light onto Lydecker Street. Follow Lydecker to 4-way stop. Turn right onto Booth Avenue. Head up hill and turn left onto the first road, Morrow Road. Go to top of hill. The house, #401 Morrow Road, is on the right. From Palisades Interstate Parkway, take the Englewood Exit. Turn right onto Palisades Avenue and go to the fifth traffic light. Turn right onto Lydecker Street and follow as above.

Pitney Farm

1 Cold Hill Road, Mendham

This house has been in the same family since the early 1700s. The present-day property has a cutting garden in front of the house where cows once grazed. There is a bird garden off the breakfast room, espaliers on three sides of the woodshed, and a garden featuring evergreens off the screened porch. Further off are a walled garden and a vegetable garden adjacent to the greenhouse.

Saturday, June 10, 10 a.m. - 4 p.m.

From I-287 South take Exit 32. Follow Route 510 around Morristown Square to old Route 24/Route 510. Six miles from the square at the traffic light, turn right onto Cold Hill Road. The second right is Pitney Farm. From Peapack, take Roxiticus Road north to Route 24. Go right (east) to the second traffic light and turn left. The second right is Pitney Farm. Please park on side street or in development.

Richard & Ronnie Klein

133 Essex Drive, Tenafly

An informal, one-acre plant collector's garden with many rare and unusual flowering shrubs and trees (the garden's primary focus), including collections of magnolias, cercis, styrax, and dogwoods. There are also Japanese maples, fruit trees, and perennial borders in both sun and shade. One-third of the garden is a shady wood-land and bog area with paths and elevated walks. Garden gates and paths lead the visitor into the next, unseen part of the garden.

Saturday, June 10, 10 a.m. - 4 p.m.

From the Palisades Interstate Parkway take Exit 1/Englewood Cliffs. Circle under the highway and continue straight to first traffic light. Turn right onto Route 9W North. Travel north on Route 9W to the fourth traffic light (approximately 1.6 miles) to East Clinton Avenue. Turn left onto East Clinton and travel 1 short block and take the next left onto Essex Drive. Go to the second house on the right, 133 Essex Drive. From the Tappan Zee Bridge take first exit on the right after crossing bridge onto Route 9W South. Follow Route 9W into New Jersey and turn right at East Clinton Avenue. Follow directions above. From Route I-95/I-80 East (local lanes) exit at Broad Avenue/Englewood. Follow Broad Avenue north until it ends at a traffic light at Palisades Avenue. Turn right onto Palisades Avenue and travel 1-2 miles to second traffic light at Route 9W. Follow directions above. Please park on the street.

Proceeds shared with Trout Unlimited.

RIVERWOOD CORNERS

WILDWOOD AVENUE, BEDMINSTER

Year-round interest is found in this space-limited garden. The four separate planting areas also incorporate pea-stone paths, brick terraces, trellis work, arbors, container gardens, and antique garden furniture.

Saturdays; May 13, June 10; 10 a.m. - 2 p.m.

Take I-287 to Exit 22 (or 22B from I-287 South). Follow 206N to the third traffic light. Turn right onto Lamington Road. Go to the next traffic light. Turn left onto Hillside Avenue. Turn right onto the second street, Wildwood Avenue. The entrance to the garden is on the left beyond the fence. Please park along the street.

TALL TREES — GARDEN OF JANET SCHULZ

16 COLONIAL ROAD, WYCKOFF

My creation, Tall Trees, is a wonderful woodland garden featuring shade-loving perennials, bulbs, vines, and shrubs. There is an extensive collection of hosta as well as trough gardens, homemade arbors, and garden statuary. Places to sit have been created so that the many garden features can be enjoyed from many areas. Almost all of the plants are labeled. Many of the clematis are growing in other shrubs which produces an elongated season of interest in plants that would have bloomed at another time. An avid plant collector, I am always searching for, and trying to find, plants that may do well in my garden. Plants must be strong to succeed here at Tall Trees, for I do not believe in growing plants that require a lot of spraying or stalking.

Saturdays; May 13, June 10; 10 a.m. - 4 p.m.

Take the George Washington Bridge to Route 4 West to Route 208 North/Oakland, approximately 7.5 miles to Ewing Avenue. Go down ramp and turn right onto Ewing Avenue. Go to traffic light and turn right onto Franklin Avenue. *Go through 2 traffic lights to first street on the right, Godwin Drive, and turn right. The first left is Colonial Drive. The garden is at #16 on the right. From Route 287 take Route 208 South. Exit onto Ewing Avenue. Turn left at the stop sign and go to traffic light. Turn right onto Franklin Avenue. *Proceed as above.

THE HANDLEY GARDEN

342 FRANKLIN TURNPIKE, RIDGEWOOD

John and Sue Handley's garden is set on a one-acre property. The front foundation planting is a mixed border of ornamental trees, shrubs, and flowers and prepares you only somewhat for the beauty of the garden behind the house. A water-and-rock garden is beside the deck. Sunny perennial borders punctuated by garden ornaments extend the length of the path that draws you to the open lawn. Sue Handley has planted a great variety of wonderful plants, some of which may be new to you.

Saturday, June 10, 10 a.m. - 4 p.m.

From Route 17 South, proceed past Ramsey, Allendale, and Waldwick to the right turn at Hohokus/Racetrack Road Exit. Proceed west for 3 blocks and turn left onto Nagel. Proceed to the Franklin Turnpike and turn right. The garden is on the left. From Route 17 North, go approximately 4 miles from Route 4 to the Linwood Avenue overpass. Go under the overpass and turn right. Continue to the second traffic light at Pleasant Avenue and turn right. Follow Pleasant Avenue to the end and turn right onto Glen Avenue. Pass the cemetery on the left to a hairpin turn at the beginning of Franklin Turnpike. The Handley Garden is approximately .75 mile on Franklin Turnpike, on the left. Park on the front lawn.

WATNONG GARDENS

2379 WATNONG TERRACE, MORRIS PLAINS

Watnong Gardens is the former Watnong Nursery made famous by Don and Hazel Smith. The garden now consists of two and one-half acres of collections, including conifers, shrubs, hostas, ferns, perennials, and a water garden. Special plants are added each year. A train, complete with four railroad cars, was made into six- and eight-foot-long troughs, all handcrafted by the owner and planted with mini-plants and alpines.

Saturdays; May 13, June 10; 10 a.m. - 4 p.m.

From Route 80 West, take Exit 43 to Route 287 South. Take Route 287 South to Route 10 West/Exit 39B. Go approximately 3 miles west to the third traffic light, Powdermill Road. Take "jug handle" turn and head east on Route 10. After passing Mountain Club Garden Homes go slow. Watnong Terrace angles off to the right, and parallels Route 10 like a service road. It is .7 mile from the "jug handle" turn. Please park on the street.

WINTER'S GARDEN

28 DRYDEN TERRACE, SHORT HILLS

This garden is densely packed with conifers ranging from miniature to dwarf, intermediate and full size. Ground covers, perennials, shrubs, and deciduous trees including Japanese maples are incorporated. Weathered limestone is extensively integrated throughout for contrast with plantings. The arrangements are personal choices for spiritual and aesthetic effect and include many rare specimens.

Saturdays; May 13, June 10; 10 a.m. - 4 p.m.

From Route 24 West take Exit 9/Hobart Avenue. Go to the traffic light, and turn right. Continue about 6 blocks and turn left onto Dryden Terrace. From Route 24 East take Exit 8 at Summit. Go to second traffic light, turn left onto Hobart Avenue. Go about 6 blocks to Dryden Terrace. Local: Dryden Terrace is off of White Oak Ridge Road between Parsonage Hill Road and Route 24. Please park on the street.

ACORN HALL &

68 MORRIS AVENUE, MORRISTOWN, NJ 07960. (201) 267-3465.

Acorn Hall, the headquarters of the Morris County Historical Society, is a Victorian Italianate mansion (c. 1853-1860). The gardens have been restored by the Home Garden Club of Morristown to reflect of the 1853-1888 period. Features include spring flowering trees, shrubs and bulbs; more than 30 varieties of authentic Victorian roses; an herb garden and traditional knot garden; and a fern garden.

Year round, daily, dawn - dusk.

From I-287 South, take Exit 37 / Route 24 East / Springfield to first exit (2A) and follow signs to Morristown. Follow Columbia Road to the end traffic light (in front of the Governor Morris Hotel). Make a left at the traffic light to the second driveway on your right. From I-287 North, take Exit 36A onto Morris Avenue. Take first right-hand fork onto Columbia Turnpike and make an immediate left to traffic light. Turn left to second driveway on right.

COLONIAL PARK ARBORETUM &

METTLERS ROAD, EAST MILLSTONE, NJ 08873. (732) 873-2459.

The 144-acre Arboretum contains labeled specimens of flowering trees, evergreens, shade trees, and flowering shrubs that grow well in central New Jersey, making this area a valuable source for homeowners and landscape professionals. The Perennial Garden provides year-round interest for the enjoyment of gardeners and park visitors alike. A gazebo in the center of the garden is surrounded by beds displaying a selection of flowering bulbs, perennials, annuals, and flowering trees and shrubs. The Rudolf W. van der Goot Rose Garden offers a formal display of more than 3,000 roses of 285 varieties. From late spring into autumn, this accredited All-American Rose Selections Garden features labeled specimens of a wide variety of roses. Located behind the Rose Garden is a Fragrance and Sensory Garden, a circular garden with raised beds accessible for persons with disabilities so that all our visitors can enjoy the flowers, shrubs, herbs, and scented plants that grow there.

Year round, daily, 8 a.m. - dusk. Guided tours available..

Located within Colonial Park in East Millstone, Franklin Township, NJ. From I-287 take Exit 12 at Weston Canal Road. Go south on Canal Road. Do not cross the canal, turn left before the bridge and continue along canal until the road turns left on Weston Road. Take first right onto Mettlers Road. Continue to Colonial Park. The Arboretum is on the first right. From Route 206 in Hillsborough, turn east onto County Route 514, Amwell Road. Follow Route 514 through the town of East Millstone then turn left onto Mettlers Road. Arboretum is on the first left.

Davis Johnson Park & Gardens ❧

137 ENGLE STREET, TENAFLY, NJ 07670. (201) 569-7275.

Featuring an award-winning rose garden recognized by the American Rose Society, this seven-and-one-half-acre park has many floral beds, paths and benches. Our gazebo is a favorite place for wedding ceremonies and photos. This former estate has several mature beech trees.

Year round, daily, dawn - dusk

Take Route 9W to East Clinton Avenue. Go west down hill to first traffic light (Engle Street). Turn left. Park entrance is on right, .25 miles from Clinton Avenue.

Delbarton ❧

ST. MARY'S ABBEY, DELBARTON MENDHAM ROAD, MORRISTOWN, NJ 07960. (201) 538-3231.

Delbarton, the largest estate of Morris County's Gilded Age, was the country home of Luther Kountze, international banker. Now a private boy's school run by the Benedictine Fathers of Saint Mary's Abbey, the campus occupies 340 acres of the original 4,000. A splendid Italian garden with a pergola and statuary flanks the west side of Old Main, the imposing residence built for the Kountze family. Also on the grounds is the striking Abbey Church, designed by Victor Christ-Janer and completes in 1966.

Year round, weekdays, 9 a.m. - 5 p.m.; weekends, 9 a.m. - dusk.

From I-287, take Exit 35 / Route 124 / Madison Avenue. Bear right at the end of the ramp onto Route 124 West / South Street. Proceed straight to the Morristown Green. Follow signs for 510 West / Washington Street. This becomes Route 24 / Mendham Road. Delbarton is on the left, 2.5 miles from the Morristown Center.

Devereux Deerhaven ❧

PO BOX 520, CHESTER, NJ 07930. (908) 879-4500.

Devereux Deerhaven, a rural residential treatment center for adolescent girls with emotional disorders, was once Elizabeth and Alfred Kay's estate, "Hidden River Farm." The original 1920s design was inspired by Lutyens, Jekyll, and the Cotswolds cottages. Original fieldstone walls, terraces, fountains, pools, a pergola, and a moongate are largely intact. The garden was replanted and is cared for by students in the landscape and horticulture program. Visitors will see our large collections of shrub roses around an antique garden of lotus and water lilies. There are two cottage gardens filled with late-spring-blooming perennials near a stream with naturalized plantings. The greenhouse is filled with plants, and a selection will be for sale.

Garden Design magazine recognized our program with a Golden Trowel Award for the "Best Healing Garden" in 1995-1996.

Open for Open Days visitors on June 10, 10 a.m. - 3 p.m.

Pottersville Road is just off of Route 206, south of the intersection of Route 206 & 24 in Chester, New Jersey.

DURAND HEDDEN HOUSE & GARDEN ⚘

523 RIDGEWOOD ROAD, MAPLEWOOD, NJ 07040. (973)763-7712.

The house is being restores to reflect the continuum of its life as a farmhouse and residence from the late eighteenth through the mid-twentieth centuries. The Durand-Hedden House sits on two picturesque acres that include a sloping meadow edged by trees, shrubs, and annuals, and perennial beds. The centerpiece is the award-winning educational herb garden maintained by the Maplewood Garden Club. It boasts one of the largest herb collections in the Northeast, with many species and cultivated varieties of thyme, sage, lavender, and mint.

Year round, daily, dawn - dusk.

From Route 78 and 24, take Exit 50B/Millburn/Maplewood. At the top of the ramp, turn right onto Vauxhall Road. Continue to the intersection of Millburn Avenue at the third light. Cross Millburn Avenue onto Ridgewood Road. Go 1 mile, past the blinking light. The house is the first on the left after Durand House and opposite Jefferson School. Please park on the street.

FRELINGHUYSEN ARBORETUM ⚘

53 EAST HANOVER AVENUE, MORRIS TOWNSHIP, NJ 07960-1295. (973) 326-7600.

The 127-acre Frelinghuysen Arboretum in Morris Township displays a wide range of native and exotic plants in home demonstration gardens of perennials, annuals, plants for shade, ferns, vegetable and roses. Collections include peonies, dogwoods, crab apples, cherries, and a pinetum. Interpretive materials are available in the Education Center.

Year round, daily, 8 a.m. - dusk . Closed Thanksgiving, Christmas, and New Year's Day.

From I-287 North, take Exit 36A. Proceed to Whippany Road. At second traffic light turn left onto East Hanover Avenue. Entrance is on left. From I-287 South, take Exit 36. Make right onto Ridgedale Avenue. Make right at first traffic light onto East Hanover Avenue. Entrance is on the left.

HISTORIC MORVEN ❧

55 STOCKTON STREET, PRINCETON, NJ 08540. (609) 683-4495.

Home to a signer of the Declaration of Independence and many of New Jersey's governors, the Morven landscape is a composite of 200 years of American history. Set amidst stately lawns and trees in downtown Princeton, a colonial revival garden is the focus of current preservation efforts.

Call for information about tours and open hours.

⚜ *A preservation project of The Garden Conservancy.*

LEONARD J. BUCK GARDEN ❧

11 LAYTON ROAD, FAR HILLS, NJ 07931. (908) 234-2677.

The Leonard J. Buck Garden is a nationally known rock garden, developed by its namesake in the 1930s. Designed to be ecologically correct and visually appealing, the garden is as pleasant to walk through as it is to sit in. Buck Garden lies in a woodland stream valley where natural rock outcroppings have been uncovered, providing visual interest as well as planting niches. There are extensive collections of pink and white dogwoods, azaleas, rhododendrons, wildflowers, ferns, alpines, and rock-loving plants. The many outcroppings provide different microclimates and exposures, making this a year-round garden. The Garden was presented to the Somerset County Park Commission in 1976.

Monday - Friday, 10 a.m.-4 p.m. Saturday 10 a.m.-5 p.m. Closed weekends and major holidays in December through February.

From I-287, take Exit 22. If approaching from the south the exit is marked 228. If approaching from the north, the exit is marked 22. From exit ramp, take Route 202 / 206 North, staying right to continue north on 202. Follow signs to Far Hills and Morristown. At Far Hills train station, turn right before the tracks onto Liberty Corner—Far Hills Road. Travel .9 mile to Layton Road, turn right. Garden is on left side.

MINDOWASKIN PARK ❧

425 EAST BROAD STREET, WESTFIELD, NJ 07090. (908) 233-8110.

Mindowaskin Park, in the heart of Westfield, was named for a Lenai-Lenape Indian Chief and was established in 1918. In 1994, concerned citizens, The Friends of Mindowaskin Park, raised money to improve the facilities and continue its care. Individuals, corporations, and foundations contributed toward the new Victorian iron lamps, iron & mahogany benches, new signage, and various gardens planted with shrubbery, trees, perennials, and annuals. A large lake, fountains, waterways, winding paths, hardwood trees, a bird sanctuary, new playground equipment, flowering gardens, and a large gazebo offer opportunities for walking and watching, ice skating, model boat sailing, performances, art shows, picnics, and relaxation.

Year round, daily, 7 a.m. - 10 p.m.

From the Garden State Parkway, take Exit 137 and head toward Westfield on North Avenue. After 3.1 miles, turn right on Elmer Street and right again onto East Broad Street. Mindowaskin Park is within one block on the left.

Moggy Hollow National Landmark &

Upper Raritan Watershed Association, Larger Cross Road, Box 273, Gladstone, NJ 07934. (908) 234-1852.

Moggy Hollow was once the outlet of the ancient Lake Passaic before the last glacier receded. Of interest to visitors are the rock outcroppings that formed a spillway for the outflow. The swamp below and the concentric rings of vegetation around the quaking bog are of special interest.

Year round, daily, dawn - dusk

Moggy Hollow is located next to the Leonard J. Buck Garden, listed above. Please see the Buck listing for directions.

New Jersey State Botanical Garden at Skyland &

P.O. Box 302, Ringwood, NJ 07456. (973) 962-9534. INFO@NJBG.ORG.

Skylands is a ninety-six-acre Historical Landmark Garden, surrounded by 4,084 acres of woodland with hiking and biking trails. The garden includes a forty-four-room Tudor manor house, generally open on the first Sunday of the month; arboretum, formal gardens, lilac garden, crabapple allée, water gardens, statuary, wildflower area, rhododendron garden and heath and heather garden.

Year round, daily, 8 a.m. - 8 p.m.

Via #208 and Skyline Drive: Turn right at end of Skyline Drive onto #511. Take the second right onto Sloatsburg Road. Pass Hewill School and Carletondale Road. Turn right onto Morris Road; Skylands is 1.5 miles up Morris road. Via I-287 north or south: At Exit 57, follow the signs to Skyline Drive and proceed as above. Via N.Y. Thruway (I-87/287) & Route 17: NY Thruway to Exit 15-A/Route 17; Route 17 to Route 72 West, which becomes Sloatsburgh Road in New Jersey. Take Sloatsburgh Road past Ringwood Manor; Morris Road is on the left, and proceed as above.

OAKESIDE — BLOOMFIELD CULTURAL CENTER &

240 BELLEVILLE AVENUE, BLOOMFIELD, NJ 07003. (973) 429-0960.

A three-acre garden near the center of the Township of Bloomfield, Oakeside is on the state and national registers of historic places. The grounds are currently undergoing restoration with assistance from the New Jersey Historic Trust. The Colonial Revival-style mansion was built in 1895. A formal rose garden (1913) and large kitchen garden (1922) were designed by Vitale, Brinckerhoff and Geiffert. A naturalistic water garden and terrace garden near the solarium date from approximately 1929.

Year round, daily, dawn - dusk. Groups by appointment.

From the Garden State Parkway South take Exit 148. Stay straight on J.F. Kennedy Drive to end, then turn left and a quick right back onto JFK Drive. At first traffic light, turn right onto Belleville Avenue. Take the second entrance on the right for parking. From GSP North, take Exit 149. Turn right off the ramp onto JFK Drive. Follow as above.

REEVES-REED ARBORETUM &

165 HOBART AVENUE, SUMMIT, NJ 07901. (908) 273-8787.

A twelve and one-half-acre former country estate, the Reeves-Reed is a national and state historic site and nature conservancy with a focus on horticultural and environmental education for children and adults. It features the newly restored historic 1889 Wisner House. There are azalea, rose, rock, and herb gardens. Thousands of April daffodils are widely naturalized. A double perennial border flowers April through October. Naturalistic areas, a pond, and a glacial kettle provide wildlife habitat.

Year round, daily, dawn - dusk.

From the New Jersey Turnpike, take Exit 14 / Newark Airport onto I-78 West. After several miles on I-78 West, take Exit 48 / Springfield / Millburn onto Highway 24 West. Take the Hobart Avenue exit off Route 24 (Route 124 runs parallel). Go left over the highway and continue straight past the traffic light. Up the hill on the left will be signs for "Reeves-Reed Arboretum."

THE EMILIE K. HAMMOND WILDFLOWER TRAIL &

MCCAFFREY LANE, BOONTON, NJ 07962-1295. (973) 326-7600.

The Dutch word tourne, meaning "lookout" or "mountain," aptly describes this 463-acre park of hilly terrain and huge granite boulders. Several mountain trails wind their way through a forest of white oaks, maples, beeches, and hemlocks. A series of niches provides specific microclimates suitable for a wide variety of plantlife. There are low, boggy spots and drier upland areas, moist slopes in sun and others in heavy shade, and a fast-flowing brook. Suitable habitats have been found for more than 250 different wildflowers and shrubs native to the eastern United States.

Year round, daily, 8 a.m. - dusk

From Route 80 West, take Route 46 / Denville Exit. Take Route 46 East to Mountain Lakes Exit. Turn left onto the Boulevard. Bear left onto Powerville Road. Take first left, McCaffrey Lane.

THE JAMES ROSE CENTER ❧

506 EAST RIDGEWOOD AVENUE, RIDGEWOOD, NJ 07450. (201) 444-2559.

James Rose (1913-1991) was one of the pioneers of bringing modern design principals to landscape architecture in the 1930s. Built in 1953, his house and garden were designed to change over time and now reflect more than forty years of evolution at the hands of this creative genius. Stabilization of the house and garden has begun with the help of the Garden Conservancy. The property is a unique environment of interwoven garden spaces formed by structure, plants, and water that create a strong fusion between house and garden. In the garden there are scrap metal sculptures and reflecting pools on a floor of fractured bluestone that can only be seen after one has entered the confines of the compound, which seems a world apart from the surrounding suburban landscape.

From New York City take the George Washington Bridge to Route 4 West to Route 17 North. Take 17N to Ridgewood Avenue/Ridgewood Exit. Follow East Ridgewood Avenue towards Ridgewood. House is on the corner of East Ridgewood Avenue Southern Parkway.

❖ *A preservation project of The Garden Conservancy.*

THE PRESBY MEMORIAL IRIS GARDEN ❧

474 UPPER MOUNTAIN AVENUE, UPPER MONTCLAIR, NJ 07043. (973) 783-5974.

The Presby Memorial Iris Gardens is the world's largest display garden of irises with over 200,000 blooms at peak. The collection of over 4,000 varieties in twenty-nine beds, mostly tall beardeds, also contains miniature dwarf beardeds, Louisianas, Siberians, Japanese, remontants, and historic irises. A display bed demonstrates the varied landscapes in which irises can grow. Dwarf varieties bloom earlier and some species, such as Japanese and Siberian, bloom through June. Remontants bloom late August through October. The Gardens adjoin the Victorian Walther House property, Presby headquarters, and its beautiful surrounding gardens, also open to the public. A small sales area offers iris motif and garden items and rhizomes during the Bloom Season. Free Admission. Group tours are available for a nominal charge.

Tall bearded display: May 18 - June 4, dawn - dusk.

Upper Mountain Avenue is bounded by Route 46 on the north, Route 23 to the west, Bloomfield Avenue, Montclair, on the south and is easily reached from Routes 3, 80, 280, 287, and the Garden State Parkway.

The Upper Raritan
Watershed Association &

2121 LARGER CROSS ROAD, BEDMINSTER, NJ 07934. (908) 234-1852.

The Upper Raritan Watershed Association has established a garden on Fairview Farm Wildlife Preserve to promote the conservation of birds and butterflies, to provide environmental and horticultural education and to foster an appreciation of nature. The garden offers food, water, protective cover and a sheltered place for reproduction. A project goal is for visitors and participants to be inspired to add specific plants to their own backyard, creating a habitat for songbirds, humming-birds, and butterflies.

Year round, daily, dusk - dawn

From Rt. 287 take the Bedminster exit to Routes 202 & 206 North. After the first light, bear left to stay on 206 north toward Chester/Netcong. Go through three lights and at the fourth light, turn left onto Pottersville Road. Go .8 mile and turn left onto Larger Cross Road. Go .5 mile to URWA's stone pillars on the right.

Van Vleck House & Garden &

21 VAN VLECK STREET, MONTCLAIR, NJ 07042. (973) 744-4752.

Begun at the turn of the century, these gardens have been developed by several generations of a family of committed horticulturists. The plan is largely formal, responding to the Mediterranean style of the house. The extensive collection of rhododendrons and azaleas, including several named for family members, is re-nowned. Also of note are the many mature plant specimens.

May - October, daily, 1 p.m. - 5 p.m.

From the Garden State Parkway North, Exit 148 Bloomfield Avenue. Stay in left lane of exit ramp through the first traffic light, take jug-handle under Garden State Parkway back to Bloomfield Avenue and turn right (west) at traffic light. Proceed on Bloomfield Avenue for 2.5 miles through Bloomfield, Glen Ridge, and Montclair town centers. Turn right at North Mountain Avenue. (Montclair Art Museum on left). Proceed through 1 traffic light (Claremont Avenue) and take the next left onto Van Vleck Street - Van Vleck House & Gardens is on the left.

🌿 *A preservation project of The Garden Conservancy.*

NEW YORK

Lake
Champlain
Area

Saratoga Springs ★

★ Cambridge

★ Albany

Southeastern
New York &
Connecticut

Long Island
(North Shore)

Eastern
Long Island

NEW YORK OPEN DAYS

April 29, June 17, July 15, & September 16: Eastern Long Island
May 7, 21 & 28, June 4 & 25, July 9 & 23
September 10 & 24, October 15: New York & Connecticut
May 7, May 21, June 4, June 25, July 9, July 23,
September 10, & September 24: North Shore of Long Island
June 17: Saratoga Springs
June 18: Albany
July 9: Cambridge
July 15: Lake Champlain

Albany Open Day

Mrs. James H. Lenden & Mrs. Henry Ferguson

Sunday, June 18

FEURA BUSH
Carl & Nancy Touhey, Onesthequaw Creek Road: 10 a.m. - 4 p.m.

LOUDONVILLE
. Bella's Garden, 16 Chestnut Hill Road: 10 a.m. - 4 p.m.
Denise & Tony Gorman, 5 Loudon Heights: 10 a.m. - 2 p.m.
Fred Miller, 5 Chestnut Hill South: 10 a.m. - 4 p.m.
Joan & Henry Ferguson, 5 Chestnut Hill North: 10 a.m. - 4 p.m.

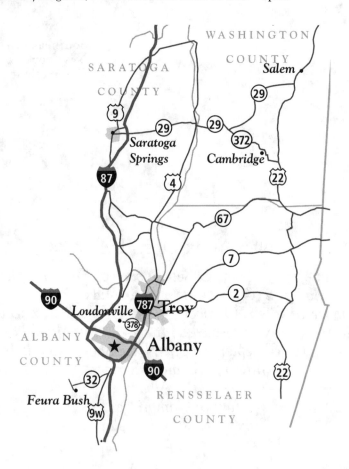

BELLA'S GARDEN

16 CHESTNUT HILL ROAD, LOUDONVILLE

A shaded pathway ruffled by an assortment of perennials leads you to a gathering of rose bushes and an intimate rose court ruled by a lovely maiden. A garden "Welcome" beckons you through the arbor to the main garden that winds all around the property. There is a "secret garden room" along the way, lovingly enclosed in the boughs of old hemlocks. A small pond keeps company with iris, daylilies, cleomes, roses, herbs, ornamental grasses and whatever happens to grow there. Another expanse of garden awaits you on the other side where a wonderful raspberry patch shares space with a vegetable, herb and cutting garden. Hummingbirds took up residence over the summer to feast on the abundant Monarda and the Asiatic lilies that grew to eight feet. The garden, which I started five years ago, is a labor of love, abounding with happy birds and butterflies. This is a happy garden because it is cultivated with love and concern for its inhabitants.

Sunday, June 18, 10 a.m. - 4 p.m.

From I-90, take Route 9 North 2 miles to Chestnut Hill Road, the second left after the first traffic light. At the top of a short hill, bear left. Look for 16 Chestnut Hill South, a taupe colored ranch, a short way down on the left immediately past a row of hedges. Please do not block driveway; park along the street. The area is a big rectangle and you can drive right around and back out to Route 9. From Route 87 North take Exit 5/ Latham/Route 155. Turn left at the traffic light and take the first right onto Old Niskayuna Road. At the second light, a few miles down, go straight across (one block) and merge right onto Route 9/Loudon Road and proceed 2 blocks to Chestnut Hill Road. (See above)

CARL & NANCY TOUHEY

ONESTHEQUAW CREEK ROAD, FEURA BUSH

Our home, built in 1754 by Steven Van Rensselaer, an early Dutch Patroon, is situated in the picturesque valley of the Helderberg Mountains, and bordered by the ever-flowing Onesquethaw Creek. Our 150 acres are steeped in Indian and early-American history. The landscaping is a reflection of the natural flowing and meandering contours of the valley. The gardens and grounds are designed for all seasons. The vistas are a symphony of natural rock and boulders sheltering intimate garden beds, covered in ivy and cantilevered over shaded gardens. The rocks and boulders are also the focal point of the pool area, creating more a pond effect than a pool. We moved an original eighteenth-century Dutch barn to our property.

Sunday, June 18, 10 a.m.- 4 p.m.

Take Route 787 south to its end. Turn right on Route 9W and go 5 miles. Take Route 32 south to Delmar, veering to the right. Continue on Route 32 for 3 miles, making a sharp left at the third traffic light, which is still Route 32. Follow this through Feura Bush to Onesquethaw Creek Road. One mile from the bridge, Onesquethaw Creek Road veers to the left immediately after sign on the left reading "New Scotland Beagle Club." From the start of this road to our house is .7 miles. It is on the left after crossing the bridge. Follow parking signs.

Proceeds shared with The Fort Orange Garden Club

DENISE & TONY GORMAN

5 LOUDON HEIGHTS, LOUDONVILLE

This garden is my interpretation of a casual English garden of the nineteenth-century. You enter through a brick arched garden wall to a stoned paved courtyard surrounded by old a new plantings. With the use of a slate pathway you walk from one garden to another. Color is important to me in making the eye comfortable with the use of color, texture and pattern. Some of my special plantings include my yellow princess rose for which I won first prize in the Fort Orange Garden Club flower show. My special interest has always been floral arranging which I have incorporated into my permanent gardens. I hope you will enjoy my efforts.

Sunday, June 18, 10 a.m. - 2 p.m.

Take Thruway to Exit 23. Take 787 North to I-90 West. Get off the first exit, Route 9 North to Loudonville. Turn left onto Loudon Heights south. Bear to the right, go up a small hill and bear to the left. The Gorman house is the second driveway to the left. Please park in back of house, also front of house

Fred Miller

5 CHESTNUT HILL SOUTH, LOUDONVILLE

This small garden "small" is a work-in-progress inspired by the nearby Japanese gardens of Joan and Henry Ferguson (and their enthusiasm), lots of photographs of faraway gardens, and the owner's visits to Japanese and Chinese gardens in the United States and Canada. This landscaping project began in 1998 with the reclamation of an overgrown corner yard. The goal is nothing fancy; just a private outdoor space with an oriental focus in which to capture the dancing of light and air on things green and vulnerable, morning and afternoon, in all seasons.

Sunday, June 18, 10 a.m. - 4 p.m.

From I-90 take Route 9 north 2 miles to Chestnut Hill Road, the second left after the first traffic light. At the top of a short hill, bear left and park on the street. This garden is located at the rear of the house at 5 Chestnut Hill South, a short stroll from the Ferguson garden at 5 Chestnut Hill North.

Joan & Henry Ferguson

5 CHESTNUT HILL NORTH, LOUDONVILLE

Intrigued by Japanese gardens, we have researched, designed, and built entirely by ourselves three separate, visually spacious gardens filling our residential lot of less than half an acre. Each is carefully reflective of Japanese garden tradition in form, philosophy, and the aesthetic principles of antiquity, mystery, and surprise. To step into these gardens to find oneself is the philosophical purpose of this purely American creation. As in Japan, these gardens are for all seasons-winter included. Thus, forms, textures and colors of foliage are more important than blossom.

Sunday, June 18, 10 a.m. - 4 p.m.

From I-90, take Route 9 north 2 miles to Chestnut Hill Road, the second left after the first traffic light. At the top of a short hill, bear right and park on the street before reaching the "Dead End" sign. Please do not enter or block the driveway. Gardens begin at the head of the driveway to the right of the "Dead End" sign. Do not go beyond the sign.

George Landis Arboretum &

P.O. Box 186, Esperance, NY 12066-0186. (518) 875-6935.

The George Landis Arboretum is a ninety-seven-acre public garden, arboretum and woodland located about twenty-five miles west of Albany, NY. Included are beech, oak, maple, and crab apple collections, as well as a significant lilac collection. The Arboretum also includes the Van Loveland perennial Garden, a large terraced collection of three-season bulbs and perennials. Trails traverse the Arboretum collections and the native woodland. The George Landis Arboretum is a naturalistic garden in a rural setting, on the site of founder Fred Lape's family farm.

Year round, daily, dawn -dusk

West from Albany, NY on Highway 20 to the village of Esperance. The Arboretum is located about 1 mile outside the village, and the route is well marked. From the New York State Thruway, south on Route 30 to Route 20, and then west on Route 20.

Pruyn House &

P.O. Box 212, Newtonville, NY 12128. (518) 783-1435.

Centrally placed between the 1830 Federal/Greek revival-style Pruyn House, the 1850 Buhrmaster Barn, and the 1910 Verdoy Schoolhouse are lovely and complementary gardens designed and maintained by two garden clubs. There is a traditional herb garden appropriate to the nineteenth century. The other garden includes perennials and annuals, providing cut flowers for the house and demonstrating plant material that thrives in sandy soil and the severe winters of upstate New York.

Year round, daily, dawn - dusk.

From I-90 take Exit 24 to I-87 North. Take Exit 5 and turn right at the traffic light to Route 155. Take the second left, Old Niskayuna Road, before the bridges. Proceed 1 mile; the Pruyn House complex in on the left.

Cambridge Open Day

Regional Representative Mrs. James H. Lenden & Mrs. Henry Ferguson

Saturday, July 8

CAMBRIDGE
Garden of Paul & Dot Schneider, 122 Main Street: 10 a.m. - 4 p.m.

GRANVILLE
Mary Obering, 7148 State Route 22: 10 a.m. - 4 p.m.

SALEM
Garland Garden, 42 Blind Buck Road: 10 a.m. - 4 p.m.

GARDEN OF PAUL & DOT SCHNEIDER

122 MAIN STREET, CAMBRIDGE

Over the past ten years, we have built a collector's garden featuring nearly 1,000 different species, including bamboo, ornamental grasses, sedges, willows, alliums, dwarf conifers, Asian native trees and shrubs. Located on a village lot (eighty-five feet x 350 feet) our collection is set up as a stroll garden with paths, native stone, sculpture, meditation hut, and water features. Many tropical plants are wintered over in a solar greenhouse for summer use as accent plants. Our aim has been to show people how much garden can be developed in a relatively small space.

Saturday, July 8, 10 a.m. - 4 p.m.

From the intersection of Route 22 and Route 372 travel west on Route 372/Main Street for .75 mile to the sign for the hospital. Turn left onto Myrtle Avenue and park on the right side of the street. Walk back across Main Street to 122 West Main Street.

Garland Garden

This informal, highly idiosyncratic garden is in a country setting along a busy stream. The terraces and grounds are defined by extensive stone walls and beds of hardy perennials, both native and cultivated, supplemented by annuals. The large vegetable garden is contained primarily in twelve raised beds. The focus of the grounds is the rock garden, which includes more than thirty miniature and dwarf evergreens, more than forty varieties of hosta, various ferns, small shrubs, perennials, ground covers, and a spring-fed pond in an exuberant mix.

Saturday, July 8, 10 a.m. - 4 p.m.

From Route 22 North, turn right at the traffic light onto Route 153/East Broadway. Continue to the first paved road on the right beyond the school and courthouse. Turn right onto Blind Buck Road and go to #42, a converted barn, well hidden behind evergreens. Please park in the field above the house.

Mary Obering

7148 State Route 22, Granville

My garden is a traditional American garden, somewhat related to English designs of both cottage gardens and those with a more formal layout. I am neither a landscape architect nor a horticulturist. I am a painter; in my mind I am dealing primarily with shapes and colors. I use both perennials and annuals, whatever works best to create the "picture" I imagine. I also like to think of the garden as a series of rooms or areas, with places to sit, relax, and experience views from differing vantage points.

Saturday, July 8, 10 a.m. - 4 p.m.

Located on Route 22, this garden is 6.7 miles south of Granville; 1.2 miles south of Saw Mill Road, which is on the east side of Route 22, and 9.9 miles north of the traffic light in Salem, New York. Please park on the front lawn.

Eastern Long Island Open Days

Regional Representative: Lalitte Scott

Saturday, April 29

AMAGANSETT
Cobb & Stanwell Garden, 239 Old Stone Highway: 2 p.m. - 6 p.m.

CUTCHOGUE
Manfred & Roberta Lee, 26850 Main Road: 10 a.m. - 4 p.m.

EAST HAMPTON
Dianne Benson's Garden, 6 Baiting Hollow Road: 2 p.m. - 6 p.m.
Margaret Kerr & Robert Richenburg, 1006 Springs Fireplace Road: 10 a.m. - 4 p.m.
Mrs. Donald Bruckmann, 105 Ocean Avenue: 10 a.m. - 2 p.m.

Saturday, June 17

CUTCHOGUE
Alice & Charles Levien's Garden, Antler Lane: 10 a.m. - 2 p.m.
Manfred & Roberta Lee, 26850 Main Road: 10 a.m. - 4 p.m.

EAST HAMPTON
Carol Mercer, 33 Ocean Avenue: 10 a.m. - 4 p.m.
Cobb & Stanwell Garden, 239 Old Stone Highway: 2 p.m. - 6 p.m.
Dianne Benson's Garden, 6 Baiting Hollow Road: 2 p.m. - 6 p.m.
Margaret Kerr & Robert Richenburg, 1006 Springs Fireplace Road: 10 a.m. - 4 p.m.

MONTAUK
Richard Kahn & Elaine Peterson, 224 West Lake Drive: 2 p.m. - 6 p.m.

SOUTHAMPTON
Joy Cordery, 14 Atterbury Road: 10 a.m. - 4 p.m.
Ron Peterson, 699 Hill Street: 10 a.m. - 2 p.m.

SOUTHOLD
Milford Garden, 1200 Bay View Road: 10 a.m. - 2 p.m.

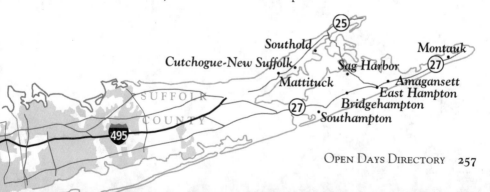

Saturday, July 15

BRIDGEHAMPTON
Villa des Amis-Larry, Jody, Catherine, Christopher, & Spencer Carlson, Scuttlehole Road: 10 a.m. - 4 p.m.

CUTCHOGUE
Alice & Charles Levien's Garden, Antler Lane: 10 a.m. - 2 p.m.

EAST HAMPTON
Bob & Mimi Schwarz, 8 Lilla Lane: 10 a.m. - 2 p.m.
Dianne Benson's Garden, 6 Baiting Hollow Road: 2 p.m. - 6 p.m.
Ina Garten, 46 Newtown Lane: 10 a.m. - 2 p.m.

MATTITUCK
Maurice Isaac & Ellen Coster Isaac, 4835 Oregon Road: 10 a.m. - 2 p.m.
Dennis Schrader & Bill Smith, 1200 East Mill Road: 10 a.m. - 4 p.m.

SAGAPONACK
Susan & Louis Meisel, 81 Wilkes Lane: 10 a.m. - 2 p.m.

SAG HARBOR
Lois Beachy Underhill, 68 Bay Street: 2 p.m. - 6 p.m.
Mac Keith Griswold, 57 Howard Street: 2 p.m. - 6 p.m.

SOUTHAMPTON
Dr. & Mrs. William L. Donnelly, 156 Meadowmere Lane: 10 a.m. - 4 p.m.

Saturday, September 16

BRIDGEHAMPTON
Mr. & Mrs. Dinwiddie Smith, 158 Quimby Lane: 10 a.m. - 2 p.m.

MATTITUCK
Dennis Schrader & Bill Smith, 1200 East Mill Road: 10 a.m. - 4 p.m.

Alice & Charles Levien's Garden

ANTLER LANE, CUTCHOGUE

This garden is designed for living-children, grandchildren, guests, frequent outdoor parties. A two-acre mixed border and woodland garden has been planted to provide year-round privacy, continuous blooms in season, many-faceted views, and tranquility during winter. Multilevel decks with a variety of container plantings serve the main house, guesthouses, elevated gazebo and pool, and children's playhouse. Occasional salt water flooding from Peconic Bay Creek made the swimming pool, fish pond, lotus pond, and lawn areas a creative challenge for the designer, Alice Levien.

Saturdays; June 17, July 15; 10 a.m. - 2 p.m.

Traveling east on Route 25, turn right at the second traffic light in Cutchogue onto Eugene's Road. Turn right at Beebe Road. Bear right at the fork in the road, Antler Lane is the first street on the right. Look for a hemlock hedge. Please park along the road.

Proceeds shared with The Horticultural Alliance of the Hamptons

Bob & Mimi Schwarz

8 LILLA LANE, EAST HAMPTON

An explosion of color! The rainbow daylily garden is a sight to see in mid-July. More than 600 named varieties of daylilies are grown in undulating herbaceous borders, backed by cedars, hemlocks and masses of rhododendrons. More than 5,000 of our own seedlings bloom in the seedling patch. There is also an ornamental grass garden with clumps of miscanthus, panicum and other grasses. The entire garden has inviting benches and shade.

Saturday, July 15, 10 a.m. - 2 p.m.

From Montauk Highway/Route 27, go to East Hampton. Pass the movie theater and continue to the traffic light. Turn left after the traffic light, going under the railroad bridge, leaving windmill on right. Continue .5 mile, bearing right at fork, onto Springs/County Road 41. Go 3 miles and turn right on Hildreth Place. At end, turn left onto Accabonac. Go .25 mile and turn right onto Lilla Lane. The house (#8) is 200 yards down on the right. Please park on street.

CAROL MERCER

33 OCEAN AVENUE, EAST HAMPTON

An undeniable partnering of pattern, movement and color makes this garden seem to glow and come alive. Mercer and her partner, Lisa Verderosa, have a thriving garden design business called The Secret Garden, and they have received several gold medals at New York City flower shows. The garden was a cover story in *Garden Design* magazine. It appeared in *House Beautiful* magazine, *Design Times* magazine, Time/Life book series' *Beds and Borders, Gardening Weekends and Shade Gardening*, as well as *Martha Stewart Living, The Natural Shade Garden*, and *Seaside Gardening*. It was also featured in *Newsday* 1999, and *Victoria* magazine, Spring 2000.

Saturday, June 17, 10 a.m. - 4 p.m.

From Montauk Highway/Route 27, follow east through Water Mill, Bridgehampton, and Wainscott to East Hampton. At traffic light at head of pond, turn right onto Ocean Avenue. The house, #33, is fourth on the left. The white stone driveway is marked by a small gray sign. Please park as directed.

Proceeds shared with The East End Hospice.

COBB & STANWELL GARDEN

239 OLD STONE HIGHWAY, AMAGANSETT

This informal cottage garden's landscaping has occurred by chance and whim. In the spring all of the flowerbeds are filled with tulips and a few choice daffodils which give way to perennials such as you might see in an English cottage garden, with an assortment of annuals. The driveway and the woods are scattered with countless varieties of daffodils. The graves of our pets are planted as little individual gardens.

Saturdays; April 29, June 17; 2 p.m. - 6 p.m.

From Montauk Highway/Route 27, go east through the village of Amagansett, past the firehouse on left. The Amagansett railroad station will appear on the left, and a railroad crossing sign ahead. Bear left at the sign, cross the tracks and turn left immediately onto Old Stone Highway. The golf course is on the right. Proceed 1.5 miles from the railroad crossing, then at the fork, keep left. Pass St. Peter's Chapel on the right, and after 1 mile there is another fork with a sign that reads "Louse Point Road." Keep left on the Old Stone Highway for .4 mile. Number 239 will be on the right just after a stockade fence and driveway. Number 239 is displayed on a big wooden gate. The house is 2.8 miles from the railroad crossing. Please park on Old Stone Highway outside of the gate.

Proceeds shared with The Horticultural Alliance of the Hamptons.

Dennis Schrader & Bill Smith

1200 EAST MILL ROAD, MATTITUCK

Set in the heart of the North Fork wineries, the two-plus acre garden surrounds a restored 1850 farmhouse. The gardens are encircled by fourteen acres of fields. There are perennial borders, ponds, a rustic arbor, a hosta collection, and many groupings of container plantings. We make extensive use of annuals, tender perennials, and tropicals in our landscape.

Saturdays; July 15, September 16; 10 a.m. - 4 p.m.

Take the Long Island Expressway to the last exit, Exit 73 for Route 58. Take Route 58 to Route 25. Go through the town of Mattituck past Love Lane to Wickham Avenue. Turn left onto Wickham, go past the train tracks and traffic light. Stay straight on Wickham and it will turn into Grand Avenue. Take Grand Avenue about .25 mile to East Mill. Turn left onto East Mill and look for #1200. Please park along the street.

Proceeds shared with The Horticultural Alliance of the Hamptons.

Dianne Benson's Garden

6 BAITING HOLLOW ROAD, EAST HAMPTON

There are no annuals, no vegetables, and no bedding plants here. This very personal garden is a melange of color coordination, texture variation, and unique plants situated in a chamber-like setting. This environment is host to an assemblage of statuary and other treasures that have been culled from around the world. This continually evolving acre totally engages its gardener twelve months a year. Not only is there the endless search for distinguished and exotic plants, but the rigors of caring for a high-summer tropical garden in Zone 6 are nonstop. Many gorgeous specimen trees too.

Saturdays; April 29, June 17, July 15; 2 p.m. - 6 p.m.

From Montauk Highway/Route 27 pass signs for the Town of East Hampton, then the Village of East Hampton. At the blinking traffic light (Georgica Getty station on the left), turn right onto Baiting Hollow Road. The garden is on the second corner on the right. Park on adjacent roads and NOT against the direction of traffic (East Hampton police adore giving tickets for that).

Proceeds shared with The Watermill Center, Byrd Hoffman Foundation

Dr. & Mrs. William L. Donnelly
156 Meadowmere Lane, Southampton

This informal one-acre garden was designed, planted, and maintained by the owners. It features unusual plants, many that are grown from seed and cuttings.

Saturday, July 15, 10 a.m. - 4 p.m.

From the west, take Route 27 to Southampton College Exit. Turn right and go 1 block. Turn left onto Montauk Highway, which becomes Hill Street after passing blinking traffic light. Turn right at the third street, Halsey Neck Lane. After second stop sign, turn left onto Meadowmere Lane. The house, #156, is on the corner of Halsey Neck Lane and Meadowmere Lane. Please park on Meadowmere Lane.

Ina Garten
23 Buell Lane, East Hampton

This garden, designed by Edwina von Gal, is arranged in squares like a kitchen garden, but is planted with perennials, annuals, roses, vegetables and herbs. It includes a crab apple orchard and rose and hydrangea gardens and is designed to feel like a traditional East Hampton garden.

Saturday, July 15, 10 a.m. - 2 p.m.

From the pond in East Hampton, go north on Route 114 towards Sag Harbor. This is called Buell Lane. The house is third on the left, #23, past the field. Park on the street.

Joy Cordery
14 Atterbury Road, Southampton

Created by the late Brenda Baldwin to highlight her love of roses, this small garden has rhododendrons, Japanese junipers, cotoneasters, oaks, pines and other evergreens to provide a backdrop against which the roses are set. (The climbing roses on the rear facade of the house should be in full flush on this date). Nestled in Shinnecock Hills around a dark swimming pool, it is a very private space in which the views of the garden from several levels lead to contemplation and calm. In maintaining this garden, organically as much as possible, I have added daffodils for the spring, attractions for birds and butterflies and am encouraging a moss walk and garden.

Saturday, June 17, 10 a.m. - 4 p.m.

From the west take Route 27 to Exit 66/North Road/Shinnecock. Then turn left at Route 39, then left again onto Montauk Highway. Continue for 2 miles to Crossroads of Hill Station Road and Atterbury Road. Turn right onto Atterbury Road; #14 is second visible house on the left. From the east, take Montauk Highway past Southampton College 1 mile to Crossroads. Turn left onto Atterbury Road. Please park on Atterbury Road.

Lois Beachy Underhill

68 BAY STREET, SAG HARBOR

In this hillside garden, a series of brick paths and terraces are bordered by beds planted for year-round foliage color. Pink flowers echo the soft tones of the old bricks. The south and west terraces overlook the harbor. An old granite retaining wall built from ships' ballasts forms an "L" around the south corner of the house. Its border emphasizes blues and yellows. The garden features mostly hydrangeas and select varieties of daphnes. The outlying hillside includes an old apple tree, a nineteenth-century chestnut, a lilac, grapevines, as well as a more recent mini-orchard, a bamboo allée, and a series of boundary borders.

Saturday, July 15, 2 p.m. - 6 p.m.

From Montauk Highway/Route 27, go to Bridgehampton. At the monument, take the Sag Harbor-Bridgehampton Turnpike to Sag Harbor. From Main Street, continue to Long Wharf. Turn right onto Bay Street. Go through blinking traffic light, past harbor and yacht yard on left. The house (#68) is a two-story shingle structure on the right. From East Hampton, turn onto Route 114 towards Sag Harbor and follow directions above. Please park along Bay Street.

Proceeds shared with The Committee for Sag Harbor's Old Burying Ground Fund

Mac Keith Griswold

57 HOWARD STREET, SAG HARBOR

This village garden is composed of three parts. The front yard greets visitors and protects our privacy with a privet hedge and picket and lattice fences. The square side garden is a full-sun, hot micro-climate filled with experiments—how much drought can these plants stand? Figs, *Rose banksia 'Lutea'* and *Rosa chinensis 'Mutabilis'* grow in side beds. Behind the hose is a forty-foot long perennial border fourteen feet deep planted in four bays. At the end of the lawn, two mulberries make an arch over the garden shed, and under our neighbor's privet hedge, a shade bed surrounds an old 'Clapp's Favorite' pear tree.

Saturday, July 15, 2 p.m. - 6 p.m.

From Montauk Highway/Route 27, go to Bridgehampton. Take the Sag Harbor Turnpike north 5 miles to Sag Harbor. On entering town, pass the Cove Deli on the right and Bayview Station on the left. Take the next left onto Howard Street. The garden is at the third house from the end on the left. Please park on the street or in the municipal lot behind Main Street.

Manfred & Roberta Lee

26850 Main Road, Cutchogue

Located in the village of Cutchogue, these two-and-one-half acres of gardens complement the Victorian house and the outbuildings. Four large tulip trees punctuate the front lawn. Deep perennial gardens surround the property. Mature azaleas, rhododendrons, roses, hydrangeas, and lilacs are spread throughout the garden. There are unusual conifers and Japanese maples as well as golden chain trees.

Saturdays; April 29, June 17; 10 a.m. - 4 p.m.

Take the Long Island Expressway to Exit 73 for Route 58, which leads into Route 25. Continue to Cutchogue. We are 5 houses past the North Fork Country Club on the right (south) side of Route 25. Please park on the street.

Margaret Kerr & Robert Richenburg

1006 Springs Fireplace Road, East Hampton

The garden, designed by Kerr, surrounds their house and studios on two acres that extend down to the wetlands of Accabonac Harbor. Kerr's brick rug sculptures, inspired by tribal Middle Eastern carpets, are placed throughout the garden. One, a brick prayer rug, lies in a contemplative glade below the studios. Kerr collects plants grown in the Middle Ages in a courtyard around a fountain and lily pool highlighted with espaliered pear trees. In the spring drifts of thousands of daffodils bloom in the fields around the house and are left unmowed until late fall. Native grasses and wildflowers make islands of meadow during the summer.

Saturdays; April 29, June 17; 10 a.m. - 4 p.m.

From Montauk Highway/Route 27, turn left at the traffic light in East Hampton. Pass town pond. Continue .9 mile past next traffic light, taking immediate left onto North Main Street. Pass windmill on the right. Go .3 mile, bearing right at fork onto Springs Fireplace Road. Go 5 miles. The driveway is marked by mailbox #1006. Please park along Springs Fireplace Road, and walk down dirt road to second house on the left.

Proceeds shared with The Horticultural Alliance of the Hamptons & Bridge Gardens Trust.

Maurice Isaac & Ellen Coster Isaac

4835 Oregon Road, Mattituck

This early 1900s country farmhouse has been designed with two major borders incorporating extensive plantings of unusual combinations of bulbs, perennials, trees, shrubs, and annuals. A pond well-stocked with Koi and water plants adds a beautiful and soothing touch. A path leads to a swimming pool and plantings, as well as an old restored barn adjacent to an arbor planted with wisteria, clematis, and several vines offering tranquility, shade, and a view of the extensive nearby farm fields.

Saturday, July 15, 10 a.m. - 2 p.m.

Take the Long Island Expressway to Exit 73 for Route 58. Take Route 58 to Route 25. Go through Mattituck past Love Lane to Wickham Avenue. Turn left onto Wickham Avenue, go past the train tracks and traffic light. Stay straight on Wickham Avenue and it will turn into Grand Avenue. Take Grand Avenue about .25 mile to East Mill. Turn right onto East Mill, keeping to the left, and this will turn into Oregon Road. Look for signs for parking.

MILFORD GARDEN
1200 BAY VIEW ROAD, SOUTHOLD

Our garden is an integral part of our old farmhouse, barn, and field complex. We have a little pond, a number of perennial gardens, a rose garden, a vegetable garden, an orchard, and an herb and cutting garden.

Saturday, June 17, 10 a.m. - 2 p.m.

Located between the hamlets of Peconic and Southold, just off of Route 25 on Bay View Road. Turn at the Gulf Station and drive .3 mile to the Indian Museum on the right. We are the next house, #1200. Please park along the road.

MR. & MRS. DINWIDDIE SMITH
158 QUIMBY LANE, BRIDGEHAMPTON

Largely grasses with groupings of lilies, irises, sedums, and evergreens.

Saturday, September 16, 10 a.m. - 2 p.m.

From Montauk Highway/Route 27, travel east through Bridgehampton to traffic light at Ocean Road. Turn right, continuing 1.75 miles to Quimby Lane. Turn left. Make a quick right and another left (This is still Quimby Lane). The house is on the left.

MRS. DONALD BRUCKMANN
105 OCEAN AVENUE, EAST HAMPTON

This seaside location emphasizes traditional and informal plantings of herbaceous borders, woodland, meadow, and rose gardens. Two ponds are surrounded by iris, aster, and other sun-loving plants. An ocean terrace and adjacent dune combine beach vegetation with bright annuals for an interesting contrast of the cultivated and naturalistic.

Saturday, April 29, 10 a.m. - 2 p.m.

From Montauk Highway/Route 27, follow to East Hampton. At the traffic light at the head of the pond, turn right onto Ocean Avenue. Take the third right onto Lily Pond Lane. Go .5 mile to driveway (#105) on the left (oceanside) marked with brick posts and a white gate. Please park along Lily Pond Lane.

RICHARD KAHN & ELAINE PETERSON

224 WEST LAKE DRIVE, MONTAUK

Stately old oaks and maples frame our three-acre property on Lake Montauk. The gardens meander around a romantic brick and shingle Tudor-style house built in 1930. A diversity of species reveals itself in collections of hosta, heath and heather, conifers, broadleaf evergreens, alpines and iris. An upper garden contains herbs, a potager and various flowering shrubs and trees, beyond which is a meadow with a mowed labyrinth. All plants are chosen for their ability to withstand the persistent challenges of heavy wind and salt spray. Year-round residents, we design and maintain the gardens ourselves, with deference to the ecology of the lake.

Saturday, June 17, 2 p.m. - 6 p.m.

From Montauk Highway/Route 27 go past the village of Montauk about 1 mile. Turn left onto West Lake Drive (signs for Montauk Harbor/Route 77/Montauk Downs). The garden, #224, is 1.2 miles on the right. Please park along the road, not in the grass.

RON & LINDA LUCY PETERSON

699 HILL STREET, SOUTHAMPTON

"Secret Garden" is designed and maintained by the owner on weekends. At the middle of the drive, the garden opens to a series of rooms surrounded by evergreens and hedges. An 1866 carriage house sits in the center of the property and is surrounded by perennial island borders filled with roses. A water garden is at the rear of the house, and an herb garden with low boxwood edging lies in front of the living room window. A white garden and perennial beds enclose the pool area. A clipped boxwood path leads to the front door. This is a most varied garden in all seasons.

Saturday, June 17, 10 a.m. - 2 p.m.

From the West, take Route 27 to the Southampton College Exit. Turn right 1 block to stop sign. Turn left onto Montauk Highway, which becomes Hill Street. Look for the blinking traffic light. Go to Lee Avenue on right side only. The garden is directly across from Lee Avenue. Park on Lee Avenue.

Susan & Louis Meisel

81 Wilkes Lane, Sagaponack

Our property encompasses more than 100 specimen trees, with a focus on special beeches. Susan uses flower color of several hundred perennials as if it were paint on canvas to create the visual effects I enjoy seeing.

Saturday, July 15, 10 a.m. - 2 p.m.

From Montauk Highway/Route 27, go to intersection at Sagg Main Street. Turn south. Go past the red schoolhouse on right and the general store. Turn left onto Hedges Lane. Go .5 mile and take the next left onto Wilkes Lane. The house (#81) is the second house on the right. Please park along the road.

Villa des Amis — Larry, Jody, Catherine, Christopher, & Spencer Carlson

1428 Scuttlehole Road, Bridgehampton

A former potato field has been transformed into a house and garden by the owner, who designed both in 1987. Built for family and friends, it has a relaxed air and transports the visitor to somewhere in Tuscany. From the blue gates, walk past olive trees on one side of the drive and apple trees on the other. Take the steps to a sunken tennis court bordered by an arbor with climbing roses and trumpet vine. The front steps lead to a veranda where, on a clear day, the ocean skips across the horizon. Walk around the brick way to the center courtyard and discover a pool, rose garden, and wisteria arbor. Explore a series of garden rooms with a reflecting pool, stone statuary, and finally, a walled garden and art studio.

Saturday, July 15, 10 a.m. - 4 p.m.

Take the Montauk Highway/Route 24 to Bridgehampton. At the flashing traffic light just west of the village center go north on Butter Lane. Go .25 mile, under railroad tracks, and stay right. Continue on Butter Lane until it deadends into Scuttlehole Road. Turn left onto Scuttlehole Road to tall hedges on the right. Just past the hedges turn right onto a long driveway. Take the driveway to the end and park just outside the 2 stone pillars.

Bridge Gardens Trust &

P.O. Box 1194, Bridgehampton, NY 11932. (516) 537-7440

The garden on these five acres were designed and installed by Jim Kilpatric and Harry Neyens. They include a formal knot surrounded by herbal beds; perennial mounds; topiaries; specimen trees; expansive lawns; aquatic plantings; woodland walks; a bamboo "room;" a lavender parterre; and hundreds of roses. A 750-foot double row of privet hedge —with fifteen viewing ports in its fifteen-foot-high walls—encloses a pavilion-like garden house (not open to the public). Bridge Gardens Trust, a charitable foundation, was created in 1997 to preserve the gardens and to encourage the accumulation of gardening knowledge.

Late-May - late September, Wednesdays and Saturdays, 2 p.m.- 5 p.m. Open for Open Days visitors on September 16. Admission is $10. Proceeds will be shared with The Garden Conservancy.

From the Montauk Highway/Route 27, go to Bridgehampton. At the blinking traffic light at the western edge of the village, turn left onto Butter Lane. Go .25 mile and under the railroad bridge; turn left immediately onto Mitchell Lane. Bridge Gardens, #36, is the first driveway on the left. Please park on Mitchell Lane.

LongHouse Reserve &

133 Hands Creek Road, East Hampton, NY 11937. (516) 329-3568.
WWW.LONGHOUSE.ORG.

Sixteen acres of gardens are punctuated with contemporary sculpture. Landscape features include a pond, numerous allées and walks, a dune garden, and 1,000 foot hemlock hedge that follows boundaries of farm fields that occupied the site until it was abandoned for agricultural use in the nineteenth century. There are collections of bamboo and grasses, 200 varieties of daffodils with more than one million blooms, and numerous irises, conifers, and broadleaf evergreens. The large new house (not open to the public) was inspired by the seventh-century Shinto shrine at Ise, Japan. LongHouse Reserve was established in 1991 to reflect founder Jack Lenor Larsen's professional interests and his desire to encourage creativity in gardening, collecting and everyday living with art. A majestic twenty-five-feet-tall, thirty-three-feet-in-diameter Fly's Eye Dome by Buckminster Fuller has been added to a selection of almost fifty sculptures throughout the gardens.

May - mid-September, Wednesdays and 1st & 3rd Saturdays. Open for Open Days visitors on April 29 & July 15, 10 a.m. - 2 p.m.

From East Hampton Village, turn onto Newtown Lane from the intersection at Main. Go to Cooper Street, turn right and go to the end. Turn left onto Cedar Street and bear right at fork in the road onto Hands Creek Road. Go .7 mile to #133 on the left.

Madoo Conservancy &

618 Main Street, PO Box 362, Sagaponack, NY 11962. (516) 537-8200.

This two-acre garden is a virtual compendium of major garden styles, including oriental bridge, a box-edged potager, a Renaissance-perspective rose walk, a knot garden, laburnum arbor, hermit's hut and a grass garden, as well as an Italianate-style courtyard and a user-friendly maze. It is fountained, rilled and pooled. It is noted for its innovated pruning techniques and striking colors (a gazebo is in three shades of mauve). Sculptures are by Matisse, Bourdelle, and Soriano. Rare trees and plants abound. A copse of fastigiate ginkos rises above box balls like the handles of mallets about to strike boules or hedgehogs. A staircase going nowhere is another of its whimsical features. The garden has been much published.

May - September, Wednesdays and Saturdays, 1 p.m.- 5 p.m.

Sagaponack is on Route 27, 1 mile east of Bridgehampton. Turn right at the traffic light (first light east of Bridgehampton on Route 27). The Madoo Conservancy is just over 1 mile from the highway and is 3 driveways after the post office on the right.

Rachel's Garden (c. 1790) &

Mulford Farm, East Hampton Historical Society, 101 Main Street, East Hampton, NY 11937. (516) 324-6850.

Located on the landmark eighteenth-century Mulford Farm, Rachel's Garden, is an authentic "period setting" garden (circa 1790) created by Isabel Furlaud and the Garden Club of East Hampton. The raised bed dooryard garden highlights the plants for medicine, food, dyes and housekeeping. Eighteenth Century costumed staff interpret the garden in the context of the life of Rachel Mulford in 1790, a young mother with three small children, a new baby and her husband David, a weaver. Rachel's Garden was a finalist for the Garden Club of America Zone III 1996 Founder's Fund award. A new weaving and spinning workhouse demonstration exhibit, country garden and orchard was opened in 1999 with The Garden Club of East Hampton.

Year round, daily, dawn - dusk.

Take Long Island Expressway, I-495, eastbound to Exit 70. Proceed south on Route 111 to Sunrise Highway/Route 27. Proceed East on Sunrise Highway/Route 27 to East Hampton. Turn left at the light at the beginning of the East Hampton Village Historic District. Proceed past the Town Pond and immediately after the burying ground, make the first right across the Village Green. Turn left onto James Lane (reference: St. Luke's Episcopal Church directly in front of you). The Mulford Farm will be on your right.

Lake Champlain Open Days

Regional Representative: Mrs. James T. Flynn

Saturday, July 15

CHARLOTTE
Converse Bay Farm, 1028 Converse Bay Road: 10 a.m. - 4 p.m.
Shelburne Farms—The Gardens at Golden Apple Orchard,
1052 Whalley Road: 10 a.m. - 4 p.m.

HINESBURG
The Hidden Garden of Lewis Creek Road,
693 Lewis Creek Road: 10 a.m. - 4 p.m.

KEENE VALLEY
Woodland Gardens of Mr. & Mrs.
   Wynant D. Vanderpoel,
Interbrook Road: 2 p.m. - 6 p.m.

VERGENNES
The Gardens of Peter Morris
   & Pennie Beach,
8 Roundtree Way: 10 a.m. - 4 p.m.

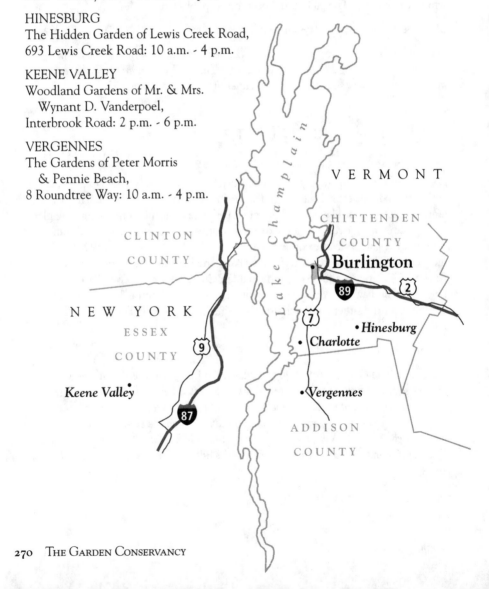

Converse Bay Farm

1028 Converse Bay Road, Charlotte

This garden is composed of several different elements on two levels, each focusing on the view of Lake Champlain. On the upper level the main feature is a pergola. There are several accesses to the next level. There is a parterre rose garden with an iron arbor as a backdrop. A sixty- by ten-foot perennial border is at the next level. There is also a lily pond surrounded by shade plants and rose gardens, an herb garden, and another perennial border. In the area of the barns is a parterre potager.

Saturday, July 15, 10 a.m. - 4 p.m.

Take I-89 North to Vermont Exit 13. Head south on Route 7 through the town of Shelburne approximately 5 miles to Charlotte intersection. Turn right onto F-5 West/ Ferry Road. Continue straight over the railroad tracks. At Lake Road intersection, turn left. Go .8 mile. Turn right onto Converse Bay Road. Fourth driveway on the left. Park along the driveway to the barn (third drive on the left).

Shelburne Farms—
The Gardens at Golden Apple Orchard

1052 Whalley Road, Charlotte

Overlooking Lake Champlain and the Adirondacks, the house is centered within an eighteen-acre apple orchard. Gardens planted in front of and behind a picket fence define the public and private spaces. Robin's white clapboard studio sits within a large walled garden. The garden is divided into rooms by hedges of gray-stemmed dogwood, arborvitae, yew, blueberry, winterberry, roses and asparagus. It includes a center knot garden, which is flanked on both sides by perennial borders. Korean boxwood, hardy in Vermont, is the formal hedge in the herb garden. The conifer garden, featuring many dwarf species, adds interest in the snowy landscape. Koi and many kinds of frogs survive the winter in two lily ponds. A path winding through a rock garden leads to an arbor-covered terrace behind the main house. Most of the gardens are accessible across pebbled paths and lawns.

Saturday, July 15, 10 a.m. - 4 p.m.

From Route 7 in Charlotte, take Ferry Road/F-5 west toward the ferry for 1.5 miles. Turn right onto Lake Road. Go 1 mile and turn left onto Whalley Road. The Golden Apple Orchard is .5 mile down on the left.

THE GARDENS OF PETER MORRIS & PENNIE BEACH

8 ROUNDTREE WAY, VERGENNES

These private gardens are a passion and ongoing experiment for architect and landscape designer Peter Morris. The upper garden is designed and laid out first to complement and "ground" Pennie and Peter's house. While many visitors stop here, the larger "garden imagined" lies to the south into, around, and along a sinuous waterway/marsh known as "the Run," a naturalized drainage outlet into Lake Champlain that forms about 250 acres. Despite the challenges of building paths and gardening its steep banks, Peter is attracted to the Run's natural beauty, curves, and mystery. The overall concept is a somewhat Chinese stroll garden with distinctive "rooms," transitions, and stations. The gardens amplify the changes and contrasts of the site.

Saturday, July 15, 10 a.m. - 4 p.m.

From the Essex, New York-Charlotte, Vermont ferry follow Route F5 East to Route 7. Turn right, and go south on Route 7. Turn right onto Route 22A into Vergennes. Go through town, down hill, over the bridge and take second right at flashing traffic light onto Panton Road. Follow signs to Basin Harbor Club and Lake Champlain Maritime Museum. Go west about 1 mile and turn right onto Basin Harbor Road. Proceed 6 miles to Basin Harbor Club entry sign. Take first left after grass airstrip. Park in field to right. From Lake Champlain Bridge on Route 17, continue northeast on Route 17 for about 2 miles. Take left fork at Addison Gas Station and Store onto Lake Street. Follow signs to Lake Champlain Maritime Museum. Stay on paved road about 5 miles and fork left at Panton Store and gas pump. Stay left and go about 1 mile past Button Bay State Park. Turn left onto Basin Harbor Road and go to Basin Harbor entry sign and Lake Champlain Maritime Museum. Take first left after grass airstrip. Park in field to right. The Upper Gardens are accessible over grass paths.

Proceeds shared with The Vermont Arts Council.

THE HIDDEN GARDEN OF LEWIS CREEK ROAD

693 LEWIS CREEK ROAD, HINESBURG

Carved out of woods and wetlands, this very original garden is one of the largest private gardens in Vermont. It is laid out on two levels. The upper garden surrounds the house. Curving paths wind through an extensive collection of hostas, shrubs and perennials that lead to open lawn, a richly varied conifer garden and a sunken walled garden. The lower garden is reached by a path past a stone wall and down under a canopy of mature evergreens that is underplanted with woodland flowers, ferns, and shrubs. Here collections of heather, ornamental grasses, damp-loving plants, conifers and waterlilies have transformed a meadow into an abundant garden embracing a reflecting pond, trout pond and "fishing camp," all enclosed in a canyon of woods.

Saturday, July 15, 10 a.m. - 4 p.m.

Take I-89 North to Exit 12. Turn left onto Route 2A and go south for 5.2 miles until road ends at Route 116. Turn left onto Route 116 South and go 2.1 miles to traffic light in Hinesburg. Go 1 mile to the intersection of Route 116 (sharp left curve) and Silver Street (straight). Proceed straight on Silver Street, for 2.9 miles to Lewis Creek Road. Turn left onto narrow gravel road. The driveway, #693 is .7 mile on the left. Continue up the driveway to parking. From Route 7 traffic light in Charlotte, go right on Church Hill Road. (or, if on Ferry Road, go straight across Route 7) and continue .7 mile to stop sign, make right and turn onto Hinesburg Road, go .6 mile to a 4-way stop at Mt. Philo Road, continue for 2.4 miles to 4-way stop at Spear Street. Continue for 4.4 miles where road will terminate across from the Hinesburg IGA. Make a right turn onto Route 116 and go .2 mile to intersection of Route 116 (sharp left curve) and Silver Street (straight).

WOODLAND GARDENS
OF MR. & MRS. WYNANT D. VANDERPOEL

INTERBROOK ROAD, KEENE VALLEY

Overlooking an alpine brook with a scenic mountain view and framed by a stand of towering white pines, the gardens cascade down three levels displaying mixed shrub and perennial beds with annual borders. Flower colors range from blue, purple, white, and deep pink to chartreuse and burgundy shrubs.

Saturday, July 15, 2 p.m. - 6 p.m.

From the Northway/Route 87 take Exit 31/Route 9N, west through Elizabethtown to intersection with Route 73. Turn left onto Route 73 to Keene Valley, approximately 3 miles. Turn right onto Adirondack Street (turns into Interbrook Road) 1 mile. Do not bear off the street. The house is at the third driveway on the left at Camp Comfort sign.

Colonial Garden at Adirondack History Center 🐾

Adirondack Center Museum, Elizabethtown, NY 12932.
(518) 873-6466.

A formal garden adjacent to the Adirondack Center Museum, the Colonial Garden borrows brick paving and walls, decorative fencing and gates, a summerhouse, fountain and sundial from Colonial Gardens of Williamsburg. A formal arrangement of hedges, flowering trees, shrubs, and perennials enclose the annual borders that are planted and maintained by the Essex County Adirondack Garden Club.

Year round, daily, dawn - dusk

Northway (I-87) to Exit 31. Proceed west on 9N approximately 4 miles to Elizabethtown. Turn left at the flashing light. Take the first left onto Church Street. From Essex Ferry via Westport: Exit the ferry parking lot. Turn left onto Route 9 and proceed south (the road is also called Lake Shore Drive in Westport). At the stop sign, turn left. Turn right onto Sisco. Follow to stop sign. Bear right (fairgrounds are on your right) onto 9N and continue past Westport Depot to I-87. Continue as above.

The Depot Theatre Gardens 🐾

P.O. Box 414, Westport, NY 12993. (518) 962-4449.

Framing the Westport landmark railroad station, which underwent major restoration in 1997-1998, are flowerbeds with a mixture of annuals, perennials, and shrubs. The station, also known as the Depot Theatre, seats 135 for its summer season equity actor's performances between mid-June and mid-September. Overlooking Lake Champlain, the site is truly unique.

June - September, daily, dawn - dusk.

From the Northway (I-87) take Exit 31. Go east on Route 9N approximately 3 miles until 9N passes under railroad tracks. Westport Railroad Station, aka The Depot Theatre, is on the right on the west side of the tracks. From the town of Westport, take Route 9N west approximately 2 miles until 9N passes under the railroad tracks. Westport Railroad Station is on the left on the west side of the tracks.

THE INN AT ESSEX ❧

70 ESSEX WAY, ESSEX JUNCTION, VT 05452. (802) 878-1000.
WWW.INNATESSEX.COM

The Inn at Essex, a AAA four diamond hotel built in 1989, is also home to the Essex campus of the acclaimed New England Culinary Institute. More than thirty-five flower boxes grace the windows of the Governor's Mansion, the Inn, and the Manor-on-the-Green. Behind the Inn is a large tented atrium/patio with stone steps leading down to the East Lawn, a welcoming expanse bordered by eighty-foot-long, hedge-lined perennial beds with a wedding gazebo at the far end. Between the patio and Butler's Restaurant is a formal herb garden with a stone wall at one end and steps leading down to an allée of Green Ash trees. On the other side of the patio is a partially shaded bed with a mix of woody flowering shrubs, roses, and phlox complemented by flowering shrubs, and roses. A fountain, sculpted by the late Paul Aschenbach (his last work), is accentuated by a semi-circle of flowering annuals.

Saturday, July 15, 10 a.m. - 4 p.m.

Take I-89 South to Exit 17. Turn left off the exit and at the traffic lights turn right onto Routes 2 & 7 south for approximately 3 miles. Bear left at the flashing yellow light onto Route 2A South and follow to Route 289. Turn left onto Route 289 and follow to Exit 10/Essex Way. Turn right off exit and the Inn will be approximately .25 mile on the left.

THE INN AT SHELBURNE FARMS ❧

1611 HARBOR ROAD, SHELBURNE, VT 05482. (802) 985-8686.

The gardens at the Inn at Shelburne Farms, originally designed by Lila Vanderbilt Webb, feature lush perennial borders inspired by the English cottage style of Gertrude Jekyll. The peak of the garden's bloom is early June when the Queen Victoria peonies are in their glory, through July when delphiniums bloom in front of a tall plume of poppies. Low brick walls provide the formal architectural structure to define the "rooms" within the garden and create multiple levels for the rose garden, the lily pond, surrounded by Dutch and Japanese iris, and an herb garden. Continuing Lila's tradition to welcome the community into her garden, we invite you to visit. Shelburne Farms is a 1,400-acre working farm, national historic site, and nonprofit environmental education center whose mission is to cultivate a conservation ethic by teaching and demonstrating the stewardship of natural and agricultural resources.

Saturday, July 15. Please call for hours.

From I-89 take Exit 13 to Route 7 West at the traffic light in the center of Shelburne. Go 1.6 miles to the entrance of Shelburne Farms. Turn right into the Welcome Center parking area before entering the gates.

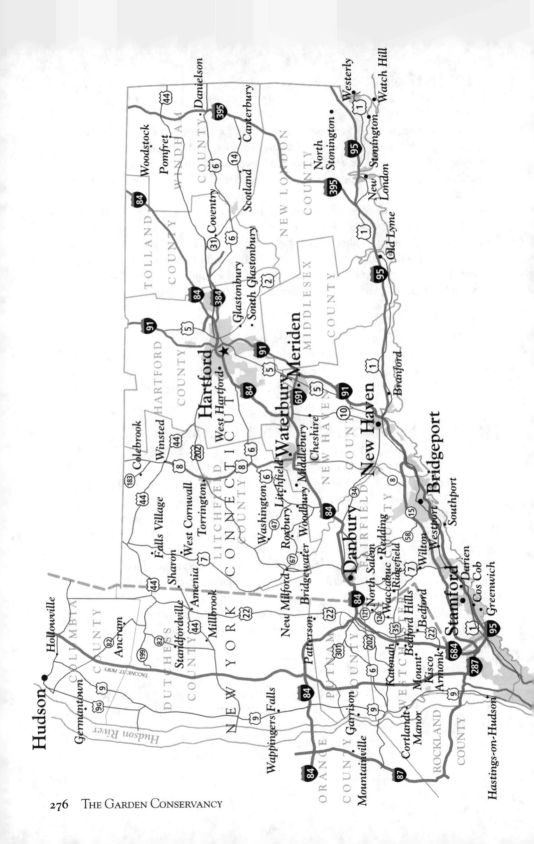

New York & Connecticut Open Days

Sunday, May 7

FARMINGTON, CT
Kate Emery & Steve Silk, 74 Prattling Pond Road: 2 p.m. - 6 p.m.

REDDING, CT
Highstead Arboretum, 127 Lonetown Road:
   Guided walks 10 a.m., noon, 2 p.m. and 4 p.m.

SCOTLAND, CT
Richard Redfield, 379 Brook Road: 10 a.m. - 4 p.m.

STAMFORD, CT
Ruth & Jim Levitan, 26 Wake Robin Lane: 10 a.m. - 4 p.m.

WESTPORT, CT
Malcolm's Way, 17 Hockanum Road: 2 p.m. - 6 p.m.
Paul Held & Jane Sherman, 195 North Avenue: 10 a.m. - 6 p.m.

WETHERSFIELD, CT
Gary Berquist, 125 Jordan Lane: 2 p.m. - 6 p.m.

HASTINGS-ON-HUDSON, NY
Midge & Dave Riggs, 112 Lefurgy Avenue, Hastings-on-Hudson: 10 a.m. - 4 p.m.

MOUNTAINVILLE, NY
Cedar House—Garden of Margaret Johns & Peter Stern, Otterkill Road at
   Anders Lane: 10 a.m. - 6 p.m.

MOUNT KISCO, NY
Jane Keiter, 43 Taylor Road: 10 a.m. - 4 p.m.
Judy & Michael Steinhardt, 433 Croton Lake Road: 10 a.m. - 4 p.m.

WAPPINGERS FALLS, NY
Anne Spiegel, 299 Maloney Road: 10 a.m. - 4 p.m.

Sunday, May 21

MIDDLEBURY, CT
John N. Spain, 69 Bayberry Road: 10 a.m. - 6 p.m.

RIDGEFIELD, CT
Garden of Ideas, 647 North Salem Road: 10 a.m. - 4 p.m.

SOUTH GLASTONBURY, CT
Brad & Toni Easterson, 124 High Street: May 21, 10 a.m. - 4 p.m.

AMENIA, NY
Broccoli Hall—Maxine Paetro, 464 Flinthill Road: 10 a.m. - 4 p.m.

ARMONK, NY
Cobamong Pond, 15 Middle Patent Road: 10 a.m. - 2 p.m.

BEDFORD, NY
Penelope & John Maynard, 210 Hook Road: 10 a.m. - 6 p.m.
Phillis Warden, 531 Bedford Center Road: 10 a.m. - 4 p.m.

COPAKE FALLS, NY
Margaret Roach: 10 a.m. - 4 p.m.

GERMANTOWN, NY
Tailings—David Whitcomb & Robert Montgomery,
    404 White Birch Road: 10 a.m. - 2 p.m.

WAPPINGERS FALLS, NY
Anne Spiegel, 299 Maloney Road: 10 a.m. - 4 p.m.

Saturday, May 27

MOUNT KISCO, NY
Henriette Suhr, 95 Old Roaring Brook Road: 2 p.m. - 6 p.m.

Sunday, May 28

REDDING RIDGE, CT
The Peonies at Poverty Hollow, Poverty Hollow Road: 9 a.m. - 6 p.m.

Sunday, June 4

BRANFORD, CT
Nickolas Nickou, 107 Sunset Hill Drive: 1 guided tour at 10 a.m.
  No wandering alone.

COLEBROOK, CT
Marveen & Michael Pakalik, 46 Stillman Hill Road: 2 p.m. - 6 p.m.

DANIELSON, CT
Robert Bonneville, 10 Morin Avenue: 10 a.m. - 4 p.m.

FALLS VILLAGE, CT
Martha A. & Robert S. Rubin, 55 Hautboy Hill Road: 2 p.m. - 6 p.m.

FAIRFIELD, CT
Nancy & Tom Grant, 4014 Redding Road: 10 a.m. - 4 p.m.
Sarah & Jonathan Seymour, 1534 Redding Road: 10 a.m - 4 p.m.

FARMINGTON, CT
Arline & Buzz Whitaker, 4 High Street: 10 a.m. - 4 p.m.

GREENWICH, CT
Stonybrooke, 29 Taconic Road: 10 a.m. - 4 p.m.

LITCHFIELD, CT
Dan & Joyce Lake, 258 Beach Street: 3 p.m. - 7 p.m.
Mr. & Mrs. David Stoner, 183 Maple Street: 2 p.m. - 6 p.m.

MIDDLEBURY, CT
John N. Spain, 69 Bayberry Road: 10 a.m. - 6 p.m.

REDDING, CT
Highstead Arboretum, 127 Lonetown Road:
  Guided walks 10 a.m., noon, 2 p.m., and 4 p.m.

RIDGEFIELD, CT
David Barnhizer, 153 South Salem Road: 10 a.m. - 4 p.m.

WEST CORNWALL, CT
Julia & John Scott, 52 Cream Hill Road: noon - 4 p.m.

WEST HARTFORD, CT
Sara M. Knight, 18 High Farms Road: 10 a.m. - 2 p.m.

WESTPORT, CT
Anita & Jim Alic, 6 Snowflake Lane: 10 a.m. - 4 p.m.
Barbara Carr's Garden, 31 Westway Road: 10 a.m. - 4 p.m.

WATCH HILL, RI
The Gardens at Graigie Brae, 6 Aquidneck Avenue: 10 a.m. - 4 p.m.

WILTON, CT
Beverly Frank—Foxglove Meadow, 203 Sharp Hill Road: 10 a.m. - 3 p.m.

ANCRAM, NY
Adams-Westlake, 681 Route 7: 10 a.m. - 4 p.m.

ARMONK, NY
Mrs. John C. Sluder, 9 Half Mile Road: 10 a.m. - 2 p.m.

BEDFORD, NY
Ann Catchpole-Howell, 448 Long Ridge Road: 10 a.m. - 4 p.m.

AMENIA, NY
Broccoli Hall—Maxine Paetro, 464 Flinthill Road: 10 a.m. - 4 p.m.

COPAKE FALLS, NY
Margaret Roach: 10 a.m. - 4 p.m.

GERMANTOWN, NY
Mark A. McDonald—Runningwater, 67 Wire Road: noon - 6 p.m.

GHENT, NY
David Lebe & Jack Potter, 104 May Hill Road: 2 p.m. - 6 p.m.

HOLLOWVILLE, NY
Adele & John Slocum, 119 Catskill View Road: 10 a.m. - 2 p.m.

KATONAH, NY
Barbara & Tom Israel, 296 Mount Holly Road: 10 a.m. - 4 p.m.
Cross River House, 129 Maple Avenue: 10 a.m. - 2 p.m.
Roxana Robinson—Willow Green Farm, 159 North Salem Road: 10 a.m. - 4 p.m.

NORTH SALEM, NY
Carol Goldberg—Artemis Farm, 22 Wallace Road: 10 a.m. - 4 p.m.
Duck Hill, 23 Baxter Road: 10 a.m. - 6 p.m.
Keeler Hill Farm, North Salem: 10 a.m. - 4 p.m.

Sunday, June 25

BETHLEHEM, CT
Baker/Linder Garden, 217 Arch Bridge Road: 2 p.m. - 6 p.m.

BRIDGEWATER, CT
Maywood Gardens, 52 Cooper Road: 10 a.m. - 2 p.m.

CANTERBURY, CT
Westminster Gardens—Eleanor B. Cote & Adrian P. Hart,
    26 Westminster Road: 1 p.m. - 5 p.m.

CORNWALL BRIDGE, CT
Michael Pollan, Pritchard Road: 2 p.m. - 6 p.m.

FAIRFIELD
Nancy & Tom Grant, 4014 Redding Road: 10 a.m. - 4 p.m.

NEW CANAAN, CT
Sandra & Richard Bergmann, 63 Park Street: 10 a.m - 6 p.m.

POMFRET, CT
Lt. Col. Paul G. & Mrs. Ann B. Hennen, 52 Putnam Road: 10 a.m. - 6 p.m.
Robert & Joan Macneil, 73 Cooney Road: 10 a.m. - 4 p.m.

RIVERSIDE, CT
Susan Cohen, 7 Perkely Lane: 3 p.m. - 6 p.m.

STONINGTON, CT
Mr. & Mrs. Juan O'Callahan, 40 Salt Acres Road: 10 a.m. - 2 p.m.

SOUTHPORT, CT
Enid & Harry Munroe, Fleming Lane: 2 p.m. - 6 p.m.

WARREN, CT
May Brawley Hill, 184 Brick School Road: 10 a.m. - 2 p.m.

WASHINGTON, CT
Charles Raskob Robinson & Barbara Paul Robinson, 88 Clark Road: 2 p.m - 6 p.m.
George Schoellkopf, Nettleton Road: 2 p.m. - 6 p.m.
Gael Hammer, 63 River Road: 10 a.m. - 4 p.m.
Linda Allard, 156 Wykeham Road: 10 a.m. - 4 p.m.

WEST REDDING, CT
Hughes-Sonnenfroh Gardens, 54 Chestnut Woods Road: 2 p.m. - 6 p.m.

WOODSTOCK, CT
Judith & Robert Gries, 486 Route 169: 10 a.m. - 4 p.m.

BEDFORD, NY
Phillis Warden, 531 Bedford Center Road: 10 a.m. - 4 p.m.

GARRISON, NY
Ross Gardens, Snake Hill Road, Travis Corners: 10 a.m. - 4 p.m.

KATONAH, NY
Cross River House, 129 Maple Avenue: 10 a.m. - 2 p.m.

MILLBROOK, NY
John H. Whitworth Jr., 506 Altamont Road: 2 p.m. - 6 p.m.

Sunday, July 9

COLEBROOK, CT
Steepleview Gardens—Kathy Loomis, Route 182: 10 a.m. - 4 p.m.

COVENTRY, CT
David & Julia Hayes, 905 South Street: 10 a.m. - 4 p.m.

EASTFORD, CT
Emberborne—Garden of Susan Burns & Bob Williams,
    126 Halls Pond Road: 10 a.m. - 4 p.m.

GREENWICH, CT
Mrs. Philip McCaull, 221 Round Hill Road: 2 p.m. - 6 p.m.

SHARON, CT
Kathleen & James Metz, Cobble Pond Farm: 2 p.m. - 6 p.m.
Lee Link, 99 White Hollow Road: 2 p.m. - 6 p.m.

WEST CORNWALL, CT
Michael Trapp, 7 River Road: 10 a.m. - 4 p.m.

WOODSTOCK, CT
Judith & Robert Gries, 486 Route 169: 10 a.m. - 4 p.m.
Upperbrook Farm, 170 Lyon Hill Road: 10 a.m. - 5 p.m.

AMENIA, NY
Jade Hill, 13 Lake Amenia Road: 10 a.m. - 4 p.m.

BEDFORD, NY
Mrs. John E. Lockwood, 32 St. Mary's Church Road: 10 a.m. - 2 p.m.

MOUNT KISCO, NY
Jane Keiter, 43 Taylor Road: 10 a.m. - 4 p.m.
Judy & Michael Steinhardt, 433 Croton Lake Road: 10 a.m. - 4 p.m.

GERMANTOWN, NY
Mark A. McDonald—Runningwater, 67 Wire Road: noon - 6 p.m.

HOLLOWVILLE, NY
Laurence Sombke & Catherine Herman Garden, 258 Connecticut: 10 a.m. - 4 p.m.

Sunday, July 23

AVON, CT
Green Dreams—Garden of Jan Nickel, 71 Country Club Road: 10 a.m. - 4 p.m.

FALLS VILLAGE, CT
Bunny Williams, Point of Rocks Road: 2 p.m. - 6 p.m.

MERIDEN, CT
George Trecina, 341 Spring Street: 10 a.m. - 2 p.m.

RIDGEFIELD, CT
Donna Clark, 264 North Salem Road: 10 a.m. - 4 p.m.
Garden of Ideas, 647 North Salem Road: 10 a.m. - 4 p.m.

SHARON, CT
Lynden B. Miller, 1 Williams Road: 10 a.m. - 2 p.m.

SOUTHPORT, CT
Enid & Harry Munroe, Fleming Lane: 2 p.m. - 6 p.m.

STONINGTON, CT
Mrs. Frederic C. Paffard, Jr., 389 North Main Street: 10 a.m. - 2 p.m.

WASHINGTON, CT
Gael Hammer, 63 River Road: 10 a.m. - 4 p.m.
George Schoellkopf, Nettleton Road: 2 p.m. - 6 p.m.

BEDFORD, NY
Phillis Warden, 531 Bedford Center Road: 10 a.m. - 4 p.m.

MILLBROOK, NY
Belinda & Stephen Kaye, Deep Hollow Road: 10 a.m - 4 p.m.

CORTLANDT MANOR, NY
Carol & Raymond Rocklin's Garden, 20 Rocky Ridge: 10 a.m. - 2 p.m.
Vivian & Ed Merrin, 2547 Maple Avenue: 10 a.m. - 5 p.m.

STANFORDVILLE, NY
Ellen & Eric Petersen, 378 Conklin Hill Road: 10 a.m. - 2 p.m.
Zibby & Jim Tozer, Uplands Farm, Hunns Lake Road: 10 a.m. - 2 p.m.

SALT POINT, NY
Ely Garden, Allen Road: 10 a.m. - 2 p.m.

Sunday, September 10

AVON, CT
Green Dreams—Garden of Jan Nickel, 71 Country Club Road: 10 a.m. - 4 p.m.

COS COB, CT
Florence & John Boogaerts—Mianus Dawn, 316 Valley Road: 1 p.m. - 5 p.m.

FARMINGTON, CT
Kate Emery & Steve Silk, 74 Prattling Pond Road: 2 p.m. - 6 p.m.

LITCHFIELD, CT
Mr. & Mrs. David Stoner, 183 Maple Street: 2 p.m. - 6 p.m.

MERIDEN, CT
George Trecina, 341 Spring Street: 10 a.m. - 2 p.m.

RIDGEFIELD, CT
Garden of Ideas, 647 North Salem Road: 10 a.m. - 4 p.m.

SOUTHPORT, CT
Enid & Harry Munroe, Fleming Lane: 2 p.m. - 6 p.m.

WESTPORT, CT
Barlow Cutler-Wotton, 79 King's Highway North: 10 a.m. - 4 p.m.
Malcolm's Way, 17 Hockanum Road: 2 p.m. - 6 p.m.

WETHERSFIELD, CT
Gary Berquist, 125 Jordan Lane: 2 p.m. - 6 p.m.

WINSTED, CT
Rita & Steve Buchanan, 317 Colbrook Road: 2 p.m. - 6 p.m.

ANCRAM, NY
Adams-Westlake, 681 Route 7: 10 a.m. - 4 p.m.

BEDFORD, NY
Ann Catchpole-Howell, 448 Long Ridge Road: 10 a.m. - 4 p.m.
Laura Fisher, Wildflower Farm, 44 Broad Brook Road: 10 a.m. - 4 p.m.

COPAKE FALLS, NY
Margaret Roach: 10 a.m. - 4 p.m.

GHENT, NY
David Lebe & Jack Potter, 104 May Hill Road: 2 p.m. - 6 p.m.

HUDSON, NY
Hudson Bush Farm, 154 Yates Road: 10 a.m. - 4 p.m.

LEWISBORO, NY
The White Garden, 199 Elmwood Road: 10 a.m. - 4 p.m.

NORTH SALEM, NY
Dick Button, Ice Pond Farm, 115 June Road: 10 a.m. - 6 p.m.

PATTERSON, NY
The Farmstead Garden, 590 Birch Hill Road: 10 a.m. - 2 p.m.

WACCABUC, NY
James & Susan Henry, 36 Mead Street: 10 a.m. - 4 p.m.

Sunday, September 24

WESTPORT, CT
Barlow Cutler-Wotton, 79 King's Highway North: 10 a.m. - 4 p.m.

WINSTED, CT
Rita & Steve Buchanan, 317 Colbrook Road: 2 p.m. - 6 p.m.

Sunday, October 15

ARMONK, NY
Cobamong Pond, 15 Middle Patent Road: 10 a.m. - 2 p.m.

ADAMS-WESTLAKE

681 ROUTE 7, ANCRAM

A number of gardens-including a walled swimming pool garden, several mixed borders, a small frog pond, an herb garden, and an extensive vegetable garden-surround an 1835 farmhouse in a pastoral Columbia County valley. There is also a large spring-fed pond in a natural ravine.

Sundays; June 4, September 10; 10 a.m. - 4 p.m.

From the Taconic Parkway, exit at Jackson Corners; go east on Route 2. At first "Y," turn left onto Route 7, following signs for Ancram. At the second "Y," turn left, staying on Route 7. Approximately 7 minutes from the Taconic, the Gallatin Town Hall will be on the left. The garden is next, on the left; look for #681 on a red mailbox. Park across the road.

ADELE & JOHN SLOCUM

119 CATSKILL VIEW ROAD, HOLLOWVILLE

This country garden surrounds an eighteenth-century farmhouse and includes roadside beds planted with ground covers, bulbs, and flowering shrubs. The stream-side woodland is planted with wildflowers and enhanced by a small waterfall. Bridges lead to a pond in a naturalistic setting. A more formal perennial sun garden is enclosed by a rustic fence. There is also a rock garden and a fragrance garden. Special interests include clematis, primulas, and unusual shrubs.

Sunday, June 4, 10 a.m. - 2 p.m.

From the Taconic Parkway, exit at Route 23 west. Travel toward Claverack 1.7 miles to Route 16, (veer left at the bottom of long hill). Go 1.5 miles to Route 27B. Continue .5 miles to Catskill View Road on the left. Go .5 miles to fourth house on the left, signed Slocum #119. Please park along Catskill View Road.

ANN CATCHPOLE-HOWELL

448 LONG RIDGE ROAD, BEDFORD

This garden features large perennial borders. It is designed on a central axis, with terrraces, stone walls, and hidden steps leading to an unusual shrub garden. It was featured in Melanie Fleischmann's *American Border Gardens.*

Sundays; June 4, September 10; 10 a.m. - 4 p.m.

From Bedford Village, take Route 172 toward Pound Ridge. Turn right at Mobil Station onto Long Ridge Road (road to Stamford). Follow 2 miles to the house, #448, on the right. Please park in the meadow as directed.

Anne Spiegel

299 MALONEY ROAD, WAPPINGERS FALLS

This dramatic natural rock garden, planted on a series of rugged stepped ledges and cliffs include screes, sand beds, a lime bed, and troughs. The slowly expanding garden is open, sunny, and windy. Plants from Turkey, the Great Basin and our western mountains, especially the Rockies, are a specialty. The garden is never watered due to an inadequate well, so there is continuing experimentation with xerophytes and drought-tolerant plants.

Sundays; May 7 & 21, 10 a.m. - 4 p.m.

From the Taconic Parkway, take the Arthursburg Road Exit and follow Arthursburg Road 3.2 miles to Maloney Road. Turn left and continue 1.5 miles. The house (#299) is the second driveway on the left after passing Laurel Road. Please follow parking signs and drive past house only when exiting.

Proceeds shared with The North American Rock Garden Society

Barbara & Tom Israel

296 MOUNT HOLLY ROAD, KATONAH

This property includes a charming box-hedged perennial border, a retreat garden, a large vegetable garden, an orchard, many specimen trees and examples of garden statuary.

Sunday, June 4, 10 a.m. - 4 p.m.

From I-684, take Route 35 East. Turn left onto Holly Branch Road. Go to end. The Israel property (#296) is just ahead through double white picket gates. Please park along the driveway.

Belinda & Stephen Kaye

DEEP HOLLOW ROAD, MILLBROOK

This farmhouse garden, designed around a lily pond and Carpenter Gothic-style potting shed, incorporates unusual combinations of annuals, ornamental vegetables, herbs, and perennials. Along the nearby roadside, junipers, native shrubs, grasses and favorite weeds are naturalized to provide a screen. The property also includes several strictly functional market gardens that produce boutique potatoes and other certified organic edibles for the restaurant trade.

Sunday, July 23, 10 a.m - 4 p.m.

From Millbrook, take Route 44 East towards Amenia. Continue through Mabbettsville and, approximately 3 miles beyond, look for Allyn's Restaurant on the right. Take the next right onto Deep Hollow Road. The farm is the first on the left after the church. It is yellow with a yellow barn. From Amenia, take Route 44 West towards Millbrook, approximately 5 miles to the hamlet of Lithgow. Turn left onto Deep Hollow Road. Please park along Deep Hollow Road.

Proceeds shared with The Dutchess Land Conservancy

Broccoli Hall—Maxine Paetro

464 FLINTHILL ROAD, AMENIA

Visitors to Broccoli Hall describe this English-style cottage garden as "delightful," "whimsical," "magical"—and they come back again and again. Starting in 1986 with an acre and a half of bare earth, Maxine Paetro collaborated with horticulturist Tim Steinhoff to create a series of enchanting garden rooms. Broccoli Hall offers an apple tunnel, a brick courtyard, a lavish display of spring bulbs blooming with crab apples in May, an extensive border of iris, peonies and old shrub roses flowering in June, a tree house with long views, and a secret woodland garden.

Sundays; May 21, June 4, 10 a.m. - 4 p.m.

From Route 22 North, go toward Amenia. Go west on Route 44 to Route 83 North/ Smithfield Road. Go 2.5 miles to dirt road on right, Flint Hill Road. Turn right. The house (#464) is the first on the left. Please park on Flint Hill Road. Be careful of ditches.

Carol Goldberg—Artemis Farm

22 WALLACE ROAD, NORTH SALEM

A year ago I dismantled a barn on our farm and spent this past winter designing a new garden for the site. I created a furnished Victorian garden room featuring many unusual garden antiques that complement our mid-nineteenth-century farmhouse. The property includes a gravel courtyard trough garden, two other large border gardens with a sweeping view of the back pasture, and a kitchen garden. The front of the house, surrounded by maple trees, has primarily shade-loving plants.

Sunday, June 4, 10 a.m. - 4 p.m.

From I-684, take Exit 7. Follow Route 116 East bearing left where it joins Route 121 North. Travel approximately 2 miles and turn right onto Route 116 East. Auberge Maxime Restaurant is on this corner. Continue .1 mile to Wallace Road and turn left. It is the first house on the left. Note the Artemis Farm sign on the tree. Please park as directed.

Proceeds shared with The North Salem Open Land Foundation.

CAROL & RAYMOND ROCKLIN'S GARDEN

20 ROCKY RIDGE, CORTLANDT MANOR

This garden, on a five-acre property, sits at the top of a boulder-strewn hill. The owners, a sculptor and his wife, have designed the garden as a series of rooms shaped to follow the contours of the land. There are many walls and pebble-strewn paths that lead the visitor from one section to another. Each room has its own character. A water garden and a black pool, each with a waterfall, add interest. Sculpture is artfully placed throughout.

Sunday, July 23, 10 a.m. - 2 p.m.

From Route 9N, take the Montrose/Buchanan Exit. Turn left onto 9AN. Go .4 mile and turn right onto Watch Hill Road. Go 2.2 miles and turn right onto Rocky Ridge. Number 20 is the second driveway on the right. Please park on Rocky Ridge.

CEDAR HOUSE — GARDEN OF MARGARET JOHNS & PETER STERN

OTTERKILL ROAD AT ANDERS LANE, MOUNTAINVILLE

Mixed perennial borders, "enhanced" meadows, informal flowerbeds, specimen trees, berries, lilacs, tree peonies, old clipped boxwood, espaliered fruit trees, and a white wisteria-draped pergola are connected by stone walls, trellises, and grass paths. The garden overlooks 200 acres of orchard, farmland, and dogwood-rich forest, as well as the Hudson Highlands to the east and the Moodna Valley to the west.

Sunday, May 7, 10 a.m. - 6 p.m.

From the New York State Thruway/I-87 North, take Exit 16 /Harriman/Monroe. Turn right onto Route 32. Travel north for 10 miles to the green metal bridge. Cross the bridge and immediately turn left onto Orrs Mill Road. Take the third left onto Otterkill Road. Follow Otterkill Road .6 mile to Anders Lane (the driveway on the right). Go up the driveway to the house. From the Hudson Valley and Connecticut, travel west on I-84 cross the Newburgh-Beacon Bridge. Take Exit 10 South. Travel south on Route 32 for 7 miles. Before you cross the green metal bridge, turn right onto Orrs Mills Road. Follow above directions to Cedar House.

Proceeds shared with The Cornwall Garden Club.

COBAMONG POND

15 MIDDLE PATENT ROAD, ARMONK

This is one of the great woodland gardens of the world-a twelve-acre pond is surrounded by twelve acres of naturalistic woodlands with an abundance of flowering shrubs that have been enhanced for almost forty years. It is featured in The Beckoning Path, with eighty color photographs. The garden has an abundance of rhododendrons, flowering trees, shrubs, and Japanese maples. The garden was also developed to emphasize New England fall color.

Sundays; May 21, October 15; 10 a.m.-2 p.m.

From I-684 South, take Exit 4/Route 172. Turn left (east) and continue to the end. Turn right (south) at the Shell station onto Route 22. Go 2.2 miles, then turn left onto Middle Patent Road. Take the second driveway on right, marked by four mailboxes. The house, #15, is at end of a long driveway. From I-684 North, take Exit 3N and go north on Route 22 for 4 miles then turn right onto Middle Patent Road and proceed as above. Please park along driveway near house.

Proceeds shared with The Mount Kisco Day Care Center.

CROSS RIVER HOUSE

129 MAPLE AVENUE, KATONAH

Cross River House's gardens are situated on seventeen acres overlooking the Cross River Reservoir in northern Westchester County. The gardens unfold through woodland paths filled with ferns, wildflowers, and large rhododendrons. From the paths you enter the first of the garden rooms. The hosta or shade garden is surrounded by trellises covered in clematis and wisteria. From the hosta garden you enter the perennial garden. Low fencing and stonework separate the border from a white azalea allée and a small crescent shade area under the magnolias.

Sundays; June 4 & 25, 10 a.m. - 2 p.m.

From Bedford Village: Take Route 22 North out of Bedford approximately 3.3. miles. Maple Avenue is a right turn onto a dirt road at a curved intersection. There are signs for Caramoor at this point, although you don't go towards Caramoor. Once on Maple Avenue, we are .5 mile on the right, #129. From I-684 North take Exit 6/Route 35/ Cross River/Katonah. Turn right at the end of ramp onto Route 35 East. Take the next right onto Route 22 South. Go 1.8 miles. Turn left at the intersection in the curve onto Maple Avenue (a dirt road), go .5 mile and the garden is on the right, #129. Please park along Maple Avenue on either side of the white gates.

David Lebe & Jack Potter

104 May Hill Road, Ghent

Our one-acre hillside meadow of native wildflowers and prairie grasses is nestled in woodland but offers wide views across Hawthorne Valley to the Taconic Hills. Wild lupines and coreopsis light the meadow in June. A gravel courtyard, small pond, and areas of improved soil near the house include a wide range of deer-resistant plants (especially alliums, poppies, roses, and euphorbias). September here features cardinal flower hybrids, late euphorbias, a large heptacodium, and a fenced garden where Griffith Buck and Austin roses mingle with more perennials and a few remnant edibles. A stone garage and garden walls link our efforts to May Hill's mysterious network of ancient (probably Native American) walls. Jack Potter was the curator of the Scott Arboretum; David Lebe is a photographer and garden designer.

Sundays; June 4, September 10, 2 p.m. - 6 p.m.

From the Taconic Parkway, take the Philmont/Harlemville Exit. Turn right (west) toward Harlemville on Route 21C. Go 1 mile to the first left, May Hill Road, then .5 mile to #104 on the right. Please park on May Hill Road.

Proceeds shared with The Aids Council of Northeastern New York, Hudson Office.

Dick Button — Ice Pond Farm

115 June Road, North Salem

Ice Pond Farm has beautiful views over meadow and pond. There is a kitchen garden-a mixture of vegetables, annuals, perennials, and roses. A bocce court has an allée of crab apples. A long flower border by the swimming pool, references to the fine art of figure skating, a stone bridge, and a wildflower walk complete this lovely garden

Sunday, September 10, 10 a.m. - 6 p.m.

Traveling South on I-684 take Exit 8/Hardscrabble Road. Turn right onto Hardscrabble Road and go east about 5 miles to June Road/Old Route 124. Turn right onto June Road and go .75 miles to #115. Traveling North on I-684 take Exit 7/Purdys. Take Route 116 East for about 3 miles to North Salem. Turn left onto June Road/Old Route 124. Go .5 miles to #115. Please park in field,

Duck Hill

23 BAXTER ROAD, NORTH SALEM

A series of hedged-in gardens are related to the ninteenth-century farmhouse they surround. They include an herb garden, a white garden, and a nasturtium garden, described in Duck Hill Journal and Breaking Ground by the author/owner.

Sunday, June 4, 10 a.m. - 6 p.m.

From I-684, take Exit 7. Follow Route 116 east to North Salem. After Route 121 joins Route 116 go approximately .5 mile. Turn left onto Baxter Road. Go to the top of the hill and turn right onto a private road. Duck Hill, #23, is the second house on the left. Please park along the road.

Ellen & Eric Petersen

378 CONKLIN HILL ROAD, STANFORDVILLE

This is a sunny sprawling country garden maintained by the owners. We have been adding some structure and shelter over the last few years with rocks, walls and arbors. I try to blend the garden into its wild surroundings with vigorous native shrubs and perennials, such as bottlebush buckeye, Joe Pye weed and butterfly weed. I like plants that seedin, such as feverfew, poppies, dill, chamomile, anise, hyssop and native bleeding heart, bluebells, columbine, goldenrod, and white wood aster. They provide continuity and act as informal ground covers. I'm planting for winter interest with beautiful bark and conifers; broad-leaved evergreens really struggle on this windy exposed site. I love yellow, purple, silver, and variegated foliage and any perennial that tops six feet.

Sunday, July 23, 10 a.m. - 2 p.m.

From Route 82 North, pass the firehouse in Stanfordville. Go 5 miles to Conklin Hill Road and turn right. Continue 2 miles up hill. The house is on the right after a sharp turn. Please pass the drive and pull into the field. The entrance will be marked.

Proceeds shared with The American Society of Botanical Artists.

Ely Garden

28 ALLEN ROAD, SALT POINT

Our contemporary gardens have evolved within the original nineteenth-century setting of the house, barn, and woods. These elements are set amid a rolling terrain which runs down to a five-acre pond surrounded by both native and "invasive" plants. Between the house and barn we placed large, deep, robust beds which are bordered by a pergola on one side and an Italianate upper garden on the other. A spring long border leads from the house to the pond.

Sunday, July 23, 10 a.m. - 2 p.m.

Take the Taconic State Parkway to the Salt Point Turnpike. Go west onto Salt Point Turnpike/Route 115 for 1.75 miles into the town of Salt Point. Turn right onto County Route 18. Bear right at the fork in the road onto Allen Road. The house is the first on the right. There is a five-foot-tall white fence along the road in front of the property. Please enter the south gates and park in the field.

Henriette Suhr
95 Old Roaring Brook Road, Mount Kisco

"Rocky Hills" is an appropriate name for this property-with hills, rocks of all sizes, and a lovely brook. The garden was started by the owner and her late husband about forty years ago. The azalea and rhododendron plantings number in the thousands. There is an extensive tree peony collection, a woodland garden, a fern garden, a wildflower garden, lots of bulbs, and irises of all descriptions. An interesting group of evergreens is planted among rocks. This is a most varied garden in all seasons.

Saturday, May 27, 2 p.m. - 6 p.m.

From the Saw Mill Parkway, travel north to Exit 33/Reader's Digest Road. At the traffic light turn left and then make a sharp right onto Old Roaring Brook Road. "Rocky Hills" is 1 mile on the right. From the Merritt Parkway, travel to the Cross County/Route 287 West. Exit the Cross County at the Saw Mill Parkway North. Travel to Exit 33/Reader's Digest Road. Follow directions above. Please park along Old Roaring Brook Road or Lawrence Farms Crossways as directed.

Proceeds shared with the Friends of Lasdon Arboretum.

Hudson Bush Farm
154 Yates Road, Hudson

Formal gardens surrounding the eighteenth-century house include color-oriented parterres, a double red border, a rock garden, and a long walk leading to a summer-house, small pool, and vegetable garden on three acres surrounded by old-growth woods.

Sunday, September 10, 10 a.m. - 4 p.m.

From the Taconic Parkway, take the Hudson-Ancram Exit. Take Route 82 West to the traffic light at Bells Pond. Continue west on Route 9/Route 23 to Yates Road, about 1 mile. Turn right onto Yates Road. Go .25 mile to driveway on the right at old brick house. Please park at the top of, or along the drive.

JADE HILL

13 LAKE AMENIA ROAD, AMENIA

Jade Hill is a hillside stroll garden with a varied collection of exotic plant material. A partial list includes dwarf yellow-stripe bamboo, fountain bamboo, lotus, magnolias, Japanese maples, and conifers. Trees, shrubs and perennials have been planted to form a tapestry of color and texture. Features include a walk-through bamboo grove and goldfish ponds. A new project, now in its early stages, is an Oriental viewing pavilion cantilevered over a ledge and overlooking a new specimen garden.

Sunday, July 9, 10 a.m. - 4 p.m.

From the traffic light in Amenia at the intersection of Routes 22, 44 and 343, take Route 44 West. Make the first left after the 55 mph sign, onto Lake Amenia Road. Gated driveway is after the fifth house on the right. Park on Lake Amenia Road.

JAMES & SUSAN HENRY

36 MEAD STREET, WACCABUC

A nineteenth-century farm is the setting for perennial gardens, specimen trees, a walled garden, cordoned apple trees, a vegetable garden, berries and fruits, a pond in a meadow, and a vineyard producing red and white wines.

Sunday, September 10, 10 a.m. - 4 p.m.

From I-684/Saw Mill Parkway, take Exit 6. Follow Route 35 East for 5 miles. After a long hill, look for Mead Street on the left. Take Mead Street .25 mile to #36 on the left. Turn left into the driveway and then left into the parking area. From Connecticut, Mead Street is 4 miles from the traffic light at Route 35 and Route 123. Please park in the field behind the vineyard.

Proceeds shared with The South Salem Fire Department.

JANE KEITER

43 TAYLOR ROAD, MOUNT KISCO

Various types of gardens surround my Colonial house on three acres. In the back yard, paths winding through an informal perennial and wildflower bed lead to a gazebo in a woodland setting. An assortment of ground covers set off collections of ferns, hostas, and hydrangeas.

Sundays; May 7, July 9, 10 a.m. - 4 p.m.

From I-684, take the Route 172 Exit and go west toward Mount Kisco. At the intersection with Route 117, turn left. At the next traffic light, turn east (left) onto Route 128 and travel for .6 mile. At the gatehouse, turn right onto Taylor Road. The house (#43) is seventh on the right. From Saw Mill Parkway, exit at the Reader's Digest Road. At the intersection with Route 117, turn north (left) and go to next traffic light. Turn right onto Route 128 and follow directions above. Please park in the street.

John H. Whitworth Jr.

506 Altamont Road, Millbrook

Far A-Field, most of all, is a collection of ornamental trees surrounding a small brick Adam-esque house built in 1931. The woods that protect the garden and give it privacy and quiet contain a variety of trees indigenous to Dutchess County, mainly deciduous hardwoods. A principal design feature of the garden is the long curving mixed border richly planted atop and beneath an old stone retaining wall. There is also a yellow-blossom, silver-foliage garden, a collection of large conifers, cutting/kitchen gardens, and a secret hot colors garden. Up the hill from the entrance front of the house is a slight bow to the Orient, and down the hill from the garden front is a touch of formality. Beyond, a near view of a horse farm and distant views of the Shawangunk Mountains take one's eye thirty miles across the Hudson. As you walk back toward the gate on the left is a small garden of dwarf conifers planted in moss beneath native gray birches.

Sunday, June 25, 2 p.m. - 6 p.m.

From the traffic light at the intersection of Routes 44, 82, and 343 in Millbrook, travel east on Route 343 toward Dover Plains, passing the Millbrook Golf and Tennis Club and a cemetery on the left. Then turn right onto Altamont Road/Route 96. Follow for 1.7 miles, then turn left onto Overlook Road. Then travel only .3 mile and turn left into a gravel drive marked "Far A-Field." Please park as posted.

Proceeds shared with Saint Peter's Episcopal Church

Judy & Michael Steinhardt

433 Croton Lake Road, Mount Kisco

The Steinhardt's love of plants is evident throughout this fifty-five-estate. More than 2,000 species of trees, shrubs, and perennials have been incorporated into the gardens. Landscape designer Jerome Rocherolle has created a naturalistic setting with walkways, stream beds, bridges, and ponds where plants can be aprreciated and nurtured. There are diverse orchards, a mature perennial bed, and a newly-developed alpine and wall garden. Much of the plant material is labeled for the viewer's benefit. Look for extensive use of ferns, moss (a moss bridge), more than 200 cultivars of Japanese maples. Wildlife and not-so-wildlife include exotic waterfowl, cranes, and peacocks.

Sundays; May 7, July 9, 10 a.m. - 4 p.m.

From the Saw Mill Parkway take the Kisco Avenue Exit (1 exit beyond Mount Kisco). Turn right at end of exit and after a few hundred feet, turn right onto Croton Lake Road. Number 433 is 1.8 miles to the mailbox on the left. Please park where directed.

KEELER HILL FARM

KEELER LANE, NORTH SALEM

Although the land has been farmed since 1731, it is just in the last ten years that gardens have been developed, including the perennial, the green, and the white garden. A friendship garden, which provides swimming pool privacy, was planted with friends' castoffs. The vegetable and fruit gardens were placed among the farm buildings. Cutting borders and a lilac walk were added in 1999.

Sunday, June 4, 10 a.m. - 4 p.m.

From Route 684 North take the Purdy's Exit. Turn right off exit ramp onto Route 116 East. Stay on Route 116 East for approximately 5 miles. Cross over Old Route 124/June Road. Route 116 will join up with Route 121 about 1 mile after the June Road intersection. Bear left at that intersection. About 1 mile up the road turn right onto Keeler Lane. Continue up Keeler Lane for .5 miles. On the left you will see seven yellow barns. Turn in the gate with the sign on the left pillar that reads "Keeler Hill Farm" and "Keeler Homestead" on the right pillar. Proceed up driveway to parking.

LAURA FISHER — WILDFLOWER FARM

44 BROAD BROOK ROAD, BEDFORD HILLS

The gardens at Wildflower Farm have recently been laid out to connect the large stone house, built in 1906, with the property's mature trees and open spaces. The new plantings include a Japanese-inspired azalea garden, the intimate studio flower garden, a formal boxwood parterre, and the grand staircase leading to a poolside belvedere and plantings. These are all linked by large open fields, bordered by woodlands and a series of hedges.

Sunday, September 10, 10 a.m. - 4 p.m.

Take Highway 684 to Exit 4. Turn west onto Route 172 (toward Mount Kisco). Go approximately 1 mile to West Patent Road and turn right (this is the street just after the school crossing sign). Go about 1.5 miles to the second stop sign and turn right onto Broad Brook Road. Wildflower Farm is .2 mile on the left-the second driveway on the left after turning onto Broad Brook Road. Please park on the road.

Laurence Sombke & Catherine Herman Garden

258 Connecticut Route 16, Hollowville

We have a number of mixed borders around our rural Hudson Valley Colonial home. A trout stream flows gently by. Cathy grows many tender perennials and exotics. I grow herbs and perennials that are attractive to butterflies and humming-birds. Most of our garden is dappled with shade but we do have a few sunny spots. I am the garden columnist for the Albany Times Union and a regular guest on Northeast Public Radio/WAMC.

Sunday, July 9, 10 a.m. - 4 p.m.

We are located at 258 County Route 16 in Hollowville, NY, just off Route 23 between Claverack and the Taconic State Parkway. Look for the beige Colonial house across from the post office.

Margaret Roach

Copake Falls

This ten-year-old homemade garden reflects my obsession with plants, particularly those with good foliage or of interest to wildlife (no, not deer!). Sixty species of birds visit. Informal mixed borders, water gardens, paved gardens, and meadow cover this two-and-one-half-acre hillside-a former orchard and pastureland dotted with a simple Victorian farmhouse, barn, and outbuildings, surrounded by the Taconic State Park. Recent collaborations with Glenn Withey and Charles Price of Seattle have smoothed rough edges and helped me begin to realize my hopes for the garden. Expansion continues, with several new areas created in 1999, and more dreams in mind.

Sundays; May 21, June 4, September 10, 10 a.m. - 4 p.m.

Off of Route 22 (5 miles south of Hillsdale, 13 miles north of Millerton), take Route 343 toward Taconic State Park signs. Bear right after the park and blue deli, over the metal bridge, past the camp. After the High Valley Road intersections on the left, continue right 100 feet more to the barn and house on the left.

Mark A. McDonald—Runningwater

67 Wire Road, Germantown

The sound and motion of a rocky creek lend rhythm to the Japanese spirit of this intimate, multi-level, fifteen-year-old garden. Rising above the lower creekside beds that feature weeping trees and shrubs, the naturalized steep walls of a curving ravine ultimately open to reveal a sudden view of distant Catskill peaks. A weathered fence dotted with architectural fragments and a baffle of evergreens define the roadside border of the upper garden, affording privacy and furnishing a backdrop for compact trees, mature shrubs and extensive perennial beds. This is essentially a shade garden hugging a precipitous hillside that relies on combinations and contrasts of shapes, foliage, and texture. Notable structures include a sculptor's lead-coated gate opening to expose a wisteria arbor, a rustic garden shed, and steps, walls and terraces crafted from local stone.

Sundays; June 4, July 9, noon - 6 p.m.

The garden is located at #67 Wire Road, just outside the Village of Linlithgo in Southern Columbia County. From Route 9, take 31 North from Blue Stores, 1.5 miles to Wire Road. Turn right, go approximately 3 miles to #67 on the left. From Route 9G, go south 4 miles from Rip Van Winkle bridge or 5 miles north from Germantown to Route 10 (green Linlithgo sign). Go east into village, bear right at red brick church on Wire Road. Go 300 yards across bridge to #67 on the right.

Midge & Dave Riggs

112 Lefurgy Avenue, Hastings-on-Hudson

The house is nestled into a rock ledge with natural outcroppings and niches all planted with choice alpines and rock plants covering one-third acre. A recirculating waterfall built into the ledge is edged with ferns, primroses, creeping phlox, and campanulas, planted in the chinks nearby. Alpine plants are nestled in holes drilled into the rocks in the tufa bed. Our great interest in western American plants prompted construction of sand beds to ensure perfect drainage; penstemons, townsendias, acantolimons, oxytropias, and erigoniums grow in them.

Sunday, May 7, 10 a.m. - 4 p.m.

From the Saw Mill Parkway, turn west onto Farragut Parkway. Go .9 mile to Mount Hope Boulevard. Go up hill .5 mile to Lefurgy Avenue; turn left. Go to Edgewood and turn right, then right onto Sunset. Please park on Sunset Road and walk to the right down the private road.

Proceeds shared with The Rock Garden Society.

Mrs. John C. Sluder

9 Half Mile Road, Armonk

This garden is modeled on a French jardin potager, with a decorative mixture of vegetables and flowers. The French-Norman house is surrounded by a home orchard with raspberries, apples, peaches, plums, and northern kiwi. Tubbed citrus and bay laurel trees thrive in the warmth around the swimming pool.

Sunday, June 4, 10 a.m. - 2 p.m.

From I-684, take Exit 2. Turn left onto Route 120 to Whippoorwill Road. Turn right onto Whippoorwill Road, go .7 mile to Half Mile Road (first right). The house, #9, is the first driveway on the right. Please park in circle and in driveway.

Mrs. John E. Lockwood

32 St. Mary's Church Road, Bedford

An unusual and interesting garden that makes use of its varied terrain. The path from the house leads through the apple orchard to a parterre-like garden of perennials and herbs. Specimen trees, a beautiful woodland, a collection of clematis, a large vegetable garden, and a wildflower meadow enhance the property.

Sunday, July 9, 10 a.m. - 2 p.m.

From I-684, take Exit 4/Route 172. Take Route 172 east to Route 22. Turn left onto Route 22. In Bedford Village, go right, staying on Route 172 East. Go about .5 mile and turn right at the Mobil Station onto Route 104/Long Ridge Road. Go .7 mile, turn right onto Miller's Mill Road. Turn left onto the first road, Mianus River Road. Go 1.5 miles to Saint Mary's Church Road. Turn right onto Saint Mary's Church Road and go .3 mile to beige farmhouse on the right, #332. There is a pond across the street. Please park at Saint Mary's Church at top of hill or along road.

Penelope & John Maynard

210 Hook Road, Bedford

We created a garden among rock ledges and oak woods on the steep shoulder of Mount Aspetong. The site is fragmented; thus the garden areas are designed to flow from one to another, linked together by a ribbon of stone walls. The greatest challenge has been to create some flat, restful spaces. The wide variety of plants must meet one criterion-to prove themselves in dry woodland conditions.

Sunday, May 21, 10 a.m. - 6 p.m.

From I-684, take Exit 4. Turn east onto Route 172. Go 1.5 miles to Route 22. Turn left and drive through Bedford. Just beyond the Bedford Oak Tree, 2.1 miles from Route 172 and Route 22, turn right onto Hook Road. The garden (#210) is almost at the top of the hill. Please park along road.

Phillis Warden

531 Bedford Center Road, Bedford Hills

This garden of many facets includes perennial borders, two water gardens, a formal vegetable garden, a wildflower garden, a moss and fern garden, a marsh garden, a woodland walk, and a formal croquet court. The garden extends over seven acres.

Sundays; May 21, June 25, July 23, 10 a.m. - 4 p.m.

From Bedford Village, take Route 22 towards Katonah to the intersection at Bedford Cross. The garden is on the left. Please park at Rippowam School and walk to 531 Bedford Center Road.

Ross Gardens

Snake Hill Road, Travis Corners, Garrison

This garden is a series of vignettes that flow into each other on five acres overlooking the Hudson River. The gardens are designed and maintained by the owner Arthur Ross and include a water garden, a moon (white) garden, a meditation garden, a rock garden, a fern garden, a shrub garden, cutting gardens and garden sculptures, along with a waterfall. Garden paths give easy access to many unusual flowers.

Sunday, June 25, 10 a.m. - 4 p.m.

Take Route 9 to the Garrison Golf Course. Turn west onto Snake Hill Road. The garden is .25 mile on the left. Parking available for 30 cars at any one time.

Roxana Robinson — Willow Green Farm

159 North Salem Road, Katonah

A writer's garden, Willow Green Farm has old-fashioned perennial borders, a white garden, an herb/kitchen border, a summer border, a woodland border, meadows, and stone walls on the grounds of a nineteenth-century farmhouse. All organic.

Sunday, June 4, 10 a.m. - 4 p.m.

From I-684, exit at Route 35 East (toward Cross River) approximately 2 miles. Turn left onto North Salem Road (a dirt road). Willow Green Farm, #159, is 1 mile on the right, past Mount Holly Road. Please park along the road.

Proceeds shared with The Natural Resources Defence Council.

TAILINGS—
DAVID WHITCOMB & ROBERT MONTGOMERY
404 WHITE BIRCH ROAD, GERMANTOWN

The gardens at Tailings comprise a series of bulb, perennial, and rose plantings closely integrated with the natural landscape and joined to each other by woodland paths. Axial cuts have been made through the woods to offer views in all directions and to complement the architecture. These culminate in a prospect of the Hudson River and entire Catskill Mountain range.

Sunday, May 21, 10 a.m. - 2 p.m.

From Germantown, take Route 9G North from the traffic light to the intersection of Route 10; turn right. Go .25 mile to White Birch Road; turn left. Go 1 mile to Tailings' driveway on the right. Look for #404 on the mailbox. Please park at the top of the driveway.

Proceeds shared with Friends of Hudson.

THE FARMSTEAD GARDEN
590 BIRCH HILL ROAD, PATTERSON

This garden, located on historic Quaker Hill, was planned as a rural landscape in keeping with its 1740 farmstead beginnings. A master plan was commissioned by the owners in 1985 to define the site's woodlands, wetlands, house gardens, and agricultural fields into a harmonious native plant landscape while preserving the property's horticultural heritage. An heirloom apple orchard greets you as you enter the fieldstone entrance. The driveway is the old stagecoach road, which connected Pawling, New York, with Danbury, Connecticut. Native wildflower meadows now grace the upper and lower fields after decades of haying. A grove of more than eighty mature blueberry bushes tell the story of the acid soil and summers of picking and tasting. The original vegetable garden is anchored by an old majestic quince, and the kitchen herb garden is filled with flowering thyme, catnip, lavender, with a border of germander. A two-acre wetland can be traversed to experience plant and aquatic wildlife. The roadside sloping fields have been mowed to create welcoming paths and sculptural grasslands.

Sunday, September 10, 10 a.m. - 2 p.m.

Take I-684 to Pawling. At the intersection of Route 311 turn right onto South Quaker Hill Road. At the first stop sign (2.5 miles) turn right onto Birch Hill Road. Follow the road to Box 590. The garden is on the left. From Connecticut, take Route 37 through Sherman and continue to Wakeman Road. The Akin Hall Library is on the right and the Hill Farm on the left. Turn left and continue south. This road becomes Birch Hill Road. Please park on the road.

Proceeds shared with The Conservancy for Historic Battery Park.

The White Garden

199 Elmwood Road, Lewisboro

The hardwood forest and native plants provide a "Sacred Grove" setting for the Greek Revival-style house. The gardens, designed by Patrick Chassé, are classically inspired near the house, including a nymphaeum, a pergola garden, a labyrinth, and a theater court. More exotic surprises are hidden in separate garden rooms. Sculptures and water features enrich the gardens.

Sunday, September 10, 10 a.m. - 4 p.m.

From the Merritt Parkway take Exit 38 and follow Route 123 North through New Canaan to the New York state line. The town of Lewisboro and the village of Vista are the first signs encountered. Go past the Vista Fire Department about .25 mile. Just after the shingled Episcopal Church on the right, Route 123 will bear left and Elmwood Road will bear right. Go approximately .25 mile just over a hill. At the beginning of a gray stockade fence on the right is the driveway at #199 Elmwood Road.

Vivian & Ed Merrin

2547 Maple Avenue, Cortlandt Manor

Overlooking a small lake, this garden has unfolded over a rocky wooded site over the last fifteen years, under the guidance of designer Patrick Chass,. New additions include a tempered glass-enclosed lookout over the lake and a wooden lotus bridge for perfect lotus viewing on a private pond. Mixed borders line garden rooms that flow among the landforms. Native plants form the framework for a collection that embraces many unusual and rare plants. Several water gardens enhance the site, and greenhouses and a formal kitchen garden provide additional plants, both ornamental and edible.

Sunday, July 23, 10 a.m. - 5 p.m.

From the Taconic Parkway, exit at Route 202. Turn left towards Peekskill. Go 2.5 miles, then turn left at the traffic light onto Croton Avenue, just past Cortland Farm Market. Go 1.2 miles to blinking traffic light/stop sign, and turn right onto Furnace Dock Road. Go .8 mile to blinking traffic light/stop sign, and turn left onto Maple Avenue. Go .9 mile to private road on the right. Go .2 mile to #2547 on the left. Please park at the house.

Zibby & Jim Tozer—Uplands Farm

Hunns Lake Road, Stanfordville

The gardens at Uplands Farm are surrounded by rolling hills, horse paddocks with romping miniature horses, Nubian goats and Belted Galloway cows, grand old trees, and a lush meadow of rye. Among the gardens, the Romantic Garden, with its forget-me-nots, bleeding hearts, trapezoidal loveseats by Madison Cox, and a Moorish gate is of special interest. The Wedding Folly, built in 1998, was inspired by the teahouse at Kykuit and has latticed walls and pagoda lanterns. The images of the fanciful juniper animal topiaries are reflected in the long reflecting pool. Nearby there are large arches, covered with William Baffen roses, which create a path to a meadow. The playhouse has a charming garden and its own rhubarb patch. The main garden is a seventy-foot-long herbaceous border filled with flowering perennials and grasses.

Sunday, July 23, 10 a.m. - 2 p.m.

From the Taconic State Parkway, take the Millbrook/ Poughkeepsie Exit. Turn right at the end of the ramp onto Route 44. Go about .2 mile. Turn left onto Route 82. Stay on Route 82 for about 8 miles. At the "Y" intersection from Stissing National Bank, bear right onto Route 65. Go 2 miles, passing Hunns Lake on your left. The main house is the third house past the lake on the right. Please park where indicated.

Anna B. Warner Memorial Garden

Constitution Island at the U.S. Military Academy, West Point, NY 10996. (914) 446-8676.

Old-fashioned perennial and annual border garden lining a fifty-yard path. Planted in nineteenth-century style with flowers described by Anna Warner in her book Gardening by Myself written in 1872. Cared for by dedicated volunteers, this garden received the Burlington House Award. Tours to Constitution Island are available on Wednesdays and Thursdays, mid-June to September. Reservations required.

Mid-June - October, Wednesdays and Thursday afternoons.

From the south, take Route 9W or Palisades Parkway to Bear Mountain Bridge Circle. Go 2 miles north on 9W, then take Route 218 through Highland Falls to West Point. After Hotel Thayer take first road right (Williams Road) down hill. Cross railroad tracks. Park north of South Dock. From the north, take Route 9W. Take first sign to West Point. Drive through West Point on Thayer Road. After road goes under stone bridge, take first road left (Williams Road) down hill. Follow as above.

Beatrix Farrand Garden at Bellefield &

Route 9, Hyde Park, NY 12538. (914) 229-9115.

The enclosed formal garden and surrounding wild garden were designed by the acclaimed landscape gardener Beatrix Farrand in 1912. Thought to be her earliest surviving residential project, it is now being restored. Adjacent to a magnificent eighteenth century house that was remodeled by the architects McKim, Mead & White in 1911, the garden evidences both colonial and American and formal European influences. Typical of Farrand's work , the subtle elegance of the plan and built elements are set off by lush borders in sophisticated color shemes.

Year round, daily, dawn - dusk.

Bellefield is part of the Roosevelt-Vanderbilt National Historic Sites and is located adjacent to the Franklin Delano Roosevelt Home Library. Please call (914) 229-9115 for more information.

 A preservation project of The Garden Conservancy.

Boscobel Restoration &

1601 Route 9D, Garrison, NY 10524. (914) 265-3638.

Boscobel is a museum of the Federal era, built between 1804 and 1808. Sixteen acres of landscaped grounds overlook the Hudson River and West Point and feature a formal rose garden, an orangery, and an herb garden. The herb garden is maintained by the Philipstown Garden Club. A one-mile woodland trail was opened to the public in October 1997.

April - October, daily, 9:30 a.m. - 5 p.m; November & December, 9:30 a.m. - 4 p.m.

From the New York Thruway go to Route 84 to Route 9D south to Boscobel. From the Taconic Parkway to Route 301 to Cold Spring traffic light. Turn left on 9D. From New Jersey, take the upper level of the George Washington Bridge to the Palisades Parkway north to the Bear Mountain Bridge to Route 9D.

Caramoor Gardens &

P.O. Box 816, Katonah, NY 10536. (914) 232-1253.
GARDEN@CARAMOOR.COM

Located throughout the 100 acres are the Sunken Garden, the Spanish Courtyard, the Butterfly Garden, the Sense Circle, the Cutting Garden, the Medieval Mount, the Woodland Garden, the Cedar Walk, the Renaissance Stroll Garden, and numerous antique containers planted in creative ways.

May - October, Tuesday - Sunday, 1 p.m. - 4 p.m. Individual group tours with luncheon available every Tuesday. Group tours by appointment. Call to reserve.

Girdle Ridge Road is off Route 22. Enter through Main Gate.

East Fishkill Community Library Garden ❧

380 Route 376, Hopewell Junction, NY 12533. (914) 221-9943.

Implemented, designed, and maintained by Mary Alice King, the gardens surrounding the library include a fragrance garden, which contains a vine-covered "secret garden" arbor where one can sit among statuary and fragrant plants. Additional gardens include two large perennial and annual borders, a bed of ornamental grass specimens, and a butterfly garden.

Year round, daily, dawn - dusk. Garden maps are available.

From the intersection of I-84 and the Taconic Parkway go north on the Taconic for 1.5 miles to the NYS Route 52 Exit. Turn left (west) onto Route 52 and travel for 1 mile to the traffic light at Route 376. Turn right onto Route 376. The Library is 1.5 miles on the right.

Hammond Museum
Japanese Stroll Garden ❧

Deveau Road, North Salem, NY 10560. (914) 669-5033.

A three-and-one-half-acre garden with thirteen different landscapes, there is a stroll garden, a waterfall garden, a garden of the Rakan, a fruit garden, a red maple terrace, and an azalea garden. The terrace restaurant serves lunch and provides a chance to dine among the trees and flowers.

Through October 24, Wednesday - Saturday, noon - 4 p.m.; November 1 - December 6, Friday & Saturday, noon - 4 p.m.

From 684 North take Exit 7 / Route 116 / Purdys / Somers. Go right at stop sign for .2 mile to Route 22. Turn left onto Route 22 North, bear right after .5 mile to Route 116 East and travel for 4 miles. After passing the North Salem Library, turn left at Salem center to Route 124 / June Road. Take the first right, Deveau Road, and follow to museum at end of street.

Innisfree Garden ❧

Tyrrel Road, Millbrook, NY 12545. (914) 677-8000.

Innisfree reflects an Eastern design technique called a cup garden which draws attention to something rare or beautiful by establishing the suggestions of enclosure around it. A cup garden may be an enclosed meadow, a lotus pool, a waterfall or a single dramatic rock covered with lichens and sedums. The visitors to Innisfree strolls from one three-dimensional garden picture to another.

May 1 - October 20. Closed Mondays and Tuesdays except holidays, Wednesday - Friday, 10 a.m. - 4 p.m.; Saturdays, Sundays & holidays, 11 a.m. - 5 p.m.

Innisfree is on Tyrell Road, 1 mile from Route 44 and 1.75 miles from the Taconic State Parkway overpass on Route 44.

❧ *public garden*

John Jay Homestead State Historic Site &

400 Route 22/Jay Street, Katonah, NY 10536. (914) 232-5651.

Five garden areas are maintained by the garden clubs in styles ranging from formal to natural/wilderness. The Bedford and Rusticus Garden Clubs use plantings that were popular in the 1920s and 1930s, with formal gardens following the plans of the last Jays to live on the site. The New York Unit of The Herb Society of America maintains an herb garden in a style tradional of herb gardens since medieval times. Hopp Ground Club is establishing gardens that will incorporate selections of plantings not accessable to all patrons in present garden areas, and Pound Ridge Garden Club is planting the field areas surrounding the newly opened Beech All ée. A selfguided walking tour of the site will assist the visitor in understanding all the gardens, intigrating them into the overall site history. An herb garden brochure is also available to visitors; both are free of charge.

Year round, daily, 10 a.m. - 4 p.m.

From Route I-684 take Exit 6. Take Route 35, heading east, for .25 miles to the next light. Turn right onto Route 22 (sign for John Jay Homestead). Continue for 2 miles. The site is on the left.

Kykuit &

Pocantico Hills, NY 10591. (914) 631-9491.

The extraordinary early-twentieth-century gardens at Kykuit, The Rockefeller Estate, were designed by William Welles Bosworth. Included are a formal walled garden, woodland gardens, a rose garden, fountains, and spectacular Hudson River views. Important twentieth century sculptures were added by Governor Nelson Rockefeller.

May - October, daily except Tuesdays, 10 a.m. - 3 p.m. No reservations needed.

All tours begin at historic Phillipsburg Manor, located on Route 9 in the village of Sleepy Hollow.

LYNDHURST ❧

635 South Broadway, Route 9, Tarrytown, NY 10591.
(914) 631-4481.

The grounds at Lyndhurst are an outstanding example of nineteenth-century landscape design. Elements include a sweeping lawns accented with shrubs and specimen trees, a curving entrance drive revealing "surprise" views, and the angular repitition of the Gothic roofline in the evergreens. The rose garden and fernery are later Victorian additions.

Mid-April - October, Tuesday - Sunday, 10 a.m. - 4:15 p.m.; November - mid-April, weekends, 10 a.m. - 3:30 p.m.

From the Taconic State Parkway take the Saw Mill River Parkway south to the exit for 287 West.* Follow signs to the Tappan Zee Bridge. (Do not take exit 1 for Tarrytown.) Continue to Exit 9. Turn left at the end of ramp. Turn left at the next traffic light. The entrance is .25 mile on the right. From Westchester and Connecticut, take I-95 south to Connecticut to Route 287 West. *Follow directions above.

MANITOGA ❧

P.O. Box 249, Garrison, NY 10524. (914) 424-3812.

A premier example of naturalistic landscape design, Russell Wright's woodland garden invites active participation in private path around the quarry and in the two and one half miles of trails open regularly to the public. This is a landscape not just to be seen but to be experienced. The eighty acre site, including Wright's house, is listed on National Register of Historic Places.

Open for Open Days visitors on Sunday May 21 & Sunday June 25, 10 a.m. - 2 p.m. Guided tours by appointment. Self-guided paths are open to the public. Weekdays: year round, 9 a.m. - 9 p.m. and weekends and holidays. April - October, 10 a.m. - 6 p.m.

In Garrison, NY on Route 9D, 2.5 miles north of the Bear Mountain Bridge and 2 Miles south of the intersection of Route 403 and 9D.

Mary Flagler Cary Arboretum/ Institute of Ecosystem Studies &

ROUTE 44A, MILLBROOK, NY 12545. (914) 677-5359.

The tree-acre perennial garden includes ecological demonstration beds. The fern glen is a two-acre display of native plants in natural communities. The greenhouse, open year round, is a tropical plant paradise and includes an "Economic Botany Trail." There are also trails, a picnic area, and an Ecology Shop with a plant room.

Year round except holidays. Monday - Saturday, 9 a.m. - 4 p.m.; Sunday, 1 p.m. - 4 p.m. Grounds open until 6 p.m. May - September. Greenhouse closes at 2:30 p.m.

From the Taconic State Parkway take Route 44 east for 2 miles. Turn onto Route 44A. The Gifford House Visitor and Education Center is 1 mile along Route 44A on the left. From Massachusetts and Connecticut take Route 22 to Route 44. Where Route 44 takes a sharp left to the village of Millbrook, continue straight on Route 44A. The Gifford House Visitor and Education Center is on the right, just before Route 44A (the Millbrook bypass) rejoins Route 44.

Montgomery Place &

P.O. BOX 32, ANNANDALE-ON-HUDSON, NY 12504. (914) 758-5461.

This 200-year-old estate enjoys a picturesque landscape, extolled by Andrew Jackson Downing. Included are ancient trees, and vistas of the Hudson River and Catskill Mountains. The early-century garden includes a wide variety of plants, many unusual. There are also hiking trails, pick-your-own orchards, and waterfalls.

Please call for a calendar of events.

From I-87 take Exit 19 for Kingston onto Route 209/199 east across the Kingston-Rhinecliff Bridge. Go left onto Route 9G for three miles and left again onto Annandale Road, bearing left onto River Road to the estate entrance.

Muscoot Farm &

ROUTE 100, KATONAH, NY 10536. (914) 232-7118.

Muscoot is a Westchester Country Gentleman's Farm circa 1880-1950. The herb garden on the property is cared for by the Muscoot Naturalist. The garden displays beds with tea, dye, fragrance and cooking herbs to be used for programs and workshops.

Year round, daily, 10 a.m. - 4p.m.

From Route 684 take Exit 6 (Route 35/Katonah) west on Route 35 for 1.3 miles. Turn left onto Route 100. The Muscoot Farm is on the right after 1.5 miles.

New York Botanical Garden ♣

200 Street & Kazimiroff Boulevard, Bronx, NY 10458-5126.
(718) 817-8700.

The New York Botanical Garden is one of the foremost public gardens in America and a National Historic Landmark. It has some of the most beautiful natural terrain of any botanical garden in the world, with dramatic rock outcroppings, a river and cascading waterfall, undulating hills, wetlands, ponds, and forty acres of historic, uncut forest. Within this grand 250-acre setting in the north Bronx, many gardens and special plantings offer stunning seasonal displays, from rainbows of tulips and azaleas in the spring to the rich tapestries of fall foliage. Several noteworthy buildings include America's most beautiful Victorian greenhouse, the Enid A. Haupt Conservatory.

Year round, Tuesday - Sunday, and Monday holidays. Closed Christmas. April - October, 10 a.m. - 6 p.m., November - March, 10 a.m. - 4 p.m.

From Westchester County, take the Cross County Parkway East or West to Bronx River Parkway South. Take Parkway Exit 7W / Fordham Road and continue on Kazimiroff Boulevard to Conservatory Gate on the right. From Connecticut take I-95 to Pelham Parkway West. Continue for three miles. Across from the Zoo entrance, bear right on Kazimiroff Boulevard to Conservatory Gate entrance on right. From New Jersey: Take the George Washington Bridge and Henry Hudson Parkway North to Mosholu Parkway Exit. Continue on Mosholu Parkway to Kazimiroff Boulevard, turn right, and continue to Conservatory Entrance gate on left. This site is also accessible by public transportation. Please call for details.

The Donald M. Kendall
Sculpture Gardens at PepsiCo ♣

700 Anderson Hill Road, Purchase, NY 10577. (914) 253-2900.

One hundred and twelve acres of landscape designed by Russell Page surround the world headquarters of PepsiCo, Inc. Spacious lawns and shrubs, plantings of trees, and small gardens provide settings for forty-five sculptures by renowned twentieth-century artists.

Year round, daily, dawn - dusk.

From I-84 East or West, take Route 684 South to the Westchester Airport exit. Take Route 120 South to Anderson Hill Road to PepsiCo on the right. From the Merritt Parkway South (which becomes the Hutchinson River parkway) take Exit 28 (Lincoln Avenue / Port Chester). Turn left onto Lincoln Avenue and proceed 1 mile to PepsiCo on the right.

Philipsburg Manor ♣

Route 9, North Sleepy Hollow, NY, 10591. (914) 631-3992.

This colonial-period working farm with water-powered grist mill is on the banks of the Pocantico River. The farm interprets the agricultural practices of the Hudson Valley. A recreated kitchen garden contains culinary, herb, and medicinal crops appropriate to the period. The gardens feature heirloom varieties of eighteenth-century plants.

April - December, daily except Tuesdays.

From I-87 take Exit 9 for Tarrytown and proceed north for 2 miles.

Springside Landscape Restoration ♣

P.O. Box 4915, Poughkeepsie, NY 12601. (914) 454-2060.

Springside is the only unaltered, documented work of Andrew Jackson Downing, one of the most influential landscape architects in American history. Once the summer home of Matthew Vassar (founder of Vassar College), the site was an "ornamental farm." Although unrestored, the landscape bears Downing's undeniable influence, illustrating the principles of the beautiful and the picturesque.

Year round, daily, dawn - dusk.

From the Taconic State Parkway take the Poughkeepsie/Route 44 Exit and then Route 44 west through Poughkeepsie until just before the bridge. Stay in the right lane for Route 9 South/Wappingers Falls for 1 mile to the Academy Street exit. At bottom of ramp, turn left. Go to the first entrance on the right at bottom of hill.

A preservation project of The Garden Conservancy.

Stonecrop Gardens ♣

R.R. 2 Box 371, Route 301, Cold Spring, NY 10516. (914) 265-2000.

At its windswept elevation of 1100 feet in the Hudson Highlands, Stonecrop enjoys a Zone 5 climate. The display gardens cover an area of approximately nine acres and include a diverse collection of gardens and plants, woodland and water gardens, a grass garden, raised alpine stone beds, a cliff rock garden, perennial beds, and an enclosed English-style flower garden. Additional facilities include a conservatory, a display alpine house, a pit house with an extensive collection of choice dwarf bulbs, and a series of polytunnels for overwintering half-hardy plants.

Open for Open Days visitors on May 7, June 25, & September 10, 10 a.m. - 4 p.m. April - October: Tuesday, Wednesday, & Friday as well as the first Saturday of each month, 10 a.m. - 4 p.m.

From the Taconic Parkway take Route 301 / Cold Spring Exit. Travel 3.5 miles to Stonecrop's driveway on the right. Just before the drive on the left, there is a wooden wheel and a cream-colored house with blue shutters.

Storm King Art Center &

P.O. Box 280, Mountainville, NY 10953. (914) 534-3423.

Surrounded by the undulating profiles of the Hudson Highlands, this museum, considered by many to be the leading outdoor sculpture museum in the world, celebrates the relationship between sculpture and nature. Five hundred acres of lawns, maple allées, terraces, and woodlands, surrounding a Normandy-style building, provide the site for more than 100 post WWII sculptures (many of monumental size) by leading international sculptors. Magnificent old rhododendrons, dogwood and specimen trees add to the parks beauty. J. Carter Brown, Director Emeritus of the National Gallery, has called Storm King, without question "the king of sculpture parks."

April 1 - November 15, daily, 11 a.m. - 5:30 p.m. (Hours extended to 8 p.m. Saturdays and Sundays in the summer.)

From the New York State Thruway / I-87 North, take Exit 16/Harriman/Monroe. Turn right onto Route 32. Travel north for 10 miles. Follow signs to Storm King Art Center. From the Hudson Valley and Connecticut, travel west on I-84 across the Newburgh-Beacon Bridge. Take Exit 10 South. Travel south on Route 32 for 7 miles. Follow signs to Storm King Art Center. From the Palisades Parkway, exit onto Route 9W from the Bear Mountain Circle. Travel north to the Cornwall Exit. Follow signs to Route 32. Turn right, cross covered bridge and exit left onto Orrs Mill Road. Follow signs to the Storm King Art Center.

Sunnyside &

West Sunnyside Lane, Tarrytown, NY 10591. (914) 591-8763.

The picturesque mid-nineteenth-century landscape is among the earliest, most important, and best preserved in America. It has a large, diverse collection of narcissi in April. A large kitchen garden with a varied collection of ornamentals and edibles was recreated in 1995.

Year round, daily, except Tuesdays.

From I-87 take Exit 9 for Tarrytown and proceed south for 1 mile.

The Lady Bird Johnson Demonstration Garden-The Native Plant Center &

75 Grasslands Road, Valhalla, NY 10595. (914) 785-6143.

This two acre garden, installed in 1998 on the college campus, contains only native american plants indigenous to the northeastern United States. The perennial and shrub beds are designed to show how these beautiful and vigorous American species can be used the home landscape. There are also two demonstration meadows, planted a year apart using different management techniques. The garden is designed for summer and fall color bloom, but is interesting all year. No pesticides or fertilizers are used in this garden.

Year round, daily, dawn - dusk. Guide available for Open Days visitors from noon -4 p.m. on June 18, July 16, August 13, September 17 and October 15.

The garden is located at the East Grassland entrance of the College next to the Security Building. From 287 east or west, take Exit 4 (Route 100 A). Turn north on 100 A. The college is .5 mile on right. At end of entrance road, turn right. From Northern Westchester, take Taconic to Sprain Brook Parkway. Exit at Eastview. Turn left onto Route 100. Enter at East Grasslands Gate and bear right at fork. *From Southern Westchester, take Sprain Brook Parkway Exit at Eastview. Turn right onto Rt. 100. Enter at East Grasslands Gate and bear right at fork.* *Follow road to Parking lot 1 on the right. Path through woods on far right of lot leads to garden.

The Mountain Top Arboretum &

P.O. Box 79, Tannersville, NY 12485. (518) 589-3903.

The Mountain Top Arboretum is a living museum of trees and shrubs created for the education and pleasure of the public. Its founders, the Ahrens' family designed and planted a seven acre mountain top area starting in 1977, to display the range of native and exotic trees and shrubs that successfully adapt to the rigorous climate at 2,500 feet elevation in the northern Catskill Mountains of New York State.

May - October, dawn - dusk. Gate is not locked so public may visit anytime.

From NYC: North on NYS Thruway to Exit 20/Saugerties. After toll booth, turn left at traffic light for .1 mile, then turn right onto Route 32. After 6 miles, take a left fork onto Route 32A to Palenville. At traffic light, turn left onto Route 32A to Haines Falls. Continue west on 23A to Tannersville, then turn right at traffic light onto Route 23C. After 2 miles, turn right onto dirt road (Maude Adams Road) 50 yards to Arboretum parking. From Albany: South on NYS Thruway to Exit 21/Catskill. After toll booth, turn left and proceed to Route 9W. Turn right onto 9W South to Route 23A. Continue west on Route 23A to Palenville and then to Haines Falls. From Haines Falls, follow directions above.

The Wildflower Island
at Teatown Lake Reservation ❧

1600 Spring Valley Road, Ossining, NY 10562. (914) 762-2912.
www.teatown.org. santonas@teatown.org.

The Island is a woodland garden of more than 200 species of native flowers. Several hundred pink lady's slippers make a spectacular display in May. In late summer, the sunny shores of the Island are ablaze with cardinal flowers, lobelia, iron weed, and other bright, moisture-loving flowers. A small interperative museum is at the entrance to the bridge leading to the island. Visitors are guided along narrow paths by experienced volunteers. Call for tour schedule.

May - September, Tuesday-Saturday, 9 a.m.-5 p.m.; Sunday, 1 p.m.-5 p.m. Closed Mondays. Wildflower Island tours: April to June, Saturday and Sunday, 2 p.m.; May, September, Saturday, 10 a.m. Open for Open Days visitors on May 21, 10 a.m. - 4 p.m. Available for private tours 10 a.m. - 2:00 p.m. Please call (914) 762-2912, ext. 10, for reservations.

Take the Major Deegan Expressway to Route 87 North to Exit 9 for Tarrytown (last exit before the Tappan Zee Bridge). Take Route 9 north to Ossining. Watch for Route 133 on right. At third traffic light after Route 133, turn right on Cedar Lane. Cedar Lane will become Spring Valley Road. Teatown is on the left 3.8 miles from Route 9.

Van Cortlandt Manor ❧

South Riverside Avenue, Croton-on-Hudson, NY 10520.
(914) 271-8981.

This restored Federal-period manor complex includes a border of period ornamentals of interest throughout the growing season, a large tulip display, a vegetable garden, an orchard, and narcissi naturalized at woodland edge. An extensive culinary and medicinal herb garden is also noteworthy.

April - October, daily except Tuesdays, 10 a.m. - 5 p.m.

Take Route 9 to Croton Point Avenue. Go east on Croton Point Avenue to traffic light. Turn right at traffic light onto South Riverside. Van Cortlandt manor is at the end of the road, past the Shop Rite shopping center.

Vanderbilt National Historic Site: Italian Gardens ❧

511 Albany Post Road, Route 9, Hyde Park, NY 12538-0698. (914) 229-6432.

The three-level formal garden covers three acres. The rose garden has more then 1,200 plants. The perennial garden, along the cherry walk, includes several hundred perennials, and thousands of annuals are planted each year in the upper beds.

Year round, daily, dawn - dusk. Group tours available by appointment.

Located on Route 9, on the left side of the road, just north of the Hyde Park Post Office.

Vassar College Arboretum, Native Plant Preserve, & Shakespeare Garden ❧

Vassar College, Box 25, Poughkeepsie, NY 12601. (914) 437-5686.

The Vassar College campus has a Shakespeare Garden, first planted in 1918 with plants represented in Shakespeare's writings. The garden has brick walks, statuary, knot beds, rose beds, heath and heather beds, and twelve rasied-brick beds containing herbs and cottage garden plantings. A hemlock hedge encloses the garden. There is also an arboretum with 220 species of native and non-native trees and shrubs. Aboretum maps are available.

Year round, daily, dawn-dusk

From Route 44/55 in Poughkeepsie turn onto Raymond Avenue to the Main Gate.

Wave Hill ❧

249th Street & Independence Avenue, Bronx, NY 10471. (718) 549-3200. www.wavehill.org.

Often called "the most beautiful place in New York," Wave Hill is a twenty-eight-acre public garden in a spectacular setting overlooking the Hudson River and Palisades. Formerly a private estate, Wave Hill features several gardens, greenhouses, historic buildings, lawns, and woodlands, and also offers programs in horticulture, environmental education, land management, landscape history, and the arts. All programs focus on fostering relationships between people and nature.

October 15 - April 14, Tuesday - Sunday, 9 a.m. - 4:30 p.m.; April 15 - October 14, Tuesday - Sunday, 9 a.m. - 5:30 p.m. Open until dusk Wednesday summer evenings.

From the West Side and New Jersey take the Henry Hudson parkway to Exit 21 (246-250th Street) Continue north to 252nd Street. Turn left at overpass and left again. Turn right at 249th Street to Wave Hill Gate. From Westchester take the Henry Hudson Parkway southbound and exit at 254th Street (Exit 22). Turn left at the stop sign and left again at the light. Turn right onto 249th Street to Wave Hill Gate.

WETHERSFIELD ♣

R.R. 1, Box 440, Pugsley Hill Road, Amenia, NY 12501.
(914) 373-8037.

Ten acres of formal and outer gardens surround Chauncey D. Stillman's Georgian-style brick home. The original garden around the perimeter of the house was created in 1940 by Bryan J. Lynch. Evelyn N. Poehler oversaw the maintenance of the garden from 1952 on and designed the formal classical-style gardens over a twenty-year period.

June - September; Wednesday, Friday, & Saturday; noon - 5 p.m.

From Route 44 east of Millbrook take Route 86 and turn right onto Pugsley Hill Road. Follow the signs for 1.3 miles to the estate entrance on left.

North Shore of Long Island Open Day

Regional Representative: Kyrnan Harvey

Sunday, May 21

GREAT NECK
Bodian Garden, 15 Clover Drive: 10 a.m. - 2 p.m.
Harvey Garden, 360 East Shore Road: 2 p.m. - 6 p.m.

SANDS POINT
Fern's Glade, 590 Sands Point Road, Sands Point: May 21, 10 a.m. - 2 p.m.

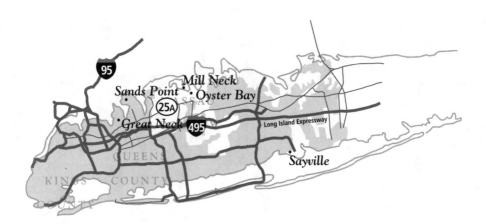

BODIAN GARDEN

15 CLOVER DRIVE, GREAT NECK

A small idiosyncratic town garden created by Kyrnan Harvey. A rectilinear plan is blurred by effusive plantings. Long Island pea-gravel paths are edged with bluestone veneer. There is a knot garden of box, variegated box, and lavender cotton; a reflecting pool garden secluded by yew hedge; and a quasi-pergola, "L"-shaped, that supports climbers and frames ever-changing tableaux. An enrapturing adaptation of the Jekyll style.

Sunday, May 21, 10 a.m. - 2 p.m.

Take the Long Island Expressway to Exit 33. Drive north on Lakeville Road, which, at the intersection with Northern Boulevard/Route 25A becomes Middle Neck Road. Take this through downtown Great Neck to Linden Boulevard on the left. Please park on Linden Boulevard.

FERN'S GLADE

590 SANDS POINT ROAD, SANDS POINT

A two-acre garden, secluded, expansive. Developed over the past decade by its owners and by Kyrnan Harvey, it features a large woodland, or shade garden; mixed beds and borders; a charming potager; or kitchen garden; a knot garden; and a beautiful old swimming pool. These are unified by a quality of design, the art of planting, and by wonderful antique garden ornaments throughout.

Sunday, May 21, 10 a.m. - 2 p.m.

Take the Long Island Expressway to Exit 36. Travel north on Searingtown Road, which, at the intersection with Northern Boulevard/Route 25A, becomes Port Washington Boulevard/Route 101, and then Middle Neck Road at Sands Point Country Club. Continue further north along Middle Neck Road to Sands Point Road and turn left. The garden is at the second driveway on the right. Park on Cedar Knoll Road just past 590 Sands Point Road.

HARVEY GARDEN

360 EAST SHORE ROAD, GREAT NECK

A rough pearl of a garden on one and one-half acres of flat land on Manhasset Bay. The dense plantings are mixed and layered throughout: maybe 200 taxa, including 30 classic roses, hydrangea, euphorbia, iris, crape-myrtle, clematis, viburnum, ilex, lilies, geranium, grasses, deutzia, spiraea under mature gray birch, black locust, and oak. A 150-foot mixed border, fifteen-feet-deep and running along the water's edge, is foiled and sheltered by Phragmites. The element of water is omnipresent, creating nuances of light and lovely views across the bay to Gatsby's East Egg.

Sunday, May 21, 2 p.m. - 6 p.m.

Take the Long Island Expressway to Exit 33 (18 miles from Manhattan. Travel north on Community Drive, which, at the intersection with Northern Boulevard/Route 25A, becomes East Shore Road. We are 3 miles north of the LIE, a mile and a half past Northern Boulevard on the water side. Please park on East Shore Road.

MEADOW CROFT,
THE JOHN E. ROOSEVELT ESTATE ❧

MIDDLE ROAD, SAYVILLE, NY 11701. (516) 472-9395.

This nature preserve, consisting of seventy-five acres of woods and tidal wetlands, was the summer home of John E. Roosevelt, a first cousin of President Theodore Roosevelt. The privet-and lattice-enclosed "kitchen garden" adjacent to the Colonial Revival home was planted and maintained by the Sayville Heritage Association and contains plant material that would have been available in 1910, the year to which the house is restores. Included are twenty-four varieties of heirloom roses, heirloom vegetables, annuals, and more than sixty varieties of perennials.

June 20 - October 24, Sunday, noon - 5 p.m. Closed July 4, September 5, & October 10.

Take Sunrise Highway/Route 27 to Lakeland-Ocean Avenue/CR 93 and exit south-bound. Proceed south on Lakeland-Ocean Avenue for approximately 2 miles to Main Street. Turn left onto Main Street and immediately bear right to South Main Street/ Middle Road. Continue on Middle Road for .5 mile and turn left at estate entrance.

Planting Fields Arboretum &

P.O. Box 58, Oyster Bay, NY 11709. (516) 922-9200

The arboretum offers a spectacular display of trees and shrubs, many imported from Europe and Asia. The extensive holly and maple collections provide year-round interest while recent plantings of magnolias combine with more than 600 different rhododendron and azalea species and hybrids to offer a kaleidoscope of color in April and May. Sweeping lawns boast majestic beech and linden trees as well as cedar, fir, elm, tulip, oak and magnolia. Along the drives are planted showy beds of daffodils and other spring flowering bulbs.

April - September, Monday - Sunday, 9 a.m. - 5 p.m.

Long Island Expressway, Exit 41N or Northern State Parkway, Exit 35N. Proceed north to Route 106. Follow Route 106 into Oyster Bay. Turn left onto Lexington Avenue and follow signs to Planting Fields Arboretum. By train from New York City, take LIRR Oyster Bay line to Oyster Bay. Taxi cabs available at station for a 5-minute ride to Planting Fields Arboretum.

The John P. Humes
Japanese Stroll Garden &

CORNER OF OYSTER BAY ROAD & DOGWOOD LANE, MILL NECK, NY (516) 676-4486.

The Humes Japanese Stroll Garden, a four-acre gem of landscape design, provides a retreat for passive recreation and contemplation. Moving through the garden, where the views, textures, and balance of elements have been planned following Japanese aesthetic principles, visitors experience a walking meditation that can lead to inner peace. The garden symbolizes a mountain beside a sea, where gravel paths represent mountain streams that form pools, eventually flowing into the ocean, represented by a pond.

April 29 - October 22, weekends, 11:30 a.m. - 4:30 p.m. Private tours and tea ceremony by appointment during the week..

Long Island Railroad to Locust Valley or Long Island Expressway to 39N. Glen Cove Road north to 25A/Northern Boulevard turn right onto 25A, pass C.W. Post, pass Route 107 to next light, Wolver Hollow Road. Old Brookville Police Station is on the left. Turn left to end, right onto Chicken Valley Road, pass planting Fields Arboretum, pass blinking light. Half mile after blinking light, tall pinkish wall on right. At that corner, Dogwood Lane, turn right, and right into parking lot. From East to West: Exit 41N on LIE to 106N to 25A. Left to second traffic light at Wolver Hollow Road. Right turn to very end. Turn right onto Chicken Valley. Pass Planting Fields Arboretum. Pass blinking light and go half mile to Dogwood Lane. Right turn and sharp right into garden parking lot.

🌐 A *preservation project of The Garden Conservancy.*

Saratoga Springs Open Day

Mrs. James H. Lenden

Saturday, June 17

Georgiana Ducas Garden, 150 Meadowbrook Road: 10 a.m. - 4 p.m.
Bruce Solenski's Garden, 182 Caroline Street: 10 a.m. - 4 p.m.

Bruce Solenski's Garden

182 Caroline Street, Saratoga Springs

The row of hemlocks was one of the first evergreens I planted after buying this Greek revival-style house (c. 1840) in 1986. The hedge not only serves to create privacy but also protection for the semi-circle of Madison Snows, which are one of the earliest blooming rhododendrons, and the dogwood *Cornus florida*. Gout weed, pachysandra, and sweet woodruff create a wonderful ground cover under the majestic Norway spruce. The circumference of this evergreen is ninety-four inches. The impatiens and browalia are satisfying in this east garden. A short stone path leads to my quiet sitting, reading, and writing area. The concord grapes grow high into the spruce, which creates a beautiful canopy for this area. My south garden is my sun garden with annuals and perennials. Deadheading is made easier by the use of a fieldstone wall. The meadow rue (*Thatictrum polyganum*) is wonderful and I will continue to nurse all the volunteers. The white picket fence is the end of my garden and nature normally dictates what is best in front of the fence.

Saturday, June 17, 10 a.m. - 4 p.m.

From I-87/Northway take Exit 14/Union Avenue into Saratoga Springs. The first traffic light is Henning Road. The second traffic light is East Avenue. The flat track is on the left. Turn right at the next traffic light onto Nelson Avenue. Please park on the street.

Georgiana Ducas Garden

15 Meadowbrook Road, Saratoga Springs

This very private hidden garden garden, surrounded by a magnificent forest of mixed hardwoods and stately white pines, has many remarkable features. Trees include weeping evergreens, dwarfed ornamental and espaliered fruit trees which provide the stage for a perennial extravaganza. Growing in the woodside garden are many native woodland plants, spring ephemerals, and horticultural delights, designed by Robin Wolfe. The main garden containsa black reflecting pool and is surrounded by two tiers of bluestone walls, behing which are perennials from around the world. Something of unusual interest is happening in all seasons.

Saturday, June 17, 10 a.m. - 4 p.m.

Travel north on I-87 to Exit 24/Albany. Continue north after toll gates. Signs will read "Montreal." Take Exit 14 and turn left onto Route 9P South. The second road on the left is Meadowbrook Road. Turn left and go approximately 2 miles. Watch for a grey mailbox on the right with #150. Turn into a hidden driveway on the right. The house cannot be seen from the road.

CONGRESS PARK &

BROADWAY/ROUTE 9, SARATOGA SPRINGS, NY 12866. (518) 584 - 4471.

Congress Park is the location of the Canfield Casino frequented by Diamond Jim Brady in the Gay Nineties. The park includes plantings and a Saratoga Spring.

Year round, daily, dawn - dusk.

Located between Broadway/Route 9 and Union Street in the center of town across from the Visitors' Center.

SARATOGA SPA STATE PARK &

BROADWAY/ROUTE 9, SARATOGA SPRINGS, NY 12866.

Includes the Hall of Springs, Saratoga Performing Arts Center, and the Gideon Putnam Hotel.

Year round, daily, dawn - dusk.

From I-87 take Exit 13N onto Broadway. Enter the park from Route 9 to drive through the Avenue of Pines.

YADDO &

P.O. BOX 3975, SARATOGA SPRINGS, NY 12866. (518) 584-0746.

Formerly the home of Spencer and Katrina Trask, this estate is presently an artists' retreat with gardens open to the public. There are extensive formal rose gardens and an informal rock garden included in this mature landscape.

Mid-June - September, daily, dawn - dusk.

From I-87 take Exit 14. Take Union Avenue/Route 9P west, crossing over the Northway. Yaddo is the first entrance on the left. Union Avenue goes into town and ends at Congress Park.

& *public garden*

OHIO

OHIO OPEN DAYS

May 20: Dayton
June 10: Columbus
June 24 & July 8: Cincinnati

Cincinnati Open Day

Regional Representative: Mrs. William R. Seaman

Saturday, June 24

Amy & John Duke, 223 Kearney Street: 10 a.m. - 4 p.m.
Hanna Schliess's Garden, 117 West Sharon Road: 10 a.m. - 4 p.m.
The Rose Garden, 5584 Palisades Drive: 10 a.m. - 4 p.m.

Saturday, July 8

Beth & Jay Karp, 5875 Mohican Lane: 10 a.m. - 4 p.m.
Julie Mahlin's Garden, 2500 Observatory Avenue: 10 a.m. - 2 p.m.
William & Mary Bramlage, 6900 Given Road: 10 a.m. - 4 p.m.

Amy & John Duke

223 KEARNEY STREET, CINCINNATI

Our American Hemerocallis Society Display Garden features 500 different cultivars of daylily, including a complete Stout Medal collection and a collection of Don C. Steven's award-winning "eyed" daylilies. Plantings are arranged around statuary, pathways and stone walls with interesting features such as the Faire Garden and Child's Garden. Perennials include seventy-five varieties of hosta and eighty varieties of woody shrubs. We plant about 2000 annuals each spring to carry color well into fall. Nearly all plants are labeled. We welcome visitors (and cameras) and provide a tour guide write-up intended to be both educational and entertaining.

Saturday, June 24, 10 a.m. - 4 p.m.

Exit I-75 at Galbraith Road/Exit #10. Turn west. The first street is Woodlawn at the traffic light. Turn left. Kearney is the next hard left turn. We are at #223, about the third house on the right. Please park on the street.

Proceeds shared with The Greater Cincinnati Master Gardener Association.

Beth & Jay Karp

5875 MOHICAN LANE, CINCINNATI

This amazing three-acre garden is maintained by Beth and Jay alone and has been created over the last five years. This garden has many separate garden rooms. A formal blue and white garden is enclosed by boxwood and brick. Raised beds with stone walls contain vegetables, herbs, and flowers. Between the raised beds, is an area with a bench, roses, and sundial. Gardens by the pond are colorful and feature plants that can survive "wet feet" during the winter. Several shade gardens feature hosta, ferns, and flowing trees and shrubs. Trees, which include stewartia, black gums, Japanese maples, bald cypress, and a weeping dogwood, are featured throughout the garden. There is a new conifer garden as well as a new raised bed next to the brick terrace which is enlivened by gorgeous containers.

Saturday, July 8, 10 a.m. - 4 p.m.

From I-71 North, take Exit 12/Montgomery Road and turn left. Go approximately .5 mile and turn right onto Galbrith Road. Continue to the second traffic light, Miami Road and turn right. Go approximately 1 mile to Euclid and Miami. Stay in the right lane and continue on Miami Road. Drive approximately 1.4 miles (past Camargo and Shawnee Run Road) and turn left onto Graves Drive. Go .6 mile and turn left onto Mohican Lane. The garden is at the third house on the left. Please park on the street.

Proceeds shared with The Cincinnati Horticultural Society.

HANNA SCHLIESS'S GARDEN

117 WEST SHARON ROAD, CINCINNATI

This is a narrow, but deep one-acre lot with a charming German cottage with overflowing window boxes. The gardens are a series of rooms. From the rear deck, step into a shady oasis, then down a path to the garden house with window boxes. Showcased here are astilbes and climbing roses, hydrangeas and three large water gardens with fountains. The garden features fifty varieties of clematis. Continue on to roses surrounding a sculpture in a bed of pebbles. The Healing Garden is filled with herbs and another water garden with lotuses and a pump dripping into the pool. The Copper Garden has you looking through the 'smoke' of a smoke tree to a copper sculpture on a bed of brown fine pine nuggets. Find color beyond with lilacs, roses, phlox and buddleia. Don't miss the 'mushroom patch' at the rear.

Saturday, June 24, 10 a.m. - 4 p.m..

From I-75 take Exit 15 (Sharon Road) and go West. Pass railroad tracks and main intersection at Congress Avenue/Princeton Pike/Route 747 and continue straight ahead to #117 on the left. Please park on the street.

Proceeds shared with The Cincinnati Horticultural Society.

JULIE MAHLIN'S GARDEN

2500 OBSERVATORY AVENUE, CINCINNATI

This is a fourteen-year-old English cottage garden enhanced by a wrought iron fence. It sits on a corner lot in a turn-of-the-century neighborhood. The garden flows in large graceful curves and is edged with silver lamb's ear. There are more than 165 different perennials including achillea, astilbe, thalictrums, helianthus, asters, boltonia, buddleia, clematis and brunnera. Each year I add about 2,000 annuals to ensure constant color in a scheme of pink, purple, white and lemon yellow. Within the beds are small trees and shrubs including Carolina silverbell, Tanyosho pine, Korean fir, vitex, chamaecyparis 'Boulevard' and 'Fernspray Gold', viburnums and cornus mas. A rear brick patio backs up to a brick garage wall which has a fountain on it. Thirty containers give color to this secret garden.

Saturday, July 8, 10 a.m. - 2 p.m.

From I-71 Northbound take Exit 5/Dana Avenue. At the end of the ramp at traffic light, turn left onto Duck Creek Road. Go .7 mile and turn right onto Dana Avenue. At the traffic light at Madison Road, Dana changes to Observatory Avenue. Go past traffic light to corner of Berry Avenue on the left. Look for house with wrought iron fence and lots of flowers. Park on either Observatory Avenue or Berry Avenue.

Proceeds shared with The Cincinnati Horticultural Society.

THE ROSE GARDEN

5584 PALISADES DRIVE, CINCINNATI

Voted the best residential rose garden (1991) in America, our garden now features more than 1000 rose bushes with more than 600 different cultivars. It is designed with soft curves which lead the eye to view the more than twenty rose beds. Our rose hybridizing skills are evident throughout the garden. Multiple large areas of annuals, perennials, conifers and tropical plants grace the estate. More than 150 varieties of hosta are planted. Strolling the brick path will finally lead the visitor to spectacular view of the Ohio River. Still a baby of thirty years, our garden grows in splendor every year.

Saturday, June 24, 10 a.m. - 4 p.m.

Take I-75 South or North to 50 West/River Road. Turn right onto Anderson Ferry Road. Turn left onto Palisades Drive. The house is the last on the right, #5584 Palisades Drive. Approximate distance from the center of Cincinnati, 11 miles. Park on Palisades Drive.

Proceeds shared with The Cincinnati Horticultural Society..

WILLIAM & MARY BRAMLAGE

6900 GIVEN ROAD, CINCINNATI

Informal cottage garden of wildflowers, bulbs, perennials, amid annuals in five acres of beech forest. Garden accents include an antique iron fence, a pond with a Robinson iron fountain, stone benches and urns, bridges and creeks, and meandering paths through the woods and gardens.

Saturday, July 8, 10 a.m. - 4 p.m.

From I-75 or I-71 take I-275 East to Loveland/Indian Hill Exit. Turn right onto Loveland Madiera Road (pass major intersection at Remington Road). Proceed .25 mile past Remington, turn left onto Spooky Hollow Road. Turn right (at stop sign) and continue on Spooky Hollow. Turn right (at stop sign) onto Given Road. Go 2.4 miles to #6900 Given Road to the Bramlage gardens.

Proceeds shared with The Cincinnati Horticultural Society.

Cincinnati Zoo & Botanical Garden 🐾

3400 VINE STREET, CINCINNATI, OH 45220.(800) 94-HIPPO.

Among the finest horticultural display gardens in the country, the Cincinnati Zoo and Botanical Garden features over 3,000 varieties of trees, shrubs, tropical plants, bulbs, perennials and annuals. Arranged in extensive landscaped gardens and in naturalistic settings simulating animal habitats, many of the plants are labeled, providing identification and interesting information for the garden enthusiast. The Zoo, celebrating its 125th anniversary, boasts one of the largest and finest spring gardens on the country with over a million spring bulbs and thousands of colorful, early-blooming shrubs and trees. The Zoo's outstanding butterfly and pollinator gardens include interpretive signs providing information about butterflies, flowers and gardening as well as the importance of the symbolic relationships of plants and pollinators. Home to the largest collection of hardy bamboo species in any Midwest botanical garden, the Zoo also has one of the largest plantings of perennials and ornamental grasses in Ohio.

Year round, daily, Summer hours (Memorial Day - Labor Day) 9 a.m. - 6 p.m. Winter hours (Labor Day - Memorial Day) 9 a.m. - 5 p.m.

From I-74, go east to I-75 North. Take I-75 North to Mitchell Avenue exit. Turn right onto Mitchell Avenue. Turn right onto Vine Street. Turn left onto Forest Avenue. Turn right onto Dury Avenue. The Auto Entrance is on the right. From I-75 North, take Mitchell Avenue exit. Turn right onto Mitchell Avenue. Turn right onto Vine Street. Turn left onto Forest Avenue. Turn right on Dury Avenue. The Auto Entrance is on the right. From I-75 South, take Mitchell Avenue exit. Turn left onto Mitchell Avenue and follow as above.

Civic Garden Center
of Greater Cincinnati 🐾

2715 READING ROAD, CINCINNATI, OH 45206. (513) 221-0981.

The Civic Garden Center of Greater Cincinnati is located in the Hauck Botanic Gardens, also known as "Sooty Acres." The property was donated to the CGC by Cornelius Hauck, who developed the property into an urban oasis. The garden includes rare, historic trees, and herb garden, a hosta garden, a dwarf conifer collection and a children's and butterfly garden.

Year round, daily, dawn - dusk.

From I-71 South, take the William Howard Taft Exit to Reading Road. Turn right and proceed one block to Oak Street. Turn left onto Oak Street and take an immediate left into the CGC parking lot. From I-71 North, take the Reading Road exit and proceed north on Reading Road to Oak Street. Turn left onto Oak Street and take an immediate left into the CGC parking lot.

Spring Grove Cemetery & Arboretum ♣

4521 SPRING GROVE AVENUE, CINCINNATI, OH 45232. (513) 681-6680.

Since its founding over 150 years ago, Spring Grove has remained a leader in cemetery design and management. The landscape "lawn plan" concept was created here and, although it was considered a radical concept of cemetery design at that time, it later became accepted almost universally as the model plan. Spring Grove remains a masterwork of the landscaping art, studied by horticulturists and admired by thousands of visitors. The Cincinnati Chamber of Commerce lists it among the city's outstanding attractions, proudly quoting the praise of an artist who once said "Only a place with a heart and soul could make for its dead a more magnificent park than any which exists for the living." With over 733 acres, fourteen lakes and one waterfall, three expansive floral borders, twenty-three champion trees and more than 1,000 labeled woody plant specimens within the Arboretum, Spring Grove truly is one of Cincinnati's best-kept secrets.

Front gate: daily; 8 a.m. - 6 p.m. North gate: daily. 8 a.m. - 5 p.m.

From downtown, I-75 North. Proceed to Mitchell Avenue Exit #6. Turn left (west) onto Mitchell Avenue. Travel Mitchell Avenue to Spring Grove Avenue, turn left onto Spring Grove (in center lane) past three traffic lights (including the light at Mitchell). Pass under third light (Winton Road) and get into curb lane as you pass under light. Entrance to cemetery is approximately 500 feet ahead on the right. From Dayton, I-75 South to Mitchell Avenue. Exit #6. Bear right (west) on Mitchell Avenue. Follow as above. From Indiana, I-74 East to I-75. Continue on I-75 to Mitchell Avenue Exit #6. Proceed as previously instructed. From Columbus, I-71 North to Norwood Lateral Exit E562. Follow lateral to I-75 South to Mitchell Avenue Exit #6. Turn right onto Mitchell Avenue and proceed as above.

Columbus Open Day

Regional Representatives: Dr. Sherran Blair & Mrs. Robert F. Hoffman Jr.

Saturday, June 10

Beth & Bob Hamilton's Garden, 1181 Millcreek Lane: 10 a.m. - 4 p.m.
Fling's Arboretum, 477 E. Dominion Boulevard: 10 a.m. - 4 p.m.
Gene & Marg Friley's Garden, 4028 Lyon Drive: 10 a.m. - 2 p.m.
Nancy & Dave Gill, 2454 West Lane Avenue: 10 a.m. - 2 p.m.

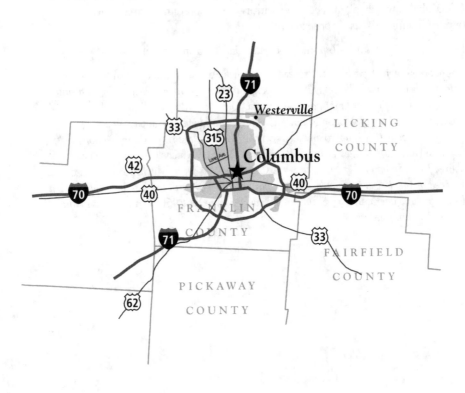

Beth & Bob Hamilton's Garden

1181 Millcreek Lane, Columbus

This warm and happy garden was designed to complement the house's architecture and to create an active play space for our family, which includes three small grand-children. Major renovations included tree removal to allow the sun to enter, privacy plantings, and slope control. More unique plants include *Carpinus betula* (ironwood), *Parrotia perisca* (Persian witch hazel), *Cercis canadensis* f. alba (white bud), and Vitis coignetiae (crimson glory grape). This is truly a "lived in" garden and a garden we love.

Saturday, June 10, 10 a.m. - 4 p.m.

Take Route 315 and exit at Lane Avenue. Travel west on Lane Avenue to Kenny Road. Turn north on Kenny Road, driving past Ackerman Road, Fishinger Road, and W. N. Broadway. There are traffic lights at each of these intersections. Continue on Kenny Road past 1 more traffic light at Tremont Road to Millcreek Lane. The Ohio State University Golf Course will be on the left. Turn right onto Millcreek Lane to 1181. The garden is at the gray house on your right. Please park on Millcreek Lane.

Fling's Arboretum

477 East Dominion Boulevard, Columbus

More than 250 conifer cultivars, mostly dwarf, are featured, interplanted with more than thirty-five maple and a dozen beech cultivars and complemented by other unusual and rare trees, shrubs and ground covers. The aesthetic design is accented by many garden sculptures, boulders, tree peonies, fifteen ornamental grass varieties, hosta, and perennials. Paths take you through sun and shade gardens and a native hillside woodland.

Saturday, June 10, 10 a.m. - 4 p.m.

From Lane Avenue, travel north on Route 315 to Henderson Road. Continue east on Henderson Road, past High Street, to Cooke Road. Continuing eastward on Cooke Road, past the two dips for Indian Springs ravine, turn on Colerain Avenue, the first road to the left. Continue north for 4 blocks until you reach Dominion Boulevard then veer left and turn west past the one-story elementary school and "no outlet" sign. We are southwest of the school at a long concrete drive. Please park on street in front.

Gene & Marg Friley's Garden

4028 Lyon Drive, Columbus

This informal do-it-yourself garden, developed over a period of many years, features more than 100 works by its retired professor of art creator. Ranging from a massive twelve-foot fountain to delicate functional ceramics, are all blended into the sun and shade multilevel landscape so that it becomes a sculptured garden rather than a sculpture garden. Backing onto a golf course, it invites a wide variety of birds and butterflies, some dozen mammal species, plus transient ducks, turtles, and frogs. Many of the vistas are whimsical or humorous in nature (a pruned palm-like silver maple with coconuts, i.e. the rare maple nut tree). Neat rather than manicured, the garden contains numerous tropical plants as well as herbs, vegetables, and wildflowers.

Saturday, June 10, 10 a.m. - 2 p.m.

Turn off Route 315 onto West North Broadway, which deadends into Kenney Road (.5 mile). Turn right onto Kenney Road. Go to McCoy Road (second traffic light, about 1 mile). Turn left onto McCoy Road. (This is N.E. corner of golf course). First street on left is Lyon Drive. Fifth house on left is 4028 Lyon Drive. Park in driveway or into adjacent vacant lot.

Nancy & Dave Gill

2454 West Lane Avenue, Columbus

This garden, featured in *Good Housekeeping* magazine in May 1997, is adjacent to a busy public street. The design of the garden complements the contemporary, full-time working lifestyle of the owners. The terrace and water garden at the rear of the home is secluded, quiet, and visible from the kitchen and the sunroom of the home. Predominantly a mid- to late-summer garden, it contains drifts of named varieties of hosta, daylilies, dwarf conifers, ornamental grasses, perennials, companion plants, and a few annuals.

Saturday, June 10, 10 a.m. - 2 p.m.

Take Route 315 to Lane Avenue. Go west approximately 3 miles (past shopping center) and turn onto Asbury Road (only one way turn). The garden is on the corner, with the driveway entrance on Asbury Road. Please park on the street.

Dawes Arboretum &

7770 Jacksontown Road SE, Newark, OH 43056-9380.
(800) 44-DAWES

Established in 1929, the Dawes Arboretum is dedicated to education in horticulture, natural history, and arboretum history. It includes 1,149 acres of horticulture collections, gardens, natural acres, a Japanese garden, the Daweswood House, and collections of hollies, crab apples, rare trees, and rhododendrons. A four-and-one-half-mile auto tour and eleven miles of trails provide easy access.

Year round, daily, dawn - dusk.

Located 30 miles east of Columbus and 5 miles south of Newark Route 13, north of I-70, off of Exit 132.

Franklin Park Conservatory & Botanical Garden &

1777 East Broad Street, Columbus, OH 43203. (614) 645-8733.

The Conservatory features the original Victorian Palm House, which was placed in the National Register of Historic Places in 1974. A large addition, which features a tropical rain forest, a desert environment and a bonsai collection, was completed in 1992. The Conservatory is surrounded by a five-acre formally landscaped grand mallway, fountains, sculptures, a Japanese garden, a victory garden and innovative educational displays.

Year round, daily, dawn - dusk.

The Conservatory and Garden are located approximately 2 miles east of the center of downtown Columbus, on the south side of Broad Street.

Inniswood Metro Gardens &

940 Hempstead Road, Westerville, OH 43081-3612. (614) 895-6216.

Originally the home of Grace and Mary Innis, Inniswood is a balance of colorful, landscaped garden and natural areas, yet it captures the warmth and serenity of a long-established estate garden. The herb, rock, and rose garden fit the contours of the land and are in harmony with the meadow and woodlands. Cultural and educational programs and tours are offered for all ages. Fall is celebrated with "An Affair of the Hort," held the last week of September.

Year round, daily, 7 a.m. - dusk.

Take Route 270 to the Westerville Exit. Turn left onto Westerville Road. Turn left at the first traffic light onto Dempsey. Turn left at the second traffic light onto Hempstead Road. The road will veer to the right after the fire station, and the entrance to the garden is on the right.

& *public garden*

THE RUSSELL PAGE SCULPTURE GARDEN
OF THE COLUMBUS MUSEUM OF ART ❦

480 EAST BROAD STREET, COLUMBUS, OH 43215. (614)221-6801.

The garden was designed in 1978 by Russell Page (1906-1985), one of the twentieth century's best-known garden designers. In a professional career that spanned more than fifty years, Page designed and worked on hundreds of public and private gardens all over the world. There are only twelve documented Page gardens in the United States. Our Museum Garden is one of three in Ohio. Toward the end of his career, Page realized that many of his gardens existed only on paper or in photographs, and he hoped very much that our Museum would preserve this garden as it does other works of art. Designed by Page to include white-blooming plants only, our Garden is tended to by Museum staff and the Museum's Garden Club.

Regular Museum Hours, Tuesday - Sunday, 10 a.m. - 5:30 p.m.; Thursday, 10 a.m. - 8:30 p.m.

The Columbus Museum of Art and Russell Page Sculpture Garden are located in the Discovery District, just 4 blocks east of the State Capitol. From I-71, take the Broad Street exit and head west. Turn right on Washington Avenue and turn left on Guy Street. The Museum parking lot is on the left.

THE TOPIARY GARDEN
AT THE DEAF SCHOOL PARK ❦

480 EAST TOWN STREET, COLUMBUS, OH 43215. (614) 645-0197.

George Seurat's famous post-impressionist painting, "A Sunday Afternoon on the Island of La Grande Jatte," is recreated in topiary of taxus and yews. There are fifty topiary people, three dogs, a monkey, and boats in a real pond representing the Seine. The largest figure is twelve feet tall. A visitor's center with facilities and a museum store are open midday seasonally except Mondays. Call for hours.

Year round, daily, dawn-dusk

From I-71 South, take the Broad Street Exit, go west and pass Washington Avenue (no left turn). Turn right on 9th Street, right on Gay Street and right on Washington Avenue. Go one block to East Town Street. From I-71 North, take the Main Street Exit and go to Rich Street (one block). Turn right onto Washington Avenue and go one block to Town Street. From I-70 East or West, take I-71 North Exit and follow directions above.

Dayton Open Day

Regional Representatives: Barbara Rion & Mrs. James Woodhull

Saturday, May 20

KETTERING
Burnap-Crotty—Wood Hollow Gardens, 3649 Wood Hollow Road: 10 a.m. - 4 p.m.

DAYTON
Ellie Shulman, 253 Schenck Avenue: 10 a.m. - 4 p.m.
Patti Demirjian, 3732 Blossom Heath Road: 10 a.m. - 4 p.m.
Sunnyside—The Deering Family Gardens, 1100 Ridgeway Road: 10 a.m. - 4 p.m.
Susan & Jim Clift, 46 Briar Hill Lane: 10 a.m. - 4 p.m.

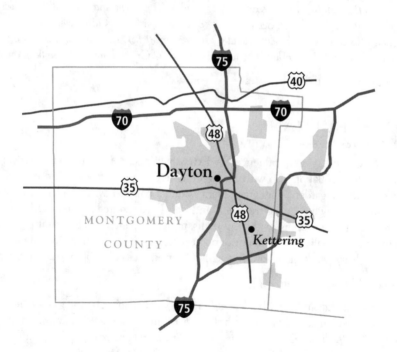

Burnap-Crotty — Wood Hollow Gardens

3649 Wood Hollow Road, Kettering

Our Wood Hollow garden was created out of an area of weeds, tangled honeysuckle and grapevines that has been designated common ground. It has evolved into a woodland garden consisting of bulbs, perennials, trees and shrubs, wildflowers, with paths of pine needles providing access. Pam Cumming, a master gardener, who helps maintain the Crotty Garden, gives it the loving care that is needed to keep it free from invasive plants and occasional deer that might decide to have a dinner of hostas and lilies. It puts on its best show in the spring. It was designed by Melinda Sloan of the Siebenthaler Co., for which she received two "American Garden Awards."

Saturday, May 20, 10 a.m. - 4 p.m.

From I-75 take Exit 50B. Turn left at end of ramp onto Route 741S. Go to third traffic light to Kettering-Dorothy Lane and turn left. Proceed on Dorothy Lane to Southern Boulevard (approximately 2 miles) to golf course on the left. Turn right onto Southern Boulevard. Proceed to Big Hill Road (approximately .75 mile). Turn right onto Big Hill Road west to Ridgeleigh Road. Turn left at Security Gate at Ridgeleigh Road. Go straight ahead on Ridgeleigh Road to Wood Hollow Road (first street on right). Burnap home is first on the left. Wood Hollow Garden is between Burnap and Crotty homes. Please park on street.

Proceeds shared with Riverscape.

Ellie Shulman

253 Schenck Avenue, Dayton

My garden style has been influenced by Extensive English, French, and American garden touring and by collaboration with garden designer Ziggy Petersons. In front is a shaded "garden within a garden"—all green plant material but no lawn. Challenges of difficult terrain and mostly full sun to the south and west have resulted in a terraced rose garden and several "garden rooms" with perennials, topiary, espalier, and a start at pleaching. There is an unusually large amount of plant material on less than an acre of property, and I am always working toward the goal of "continuous color, bloom, and fragrance."

Saturday, May 20, 10 a.m. - 4 p.m.

From I-75 take Edwin Moses Boulevard/University of Dayton Exit and go east on Edwin Moses .8 mile to Stewart Street (first traffic light). Turn right onto Stewart and proceed .6 mile (third traffic light). Turn right onto Brown Street and proceed .7 mile (4 traffic lights plus 2 more streets). Turn left onto Schenck Avenue and proceed to #253.

Patti Demirjian Garden

3732 Blossom Heath Road, Dayton

The gardens, planted in 1928 on a three-acre site, were lost until 1984 when the original design was discovered. In 1986, the restoration process began in earnest with the reconstruction of the formal rose garden, vegetable and herb gardens, and perennial beds. Most recently, the remains of a 200-foot-wide rock garden with paths, five ponds, and waterfalls have been unearthed, revealing the main features of the original one-acre woodland garden. In spring, thousands of naturalized bulbs and wildflowers bloom with those that have emerged on their own since the garden has been reconstructed.

Saturday, May 20, 10 a.m. - 4 p.m.

From Route 48/Far Hills Road go west on Dorothy Lane to Southern Boulevard (1.25 mile) Turn right onto Southern Boulevard and travel .8 mile to Blossom Heath Road. (Kettering Medical Center is on the right). Turn left onto Blossom Heath and proceed .4 mile to #3732, an English Tudor-style with circular drive and fountain in the center.

SUNNYSIDE—THE DEERING FAMILY GARDENS

1100 RIDGEWAY ROAD, DAYTON

In 1994 we rescued nearly two acres from years of neglect and made plans to restore the gardens. We found treasures—gnarled redbuds, cherry trees, a stand of lilacs, relics of a rock garden—rebuilt the terrace and stone walls, and refurbished the fountain. We planned an all-season garden, using an extensive variety of trees, shrubs, perennials, and a myriad of bulbs to have wonderful color from spring through fall. Our passion for lilacs and roses is reflected in the formal gardens. We spend many hours nurturing the shade and perennials gardens, enjoying the changes through the seasons. The ultimate compliment came from an octogenarian who knew the owner/architect in the 1920s: "The Sunnyside Garden has not looked so wonderful since Harry lived here!"

Saturday, May 20, 10 a.m. - 4 p.m.

From I-75 take the Edwin Moses Road/University of Dayton Exit. Turn east and continue to Stewart Street. Turn right, and go to Stewart Street. Turn right, cross the bridge and go to the second traffic light at Main Street. Turn right onto Main Street. After the third traffic light (5-way intersection), the next street is Harman. Turn right onto Harman, pass one traffic light (Harman School is on the right), to the next stop sign. The garden is on the southeast corner of Harman and Ridgeway. Please park on the street.

SUSAN & JIM CLIFT

46 BRIAR HILL LANE, DAYTON

Ours is an informal cottage garden with water as a focal point. Carved out of the woods, this naturalistic garden was designed to be enjoyed from various vantage points, both outside and inside our home.

Saturday, May 20, 10 a.m. - 4 p.m.

From I-75 take the Main Street Exit and go south on Route 48/Far Hills to Park Avenue. Turn right onto Park Avenue and go to stop sign (Harman Avenue) and continue down Park Avenue. Briar Hill Lane is on the left. Park on Park Avenue and walk to the lane.

AULLWOOD GARDEN &

930 AULLWOOD ROAD, DAYTON, OH 45414. (937) 898-4006.

Aullwood Garden Metro park is a 1920s country estate garden. The shady woodland combines native wildflowers, bulbs, and exotic plants. A meadow has some native prairie species. Peak bloom is in spring, especially April and May. There is something in bloom most of the year from helleborus, narcissus, mertensia, and syringa to echinacea, lycoris, hosta, and colchicum.

March 1 - November 30, Tuesday - Sunday, 8 a.m. - 7 p.m.

From I-75, take Route 40 West, take Aullwood Road South at Englewood Dam. Pass Aullwood Audubon Center; turn right into garden parking via sign.

A preservation project of The Garden Conservancy.

COX ARBORETUM & GARDENS &

6733 SPRINGBORO PIKE, DAYTON, OH 45449. (937) 434-9005.

The Cox Arboretum exhibits landscaped and natural areas on 175 rolling acres. Garden features include the Edible Landscape Garden, Herb Garden, Founders Water Garden, and the Shrub Garden. Woody plant collection includes crab apple, magnolias, lilacs, maples, oaks and conifers. Hiking trails traverse approximately seventy acres of woodlands and ten acres of prairie and wetland.

Year round, daily, 8 a.m. - dusk. Closed Christmas and New Year's Day.

From I-75 got to Exit 44. Go east on Route 725 1 mile to Route 741/Springboro Pike, south 2 miles to the entrance.

THE STILLWATER GARDENS &

STILLWATER GARDENS METROPARK/WEGERZYN CENTER, 1301 EAST SIEBENTHALER AVENUE, DAYTON, OH 45414-5397. (937) 277-9028.

These formal gardens feature Federal, English, and Victorian theme gardens, as well as rose, shade, and children's gardens, all flanking the Garden Green with ash allée. This MetroPark also features the scenic Stillwater River, the Marie Aull Nature Trail, and a mature lowland forest, or wetland wood, through which meanders a 350-foot boardwalk. The center presents programs on horticulture.

Year round, daily, 8 a.m. - dusk. Closed Christmas and New Year's Day

Located 1.5 miles west of I-75 and 4 miles south of I-70. Take I-75 to 57B, Wagoner Ford Road. Turn west to Siebenthaler Avenue, continue west on Siebenthaler and turn right into the Cultural Arts Complex, before the Siebenthaler Bridge. Follow the drive .5 miles to The Stillwater Gardens and Wegerzyn Horticultural Center.

PENNSYLVANIA

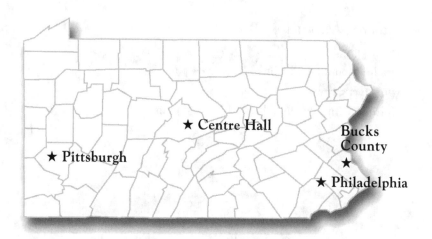

PENNSYLVANIA OPEN DAYS

May 13 & June 11: Centre Hall
May 13: Philadelphia
May 14: Bucks County
September 10: Pittsburgh

Bucks County Open Day

Regional Representative: Jack Staub

Sunday, May 14

NEW HOPE
Jericho Mountain Orchards: 10 a.m. - 4 p.m.

WRIGHTSTOWN
Hortulus Farm, Pineville Road: 10 a.m. - 4 p.m.

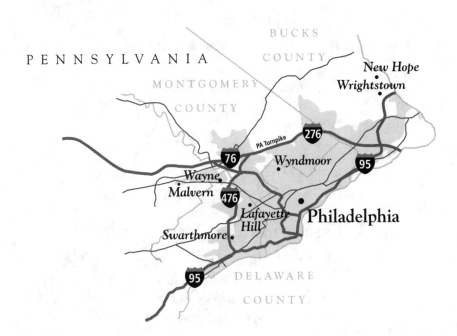

HORTULUS FARM

62 THOMPSON MILL ROAD, WRIGHTSTOWN

Our garden appears as an integral part of the Pennsylvania landscape as befits an eighteenth-century farmstead with barns and a healthy population of animals. We are lucky enough to be nestled in our own little valley, quite far off the road and unusual for a house of this age. Our seventy-two acres try to respect the integrity of the farm's historical significance and the natural landscape, with the occasional whimsical or formal statement thrown in. Lots of woods and pasture. Lots of shrubs and naturalized perennial plantings in the stream and woodland gardens, yet formal borders, follies, and gazebos, and sizeable herb and vegetable gardens. All is anchored by the formal simplicity of classic Bucks County architecture.

Sunday, May 14, 10 a.m. - 4 p.m.

From New Hope, take Windy Bush Road/Route 232 south out of New Hope for approximately 5 miles. At the "Wrightstown Township" sign on the right, turn immediately left onto Pineville Road. *Go on Pineville Road for approximately 1 mile to a right onto Thompson Mill Road. Continue over bridge through a series of steep, winding, uphill turns, and up into a clearing and straight-away. From Philadelphia take I-95 North toward Trenton for approximately 40 miles to Exit 31/New Hope. Turn left at end of ramp onto Taylorsville Road. Go north for 3 miles to Wood Hill Road on the left. Stay on Wood Hill Road for approximately 2.7 miles to the first stop sign. Turn right onto Eagle Road and go .3 mile to the first left onto Pineville Road. Follow from * above.

JERICHO MOUNTAIN ORCHARDS

BUCKMANVILLE ROAD, NEW HOPE

A delightful, terraced, country garden surrounding a seventeenth-century stone and timber farmhouse. Many varieties of old garden roses and climbers ramble over an eighteenth-century walls, barns, trellises and tuteurs leading to lovely perennial borders and formally parterred beds. There are also charming shade pond and stream gardens, as well as a sizeable nineteenth-century apple orchard.

Sunday, May 14, 10 a.m. - 4 p.m..

From New Hope: Take Route 232 South about 4 miles to Street Road. Turn left onto Street Road, then take your first right onto Buckmanville Road. Jericho Mountain Orchards will be about .5 mile down on your right. From Hortulus Farm Nursery, turn right out of drive onto Thompson Mill Road. Continue to stop sign, then left onto Pineville Road. Buckmanville Road will be about .5 mile down on your right. Turn right and continue .5 mile to Jericho Mountain Orchards on the right.

Centre Hall Open Day

Regional Representative: Dr. Richard Morgan

Saturday, May 13 & Sunday, June 11

PINE GROVE MILLS
Alice's Garden, 160 East Pine Grove Road: 10 a.m. - 2 p.m.

SPRUCE CREEK
David Pechmann's Garden, Smiley Lane: 2 p.m. - 6 p.m.

STATE COLLEGE
Deno's Garden, 139 Lenor Drive: 10 a.m. - 4 p.m.
Rae's Garden, 705 Holmes Street: 10 a.m. - 4 p.m.

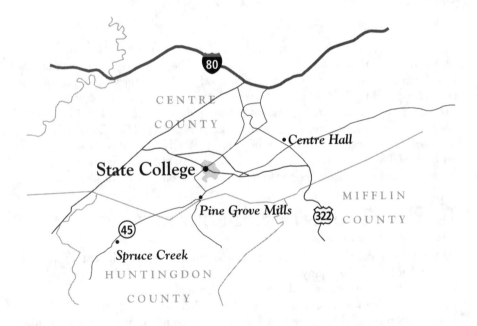

ALICE'S GARDEN

160 EAST PINE GROVE ROAD, PINE GROVE MILLS

You will be delighted with my secret garden. It is hidden behind an ordinary house on a very busy street in Pine Grove Mills. The foothills of Pine Grove Mountain are the garden's backdrop. The retaining walls throughout the small property are built of native stone. I have spent the last fifteen years creating a perennial garden that has so far attracted many species of birds, a few squirrels and chipmunks, one toad, one garter snake, and lots of strolling neighbors. Come and spend a day in beautiful Nittany Valley. I look forward to showing you my garden.

Saturday, May 13; Sunday, June 11; 10 a.m. - 2 p.m.

From Route 26 South in State College or Route 45 West in Boalsburg, travel 6 miles to Pine Grove Mills. The garden is located in the center of town, directly across from Centre Marine. Look for a white house with black shutters, a red tin roof, a large front porch, several lattice privacy fences, and a stone wall. Please park on the street.

DAVID PECHMANN'S GARDEN

SMILEY LANE, SPRUCE CREEK

A small rustic garden that walks around the house. Set magnificently below a near mountain and edged with mature white pines, this garden is constantly challenged by its wild neighbors. Still a building after 20 years, the lawn areas and beds variously contrast and blend with the wild. The plantings are relaxed in style and here and there are punctuated by more formal elements: stone wall/steps and a clipped yew hedge.

Saturday, May 13; Sunday, June 11; 2 p.m. - 6 p.m.

From State College (30 minute drive). Route 26 South to blinking traffic light in Pine Grove Mills (5 miles). Straight through blinking traffic light on Route 45 West about 12 miles to fork in road. Bear left on 45 West. Set tripometer. At 2.9 miles, see Smiley Lane on left. Turn left onto Smiley. Go to the first real lane on left (low stone wall). Turn left, last house at top of hill on right. Please park in the gravel driveway.

Deno's Garden

There will be 100 to 150 different botanical species in flower on the visitation dates. There are large colonies of many Eastern U.S. species and colonies of three endangered species. The garden has small cliffs, many rock outcroppings, steep hillsides, woods, a marsh, a spring, and more than 200 yards of trout stream.

Saturday, May 13; Sunday, June 11; 10 a.m. - 4 p.m.

The grounds are only 2 blocks from the intersection of Routes 322 & 26. From this intersection proceed 1 long block SW on Route 26 (towards State College) to Puddintown Road. Turn right onto Puddintown Road. Turn onto the first road on the left (Lenor Drive). This is a dangerous turn, as cars come up a hill. We are the second house on the right (139 Lenor Drive). Park along road in front of the house.

Rae's Garden

705 HOLMES STREET, STATE COLLEGE

My eight-year-old garden contains 350 rose varieties, most of which are old and species roses. A community of perennials, shrubs, small trees, grasses and animals, it is an organic garden in that I rely on heterogeneity, compost and manure and do not use pesticides or commercial fertilizers. The roses are large shrubs, hardy, disease-resistant, entangled with companion plants. Variety helps prevent disease and insect concentrations, and encourages pest-prey interactions. Close planting inhibits weeds, conserves moisture, moderates soil temperatures. Birds provide spirit and song, help to keep insects in check, and are as important as plants. Complexity, chaos and twisting paths allow for wonderful surprises.

Saturday, May 13; Sunday, June 11; 10 a.m. - 4 p.m.

In State College, enter East Park Avenue from North Atherton Street/Route 322 or from University Drive. Turn north off East Park Avenue on Holmes Street and go 2 blocks. Number 705 Holmes is on the right. Please park on front street.

Rhoneymeade Arboretum & Sculpture Garden ⚘

RD 1, Box 258, Centre Hall, PA 16828. (814) 364-1527.

Rhoneymeade is an intimate public garden, which provides sites for a variety of sculptures. Century-old hemlocks, spruces, arborvitae, and maples tower around massings and specimens of deciduous and evergreen trees planted since 1984. Paths reveal an old orchard, gazebos, ponds, limestone walls, a brick garden, and an 1853 brick farmhouse. These create spaces for abstract and figurative sculpture in wood, stone, and metal. Because the garden straddles a high north-south valley ridge, it offers outstanding views to surrounding farm fields, forests, and sky. The new studio is a treat too.

Open for Open Days visitors on May 13 & June 11. Otherwise open the first weekend of each month from April - October. 10 a.m. - 2 p.m.

From State College take Route 322 South/East. At the Exxon Station in Boalsburg go east on Route 45 for 4.4 miles. Make a sharp, left turn on Rimmey Road and .6 mile turn in at Rhoneymeade Arboretum & Sculpture Garden sign.

Philadelphia Open Day

Regional Representative: Mrs. Morris Lloyd, Jr.

Saturday, May 13

LAFAYETTE HILL
Mr. & Mrs. George Q. Nichols, 730 Andorra Road: 10 a.m. - 4 p.m.

PHILADELPHIA
Alice & Richard Farley, 606 St. Andrews Road: 10 a.m. - 4 p.m.
Ann & Frank Reed, 716 West Mt. Airy Avenue: 2 p.m. - 6 p.m.
Eric & Nina Schneider, 8235 Crittenden Street: 10 a.m. - 4 p.m.
Homewoods-Bill & Ann Hozack, 9002 Crefeld Street: 10 a.m. - 4 p.m.

WYNDMOOR
Mr. & Mrs. Henry F. Harris, 575 East Evergreen Avenue: 10 a.m. - 4 p.m.
Tom & Leslie Purple Garden, 611 East Gravers Lane: 10 a.m. - 4 p.m.

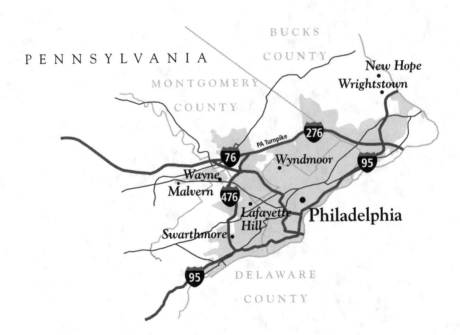

ALICE & RICHARD FARLEY

606 ST. ANDREWS ROAD, PHILADELPHIA

This landscape architect's twenty-year-old woodland garden overlooks the beautiful Wissahickon Valley of Philadelphia's Fairmount Park. Filled with many hundreds of rare treasures, the garden is used as a lab, testing plants new to the trade for hardiness, deer resistance, drought tolerance and overall garden worthiness. Paths and stairs, some steep, wind through the landscape, creating vistas and passing unusual combinations of texture, form and foliage color. Although it is at its flowering peak in the spring, the garden is designed to be interesting year-round, and utilizing its special microclimates ensures that something is in bloom 365 days a year.

Saturday, May 13, 10 a.m. - 4 p.m.

From Exit 25 of the Pennsylvania Turnpike or Exit 8 of Route 476 go east on Germantown Pike. Continue for several miles, passing through Plymouth Meeting, Lafayette Hill, and after entering Philadelphia begin driving up a long hill, Chestnut Hill. Pay attention to stay in correct lane, always staying straight on Germantown Pike/ Avenue. At the top of the hill, Chestnut Hill Hospital will be on the left. At the light, go right onto Chestnut Hill Avenue. Take second left (no stop sign), following traffic onto Seminole Avenue. Go two blocks and at traffic triangle bear right onto St. Martin's Lane. Railroad tracks will be on the left. Drive 2 blocks and turn right (no stop sign) onto Hartwell Lane. Cross over golf course, cricket club will be on the left, and take first right (no stop sign) onto St. Andrews Road. Number 606 is a modern tan stucco house on left (number over carport). Park on either side of the road. Travel time from turnpike is 15- 20 minutes.

ANN & FRANK REED

716 WEST MT. AIRY AVENUE, PHILADELPHIA

This gracious stone home was built in 1931 in the style of a country farmhouse. The property was landscaped by Frederick Peck thirty-five years ago. As the trees and shrubs matured they destroyed the feeling of light and space of the original design so the present owners decided that it was time for a major restoration. One of the redesign objectives was to use the whole two acres, to save and reuse many of the old plants, and make the property low maintenance. First the many large mature trees and shrubs were moved and properly sited to the perimeters of the property. Next the perennial garden was transformed from the Williamsburg style of four fifteen-foot squares into an open space with curving walks and manageable beds. In this process the owners moved 400 perennials from the old garden and then back into the garden that you see today. In the back yard, terraces were planted with heaths and heathers. This last year the old pond was redesigned and now features waterfalls and bog gardens, completing the restoration. Foundation plantings include drifts of astilbes and ferns, and the old box hedge has been cut back to be in scale with the house. Today a four-year-old garden flows from one space to another, using stone, brick, texture, shape and color for harmony and balance.

Saturday, May 13, 2 p.m. - 6 p.m.

Take the Pennsylvania Turnpike to Exit 25/Norristown. Exit onto Germantown Pike East and continue on Germantown Pike approximately 6 miles through Chestnut Hill to Lincoln Drive (thirteenth traffic light). Turn right onto Lincoln Drive. After the first traffic light (Allen's Lane), the next street is Mt. Airy Avenue. Turn right and continue for 4 blocks to 716 on the left. Please park on the street.

Proceeds shared with The Morris Arboretum.

ERIC & NINA SCHNEIDER

8235 CRITTENDEN STREET, PHILADELPHIA

Our garden is a densely planted one-half acre lot in the Chestnut Hill section of Philadelphia, known as the Garden District of the city. The remnants of the original 1954 plantings consist of mature Ilex opaca hedges, large sweet gum and oak trees and some sizable shrubs such as Pieris and rhododendron. These provide valuable privacy and form the backbone of multiple garden areas that we have developed over the last ten years for mixed border-type plantings. We attempt to provide four-season interest and indulge a particular interest in euphorbia, lilies, peonies, and hydrangea as well as foliage texture and color in general.

Saturday, May 13, 10 a.m. - 4 p.m.

From Germantown Avenue/take Willow Grove Avenue North through 2 stop signs; turn left onto Crittenden Street, up slight hill, house on right. Please park on the street.

HOMEWOODS—BILL & ANN HOZACK

9002 CREFELD STREET, PHILADELPHIA

Bordering Fairmount Park, our five-acre garden slopes away from the house-gently to the south, steeply to the west. The property was named Homewoods in 1930, and the gardens were reconfigured in 1949 by Umberto Innocenti. Given over to institutional use from 1969 to 1996, the house and grounds are being rehabilitated one room and path at a time by and for our family. The "hidden" garden really was by grapevine, and the fern path had stinging nettle as its element of surprise!! In spring, our azaleas framing the south lawn foam pale pink under dogwoods, enkianthus, and native rhododendron.

Saturday, May 13, 10 a.m. - 4 p.m.

From the intersection of Routes 476 & 276 (Pennsylvania Turnpike), take the Norristown Exit onto Route 422/Germantown Pike south. Travel 5 miles, past Bell's Mill Road. (Woodmere Art Museum is on left). Turn right at next street onto Hampton Road and take to dead end. Turn left onto Crefeld Street and go to #9002 on the right (brown stone wall and lanterns on gate posts). Park on Crefeld Street.

MR. & MRS. GEORGE Q. NICHOLS

730 ANDORRA ROAD, LAFAYETTE HILL

Arched roses, honeysuckle and clematis outline the entrance to this walled garden, which is defined by an eighteenth-century stone bank barn and a nineteenth-century farmhouse. Inside the walls are flowering perennial borders curving around the perimeters and paths leading to mirrored trellises, a small pond, and fields beyond wooden fences. Large specimen trees planted in the nineteenth and twentieth centuries accent the property, and there are five Chinese tree peonies more than forty years old blooming in the garden.

Saturday, May 13, 10 a.m. - 4 p.m.

Take the Pennsylvania Turnpike to Exit 25/Norristown onto Germantown Pike East. Continue on Germantown Pike through 4 traffic lights. Stay right and bear right around the Lafayette Inn. Take an immediate left onto Park Avenue. At the bottom of the hill, turn left onto Andorra Road. The tan 3-story stucco house is on the right with a stone barn at the driveway entrance. Please park on the street. Distance from Turnpike to house is about 3 miles.

Mr. & Mrs. Henry F. Harris

575 East Evergreen Avenue, Wyndmoor

A spring herbaceous border of two beds off a large flagstone terrace planted with spring bulbs and hosta under two huge Japanese weeping cherry trees. The two beds are new this year. We replaced four beds, saving all the plants, to make our lives easier! We hope, even though there are fewer gardens, they will be more effective.

Saturday, May 13, 10 a.m. - 4 p.m.

From the Pennsylvania Turnpike, take the Norristown Exit and go straight down Germantown Avenue to a left onto Evergreen Avenue. The garden is at the last house on the left on Evergreen Avenue (before it turns into Ardmore Avenue) #575. Please park on the street.

Tom & Leslie Purple Garden

611 East Gravers Lane, Wyndmoor

Although we live in a Victorian-style house, our garden is only fourteen years old. With the exception of a few ash trees, our garden was planted almost entirely by us. Because our property is small, we have created a series of small gardens that feature unusual perennials and small shrubs. The long border in the front has been a challenge, with the reward being that we now know for certain what grows under a Norway maple in a drought. We have planted more than forty cultivars of hostas in the large shade gardens on the property. The back gardens are a series of small, informal, shady woodland gardens.

Saturday, May 13, 10 a.m. - 4 p.m.

From the Pennsylvania Turnpike take Exit 25. Go east on the Germantown Pike for several miles, through Lafayette Hills and past the Whitemarsh Golf Course on the left. Cross over Northwestern Avenue (Chestnut Hill College is on the left) and across bridge. Pass Chestnut Hill Hospital on the left and enter town of Chestnut Hill. Cross Evergreen Avenue, Highland, then Gravers Lane. Turn left onto Gravers Lane and go approximately 1 mile. After crossing Ardmore, look for 611 East Gravers Lane on the left. Park on Gravers Lane.

Chanticleer ❦

786 Church Road, Wayne, PA 19087. (610) 687-4163.

This thirty-acre pleasure garden was formerly the home of the Rosengarten family. Emphasis is on ornamental plants, particularly herbaceous perennials. The garden is a dynamic mix of formal and naturalistic areas, collections of flowering trees and shrubs, a pond, a meadow, wildflower gardens, and a garden of shade-loving Asian herbaceous plants.

April 1 - October 31, Wednesday - Saturday, 10 a.m. - 5 p.m.

Take Route 76 West to Route 476. Turn south onto Route 476 toward Chester. Take Exit 5 toward Villanova. Turn right at the intersection of Route 30 and Route 320 South. Turn right at the next traffic light onto Conestoga Road. Turn left at the second traffic light onto Church Road. Go .5 miles to Chanticleer.

Fairmount Park Horticulture Center & Arboretum ❦

Belmont Avenue & North Horticultural Drive, Philadelphia, PA 19131. (215) 685-0096.

The Arboretum covers twenty-two acres and boasts an assortment of trees, many of which have been labeled with both common and botanical names. The display house is the first greenhouse you enter from the lobby. Its permanent display includes olive and fig trees, oleander, and bougainvillea. The next greenhouse contains a magnificent collection of cacti and succulents. There are also many statutes and perennial gardens on these grounds. Come and visit!

Year round, daily, 9 a.m. - 3 p.m.

From I-76 West, take Exit 35 for Montgomery Drive. Turn left at the light onto Montgomery Drive and travel one block, turning left onto Horticultural Drive. Drive through the front gates on the left; the building is on the right.

Gibraltar ❦

2501 Pennsylvania Avenue, Wilmington, DE 19806. (302) 651-9617.

Now being restored by Preservation Delaware, this classic twentieth-century urban estate designed by Marian Cruger Coffin features a formal Italian garden, a bald cypress allee, and an extensive collection of period garden ornaments.

Year - round, Tuesday - Friday, 9 a.m. - 3 p.m.

Take I-95 to Route 52 North/Pennsylvania Avenue, approximately 1.2 miles. Turn right at Greenhill Avenue. The entrance is immediately on the right.

⚙ *A preservation project of The Garden Conservancy.*

❦ *public garden*

HISTORIC BARTRAM'S GARDEN 🌺

54TH STREET AND LINDBERGH BOULEVARD, PHILADELPHIA, PA 19143.
(215) 729-5281.

Historic Bartram's Garden is America's oldest living botanical garden, founded in 1728 by John Bartram, America's first great botanist, naturalist, and plant explorer. The forty-five acre site on the banks of Schuylkill River includes the furnished Bartram house and other unique eighteenth-century farm buildings, a botanical garden, historic trees, a fifteen-acre wildflower meadow, a water garden, a wetland, a parkland, and a museum shop.

March - December, Tuesday - Sunday, 10 a.m. - 4 p.m. January - February group tours by reservation.

Located less than fifteen minutes from Center City Philadelphia and convenient to I-76 and I-95. Please call for detailed directions.

MEADOWBROOK FARM & GREENHOUSE 🌺

1633 WASHINGTON LANE, MEADOWBROOK, PA 19046. (215) 887-5900.

This beautiful garden is the life work of J. Liddon Pennock. Designed with the emphasis of outdoor rooms, each garden is unique and very comfortable, with the emphasis on design. The public display garden leads to the greenhouse where plants and garden gifts of all types are available. Meadowbrook Farm has long been known for special horticulture activities including lectures and workshops to visiting groups.

Year-round, Monday - Saturday, 10 a.m. - 5 p.m.

From Pennsylvania Turnpike: take Exit 27. Take Route 611 south, turn left onto Route 63, in approximately 1.5 miles turn right onto Washington Lane. Meadowbrook Farm sign is located approximately .75 mile on left side.

Morris Arboretum
of the University of Pennsylvania &

100 NORTHWESTERN AVENUE, PHILADELPHIA, PA 19118. (215) 247-5777.

The Morris Arboretum of the University of Pennsylvania is an historic Victorian garden and educational institution dedicated to understanding the important relationships between people and plants. Its living collection contains approximately 2,532 taxa and more than 12,000 accessioned and labeled plants from the temperate Northern Hemisphere, parts of Asia, Europe, and North America. The Arboretum collection consists of ninety-two acres that include gardens in the Victorian eclectic style. Handicapped accessible. Museum shop.

Year round, daily, 10 a.m. - 4 p.m. April-November, weekends, 10 a.m. - 5 p.m.

Take I-76 / Schuylkill Expressway to the Blue Route/476 North. Take Exit 8/Plymouth Meeting and follow signs for Germantown Pike East. Continue on Germantown Pike for 4 miles and turn left onto Northwestern Avenue. The Arboretum entrance is .25 miles on the right.

Scott Arboretum
of Swarthmore College &

500 COLLEGE AVENUE, SWARTHMORE, PA 19081-1397. (610) 328-8025.

The Scott Arboretum is a green oasis uniquely situated on the Swarthmore College campus. More than 300 acres create the college landscape and provide a display of the best ornamental plants recommended for Delaware Valley gardens. There are more than 3,000 different kinds of plants grown on the campus. Major plant collections include flowering cherries, coreopsis, crab apples, hydrangeas, lilacs, magnolias, rhododendrons, tree peonies, viburnums, wisteria, and witch hazels. Special gardens include the Rose Garden, Fragrance Garden, Teaching Garden, Entrance Garden, Winter Garden, Nason Garden, Harry Wood Courtyard garden, and Cosby Courtyard.

Year round, daily, dawn - dusk

From I-95 take Exit 7 for I-476 North / Plymouth Meeting. Take I-476 to Exit 2 for Media / Swarthmore. Turn right onto Baltimore Pike and follow signs for Swarthmore. Stay in the right lane for .25 miles and turn right onto Route 320 South. Proceed through the second traffic light at College Avenue to the first driveway on the right.

Pittsburgh Open Day

Regional Representatives: Farley Whetzel & Bernita Buncher Duber

Sunday, September 10

FOX CHAPEL
Garden at High Haven, 608 Squaw Run Road East: 10 a.m. - 4 p.m.
Jacobson/Strollo Garden, 123 Springhouse Lane: 10 a.m. - 4 p.m.
Rosemont Farms, 1950 Squaw Run Road: 10 a.m. - 4 p.m.
Soffer Residence, 710 Bending Oak Lane: 10 a.m. - 4 p.m.

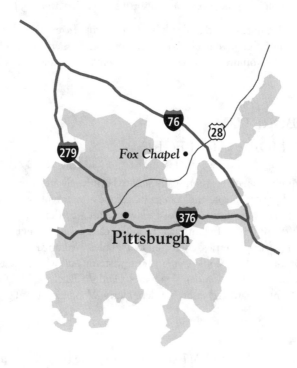

Garden at High Haven

608 Squaw Run Road East, Fox Chapel

This property is a work in progress. During the past four years, the east one-half of the seven-acre property has been modified to generate a mood of casual country including a dwarf conifer garden, crab apple orchard, the beginnings of a hybrid rhododendron and native azalea collection, an arboretum, and a meadow. The immediate entrance to the house is more intensively developed with a grassblock parking area, a small pond flanked by shrubs and perennials, and an overhanging porch softened by clematis varieties to welcome the visitor. My goal has been to use xeriscaping and to emphasize spring and fall colors and blooms. Winter winds and summer heat are both factors in this exposed hilltop location.

Sunday, September 10, 10 a.m. - 4 p.m.

Take Route 28 North to Fox Chapel Road Exit, bear to the left as you exit and at the traffic light turn left. Follow Fox Chapel Road approximately 2.5 miles and turn left by the golf course onto Squaw Run Road East. Drive .6 mile and turn right onto a private road marked by a sign for the Fox Chapel Episcopal Church. Go straight ahead through a drive with a gatehouse on the right and an open white gate on the left. Number 608 is the first drive on the left. Please park at the top of the drive.

Jacobson/Strollo Garden

123 Springhouse Lane, Fox Chapel

Our garden, throughout the growing season but especially in September, is about form and texture rather than floral profusion. It has evolved from a blank slate; no stone or brickwork, no paths or borders, no specimen trees or perennials existed on the site ten years ago. We tend to think of it as a hybrid between a Japanese and an English garden-spare in certain details, yet lush and diverse in others. When all is said and done, we are much more interested in the descriptions of others than in our own.

Sunday, September 10, 10 a.m. - 4 p.m.

From Route 28, take Exit 8/Fox Chapel Road. At the end of the exit ramps, turn left (north) onto Fox Chapel Road. Continue approximately 1.9 miles to Springhouse Lane and turn right (The Fox Chapel Presbyterian Church is visible on the right just beyond Springhouse Lane). Continue approximately .2 mile, just past the mailbox on the right that reads "121 1/2." Please park along the row of white pine trees or elsewhere on the main street. Walk down the cul-de-sac on the right to the lower driveway for access to the garden.

Rosemont Farms

Splendid panoramic views provide the backdrop for the formal and informal gardens found at Rosemont Farms, an organic private estate/working farm. From the tennis court a boxwood-lined allée leads visitors through lilac borders, hybrid tea rose beds, and a bank of New Dawn roses which cascade over a wall adjacent to the swimming pool. Along the way a Jeffersonian walled garden with serpentine brick wall provides a micro-climate for the fruits and herbs planted within. The allée also features a canopy created by eight standard Sargent crab apple trees, each in its own niche in the serpentine walls. Continuing along the allée, guests pass through perennial borders overlooking the pasture leading to the barn.

Sunday, September 10, 10 a.m. - 4 p.m.

Take Route 28 North to Fox Chapel Road/Exit 8 and stay left. At the end of the ramp at the traffic light, turn left onto Fox Chapel Road. Go 1.2 miles to Squaw Run Road/Fox Chapel Road. Bear left at fork. Travel 2.3 miles on Squaw Run Road to the Rosemont Farms driveway, which will be a very sharp left (shortly before the driveway, there is a small red house on the left.) There is ample parking on premises

Soffer Residence

710 Bending Oak Lane, Fox Chapel

The garden tour begins at the gravel gate. A stone path through an archway of viburnums brings the visitor to a Japanese Tea House with its reflective swimming pool. The sound of water piques one's curiosity to continue the tour along a liriope- and hosta-planted path. A man-made stream empties into a Koi pond and cascades into a larger pond planted with aquatics on which floats the "Meditation Pavilion." A foot bridge takes the visitor to an extended natural woodland setting where exotics are mixed with native Western Pennsylvania plant material.

Sunday, September 10, 10 a.m. - 4 p.m.

From downtown Pittsburgh, go over Seventh or Ninth Street Bridge and turn right to follow Route 28 signs. Exit Route 28 at Fox Chapel and turn left onto Fox Chapel Road. Continue for 4-5 miles and go through 1 traffic light. Bear right at the "T," and go left at the "Y." Continue about .5 mile to a mailbox marked "1120" on the right. The next driveway on right is Bending Oak Lane, a private drive. Follow drive through two switchbacks to the top of the hill. Please park as directed.

Beechwood Farms Nature Reserve/Audubon Society of Western Pennsylvania ❧

614 Dorseyville Road, Pittsburgh, PA 15238. 412/963-6100.

Beechwood Farms is a 134-acre nature reserve featuring meadow and woodland wildflowers, trees and other vegetation in a natural setting. Beechwood Farms is also home to the new Audubon Center for Native Plants, the only nursery devoted solely to the study, propagation and cultivation of western Pennsylvania's approximately 1,500 native plant species. The center serves as the focus of an educational and demonstration outreach initiative to encourage the reestablishment of native plants in home gardens, landscapes and natural areas in the region as a means of increasing the bio-diversity and ecological balance that is threatened by the encroachment of invasive exotic species. Native plants are those species which grew here before European settlement.

Year round, daily (except Mondays), dawn - dusk

From Pittsburgh: Route 28/North to the Route 8/North-Butler exit; right at the 1st light onto Sharps Hill/Kittanning Road, which becomes Dorseyville Road; Beechwood Farms is 4.3 miles from the right turn on the left side. From the east: Pennsylvania Turnpike to exit 5; south on Freeport Road; right turn onto Guys Run Road at the fourth light; left at the second stop sign onto Dorseyville Road to Beechwood Farms on the right. From the North & West: Pennsylvania Turnpike to exit 4; south on Route 8; left onto Harts Run Road and follow the Green Belt signs; right onto Dorseyville Road to Beechwood. Free parking available.

Phipps Conservatory & Botanical Gardens ❧

One Schenley Park, Pittsburgh, PA 15213. (412) 622-6914. WWW.PHIPPS.CONSERVATORY.ORG

For more than 100 years, Phipps and Botanical Gardens has delighted plant and flower enthusiasts from around the world. Pittsburgh's thirteen-room "crystal palace" is one of the largest and finest Victorian glasshouses in the country. The botanical gardens at Phipps feature lush tropical plants, palms, orchids, ferns and desert plants, as well as many special flower shows and exhibits. Outdoor, seasonal gardens include the Discovery Garden, Japanese Courtyard Garden, bonsai, butterflies, perennials, annuals, herbs and aquatics.

Year-round, Tuesday - Sunday, 9 a.m - 5 p.m. (Closed Mondays, Thanksgiving and Christmas Day).

From Downtown Pittsburgh, take I-376 to Exit 5 (Oakland): follow Forbes Avenue; turn right on Schenley Drive; turn left at the stop sign; follow Schenley Drive into Schenley Park. Phipps is on the right. A center island parking area across form the conservatory is available upon receiving a permit at the information desk. Metered parking is also available.

Rodef Shalom Biblical Botanical Garden ❧

Rodef Shalom Temple, 4905 5th Avenue, Pittsburgh PA 15213. (412) 621-6566.

This is one of three botanical gardens in North America with a Biblical theme. The design of the garden replicates the landscape of Israel: plants with Biblical names, which demonstrate popular love of Scripture, are grown. Each year the garden has a special series of plantings and programs that focus on ancient horticulture. In 1998 we will deal with beer in the ancient Near East. Lectures, literature, and exhibits accompany the plantings.

June 1 - September 15, daily, 10 a.m. - 2 p.m.

Located on Fifth Avenue and Devonshire, across the street from the Carnegie Mellon University campus and from WQED television. It is adjacent to the Rodef Shalom Temple which covers a city block.

TENNESSEE

TENNESSEE OPEN DAYS

May 13: Chattanooga
June 4: Nashville

Chattanooga Open Days

Regional Representative: Mrs. John Stout

Saturday, May 13
"Bobby's Walk"—Town Common, 933 Scenic Highway: 10 a.m. - 4 p.m.
Foy Garden, 1009 East Brow Road: 10 a.m. - 4 p.m.
Mr. & Mrs. Edward L. Mitchell, 206 Morrison Street: 2 p.m. - 6 p.m.

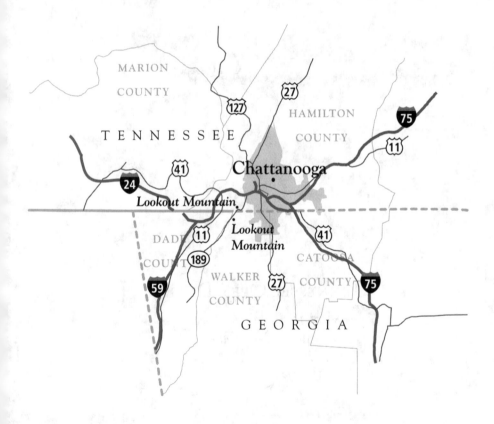

"BOBBY'S WALK"— TOWN COMMON

933 SCENIC HIGHWAY, LOOKOUT MOUNTAIN

Bobby's Walk, with side trails, leads through a wooded area of the thirteen-acre Town Commons. Featuring a wide selection of native azaleas, rhododendron, ferns, daylilies, and annual and perennial flowers, most indigenous to North America, the trails are designed for an easy and comfortable walk under the shade of a wide variety of towering native trees.

Saturday, May 13, 10 a.m. - 4 p.m.

From the end of Chattanooga's South Broad Street, proceed on to Cummings Highway (US #11) and enter Scenic Highway (#148) up Lookout Mountain, past Ruby Falls for another 2.3 miles. Enter the Town Commons gates opposite the large stone water fountain, located in the middle of the Scenic Highway. Please park on the street.

Proceeds shared with The Lookout Mountain Beautification Committee.

FOY GARDEN

1009 EAST BROW ROAD, LOOKOUT MOUNTAIN

A petite formal English garden on edge of Lookout Mountain with a view of the city and river. Boxwood, ferns and blooming plants sit against antique statuary.

Saturday, May 13, 10 a.m. - 4 p.m.

Follow signs to Ruby Falls. Continue to follow signs for incline. We are 3 houses after the incline on R-1009. Stacked stone wall around front of house and garden. Please park on the street.

Mr. & Mrs. Edward L. Mitchell

206 Morrison Street, Lookout Mountain

An English garden, terraced with wildflower and perennial beds, of which the most outstanding specimen is an old tree peony. There are beds of indigenous species of rhododendron and laurel, and groupings of four separate varieties of hydrangeas. Large plantings of hosta edge the lawn. A restored fish pond is nestled in a garden of fern and Japanese maple. A rose garden is centered in a perennial border.

Saturday, May 13, 2 p.m. - 6 p.m.

Take I-124 through Chattanooga. Take Lookout Mountain Exit, follow signs to Ruby Falls. Pass Ruby Falls and go to the top of the mountain. At top take hard right (East Brow Road). Go about 1 mile. Morrison Street turns off to the left, beside a large green bus garage. (If you come to the top of Incline Railroad, you went a half of a block too far). Take Morrison Street to the last house on the left, #206 Morrison Street (stone-and-stucco Tudor house). Park on Morrison Street.

Proceeds shared with Reflection Riding Arboretum & Botanical Garden.

Reflection Riding Arboretum & Botanical Garden ❧

400 Garden Road, Chattanooga, TN 37419. (423) 821-9582.

Reflection Riding is a 300-acre landscape park, nature preserve, and historic site nestled between the western slope of Lookout Mountain and Lookout Creek. Sixteen miles of roads and trails offer visitors an opportunity to enjoy dramatic vistas, thousands of wildflowers, flowering trees and shrubs, along the way in woodland gardens, meadows, mountain ravines, and slopes. More than 500 species and a rich selection of Southern Appalachian plant life grow here, and more than 200 are propagated on site. The Philp Garden features all the evergreen rhododendrons and all but two azaleas native to the eastern United States.

Saturday, May 13, 10 a.m. - 4 p.m.

From Downtown Chattanooga, take I-24 West. Exit at Brown's Ferry Road and turn left at the traffic light. At the next traffic light turn left onto Cummings Highway. Travel about 1 mile and turn right at the signs for Reflection Riding and the Tennessee Wildlife Center. Follow Garden Road to the end and turn left at the sign to the Humphreys House.

TENNESSEE RIVER GARDENS & WILDLIFE PRESERVE ♣

1002 SCENIC HIGHWAY, LOOKOUT MOUNTAIN, TN 37402. (423) 821-1538.

Tennessee River Gardens is a wildflower and native plant gardens on a spectacular site along the Tennessee River. More than 500 species are individually identified with colored pictures long a trail that winds through a meadow and forest, by streams, fifteen-foot waterfalls, and trout ponds. River Gardens overlooks a private fifty-acre lake with a dramatic view down the Tennessee River Gorge with 1200-foot mountains rising on each side. Here you may also see great blue herons working out of their rookery, Canadian geese, kingfishers, ospreys, and sometimes wild turkeys and bald eagles. The wildflowers in the meadows in May are spectacular.

Saturday, May 13, 10 a.m. - 5 p.m.

Go west on I-24 6 miles from Downtown Chattanooga. Take the Lookout Valley Exit and go right on Cummings Highway/Route 41. Go 2.7 miles and turn right through the stone gates to River Gardens (250 yards past TVA Raccoon Mountain Facility Road).

Nashville Open Day

Regional Representative: Mr. Bob Brackman, Mrs. Robert C. H. Mathews Jr., & Mr. Ben Page

Sunday, June 4

Cheek Garden, 4404 Honeywood Avenue: noon - 4 p.m.
Cheekwood Garden, 1200 Forrest Park Drive: 11 a.m. - 4 p.m.
Page Garden, 3801 Richland Avenue: noon - 4 p.m.
Proctor Garden, 215 Evelyn Avenue: noon - 4 p.m.
Robinson Garden, 540 Belle Meade Boulevard: noon - 4 p.m.

CHEEK GARDEN

4404 HONEYWOOD AVENUE, NASHVILLE

A walled garden encompassing three interconnected but distinct horticultural displays. The first garden, entered from the street through a wood and wrought-iron gate, reveals a multilevel herbaceous border with a diverse collection of deciduous plants. The second garden is anchored by a swimming pool with a water feature and shrubbery collections. A brick and stone terrace with an adjacent dovecote and espaliered shrubs completes the trilogy.

Sunday, June 4, noon - 4 p.m.

From I-65, take I-440 West to Exit 1/West End Avenue. Travel west 5.1 miles to Belle Mead Boulevard, and turn left. Go .5 mile to Honeywood and turn left. The house is .3 mile on the left. Parking in driveway and on street.

Proceeds shared with Cheekwood.

PAGE GARDEN

3801 RICHLAND AVENUE, NASHVILLE

An urban historic neighborhood provides the setting for this intimate walled garden. Sidewalk access through louvered wooden gates leads to the first entry garden, anchored by a pebble mosaic. A small, two-tiered fountain anchors a corner terrace richly planted with rare shrubs and herbaceous perennials. A screened dining porch looks out onto the formal lawn, featuring four stone columns salvaged from a lost local mansion. An extensive hosta, fern, astilbe, and hellebore collection is featured in the shade garden.

Sunday, June 4, noon - 4 p.m.

From I-65, take I-440 West to Exit 1/West End Avenue. Travel .6 mile to Christopher Street and turn right. Go 1 block and turn left onto Richland Street. The garden is on the southwest corner of Richland and Christopher, facing Richland. Enter the garden from the Christopher Street side of the house. Please park on the street.

Proceeds shared with Cheekwood.

PROCTOR GARDEN

215 EVELYN AVENUE, NASHVILLE

An intimate walled garden closely tied to the interior of this house, designed for ease of access and richness of horticultural diversity. Antique wrought-iron gates provide access to a lush shade garden adjacent to a small pool. A serpentine brick walk moves by collections of hydrangeas, daylilies, roses, and perennials. Commissioned pieces of art provide accents at every turn.

Sunday, June 4, noon - 4 p.m.

From I-65, take I-440 West to Exit 1. Travel west 5.1 miles to Belle Meade Boulevard, and turn left. Go .2 mile to Clarendon and turn right. Go .2 mile to Evelyn Avenue and turn right. The garden is .1 mile on the left. Please park on the street.

Proceeds shared with Cheekwood.

ROBINSON GARDEN

540 BELLE MEADE BOULEVARD, NASHVILLE

This extensive 1920s garden continuously tended by two generations of the same family, features a formal stone terrace adjacent to the house with a walled rose parterre and arbor. A stone-pedimented wooden gate leads to the summer perennial garden, with spectacular hydrangea collections, adjacent to the screened pool pavilion and pool. Extensive cutting and vegetable gardens provide flowers and fruits for the owner's table and for altar flowers.

Sunday, June 4, noon - 4 p.m.

From I-65, take I-440 West to Exit 1. Travel west 5.1 miles to Belle Meade Boulevard, and turn right. Go 1.2 miles. The garden is on the left. Please park in the field to the right of the entry drive.

Proceeds shared with Cheekwood.

CHEEKWOOD 🌸

1200 FORREST PARK DRIVE, NASHVILLE, TN 37205. (615) 356-8000.

At Cheekwood you will find collections of dogwood, wildflowers, herbs, iris, roses, peonies, magnolias, daylilies, ferns, hydrangeas, and much more. Specialty gardens include the Color Garden, showcasing gardening as a year-round activity; water garden; the Japanese Garden; and the Trial Garden where annuals are tested for performance in the mid-South. The perennial gardens are at their peak in June and July. The original Bryant-Fleming-designed gardens around the Cheek mansion are fully restored to their former elegance with lovely vistas, boxwood gardens, Italianate water features, and spectacular stonework. The mansion now house the Museum of Art.

Sunday, June 4, 11 a.m. - 5 p.m. Otherwise, year round, Monday - Saturday, 9 a.m. - 5 p.m.; Sunday, 11 a.m. - 5 p.m. Closed New Year's Day, Thanksgiving, and the third Saturday in April.

From I-65 take I-440 West to Exit 1/West End Avenue. Travel west 5.1 miles to Belle Meade Boulevard and turn left. Go 2.8 miles to Page Road. Turn right onto Page and go .2 mile. Turn left onto Forrest Park Drive. Follow .2 mile to the Cheekwood entrance.

TEXAS

★ Austin
★ Houston

TEXAS OPEN DAYS

March 19: Houston
October 14: Austin

Austin Open Day

Regional Representative: Deborah Hornickel

Saturday, October 14

Anne McGrath & David Schade, 501 Brookhaven Trail: 10 a.m. - 6 pm.
Deborah Hornickel, 3206 Oakmont Boulevard: 10 a.m. - 6 pm.
James deGrey David & Gary Peese, 8 Sugar Creek Drive: 10 a.m. - 6 p.m.
Jane Schweppe, 2316 Bridle Path: 10 a.m. - 6 pm.
Janine Mazur 1810 West 29th Street: 10 a.m. - 6 p.m.
Jennifer & Fred Myers, 1101 West 31st Street: 10 a.m. - 6 pm.
Susan Dillon & Chris Williams, 1200 Claire Avenue: 10 a.m. - 6 p.m.

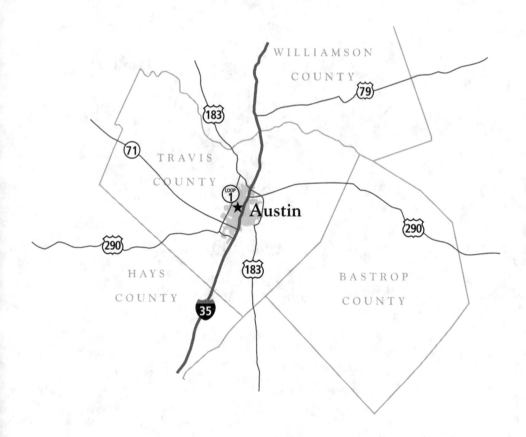

Anne McGrath & David Schade

501 Brookhaven Trail, Austin

This suburban garden consists of several distinctive theme gardens. Woodland, wildlife, white, herb, and water gardens are some of the special areas. There is a strong use of vertical accents with a vast array of plant species.

Saturday, October 14, 10 a.m. - 6 p.m.

From Loop 1, take Beecave Road to Westbrook Road, which will become Briarwood at the stop sign, and finally Brookhaven Trail. Look for #501 Brookhaven Trail. Please park along the road.

Deborah Hornickel

3206 Oakmont Boulevard, Austin

A long gravel drive lined with roses (*Rosa Chinensis mutablis*) leads you to the entry of the garden which originates in back of the house. The cool greenery and unexpected size and formality of this garden greet you as your eyes behold the ultimate surprise—a *Pyrus calleyera* allée. This is a garden with many elegant touches and made with economy in mind.

Saturday, October 14, 10 a.m. - 6 p.m.

Travel north on Loop 1 (Mopac) to the 35th Street exit. Go east on 35th Street and turn right on Oakmont Boulevard.

James deGrey David & Gary Peese

8 Sugar Creek Drive, Austin

This is a collector's garden with Mediterranean elements. It includes a series of terraces and courtyards. Water features include a native limestone water staircase extending to a creek bed. A special feature is a vegetable garden with a collection of exotic, hard-to-find edibles. The garden integrates and flows with this architecturally acclaimed home.

Saturday, October 14, 10 a.m. - 6 p.m.

Travel south on Loop 1. Go west on 2244, commonly known as Beecave Road. Turn right on Edgegrove at the Texaco Station. Turn right on Rollingwood Drive and then a quick left onto Gentry. Turn right on Sugar Creek and park along the road.

Jane Schweppe

Sea Shells from the Texas Gulf Coast accent the garden beds and hang from a large canopy of live oaks. There are two ponds bordered by honeycombed limestone and garden paths with jade pebbles and fossilized shells. Both Buffalo grass and St. Augustine cover three tiers of the garden as it slopes down into a bog of Crinum lilies. The overall effect of the choice of plants and the use of materials create a surreal and whimsical feeling of being encased in an underwater capsule.

Saturday, October 14, 10 a.m. - 6 p.m.

Take Loop 1 to the Enfield Road exit. At Enfield, exit west toward Lake Austin. The first right is Forest Lane. Turn right and proceed to the first stop sign. Turn left at the stop sign, heading west on Bridle Path. Look for #2316 on the north side of the street. Please park along the road.

Janine Mazur

This garden is a labor of love created by the resident gardener over the last several years. It might be described as a Californian's version of a Texas cottage garden. The front and side of the lot have a screening border that contains a wide variety of plant colors and textures. Large limestone stepping stones were "dropped" in an informal manner to create a path from the street to the front courtyard area. The back garden is framed with vertical yaupons and has a tranquil fish pond as the focal point. Limestone and salvaged, broken cement pieces were used to create paths and raised planters around the native juniper trees.

Saturday, October 14, 10 a.m. - 6 p.m.

From MOPAC, take the Northwood/Westover Exit. Go east 1 block to Jefferson. Turn left on Jefferson and go two blocks to 29th Street. Turn left onto 29th Street and continue to the last house on the right. The house is at the corner of 29th Street and Oakmont Boulevard. Please park on the street.

JENNIFER & FRED MYERS
1101 WEST 31ST STREET, AUSTIN

This garden is centered about a historical hang-cut limestone home. The entrance is formally informal with intense flowering plants, emphasizing color and fragrance. There are adjacent shaded woodlands. Terraced gardens, banked with limestone, casacade to a vista of Austins's Shoal Creek.

Saturday, October 14, 10 a.m. - 6 p.m.

From I-35, take Highway 290 West (changing into Koenig Lane) for 1.3 miles to Lamar Boulevard. Turn left on Lamar and travel 2.2 miles to West 31st Street. Turn right on West 31st Street and go one-half-block to #1101 West 31st Street. It is a rock house set back from the road on the left. Park along the road.

SUSAN DILLON & CHRIS WILLIAMS
1200 CLAIRE AVENUE, AUSTIN

This small charming garden, designed by Selena Souders & Dylan Robertson of Big Red Sun, in 1997, creates a private living space while embracing its urban setting. The garden, structured around a water element, combines the use of traditional and tropical plants that are accented with edibles and seasonal color. A central pergola houses several climbing varieties that provide a cool resting place through the seasons and continues fragrance and bloom. A stroll through the garden offers a pleasant surprise.

Saturday, October 14, 10 a.m. - 6 p.m.

Located at 1200 Claire Avenue. Take Mopac Highway to Northwood/Westover Exit, head east. Go past 2 stop signs (approximately .5 mile) at third stop sign turn right onto Woolridge Street. Go approximately 50 yards to a "Y" in the road, veer left onto Claire Avenue. Please park on the street.

LADY BIRD JOHNSON WILDFLOWER CENTER &

4801 LA CROSSE AVENUE, AUSTIN, TX 78739-1702. (512) 292-4100.
WWW.WILDFLOWER.ORG

The Lady Bird Johnson Wildflower Center maintains a native plant botanical garden with acres of designed gardens, courtyards, and natural areas, showcasing the magnificent native plants of the Texas Hill Country in a variety of styles from naturalistic to formal. Highlights of the grounds include a Visitors Gallery with exhibits and a video presentation, Wild Ideas: The Store, a terraced cafe, a forty-five-foot Observation Tower, a children's discovery room, home comparison gardens, and nature trails. The Center also has North America's largest rooftop rainwater collection system, with a series of aqueducts, beautiful stone cisterns, and waterways.

Year round, Tuesday - Sunday, 9 a.m. - 5:30 p.m.

From I-35, take Exit 227 for Slaughter Lane. Bear west off of the exit and travel 6 miles west to the intersection of Slaughter Lane and Loop 1. Turn left onto Loop 1 and left again onto LaCrosse.

WESTCAVE PRESERVE &

GENERAL DELIVERY, ROUND MOUNTAIN, TX 78663. (830) 825-3442.
WWW.WESTCAVE.ORG. WESTCAVE@MOMENT.NET.

Westcave preserve is a thirty-acre natural sanctuary protected for future generations. It is a delight for wildflower enthusiasts, hikers, birders, or anyone who loves the natural beauty of the Texas Hill Country.

Year round, Saturday & Sunday. 10 a.m., noon, 2 p.m., and 4 p.m. Weekday programs scheduled in advance.

Take Highway 71 West from Austin to the village of Bee Cave. Turn left onto Ranch Road 3238 (Hamilton Pool Road) and travel 14 miles, crossing the Pedernales River. Look for the first gate on the right.

372 THE GARDEN CONSERVANCY

Houston Open Day

Regional Representatives: Anne Symonds & Mrs. Seller J. Thomas Jr.

Sunday, March 19

Estes Garden, 5010 Longmont Drive: 10 a.m. - 2 p.m.
Garden of Anne & John O'Neill, 1004 Kirby Drive: 2 p.m. - 6 p.m.
Garden of Christopher Knapp, 2201 Albans Road: 10 a.m. - 2 p.m.
Garden of Melinda & Mike Perrin, 3207 Inwood Drive: 2 p.m. - 6 p.m.
Garden of Nancy & Sellers Thomas, 106 Maple Valley: 10 a.m. - 2 p.m.
Liddell Garden, 406 Hedwig Green: 10 a.m. - 2 p.m.
Matthews Garden, 3654 Olympia: 2 p.m. - 6 p.m.
Phoebe & Bobby Tudor Garden, 1405 South Boulevard: 10 a.m. - 2 p.m.
Simmons Garden, 1405 North Boulevard: 10 a.m. - 2 p.m.
The Carmichael Garden, 3315 Ella Lee Lane: 2 p.m. - 6 p.m.

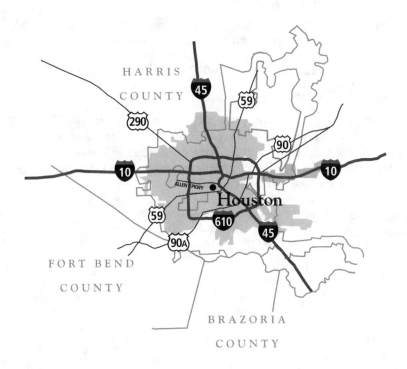

ESTES GARDEN

5010 LONGMONT DRIVE, HOUSTON

Our small walled gardens feel Mediterranean. Formal beds are informally planted with wildflowers, ginger, citrus, vines, and butterfly-attracting plants. The garden around the pool is planted for scent and color. The back garden is for cutting and herbs. The patio garden is subject to whim. At the front door there is a parterre. We garden organically and share the garden with bees, butterflies, and hummingbirds.

Sunday, March 19, 10 a.m. - 2 p.m.

Located in the Galleria area, just west of Loop 610, bordered by Woodway to the north and San Felipe to the south. It is east of Sage Road and west of South Post Oak Lane. The house sits behind a white stucco fence, which is marked #5010. Enter from Longmont Drive through the wooden gate at the southwest corner of the property.

Proceeds shared with The National Wildflower Research Center.

GARDEN OF ANNE & JOHN O'NEILL

1004 KIRBY DRIVE, HOUSTON

Many aspects of the gardens on the one-and-one-half-acre property along Buffalo Bayou give pleasure and inspire tranquility. There is a forest of sycamore and redbud trees, a charming gazebo area, azaleas and roses, as well as many flowering native plants. Landscaping was completed in 1997 by Thompson & Hanson.

Sunday, March 19, 2 p.m. - 6 p.m.

From Downtown on Allen Parkway, cross Shepherd, entering River Oaks on Kirby Drive. Turn right off Kirby after 3 blocks onto Shadder Way. House is at the corner of Shadder Way and Kirby. From Loop 610 West, exit San Felipe, heading East. After crossing RR tracks, go to fourth light and turn left on to Kirby. Take the fourth left onto Shadder Way and continue to end of street where it rejoins Kirby. From Highway 59 take the Kirby Drive Exit, heading North. After crossing Westheimer, go through 3 lights and take the second right onto Shadder Way, continuing to end of street. Please park on Shadder Way.

GARDEN OF CHRISTOPHER KNAPP

2201 ALBANS ROAD, HOUSTON

This garden, surrounding a 1927 Southampton bungalow, is a series of rooms: at the front is a shade garden planted under the canopy of three live oaks more than 100 years old. Many of the larger shrubs are original to the site, transplanted after renovation of the house in 1992. The rear garden is in full sun most of the year and surrounds a small pool/fountain, potted citrus, and fruit trees.

Sunday, March 19, 10 a.m. - 2 p.m.

Exit SW Freeway at Greenbriar. Go south on Greenbriar to Albans. Turn left onto Albans, go 1 block. Albans is 7 blocks south of the Freeway. Number 2201 Albans Road is at the SW corner of Albans Road and South Shepherd. Albans Road runs east-west and is between Bissonnet Street and Sunset Boulevard. The house is approximately 5 blocks south of Rice University via South Shepherd. Please park on Albans Road.

GARDEN OF MELINDA & MIKE PERRIN

3207 INWOOD DRIVE, HOUSTON

This classic garden was originally designed by Pat Fleming, who also designed the gardens of Bayou Bend. The entrance motorcourt, enclosed by a massive azalea hedge, contains a lovely raised rose garden. A decorative iron gate leads into the brick-walled garden, where a series of garden rooms connects the Tudor-style house to the gracious landscape. The garden's flagstone terraces are surrounded by masses of white azaleas and flowering trees. An elegant wood arbor, covered with white Lady Banksia roses, anchors one end of the pool garden. This lovely garden is primarily a white garden and is a true delight to view during the azalea-blooming season. The garden was originally designed by Ruth London, who worked in Houston in the 1930s.

Sunday, March 19, 2 p.m. - 6 p.m.

From downtown travel south on Allen Parkway. Turn right at the light on Inwood Drive and proceed two blocks. From Westheimer or San Felipe travel east from Loop 610 South. Turn left on River Oaks Boulevard. Turn right on Inwood Drive to #3207. The back gate at 1405 North Boulevard will be open for guests to walk through to 1405 South Boulevard or vice-versa. The garden gate off the driveway at 1400 South Boulevard will be open. Please park on Inwood Drive, Bellmeade or Del Monte Drive

GARDEN OF NANCY & SELLERS THOMAS

106 MAPLE VALLEY, HOUSTON

The garden is a woodland garden bordering Buffalo Bayou with many species of ferns, native plants, and trees. It is a small garden that utilizes the topography of ravines and bayou banks to augment the space. An effort has been made to have plants of unusual horticultural interest. Birds, butterflies, and people are welcome.

Sunday, March 19, 10 a.m. - 2 p.m.

Going west on Woodway turn right onto Chimney Road Road. Go to the second traffic light, Shady River, and turn right. Follow Shady River to Maple Valley and turn left. Go to first stop sign and cross over Bridge Drive. Continue to cul de sac and #106 Maple Valley. Please park on Maple Valley or Briar Drive.

LIDDELL GARDEN

406 HEDWIG GREEN, HOUSTON

This small cottage-style garden was developed over twenty-five years by Alice Staub Liddell, and has been lovingly maintained by her husband Frank A. Liddell Jr. since her death in 1997. Mrs. Liddell was a noted plantswoman and landscape designer of many of Houston's most interesting gardens. Her own garden reflects her desire to try the unusual as well as native plants. Mr. Liddell welcomes visitors to this charming garden.

Sunday, March 19, 10 a.m. - 2 p.m.

From the traffic light at Memorial Road and Voss Road go west .3 mile to the next traffic light at Greenbay. Turn right onto Greenbay and continue for 2 blocks to Hedwig Road. Turn right onto Hedwig Road and continue .5 mile to stop sign. Proceed approximately 100 feet to Hedwig Green and turn right. The Liddell garden is at the third house on the right, #406.

Matthews Garden

3654 OLYMPIA, HOUSTON

The primary garden of this classic American Federal-style home consists of a long, brick terrace divided into a series of garden rooms surrounded by azaleas, camellias, gardenias, magnolias and spring-flowering trees. The first terrace is centered around a lily pond fountain and leads to the center terrace, which is used for entertaining. The last terrace is a rose garden.

Sunday, March 19, 2 p.m. - 6 p.m.

From Downtown on Allen Parkway, cross Shepherd, entering River Oaks on Kirby Drive. At the second traffic light, turn left onto San Felipe. After crossing River Oaks Boulevard, continue on San Felipe for 3 blocks, turning right onto Olympia. The garden is on the left. From Loop 610 West, take the San Felipe Exit, heading east. After crossing railroad tracks, turn left onto Willowick at first traffic light, take first right onto Olympia. The garden is second block on left. From Highway 59 take the Buffalo Speedway Exit, heading north. After crossing Westheimer (St. John's School on corner), continue to next traffic light and turn left onto San Felipe. Take second right onto Timber Lane, first right onto Olympia. The garden is on the left.

Phoebe & Bobby Tudor Garden

1405 SOUTH BOULEVARD, HOUSTON

Our garden was designed and installed half a century ago by one of Houston's preeminent landscape architects, C. C. Pat Fleming (1909-1996). This garden has been described as an estate garden condensed into a one-acre city lot. It features a series of outdoor rooms of differing characteristics. Behind a brick wall on the east side of the house is a formal garden of clipped boxwood with a fountain and statuary. Beyond that is a secret garden or selvaggio of azaleas and large magnolias through which narrow gravel paths meander. A swimming pool now replaces the original sunken lawn terrace, which is framed by numerous huge crape-myrtles. We have incorporated *Camellia japonica* and *Camellia sasanqua* among the azaleas behind our 1998 kitchen addition to this 1924 house. The rose garden sits on the west side of the house.

Sunday, March 19, 10 a.m. - 2 p.m.

From Highway 59 take the Greenbriar-Shepherd Exit. Go south on Greenbriar to Bissonnet. Turn left onto Bissonnet and continue to third traffic light at Mandell Street. Turn left onto Mandell and then right onto the first street, South Boulevard and #1405 South Boulevard. Please park on the street and enter garden through iron gate on the left of the house.

Simmons Garden

Designed by John Staub as his first independent commission in 1924 for the Palmer Hutchesons, the house and garden was on tour during the 1939 Garden Club of America's Annual Meeting in Houston. The gazebo was built especially for the tour and the original rose garden was on the site of the swimming pool. The second and present owners, parents of five daughters, have lived in the house for fifteen years. Fischer Shalles, the landscape architects, have assisted them in creating an English-style cottage garden. The herb garden was planted three years ago. Each year the five daughters choose and plant the material for their planter boxes by the playhouse. A warm and friendly garden; enter by walking up the driveway.

Sunday, March 19, 10 a.m. - 2 p.m.

Exit SW Freeway at Greenbriar. Turn south onto Greenbriar. Take the second left onto North Boulevard. Go east 6 blocks to 1405.

The Carmichael Garden

3315 ELLA LEE LANE, HOUSTON

The garden was designed and created by the owners' landscape company, Thompson & Hanson, in 1994 following the complete renovation of the house. The front garden is a tailored brick-and-flagstone-paved motorcourt bordered by clipped boxwood. Asian jasmine and paired planters are softened by evergreen pear, Mexican plum, and masses of Mrs. G. G. Gerbing' azaleas. The back garden is a white garden and is best viewed from the raised brick and flagstone terrace that runs the length of the south facade. A generous rectangular lawn stretches to the property's edge, where informal plantings of magnolia, holly, dogwood, azaleas, hydrangeas, and camellias soften the enclosing brick wall. Flagstone pathways lead to other garden rooms partitioned by low brick walls. A rose garden runs along the east driveway wall and a small kitchen herb garden is nestled behind a curved brick wall. English and French antique garden ornaments and furniture are found through-out the garden. The Carmichael garden is a good example of a medium-scale suburban garden appropriate to this updated 1937 colonial house designed by John Staub. The plant palette is typical of southeastern American gardens. The mild Gulf Coast climate allows a succession of annual and perennial plantings year-round.

Sunday, March 19, 2 p.m. - 6 p.m.

From the 610 Loop West exit for San Felipe, turn left, heading east to River Oaks Boulevard. Turn right onto River Oaks Boulevard. Ella Lee Lane is the first right. The house is the first on the left, #3315.

BAYOU BEND COLLECTION AND GARDENS 🐾

P.O. BOX 6826, HOUSTON, TX 77007. (713) 639-7750.

Bayou Bend, now the Decorative Arts wing of the Museum of Fine Arts, Houston, is located within the fourteen-acre estate of Miss Ima Hogg. The regional bayou woodland has been interplanted with a diverse collection of native Gulf Coast and ornamental plants. The horticultural collection is framed in a series of formal garden rooms, woodland gardens, ravines, and paths. The integrated house / garden composition is a significant example of a regional historic landscape of the American Country House movement. The gardens feature one of the most extensive collections of azaleas and camellias in Texas.

Year round, Tuesday - Saturday, 10 a.m. - 5 p.m. Sunday, 1 p.m. - 5 p.m.

Approach Bayou Bend via Memorial Drive in Houston, turning south at Westcott Street. Please park in the free lot and cross the footbridge to enter the gardens.

PECKERWOOD GARDEN 🐾

ROUTE 3, BOX 103, HEMPSTEAD, TX 77445.(409) 826-3232.

Peckerwood Garden is an artist's garden set in a natural landscape. It holds an unduplicated collection of native rarities from Texas and Mexico interspersed in the garden with their Asian counterparts. This garden also serves as a horticultural laboratory where unusual plants and innovative techniques are tested. At present the cultivated garden occupies about seven acres of the twenty-acre site and includes a woodland garden along the banks of a creek, a higher dry garden on the north slope of the creek, and a recently established meadow garden and arboretum on acreage to the south. More than 3,000 species and cultivars can be found here, including significant collections of Quercus, Acer, Magnolia, Ilex, Pinus, Clethra, Styrax, Taxus, Philadelphus, Monarda, Bauhinia, Agave, rare bulbs, conifers and ferns.

Open for Open Days visitors Saturday & Sunday, March 18 & 19, 1 p.m. - 5 p.m. Open various weekends March - November. Call for details.

From Houston, take Highway 290 West past Prairie View. Before reaching Hempstead, take Exit FM359 toward Brookshire. Proceed through the traffic light at the intersection with Business 290. The garden is located 1.7 mile past this intersection, on the right. Look for a small sign. Parking will be at Yucca Do Nursery, which is located just south of the garden.

🌀 *A preservation project of The Garden Conservancy.*

Rienzi ❧

1406 KIRBY DRIVE, HOUSTON, TX 77265-9964. (713) 639-7800.

Rienzi, the European decorative arts wing of the Museum of Fine Arts, Houston, is the former home of Carroll Sterling and Harris Masterton III. The residence and its gardens opened to the public in March 1999. Set in 4.4 acres of wooded ravines on Buffalo Bayou, Rienzi's gardens are an artful combination of formal spaces compatible with its Palladian contemporary exterior and its wilder native ravines. Azaleas, camellias, ginger, and roses flourish in settings surrounded by native magnolias, conifers and oaks.

Open for Open Days visitors Sunday, March 19, 10 a.m. - 4 p.m. Otherwise September 1 - July 31, by appointment. Closed Tuesdays and Wednesdays.

Rienzi is located in River Oaks at 1406 Kirby Drive. It is west of downtown Houston and north of U.S. 59. From downtown take Allen Parkway west. As it crosses Shepherd, Allen Parkway becomes Kirby Drive. Rienzi is on the right miles west of Shepherd. From U.S. 59 take the Kirby Exit and drive north miles. Rienzi will be on the left. Bayou Bend is nearby.

VERMONT

Lake
Champlain
Area

Manchester
& Putney Area

VERMONT OPEN DAYS
June 10, July 8: Manchester

Manchester Open Days

Regional Representative: Mrs. A. V. S. Olcott

Saturday, June 10

DORSET
Old Stone House Garden, The Dorset West Road: 10 a.m. - 2 p.m.

MANCHESTER
Glebelands, Route 7A: 10 a.m. - 5 p.m.
Ondawa Farm Garden, 904 River Road: 10 a.m. - 2 p.m.
The Sunken Garden, River Road: 10 a.m. - 2 p.m.

PUTNEY
Gordon & Mary Hayward's Garden, 508 McKinnon Road: 10 a.m. - 6 p.m.

Saturday, July 8

MANCHESTER
Glebelands, Route 74: 10 a.m. - 5 p.m.
Ondawa Farm Garden, 904 River Road: 10 a.m. - 2 p.m.
The Sunken Garden, River Road: 10 a.m. - 2 p.m.
Wyndhurst, 3227 Main Street: 10 a.m. - 4 p.m.

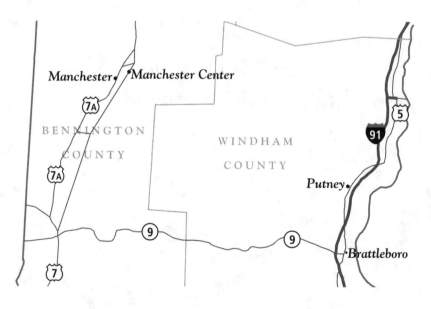

GLEBELANDS

ROUTE 7A, MANCHESTER

Our garden was started in the 1930s with perennials and a long allée of peonies. We later added marble defining walls, two gazebos (a Temple of Love and a Moorish-style with tassels), statues, and a tiled pool. I've incorporated a large reflecting pool with fountains at each end, antique iron (New Orleans) gates and grills, urns and statuary from my former house. The grounds, totaling thirty acres, encompass an orchard underplanted with narcissus (fairyland in springtime), a folly pavilion, two large ponds created by a 100-yard-long nineteenth-century marble dam (the area was a marble mill), two miles of woodland trails, brooks, and fine trees, including a Chamaecyparis collection I've raised from cuttings that I propagated.

Saturdays; June 10, July 8; 10 a.m. - 5 p.m.

Take Route 7A from The Equinox Hotel in Manchester Village. Travel north for .7 mile. Orvis Company will be on the right. Look for a dirt driveway within a spruce and pine grove on the left. A "Glebelands" sign will be in the middle of the drive. The house cannot be seen from the road. Please follow signs for parking. From the north, take Route 7A South past the junction of Routes 11 & 30 in Manchester Center. Travel .6 mile south. "Glebelands" will be on the right.

Proceeds shared with The Federated Garden Club of Vermont, Inc.

GORDON & MARY HAYWARD'S GARDEN

508 McKINNON ROAD, PUTNEY

Gordon and Mary Hayward, professional garden designers, have created a one-and-one-half acre garden centered around their 200-year-old Vermont farmhouse. Reflecting Mary's English background, they have created a garden of firm structure and relaxed plantings. The garden is comprised of nine areas: the hedged four-quadrant herb garden, the dry shade and moist shade gardens, the long borders, two ninety-foot mixed borders ending at a post-and-beam gazebo, woodland and spring gardens, a pool garden, and outdoor dining area.

Saturday, June 10, 10 a.m. - 6 p.m.

From I-91 North or South, take Exit 4 for Putney. Get onto Route 5 North and go .5 mile to the Putney General Store. Turn left after the General Store onto Westminster West Road. Go 4 miles and turn right at the second McKinnon Road sign. Turn right immediately into the field and park. Our garden is across the dirt road. Please park in the field.

Old Stone House Garden

The Dorset West Road, Dorset

Commissioned in 1914, this formal Italian garden was designed by Charles Downing Lay. The extensive flower gardens enhance a marble teahouse, marble pergola, thirty-two marble containers carved on site in 1914 and 1915, fountains, a peony walk, marble benches, tables, urns, monuments, roses, vines, and a bucolic view of Vermont meadows. The house and garden consist of three levels surrounded by marble walls and are listed on the National Register of Historical Places.

Saturday, June 10, 10 a.m. - 2 p.m.

From Manchester follow Route 30 northwest out of town to Dorset West Road. Turn left and travel 1.25 miles to the Old Stone House. There are extensive lawns with a flagpole. Please park in the west meadow and enter the garden through the front gate.

Ondawa Farm Garden

904 River Road, Manchester Village

My favorite area is an informal picket-fenced kitchen garden with herbs and flowers. I designed it to be low maintenance, with gravel walks and beds outlined with stone. There is a creek flowing through the property with a border on the higher bank. Beyond that there is a pond outlined on the far side by another border, mostly phlox, iris, daylilies, and lupine. As a magnificent background, the green mountains rise from the plain of the Battinkill River and on the other side of the valley stands the tallest mountain in the Taconic Range, (Mt. Equinox). There is a shade garden under a grove of black locusts, and a vegetable garden surrounded by treillage.

Saturdays; June 10, July 8; 10 a.m. - 2 p.m.

Starting at Historic Equinox Hotel in Manchester, go south on Route 7, for .3 mile and turn left onto River Road. Go 2.5 miles and pass Richville Road, 500 feet on left to the first house (Greek revival style with four big columns). Ondawa Farm sign in drive, 904 River Road. There will be parking directions.

The Sunken Garden

My sunken garden is an area that was previously the foundation of a greenhouse. The glass frame was taken away years ago and only the sunken stone wall remains. This area could easily have become an eyesore, and it presented a challenging problem. The stone was lovely so I decided to make a garden using the stone wall as a background. It is an old-fashioned English-style cottage garden that is attached to the brick greenhouse that is now the study. It seems to belong with the small 200-year-old cottage that is my home.

Saturdays; June 10, July 8; 10 a.m. - 2 p.m.

From Route 7A South in Manchester go 1 mile down River Road. The driveway is the second on the left past the entrance to The Wilburton Inn. Look for "J.B. Wilbur" on the stone pillars. Please park along the driveway.

Proceeds share with The Federated Garden Club of Vermont, Inc.

Wyndhurst

3227 Main Street, Manchester Village

A century ago, my family bought a Vermont farm and redesigned the formal gardens into a more romantic informal design. A second new garden is a maze of curving paths of various widths and lengths, with many entrances and exits, forming twenty-five beds of different shapes and sizes. Flowers are on all sides and views are ever-changing. My sculpture is used for accents, and black flowers and foliage have been interspersed with many vibrant colors. It is not an old-fashioned garden. Rules have been kept to a minimum and spontaneity has played a large part in the color schemes and design. When you walk through the garden, please be sure to turn and look back. Most important of all, stand off on the outer edges for a look across.

Saturday, July 8, 10 a.m. - 4 p.m.

From the North, go south on Route 7A past the Equinox Hotel in Manchester Village. Wyndhurst, #3227 Main Street, is on the right opposite River Road. From the south, go north on Route 7A. Wyndhurst is on the left shortly after you enter Manchester Village, after passing Hildene and Dellwood Cemetery on the right.

ALICE'S FLOWER GARDENS ❧

RR 1 BOX 1536, EAST MANCHESTER ROAD, MANCHESTER CENTER, VT 05255. (802) 362-3027.

Our cutting gardens / nursery were features in Organic Gardening, November 1992; Garden Design, April/May 1996; National Gardening, December 1996. A modest ranch-style house is surrounded by two acres of immaculately kept beds and borders filled with an amazing diversity of hybrid and heirloom flowers. The planting of our organic gardens began in 1954 and has been orchestrated so that something is in bloom from May to October, though the gardens are particularly spectacular in June and July.

Saturdays; June 12, July 10; 3 p.m. - 6 p.m.

On East Manchester Road, .5 mile east of the intersection of U.S. Highway 7 and Vermont 11/30.

HILDENE ❧

ROUTE 7A, P.O. BOX 377, MANCHESTER, VT 05254. (802) 362-1788.

Robert Todd Lincoln's Hildene was the home of Abraham Lincoln's descendants until 1975. This Georgian Revival mansion is situated among formal gardens that have been restored to their original beauty. Many of the original plantings remain, and the location on a promontory in the valley provides a splendid view of the mountains on either side of Hildene's meadowlands below. Cutting and kitchen gardens are in the process of being restored.

Mid-May - October; 9:30 a.m.-4 p.m. Tours available by appointment.

Located just 2 miles south of the junctions of Routes 7A and 11/30.

❧ *public garden*

WASHINGTON

★ Seattle

WASHINGTON OPEN DAYS
June 3 & 4, May 6 & 7: Seattle

Seattle Open Days

Regional Representative: Rosina McIvor

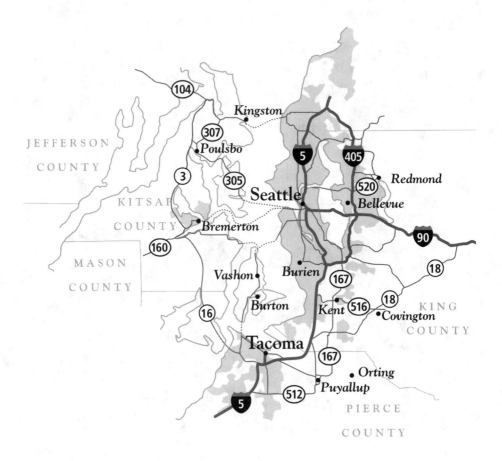

Saturday, May 6

ORTING
The Chase Garden, 16015 264th Street East: 10 a.m. - 4 p.m.

PUYALLUP
The Mulcahey Garden, 12413 136th Avenue East: 10 a.m. - 2 p.m.

Sunday, May 7

VASHON ISLAND
Edith Ostrom's Garden, 9618 S.W. Burton Drive, Burton: 10 a.m. - 4 p.m.
Thomas McNair House & Garden, 22915 107th Avenue SW: 10 a.m. - 4 p.m.

Saturday, June 3

KINGSTON
Heronswood, Heronswood Nursery, 7530 NE 288th Street: 9:30 a.m. - 3:30 p.m.

POULSBO
Elverhøj, 16813 Lemolo Shore Drive, NE: 10 a.m. - 4 p.m.

REDMOND
1332 232nd Place NE: 10 a.m. - 4 p.m.

SEATTLE
Geller-Irvine Garden, 1725 26th Avenue: 10 a.m. - 4 p.m.

Sunday, June 4

BURIEN
Shorewood Gardens, 12011 18th Avenue SW: 10 a.m. - 4 p.m.

COVINGTON
The Groeblacher Garden, 26027 158th Avenue SE: 10 a.m. - 4 p.m.

1332 232ND Place NE

REDMOND

A typical suburban lot with nothing on it has been transformed into a plantperson's paradise. There is a white garden leading to a "woods" of magnolias and sorbus. Alpines are in another area, and a double perennial border is full of surprising combinations. Containers change constantly as plants go in and out of bloom. Irises are a feature of the garden. This garden has been featured in Fine Gardening, The Seattle Times and The Natural Garden by Ken Druse.

Saturday, June 3, 10 a.m. - 4 p.m.

The garden is east of Lake Sammamish. From Highway 520 turn right (south) onto Redmond/Fall City Road. Go straight for about 2.5 miles. Turn right at the traffic light at Sahalee Way (the Grey Barn Nursery at this intersection is very good). Go up Sahalee Way 3 miles where it becomes 228 Avenue NE. Turn left onto NE 14th Street (Cimarron) just past the fire station. Turn right at 232nd Place NE. The house is the second on the right, #1332.

Edith Ostrom's Garden

9618 S.W. Burton Drive, Burton

Visit the glory of 100-year old orchard in bloom when Edith Ostrom's Centennial Orchard magnificently declares the rites of spring. You'll see all the old apples— Wagner, Macintosh, Grimes Golden, Northern Spy, Wealthy, Black Republican cherries. A garden experience rapidly disappearing.

Sunday, May 7, 10 a.m. - 4 p.m.

By car from Seattle: Take the West Seattle Ferry from the Fauntleroy Dock to Vashon Island. Travel southbound on Vashon Highway: through central business district (Vashon); across Judd Creek Bridge; to village of Burton. At stop sign (old country store Harbor Mercantile will be on the left) turn left, or east onto S.W. Burton Drive. At a 3-way intersection keep going straight. Edith's Orchard is on the left. Parking available at Edith's.

ELVERHØJ

Our three-acre garden is on a small peninsula jutting into Liberty Bay. It is a collector's garden planted with many unusual trees, shrubs, dwarf conifers, and perennials, a great many of which I have grown from seeds or cuttings. The greatest challenge has been to preserve the view of the surrounding waters and the Olympic Mountains, and at the same time grow all of the trees and shrubs that I love. The large perennial garden is slowly becoming a shady woodland-so changes are always being made.

Saturday, June 3, 10 a.m. - 4 p.m.

Take the Seattle-Bainbridge Island Ferry to Winslow. Drive north on Highway 305 approximately 7 miles over the Agate Pass Bridge. Go 1.8 miles past the bridge, and turn left onto Lemolo Shore Drive. Keep right and at 1.3 miles turn onto Elverhøj Drive. Please park in the lot at the top of the drive or along Lemolo Shore Drive.

GELLER-IRVINE GARDEN

1725 26TH AVENUE, SEATTLE

I started the garden about eighteen years ago when there were only two trees on the property. Today, the woodland cottage garden reminds me of my native New England. The placement of the main structure of trees and shrubs naturally defines the interconnected outdoor rooms. A walk through the property brings you up a steep hillside entry garden, through the woodland canopy, and onto two brick terrace gardens surrounded by perennials. The sixty-foot by 120-foot garden feels larger than it is due to the changing feeling and flow of the spaces.

Saturdays, June 3, 10 a.m. - 4 p.m.

Take I-5 to Madison Street. Turn East on Madison toward Lake Washington. Turn right onto 25th Avenue East (heading south). Turn left onto East John Street, proceed down the hill. Take the first right onto 26th Avenue and continue a couple of blocks past East Denny and East Howell. Number 1725 26th Avenue is on the right side just past East Howell. Look for a wooden staircase.

Heronswood

Heronswood Nursery, 7530 NE 288th Street, Kingston, WA 98436.

Three-plus acres of unusual perennials, shrubs, grasses, vines, trees, and conifers in varied garden conditions. A large woodland shade garden, mixed shrub and herbaceous borders, wet site and bog gardens make up this partially wooded setting in rural Kitsap County. Interesting arbors and hardscape complete the design.

Weekends; June 2 & 3, July 21 & 22, September 8 & 9, 9:30 a.m. - 3:30 p.m.

Please call or fax ahead. Voice (360) 297-4172, Fax (360) 297-8321.

Shorewood Gardens

12011 18th Avenue SW, Burien

Grand prize winner of the 1996 Seattle Times Pacific Magazine Pacific Gardens Contest, this spirited hillside overlooking scenic Puget Sound won the gardener a trip to London for the 1997 Chelsea Flower Show. An avid plant collector and variegated foliage fanatic, the owner writes a twice-monthly gardening column for local papers in western King County. Designed as a series of rooms, the garden offers foliage and texture galore, with comfortable seating to enjoy the sights and sounds of the best gardening climate in the United States.

Sunday, June 4, 10 a.m. - 4 p.m.

From the interchange of I-5 and Route 518, exit to Route 518 and travel west 6 miles to the end of the freeway, entering downtown Burien. At First Avenue South, turn right and travel north on First Avenue to 116th Street and turn left. Travel west on 116th Street to Eighteenth Avenue SW and turn left. Continue to dead end. The garden is at the last house at the end of the cul-de-sac. Do not park in cul-de-sac.

The Groeblacher Garden

26027 158th Avenue SE, Covington

This garden is designer Michaela's approach to the challenges of a suburban housing development. A blank canvas with heavy soil, a steep slope, canine pets and a child became a terraced garden flowing with good plants having tough constitutions and clear drama. Designer touches abound, with well-placed urns and other art. Glorious in spring and fall, the garden remains impressive the balance of the year due to strong foliar accents and good bones.

Sunday, June 4, 10 a.m. - 4 p.m.

From I-5 take the Kent/Des Moines Exit. Travel east on Kent/Des Moines Road to intersection with Meeker Street and turn left. Continue to the city of Kent. The arterial turns north at Lincoln just past Route 167 underpass, then continues as Smith Street. Continue east on Smith Street, which becomes SE Kent/Kangley Road. At the intersec-

tion with 104th SE continue east on 256th Street SE. Go up Kent East Hill and east to 156th Avenue SE and turn right. Go past church and enter Fairfield housing development at 260th Avenue SE. Turn right at second cul-de-sac onto 258th Place SE. The house is clearly marked at the end of the street. (The garden is 9 miles from the exit). Do not park in cul-de-sac.

THE MULCAHEY GARDEN
12413 136TH AVENUE EAST, PUYALLUP

My garden has a wonderful view of Mt. Rainier, and is of Japanese garden influence adapted to Northwest conditions. It contains a little waterfall and Koi pond, more than 150 different kinds of rhododendrons and azaleas, thirty-six named Japanese maples, small rock garden plants, and conifers, perennials, etc., to show interest year-round. Form, color, texture, light, and grouping create a complementary, restful effect to enjoy on a little more than three-quarters of an acre.

Saturday, May 6, 10 a.m. - 2 p.m.

From Highway 161/Meridian, take 37th Avenue East between Shari restaurant and Starbucks. Continue east past Pierce College to the traffic light. Turn right onto Shaw Road and continue south to 4-way stop. Exxon gas station and a mini-mart are on the right. Turn left onto 122nd Street. Go down hill to 136th Avenue and turn right. Continue to 137th Avenue. The garden is between 136th Avenue and 137th Avenue. Please park on 137th Avenue side.

THOMAS MCNAIR HOUSE & GARDEN ❧
22915 107TH AVENUE SW, VASHON

Visit a 110-year old early Victorian house in original condition, built by carpenter Thomas McNair, and be entranced by the old apple trees in bloom and the perennial garden of present owner Richard Wickberg. This homestead property was actually "proved up" by Elta McNair; Thomas worked in Tacoma and rowed across treacherous Puget Sound waters to come home once a week. In Richard's garden "Monet colors" of lavenders and pinks complement a carpet of apple blossoms, softly providing an atmosphere of timelessness for this classic historic landmark.

Sunday, May 7, 10 a.m. - 4 p.m.

From Seattle: Take West Seattle Ferry from the Fauntelroy dock and Vashon Island. Travel southbound on Vashon Highway, through central business district (Vashon). Cross Judd Creek Bridge. At the end of the bridge turn right onto 228th Street, which swings north and turns into 107th Street. The Thomas McNair House and Garden is approximately .25 mile on right behind the laurel hedge. Parking is on street only.

BLOEDEL RESERVE ❧

7571 NE DOLPHIN DRIVE, BAINBRIDGE ISLAND, WA 98110. (206) 842-7631.

The Bloedel reserve is a 150-acre former residence now public access garden and nature preserve. The primary purpose of the Reserve is to provide people with an opportunity to enjoy nature through quiet walks in the gardens and woodlands.

Year round, Wednesday - Sunday (except holidays), 10 a.m. - 4 p.m. by reservation.

The Reserve is located approximately 8 miles north of Winslow (Bainbridge Island Ferry Terminal) off Highway 305. Phone for reservations and directions.

DUNN GARDENS ❧

THE E. B. DUNN HISTORIC GARDEN TRUST, P.O. BOX 77126, SEATTLE, WA (206) 362-0933.

In 1915 the Olmsted Brothers designed a summer "country place" for the Arthur Dunn family on a bluff overlooking Puget Sound. The estate has been remained in the private ownership of the family and with the passage of time, has come to reflect the mature grace which the designers and owners desired for a rural retreat. The Olmsted ideals of naturalistic groupings of trees amid broad lawns and flowering borders of shrubs and groundcovers, continue as vibrant and compellling today as they were at the turn of the century.

Guided tours only. April - September, Thursdays at 2 p.m., Fridays at 10 a.m. and 2 p.m., and Saturdays at 10 a.m.

Please call for directions.

LAKEWOLD GARDENS ❧

12317 GRAVELLY DRIVE SW, LAKEWOOD, WA 98499. (253) 584-4106.

A beautiful ten-acre estate garden showcasing stunning formal gardens as well as naturalistic displays. This includes woodland areas, aquatic displays, waterfalls, rock and alpine gardens, a knot garden, kitchen garden, shade garden, rose garden, and fern garden. Lakewold also is a splendid example of noted landscape architect Thomas Church's residential designs.

April - September, Thursday, Saturday, Sunday, Monday, 10 a.m. - 4 p.m; Friday, noon - 8 p.m.; October - March: Friday - Sunday, 10 a.m. - 3 p.m

Take Exit 124 off I-5 (Gravelly Lake Drive). Follow signs for 1 mile. Lakewold is only 10 miles south of the Tacoma Dome.

MUKAI ♠

ISLAND LANDMARKS, P.O. BOX 13135, BURTON, WA 98013. (206) 463-2445.

Island Landmarks is working to save this site which represents a chapter in the early Japanese-American experience. In the midst of her family's prosperous strawberry farm a first-generation Issei woman created a Japanese-style garden, replete with "islands" and waterfalls surrounded by pools filled with koi and waterlilies.

Open by appoinment only.

 A preservation project of The Garden Conservancy.

THE BELLEVUE BOTANICAL GARDEN ♠

12001 MAIN STREET, BELLEVUE, WA 98005. (425) 452-2750.

The Bellevue Botanical Garden comprises thirty-six acres of display gardens, rolling hills, woodlands, meadows and wetlands offering an ever-changing panorama of greenery and color. It's a unique combination of horticulture education; scenic beauty, special events, and volunteer opportunities create a focus of community pride. Since opening in 1992, the Bellevue Botanical Garden has become a major center community activity.

Year round, daily, 7:30 a.m. - 4 p.m.

From I-405, heading either north or south: Exit onto N.E. 8th east. Follow N.E. 8th to 120th, turn left onto 120th. Turn left onto Main Street. Garden is located on the right at 12001 Main Street.

THE CHASE GARDEN ♠

ORTING, WA

Recently featured in *Earth on Her Hands: the American Woman in Her Garden*, this naturalistic style garden on four and one half acres has been created and tended by Emmott and Ione Chase since 1960. The area surrounding the house was designed by Rex Zumwalt evoking the simplicity of a Japanese garden by the use of raked pea gravel, moss-covered boulders, and reflecting pools. A forest of naive trees is carpeted with wildflowers. There are perennial shade borders, a rock garden, and a groundcover meadow inspired by the alpine meadows of Mt. Rainier. Visitors may enjoy the mountain as part of the panoramic view of the Puyallup River Valley.

Open for Open Days visitors on Saturday, May 6, 10 a.m. - 4 p.m.. Otherwise by appointment only from mid-April to mid-May. Please call (206) 242-4040.

From Highway 161 (Meridian) turn east on 264th Street East which is about one mile south of the town of Graham. Continue for 3.5 miles. Watch for the driveway at 16015-264th Street East directly across from a road sign indicating 10mph (with a crooked arrow). Puyallup/Orting area directions: All specific directions for gardens in this area are given from Highway 161 (Meridian). From Seattle, go south on Highway 167. Take the Puyallup/Olympia exit onto Highway 512 south. Remain on Highway 512, bypassing Puyallup and take the South Hill/Eatonville exit. Turn left at the light to access Highway 161 (Meridian). From the Tacoma at I-5, take Highway 512 east to the Eatonville exit. Turn right at the light to access Highway 161 (Meridian). From Olympia, follow signs to Eatonville. Go north from Eatonville via Highway 161 (Meridian).

A preservation project of The Garden Conservancy.

VILLAGE GREEN PERENNIALS

10223-26TH AVENUE SW, WEST SEATTLE, WA (206) 767-7735.

An English Country Garden and cottage nursery owned and operated by Teresa Romedo. A rich tapestry of color and texture, the garden hosts High Tea for the Daughters of the British Empire twice a year. Flowers, foliage, artworks and a soothing pond, Village Green Perennials is an oasis in a suburban neighborhood. Explore the intoxicating garden, then visit the nursery to add your favorites to your own garden.

June 4 and July 30. Otherwise Saturday 10 a.m. -5 p.m., Sunday 11 a.m.-4:30 p.m..

From Interstate 5 exit at the West Seattle Freeway heading west. Once in West Seattle, turn left at 35th Avenue SW. Continue south to intersection with SW Roxbury. Turn left onto Roxbury and travel west to 26th SW. Turn right onto 25th SW and travel south three blocks to the Village Green Perennials sign at the curb. Park along 26th Avenue SW.

WASHINGTON PARK ARBORETUM

2300 ARBORETUM DRIVE EAST, UNIVERSITY OF WASHINGTON, SEATTLE WA 98112-2300. (206) 543-8800.

The Washington Park Arboretum is a living plant museum emphasizing trees and shrubs hardy in the maritime Pacific Northwest. Plant collections are selected and arranged to display their beauty and function in urban landscapes, to demonstrate their natural ecology and diversity, and to conserve important species and cultivated varieties for the future. The arboretum serves the public, students at all levels, naturalists, gardeners, and nursery and landscape professionals with its collections, education programs, interpretation and recreational opportunities.

Year round, daily, dawn - dusk.

From I-5 northbound or southbound, take Exit 168-B (Bellevue / Kirkland) East. Take the very first exit, Montlake Boulevard / UW. At the traffic signal, go straight. You are now on Lake Washington Boulevard East. Follow for 1 miles until you come to the stop sign with the left-turn lane. Turn left onto Foster Island Road and follow signs to the Visitors Center.

WEST VIRGINIA

★ Charleston

WEST VIRGINIA OPEN DAYS
June 10: Charleston

Charleston Open Days

Regional Representatives: Mr. & Mrs. James Rufus Thomas II

Saturday, June 10

MALDEN
Kanawha Salines—Garden of Mrs. Turner Ratrie, Kanawha Salines: 10 a.m. - 4 p.m.

CHARLESTON
Mr. & Mrs. Fred H. Belden, Jr., 5 Manburn Road: 10 a.m. - 4 p.m.
The Garden of Bill Mills & Thomas Gillooly, 729 Gordon Drive: 10 a.m. - 4 p.m.
Zeb Wright's Garden, 1525 Clark Road: 10 a.m. - 4 p.m.

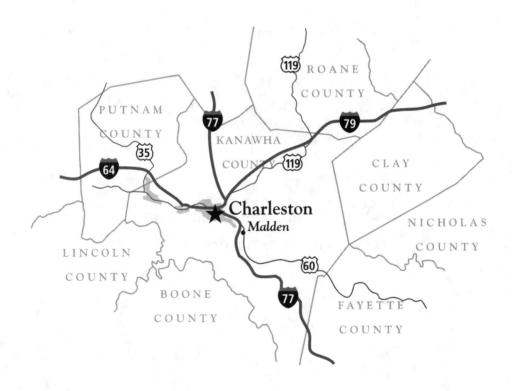

Kanawha Salines—
Garden of Mrs. Turner Ratrie

KANAWHA SALINES, MALDEN

Kanawha Salines, one of the most historic properties in the Kanawha Valley, was built by a pioneer in the exploitation of the abundant resources of salt brine beneath the earth. The original house was built in 1815 and remodeled in 1923. The owner, Mrs. Ratrie, is a direct descendent of the first salt producers and has been the garden designer since 1958. An allée of cherry trees on either side of an old brick walk leads to an enchanting white garden surrounding a rectangular pool filled with white water lilies. There is a formal rose garden surrounded by an English boxwood hedge, an extensive vegetable garden and a beautiful herbaceous border. The property encompasses one and one-half acres.

Saturday, June 10, 10 a.m. - 4 p.m.

From I-64 /I-77 take Route 60 East to the Malden Exit. Turn left after the underpass and proceed through the town of Malden. Turn right onto a gravel road east of town. Look for a sign at the gravel driveway. Park as directed.

Proceeds shared with the Kanawha Garden Club.

Mr. & Mrs. Fred H. Belden, Jr.

5 MANBURN ROAD, CHARLESTON

A wooded residential site in constant evolution. The owner makes extensive use of timbers to create planting areas and walkways within the sloping contours dictated by the terrain. A boardwalk path to a remote bench captures the serenity of the location. Plantings of rhododendron, azalea, pieris japonica, and cotoneaster dot the landscape. Some areas find dense shade and the plant material reflects these conditions: hostas, ferns, astilbe, and the like. A stone wall and steps find their way to perennial planting beds in the rear of the house, including daylily plantings in several separate locations where the summer sun can be captured. Buddleia brings in the butterflies and monarda attracts hummingbirds, and many species of birdlife are fed seasonally. Moving water exists too, both in a small pond and in a birdbath. Although the property is abundant with hardwoods, the owner has augmented the landscape with white pines started from seedlings to provide an evergreen backdrop. Evolution is the key operative term for this location as the owner does all the design and implementation, and it is continually in a state of change.

Saturday, June 10, 10 a.m. - 4 p.m.

Traveling east, take exit I-64 at Broad Street. Stay on Broad Street (third traffic light) and turn right on Quannier Street. Turn left at second traffic light (Dickinson Street) cross South Side bridge turn left and stay on Louden Heights Road until you come to Hampton Road (1.5 miles) Turn right at Holy Elementary School and continue to Longridge. Take right to dead end and a sharp right down hill, which is Manburn. In front of you will be a steep drive (which is not handicapped accessible). Park just before Manburn and walk to garden.

The Garden of Bill Mills & Thomas Gillooly

729 Gordon Drive, Charleston

As a garden designer I (Bill) greatly enjoy having my own laboratory to work in. This property of about an acre offers a pleasant range of sites, from sunny flats to hillside woodland. As one walks up the gravel drive, a series of borders, each with its own color pallet, comes into view. Through a gate, an all white circular garden with a small formal pond leads on to another border and another circular space. A walk up the hill behind the cottage rambles through many pocket gardens and on to the woodland garden. Urns, pots, and haymows are found throughout the property, rich in color and contrast.

Saturday, June 10, 10 a.m. - 4 p.m.

Take the Oakwood Exit of I-64 to Route 119. Turn right onto Cantley Drive. From Cantley turn right onto Wilkie Drive. Make the second left turn onto South Fort Drive. South Fort turns into Gordon Drive. Our residence, one mile further at #729 Gordon Drive, is on the left, a small cottage up a gravel drive. Additional parking may be found just past the residence at Weberwood Elementary School.

Zeb Wright's Garden

1525 Clark Road, Charleston

The home of garden designer, retired garden writer, and avid collector, displaying over 1300 species and cultivars of shrubs, orchids, dwarf conifers, perennials, wildflowers, and water/bog plants sited in a figure-eight pattern that meanders among rock, mixed border, carnivorous and water gardens. Especially recommended are large colonies of hardy orchids and 240 species and cultivars of conifers landscaped among companion astilbes, hostas, dwarf shrubs, heathers, and ground covers. Some areas of the garden go back as far as thirty years; the bog and water gardens are new additions. Most plants are labeled, and a computer printout will be available upon request.

Saturday, June 10, 10 a.m. - 4 p.m.

Take I-64 toward Huntington. Take the Oakwood Exit onto Route 119 to the top of the hill and the second stoplight (approximately 1 mile). Turn left onto Oakwood Road to the George Washington High School intersection. Turn right onto Clark Road, to the fourth house on the right, #1525.

Governor's Mansion — State of West Virginia 🌿

1716 Kanawha Bouleard E, Charleston, WV 25302. (344) 558-3588.

A red-brick walled garden combines woody and perennials and annuals around an open grassy courtyard. An informal dining area overlooks a small herb and rose garden in summer, chrysanthemums and Japanese anemones in the autumn. The focal point is a wall fountain painted with a faux marble finish and surrounded by blue atlas cedars. The west wall contains climbing hydrangea underplanted with hellebores, narcissus, and native creeping phlox.

Saturday, June 10, 10 a.m. - 4 p.m.

Exit I-64 at airport and State Capital Building. Turn right and at the first traffic light, turn left into parking area for cultural center. Continue on foot for one half block toward Kanawha River. The Governor's mansion faces the river and Kanawha Boulevards.

🌿 *public garden*

WISCONSIN

★ Milwaukee

WISCONSIN OPEN DAYS
July 16: Lake Country

Lake Country Open Day

Regional Representatives: Mrs. Anthony Meyer & Mrs. Harry Quadracci

Sunday, July 16

CHENEQUA
Cedarhurst, 5975 Cedarhurst Lane: 10 a.m. - 4 p.m.

HARTLAND
Florence & Harold Steen Garden, W310 N6759 Chenequa Drive: 10 a.m. - 4 p.m.

PEWAUKEE
Christopher Place, N35 W28146, Taylor's Woods Road: 10 a.m. - 4 p.m.
Perennial Joy, W283 N3366, Lakeside Road: 10 a.m. - 2 p.m.

CEDARHURST

5975 CEDARHURST LANE, CHENEQUA

Our garden greets the approach and slowly meanders until joyously encircling our Pine Lake summer home. An Italian vista with its own lake, fountain, and goat tower folly; expansive, fragrantly lush, English-style borders; a foot bridge with side glimpses of serene woodland plantings; and a unique, trough-filled vegetable and herb garden are incorporated throughout a continuous intimate, flirtation path. These garden elements are the fruition of our shared, exuberant imagination and spirit of heartfelt hospitality.

Sunday, July 16, 10 a.m. - 4 p.m.

From Highway 16 take Highway 83 north 2.2 miles to Cedarhurst. Please park as directed.

CHRISTOPHER PLACE

N35 W28146, TAYLOR'S WOODS ROAD, PEWAUKEE

This Wisconsin farm setting is visible immediately inside the fenced lilac-lined approach: a red barn laced with roses and hollyhocks; a small farmhouse highlighted with heritage plantings and lively pots of geraniums; an enclosed, formal flower-laden, pleasure garden and potager; a glass, viewing pavilion placed to catch the glow of the setting sun; a scattered informal orchard of dwarf fruit trees; an open tree-edged meadow banked by two American chestnuts. Grandfather Christopher purchased the property in 1937. The present garden was where his daughter, Margaret, planted flowers. His great grandson, Nicholas, designed the pavilion.

Sunday, July 16, 10 a.m. - 4 p.m.

From Highway 16 take KE south l mile to Old North Shore Drive. Turn left and go .6 miles to Taylor's Woods Road. Turn left and continue .25 mile. Please park along the road.

FLORENCE & HAROLD STEEN GARDEN

W310 N6759 CHENEQUA DRIVE, HARTLAND

Ours is a secret garden alive with color, variety and whimsy, reflecting the individual preferences of we two resident gardening enthusiasts. Florence's gardens feature an extensive collection of miniature roses, dwarf perennials and annuals. More than 250 modern-day lily cultivars, interplanted with perennials and annuals, fill Harold's gardens. Hosta beds nestle in several shaded areas throughout the yard.

Sunday, July 16, 10 a.m. - 4 p.m.

From the Milwaukee area, head west to Highway 83. Go north on Highway 83, (6.8 miles from I-94; 3.0 miles from Highway 16) to Beaver Lake Road, just past the entrance of the Chenequa Golf Club. Head east on Beaver Lake Road .5 miles and turn left onto Chenequa Drive for .3 mile. The driveway is at the top of the hill on the left. Please park on the street.

PERENNIAL JOY

W283 N3366, LAKESIDE ROAD, PEWAUKEE

"Perennial Joy" borders the shores of Pewaukee Lake, a haven for fisherman and sailors alike. Its changing beauty rejuvenates my spirit daily. The patio, which visually separates the inside of our house from the mysterious waters, has gardens on both sides of the wall, giving a sense of security while bringing nature's colors and textures into our home. Our children and their friends enjoy camping in the woods, scouting the pond for animal prints, as well as studying the life cycle of the many frogs that live there. Perennials abound, with texture and fragrance vying with color for importance. Benches are strategically placed, inviting moments of reflection on the beauty of creation.

Sunday, July 16, 10 a.m. - 2 p.m.

From Highway 16 take KE south 1 mile to Old North Shore Drive. Turn left and go .6 mile to Taylor's Woods Road. Once on Taylors Woods Road, turn right onto Lakeside Road. The garden is at the first driveway on the left at the bottom of the hill. Please park on the road.

BOERNER BOTANICAL GARDEN &

5879 SOUTH 92ND STREET, HALES CORNERS, WI 53130-2299. (414) 425-1130.

Internationally recognized, fifty-acre formal gardens set within a 1,000 acre arboretum park. Collections are displayed in beautifully landscaped settings including a Perennial Mall, Herb Garden, Rose Garden, Annual Garden, Rock Garden, and Shrub Mall. Seasonal displays of wildflowers, tulips, crab apples, peonies, iris, roses and daylilies are among the popular attractions. Boerner Botanical Garden's Trail

Garden is an All-America Selections Flower Trial Judging Ground, an All-America Rose Selection's Test Site, and displays All America Flower Trail and Vegetable Trail Winners.

Mid-April - November, daily, 8 a.m. - dusk.

Located southwest of Milwaukee. Take I-894 to Exit 5A (Forest Home). Take Forest Home southwest to 92nd Street and go south approximately 1 mile to the College Avenue entrance.

MITCHELL PARK
HORTICULTURAL CONSERVATORY ❧

524 SOUTH LAYTON BOULEVARD, MILWAUKEE, WI 53215.
(414) 649-9830.

Three large domes, seven stories tall, housing a rainforest, a desert, and a themed floral show. Orchids, thirty-five-foot waterfall, over 6000 plants, and cacti from around the world. Five themed floral shows featuring travel, fantasy, or history to inspire any palette or taste. One acre under glass; accessible in any weather. Lobby is air-conditioned; tropical dome is 70 degrees all winter.

Year round, daily, 9 a.m. - 5 p.m.

North on I-94 from Chicago to downtown Milwaukee; West on I-94 from Milwaukee to 1st. exit: 22nd/Clybourn. West 5 blocks to 27th Street; left to Domes on your left. East on I-94 from Madison, WI to 26th/St. Paul exit. One block West to 27th Street, left to domes on your left. South on I-43 from Green Bay, WI, to downtown Milwaukee; West on I-94 to 22nd/Clybourn. West 5 blocks to 27th Street; left to Domes on your left.

ROTARY GARDENS ❧

1455 PALMER DRIVE, JANESVILLE, WI 53545. (608) 752-3885.

A must see for the whole family! Featuring fifteen acres of internationally themed botanical gardens. Admission if free-donations encouraged. Call for information about guided tours. Join us for special events throughout the year.

Year round, Saturday and Sunday, May-October 10 a.m. - 6 a.m., November-December, noon - 4 p.m..

From I-90, exit at the 175A Janesville West Highway Exit. At the traffic light turn left onto Palmer Drive. Go approximately 1 mile and Rotary Gardens is located on the right.

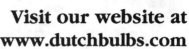

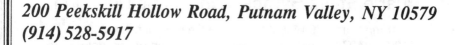

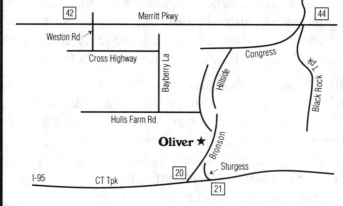

Index

Notes

Notes

Notes

NOTES

Notes

Join The Garden Conservancy

All members receive the Conservancy's quarterly newsletter; discounts on purchases of the Open Days Directory and garden admission coupon booklets; and invitations to special events and educational programs. Contributors of $100 or more are acknowledged in the Conservancy's newsletter and receive invitations to additional regional events. Donors of $1,000 or more join the Society of Fellows and are invited to attend semi-annual garden study tours highlighting the finest gardens in America.

Your membership contribution may result in additional support for the Garden Conservancy, as many companies match gifts made by their employees. Please contact your employer for further information and to obtain the necessary forms.

Please enroll me as a member of the Conservancy. My contribution is enclosed.

❏ Individual $35   ❏ Sponsor $250
❏ Family/Dual $50   ❏ Patron $500
❏ Friend $100   ❏ Society of Fellows $1,000
                          ❏ President's Circle $2,500

Open Days Discount Admission Coupons

Make garden visiting easier and save on regular admission fees.

I am a Garden Conservancy member, please send me:
_____ book(s) of 6 coupons at $16. *(2 free garden admissions)*

I am not a Conservancy member, please send me:
_____ book(s) of 6 coupons at $20. *(1 free garden admission)*

Membership Contribution: $ _____

Total Price of Discount Coupon Books: $ _____

Additional Directories (members, $10.95; non-members, $14.95): $ _____

Add $3.50 for shipping & handling when ordering Directories: $ _____

Total Enclosed: $ _____

Name: _____

Address: _____

City:_____State:_____Zip: _____

Daytime Phone Number: _____

Send To: The Garden Conservancy, P.O. Box 219, Cold Spring, NY 10516

Please make checks payable to The Garden Conservancy.
Your membership contribution is fully tax-deductible.